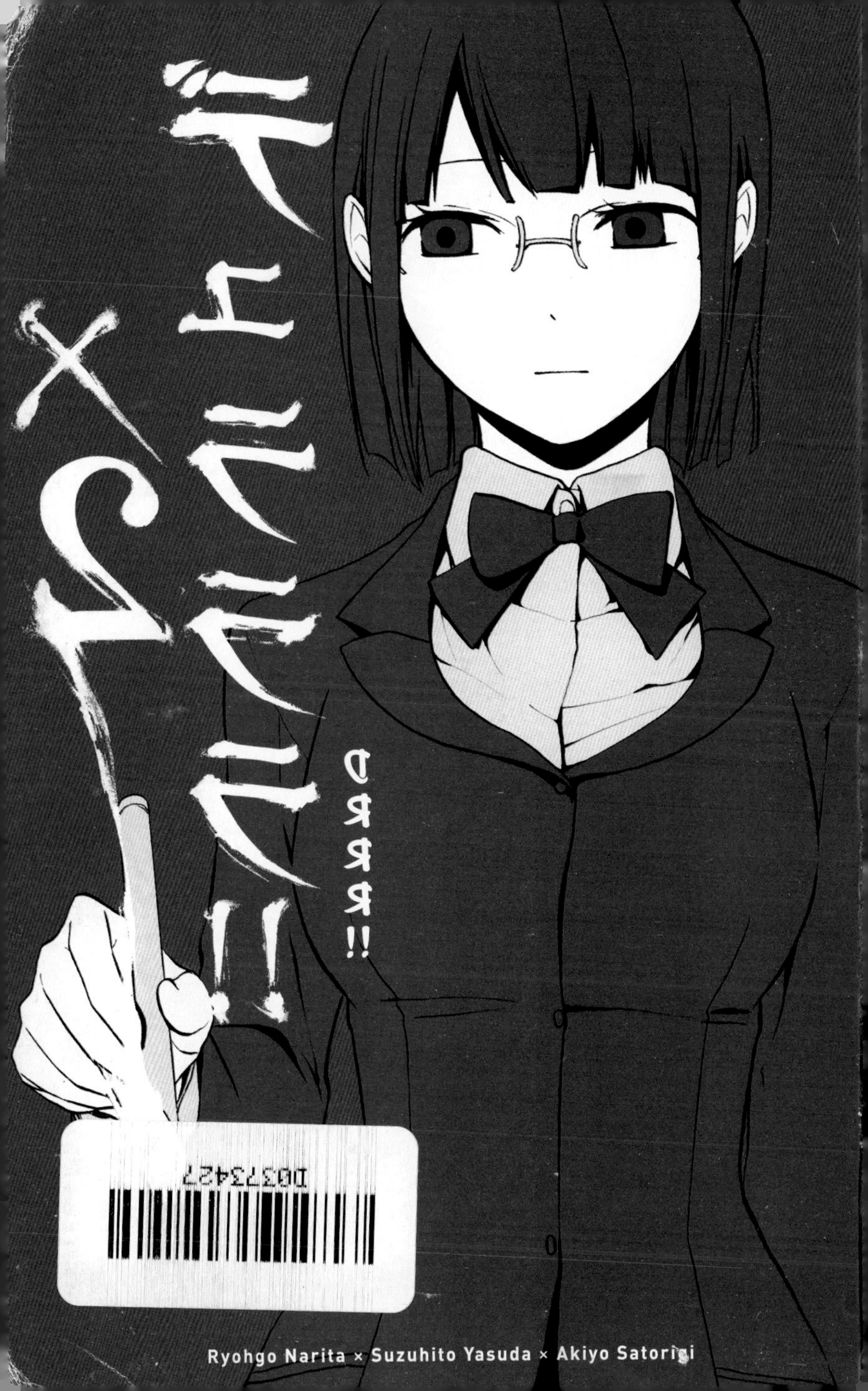
DRRR!!
Ryohgo Narita × Suzuhito Yasuda × Akiyo Satorigi

Contents

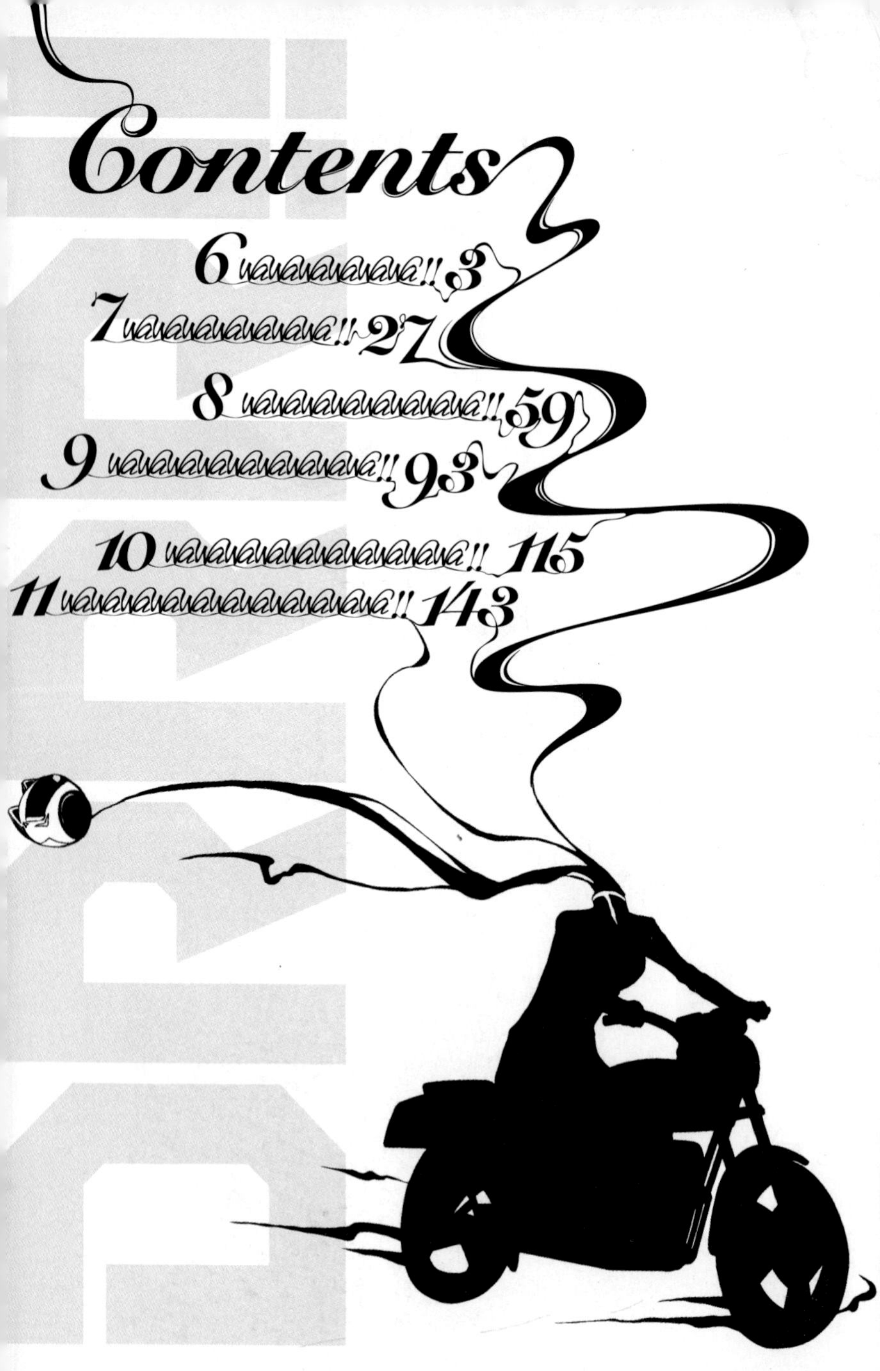

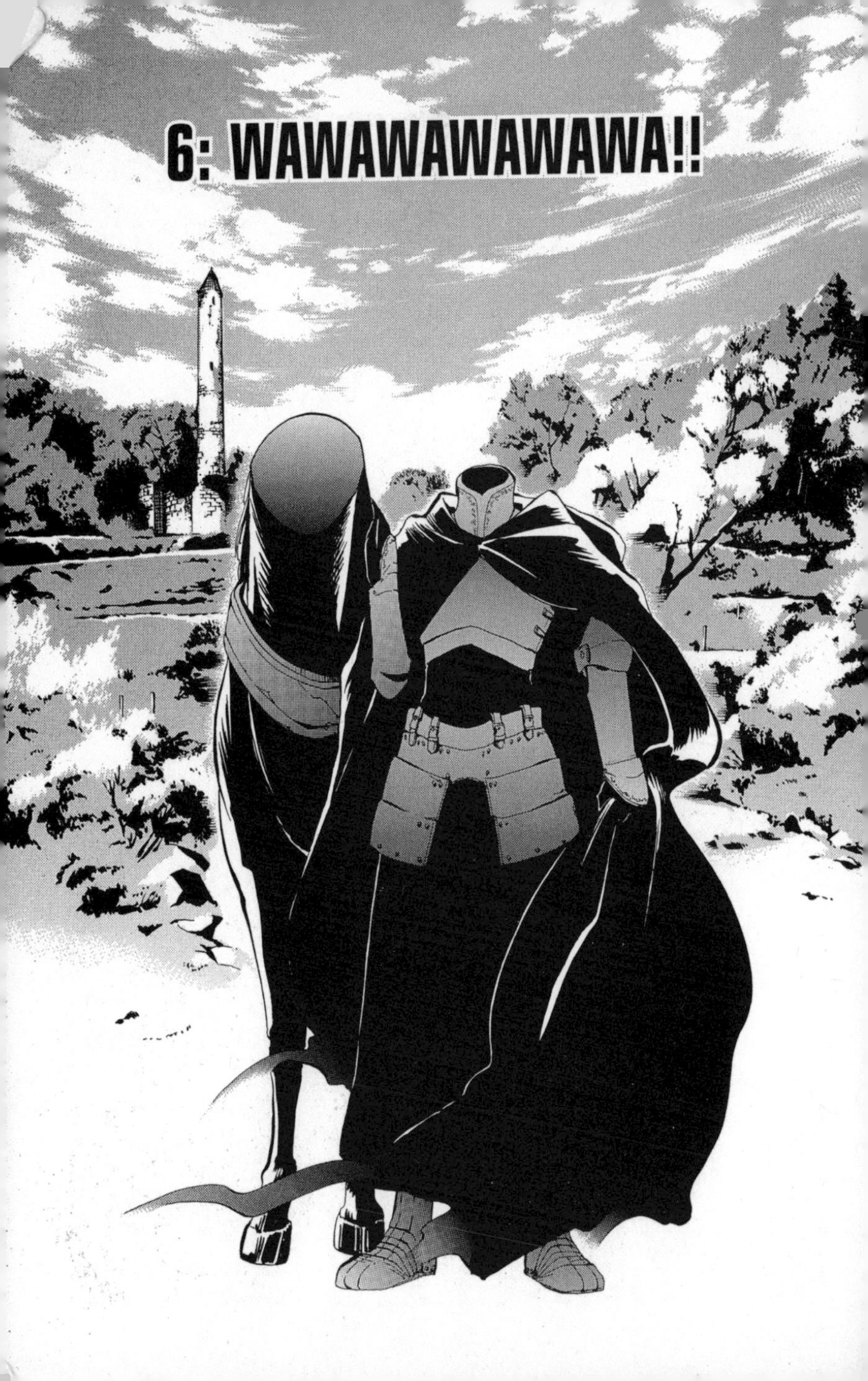
6: WAWAWAWAWAWA!!

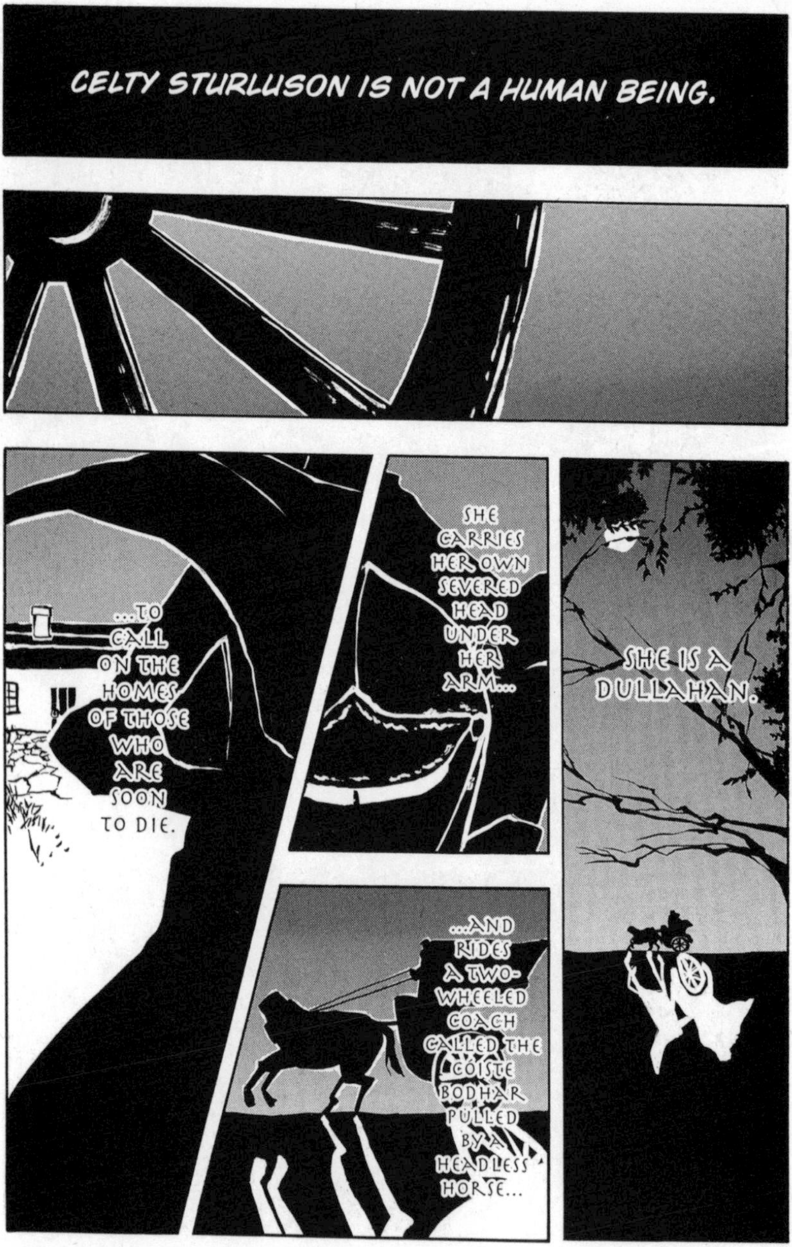
CELTY STURLUSON IS NOT A HUMAN BEING.
SHE IS A DULLAHAN.
SHE CARRIES HER OWN SEVERED HEAD UNDER HER ARM...
...AND RIDES A TWO-WHEELED COACH CALLED THE CÓISTE BODHAR PULLED BY A HEADLESS HORSE...
...TO CALL ON THE HOMES OF THOSE WHO ARE SOON TO DIE.

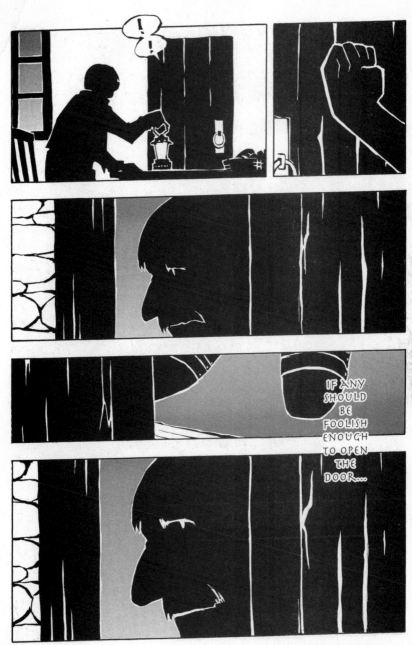

IF ANY SHOULD BE FOOLISH ENOUGH TO OPEN THE DOOR....

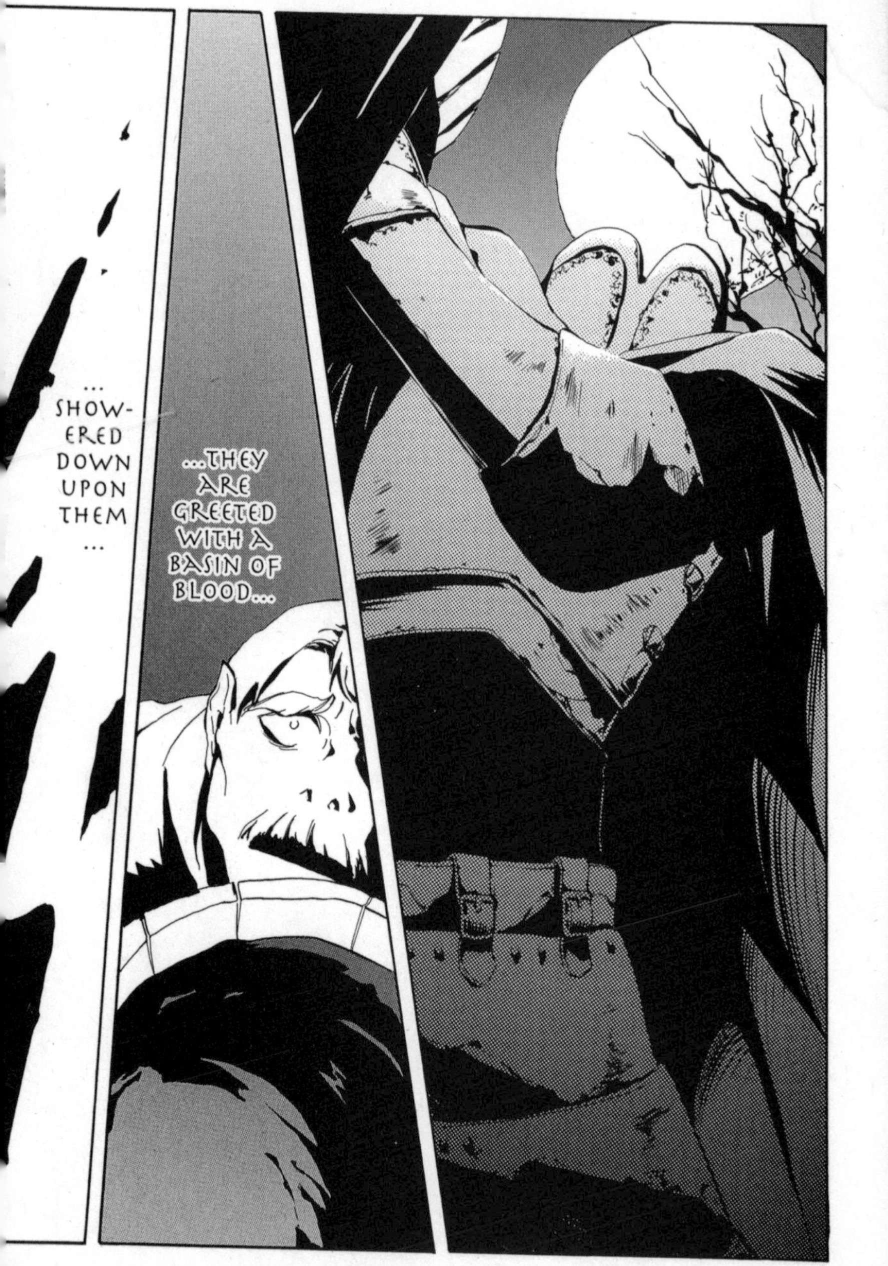
...THEY ARE GREETED WITH A BASIN OF BLOOD...
... SHOW-ERED DOWN UPON THEM ...

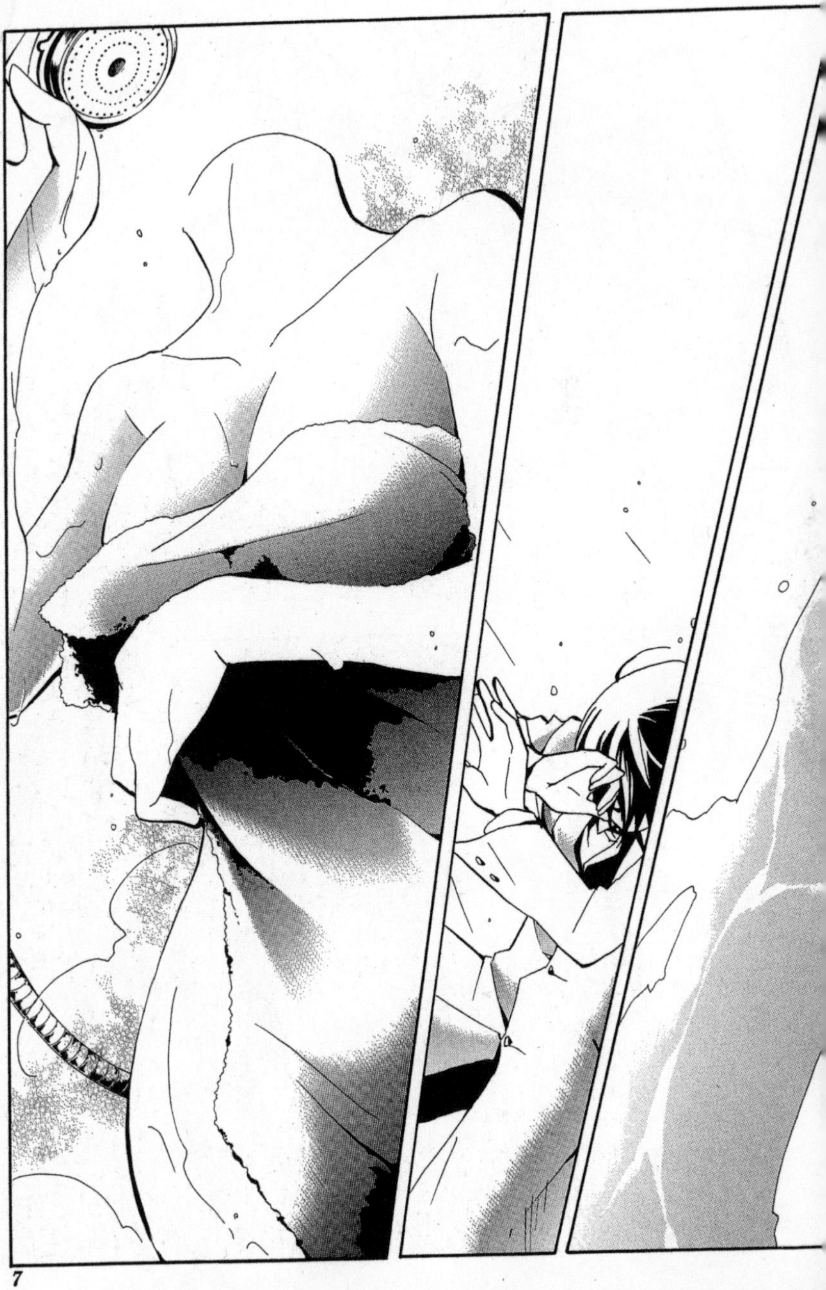

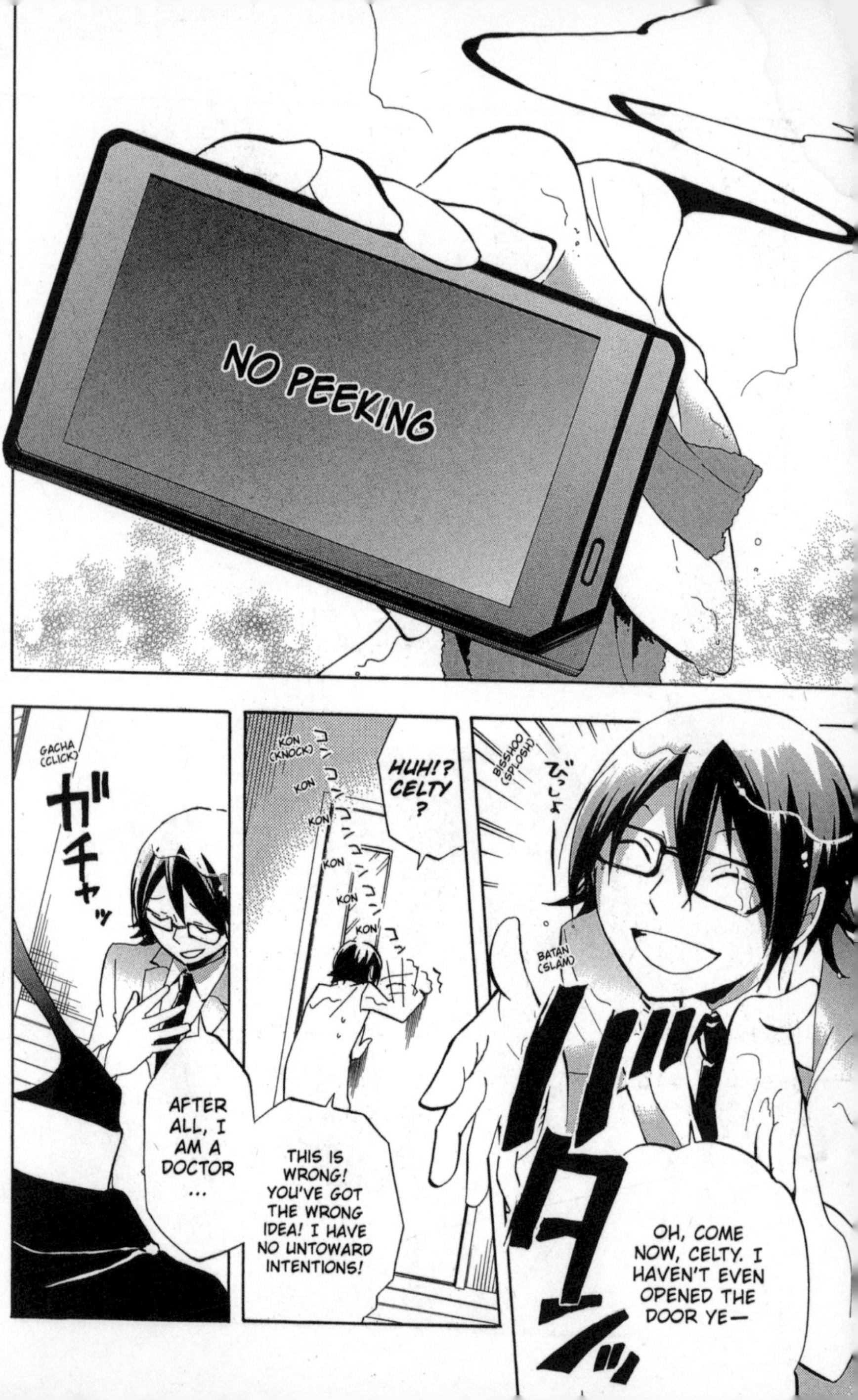
NO PEEKING
BISSHOO (SPLOSH)
BATAN (SLAM)
OH, COME NOW, CELTY. I HAVEN'T EVEN OPENED THE DOOR YE—
KON (KNOCK)
KON
KON
KON
KON
KON
HUH!? CELTY ?
THIS IS WRONG! YOU'VE GOT THE WRONG IDEA! I HAVE NO UNTOWARD INTENTIONS!
GACHA (CLICK)
ガチャッ
AFTER ALL, I AM A DOCTOR ...

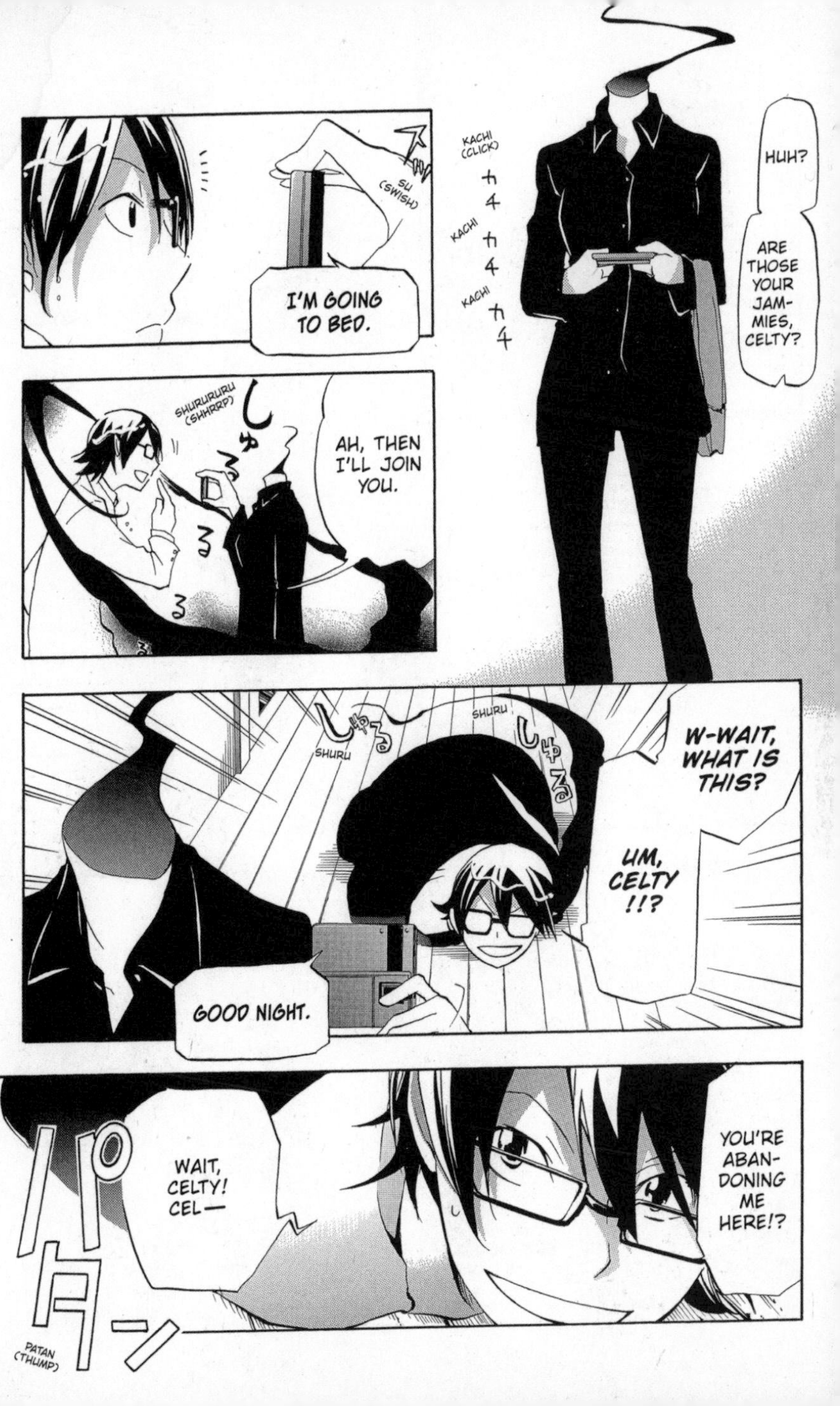

HUH?
ARE THOSE YOUR JAM-MIES, CELTY?
KACHI (CLICK)
KACHI
KACHI
SU (SWISH)
I'M GOING TO BED.
SHURURURU (SHHRRP)
AH, THEN I'LL JOIN YOU.
W-WAIT, WHAT IS THIS?
UM, CELTY !!?
SHURU
SHURU
GOOD NIGHT.
YOU'RE ABAN-DONING ME HERE!?
WAIT, CELTY! CEL—
PATAN (THUMP)

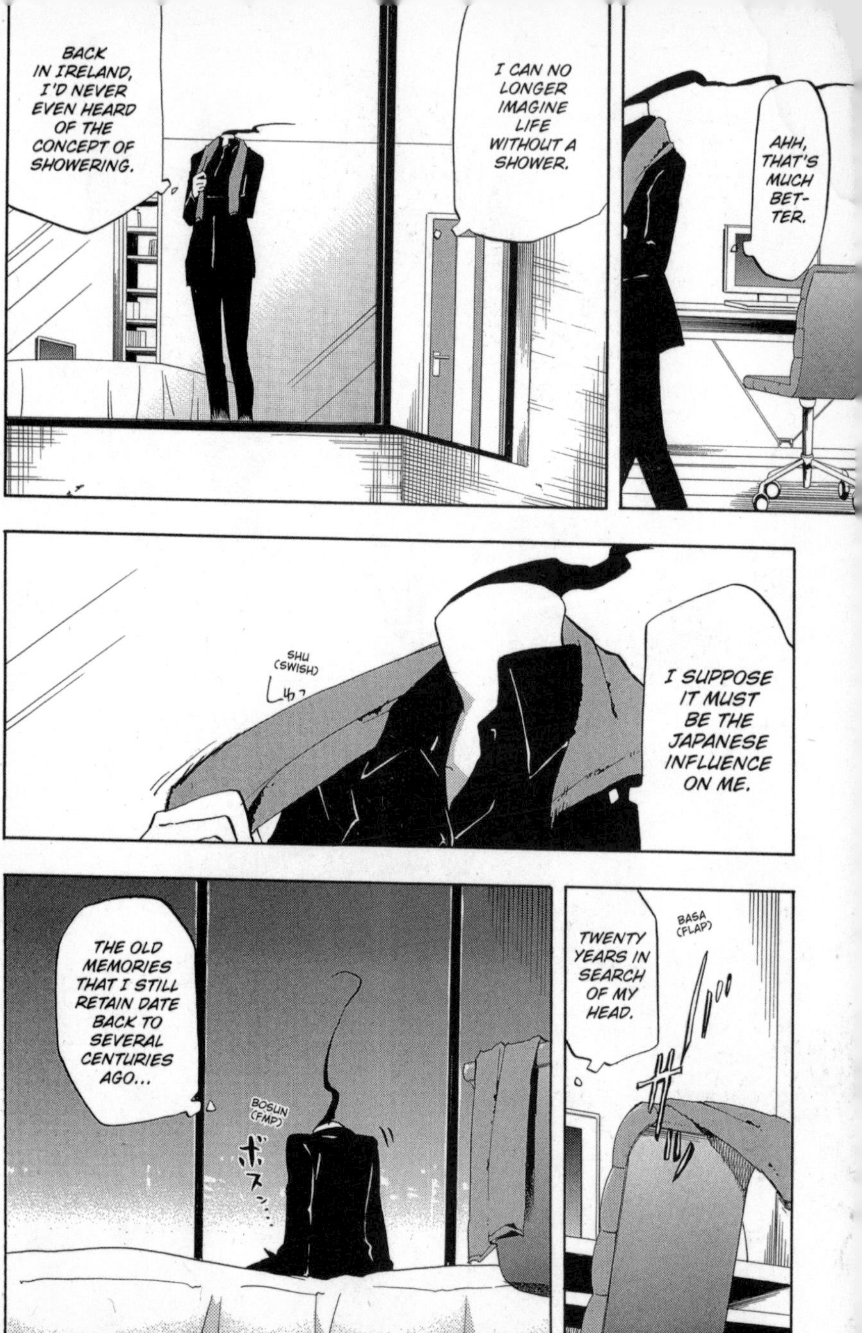
AHH, THAT'S MUCH BET-TER.
I CAN NO LONGER IMAGINE LIFE WITHOUT A SHOWER.
BACK IN IRELAND, I'D NEVER EVEN HEARD OF THE CONCEPT OF SHOWERING.
I SUPPOSE IT MUST BE THE JAPANESE INFLUENCE ON ME.
SHU (SWISH)
BASA (FLAP)
TWENTY YEARS IN SEARCH OF MY HEAD.
THE OLD MEMORIES THAT I STILL RETAIN DATE BACK TO SEVERAL CENTURIES AGO...
BOSUN (FMP)

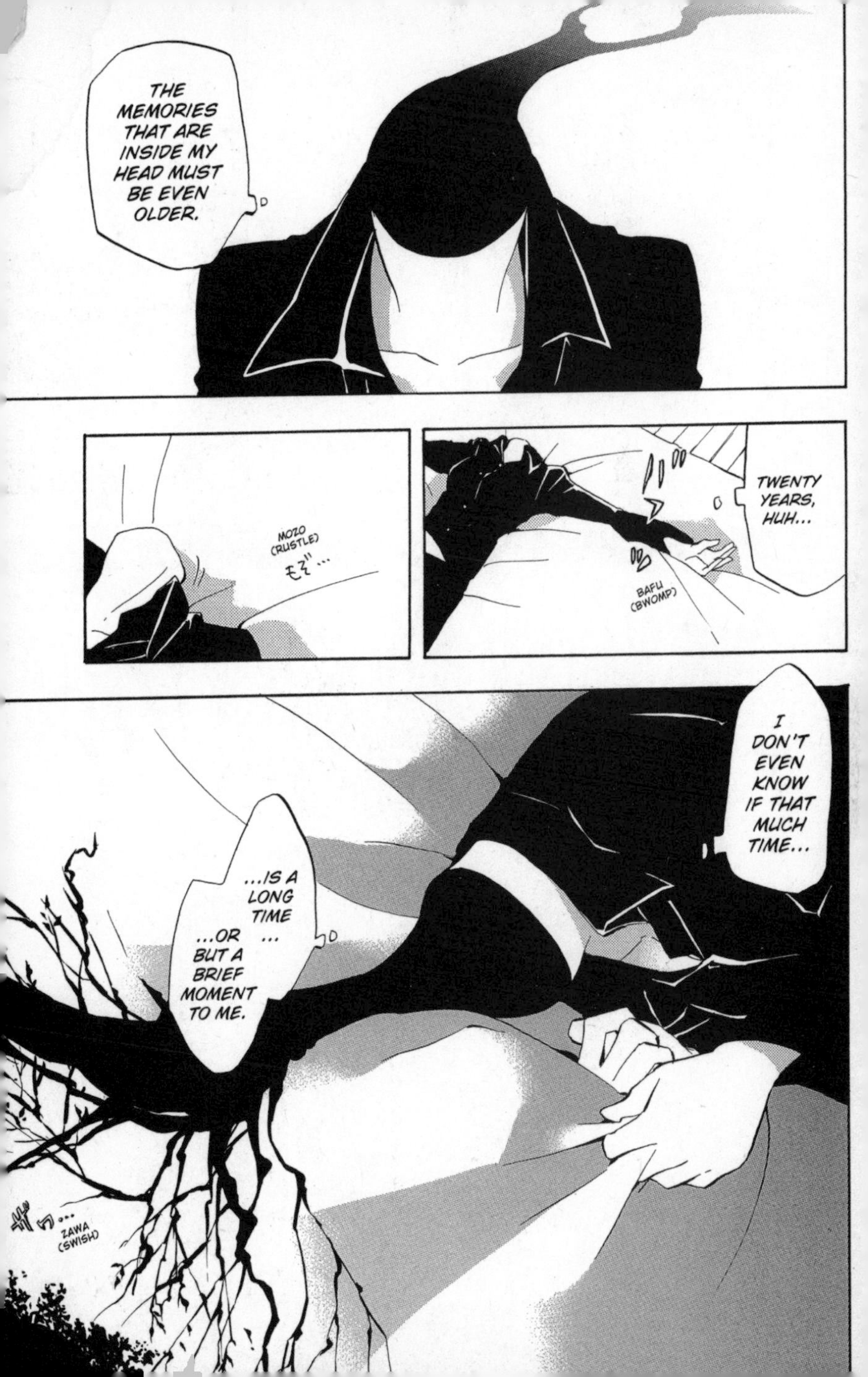
THE MEMORIES THAT ARE INSIDE MY HEAD MUST BE EVEN OLDER.
TWENTY YEARS, HUH...
BAFU (BWOMP)
MOZO (RUSTLE)
もぞ…
I DON'T EVEN KNOW IF THAT MUCH TIME...
...IS A LONG TIME...
...OR BUT A BRIEF MOMENT TO ME.
ZAWA (SWISH)

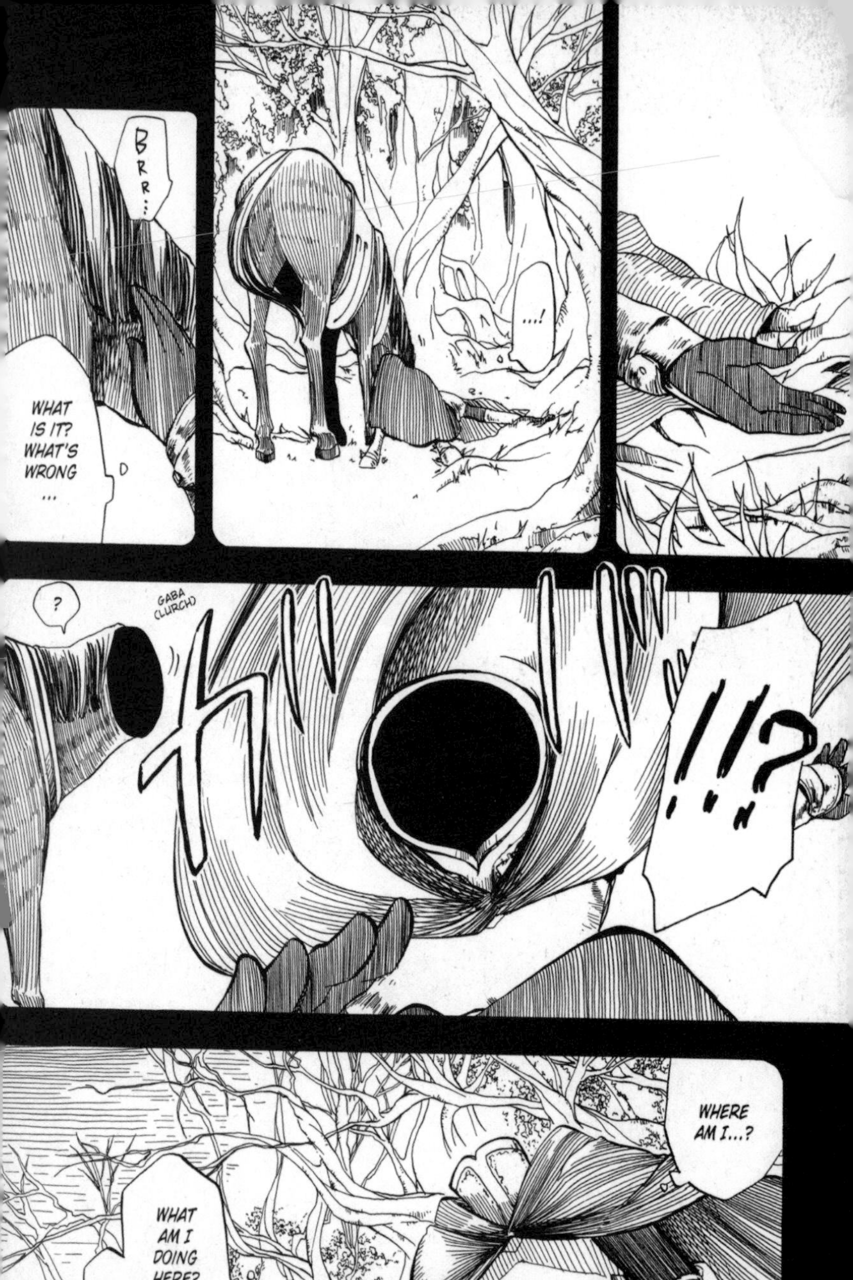
...!
BRR...
WHAT IS IT? WHAT'S WRONG ...
!!?
GABA (LURCH)
?
WHERE AM I...?
WHAT AM I DOING HERE?
HUH?

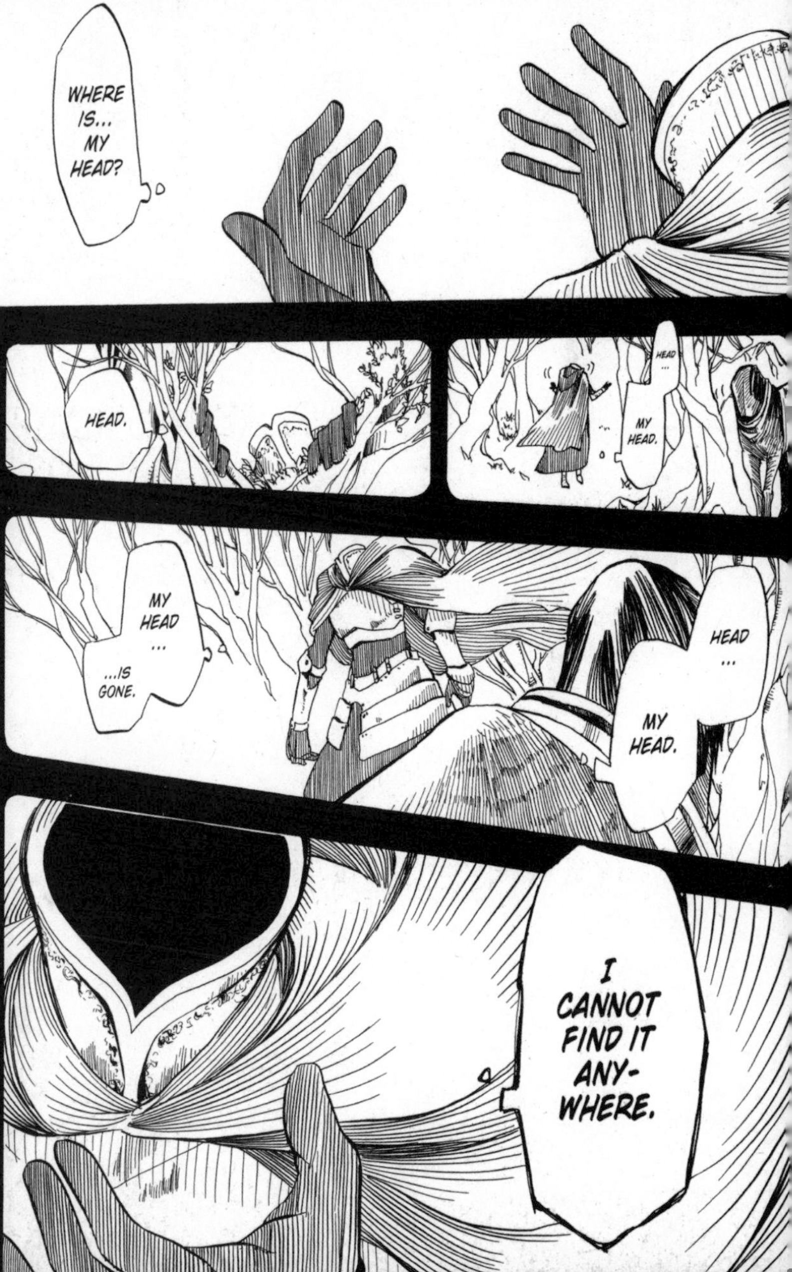
WHERE IS... MY HEAD?
HEAD ...
MY HEAD.
HEAD.
HEAD ...
MY HEAD.
MY HEAD ...
...IS GONE.
I CANNOT FIND IT ANY-WHERE.

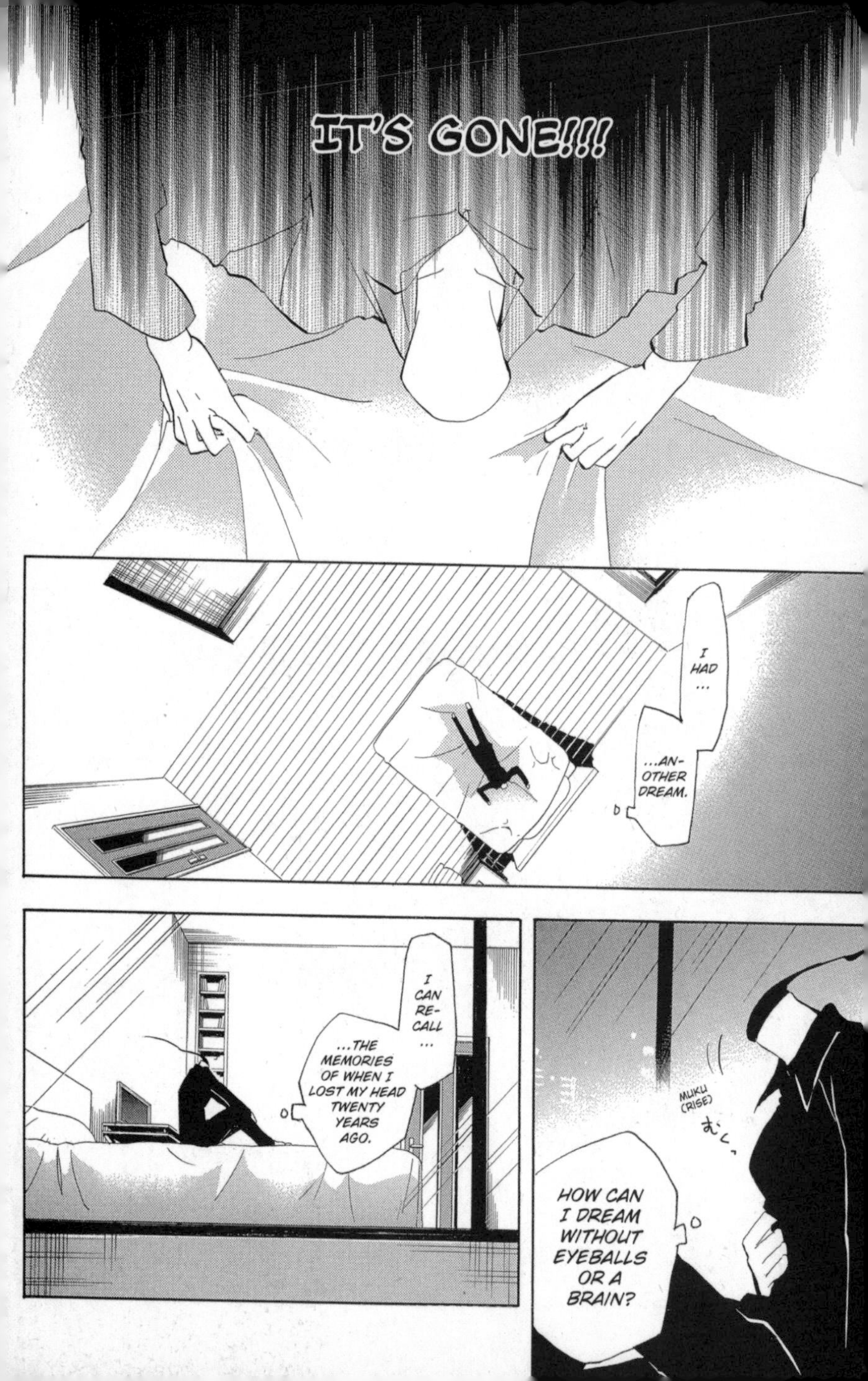
IT'S GONE!!!
I HAD...
...AN-OTHER DREAM.
MUKU (RISE)
むく、
HOW CAN I DREAM WITHOUT EYEBALLS OR A BRAIN?
I CAN RE-CALL...
...THE MEMORIES OF WHEN I LOST MY HEAD TWENTY YEARS AGO.

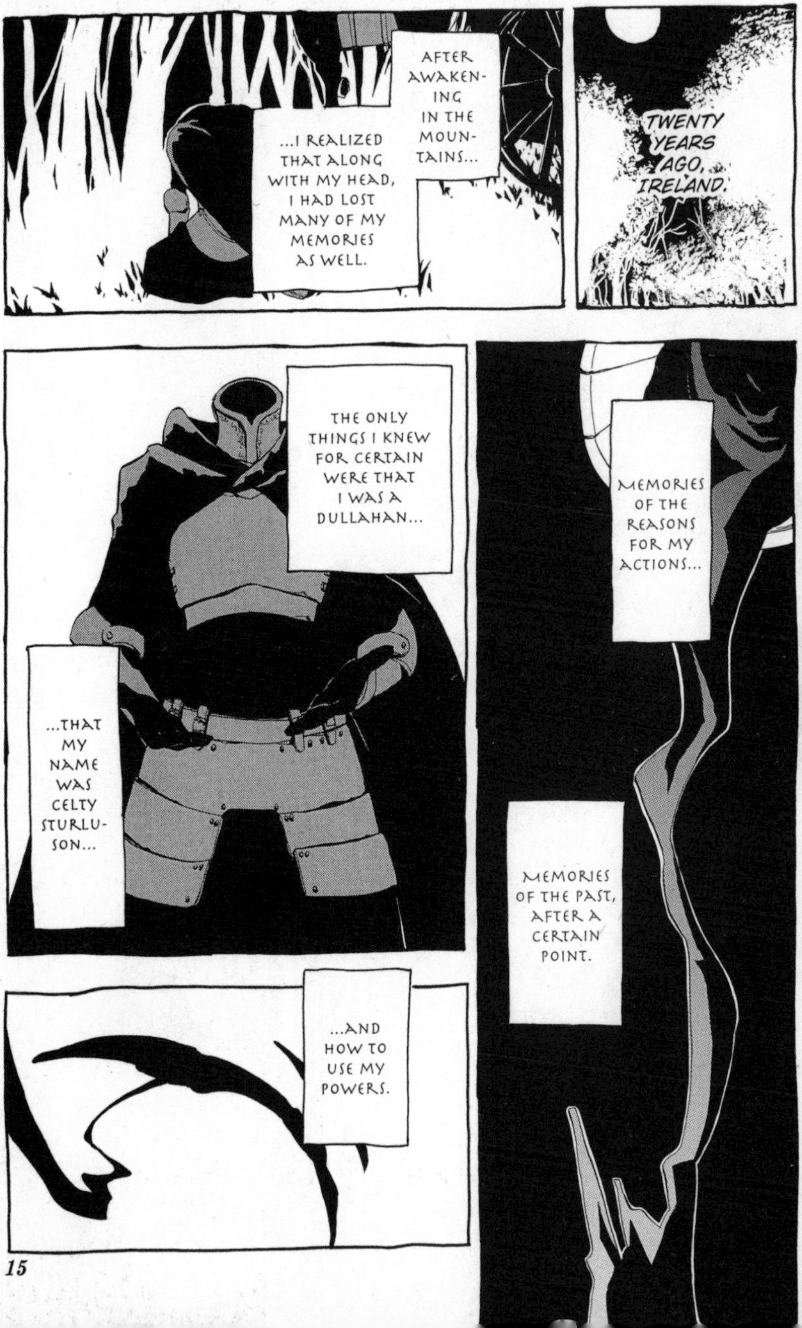
TWENTY YEARS AGO, IRELAND.
AFTER AWAKENING IN THE MOUNTAINS...
...I REALIZED THAT ALONG WITH MY HEAD, I HAD LOST MANY OF MY MEMORIES AS WELL.
MEMORIES OF THE REASONS FOR MY ACTIONS...
MEMORIES OF THE PAST, AFTER A CERTAIN POINT.
THE ONLY THINGS I KNEW FOR CERTAIN WERE THAT I WAS A DULLAHAN...
...THAT MY NAME WAS CELTY STURLUSON...
...AND HOW TO USE MY POWERS.

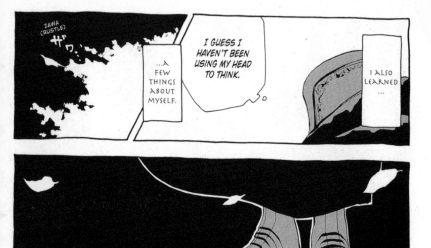

I ALSO LEARNED ...
I GUESS I HAVEN'T BEEN USING MY HEAD TO THINK.
...A FEW THINGS ABOUT MYSELF.
ZAWA (RUSTLE)
ザワ
I COULD FEEL THE PRESENCE OF SOME-THING THAT I ASSUMED WAS MY HEAD.

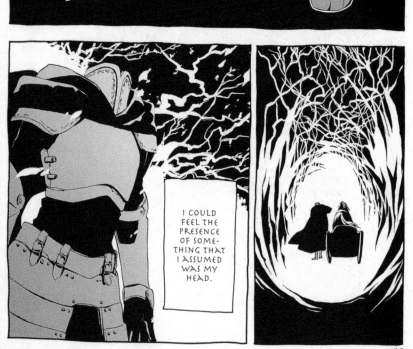

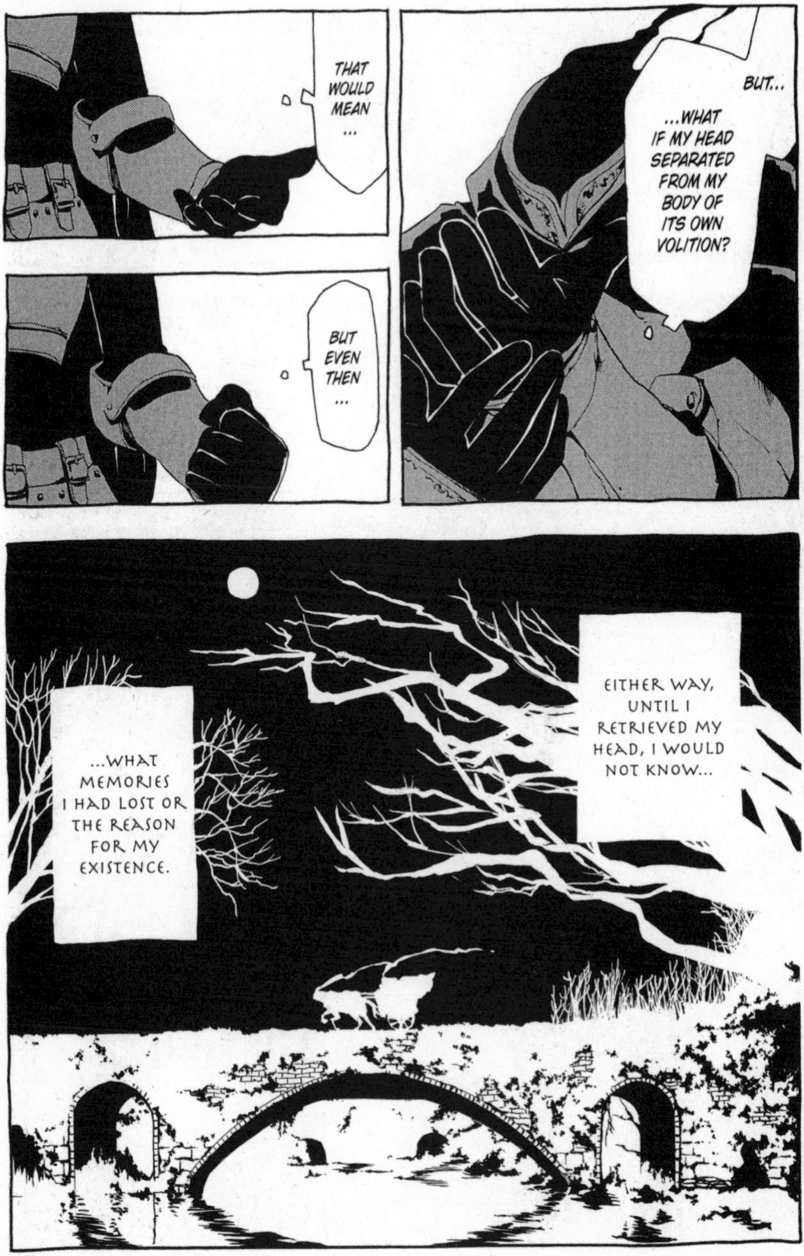
BUT...
...WHAT IF MY HEAD SEPARATED FROM MY BODY OF ITS OWN VOLITION?
THAT WOULD MEAN...
BUT EVEN THEN...
EITHER WAY, UNTIL I RETRIEVED MY HEAD, I WOULD NOT KNOW...
...WHAT MEMORIES I HAD LOST OR THE REASON FOR MY EXISTENCE.

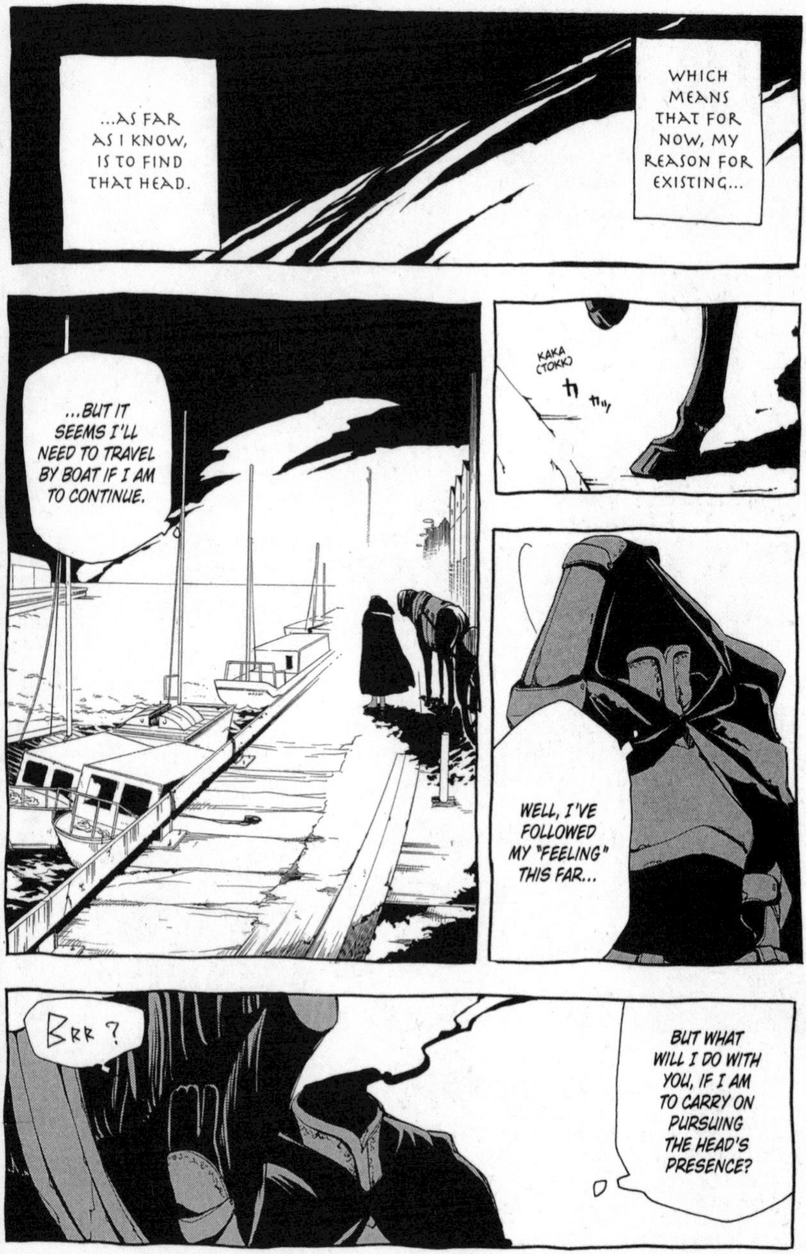
WHICH MEANS THAT FOR NOW, MY REASON FOR EXISTING...
...AS FAR AS I KNOW, IS TO FIND THAT HEAD.
KAKA (TOKK)
カ カッ
WELL, I'VE FOLLOWED MY "FEELING" THIS FAR...
...BUT IT SEEMS I'LL NEED TO TRAVEL BY BOAT IF I AM TO CONTINUE.
BUT WHAT WILL I DO WITH YOU, IF I AM TO CARRY ON PURSUING THE HEAD'S PRESENCE?
Brr ?

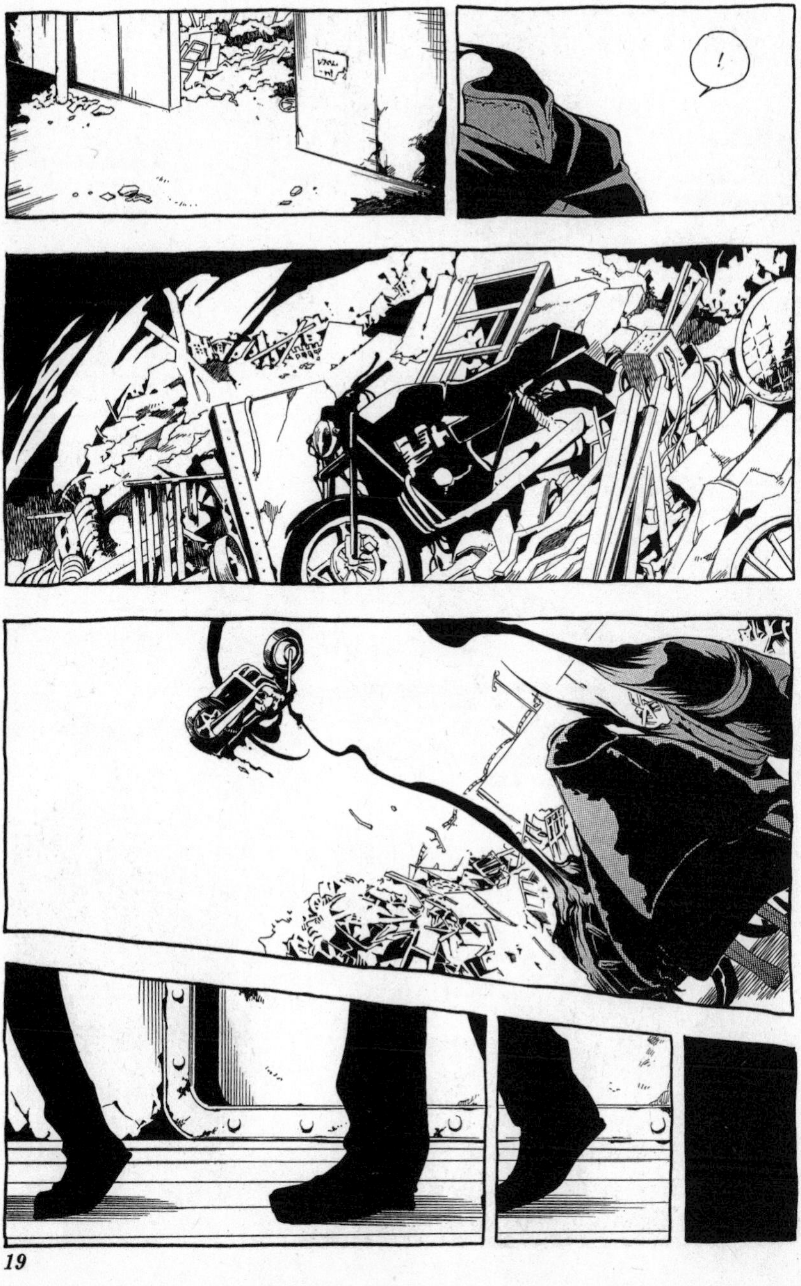
!

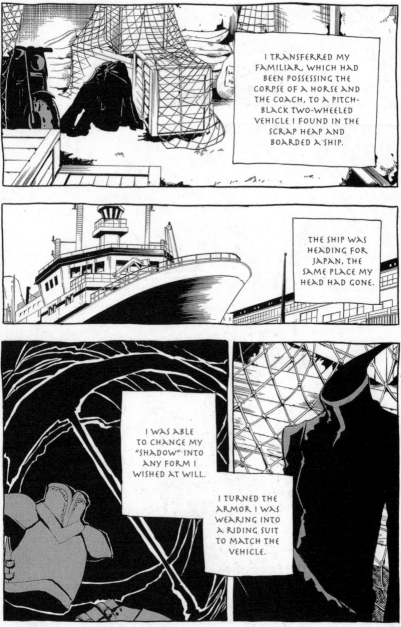

I TRANSFERRED MY FAMILIAR, WHICH HAD BEEN POSSESSING THE CORPSE OF A HORSE AND THE COACH, TO A PITCH-BLACK TWO-WHEELED VEHICLE I FOUND IN THE SCRAP HEAP AND BOARDED A SHIP.

THE SHIP WAS HEADING FOR JAPAN, THE SAME PLACE MY HEAD HAD GONE.

I WAS ABLE TO CHANGE MY "SHADOW" INTO ANY FORM I WISHED AT WILL.

I TURNED THE ARMOR I WAS WEARING INTO A RIDING SUIT TO MATCH THE VEHICLE.

20

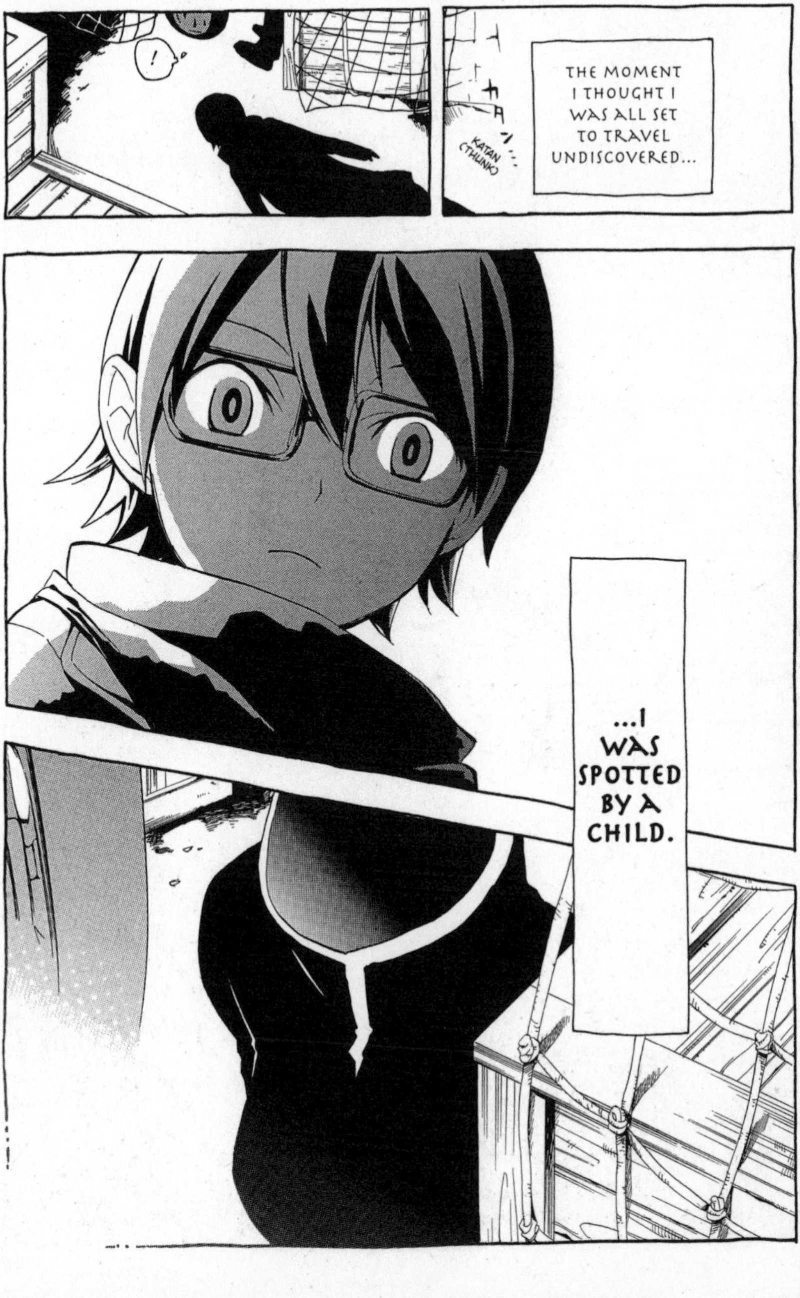
THE MOMENT I THOUGHT I WAS ALL SET TO TRAVEL UNDISCOVERED...
KATAN (THUNK)
!
...I WAS SPOTTED BY A CHILD.

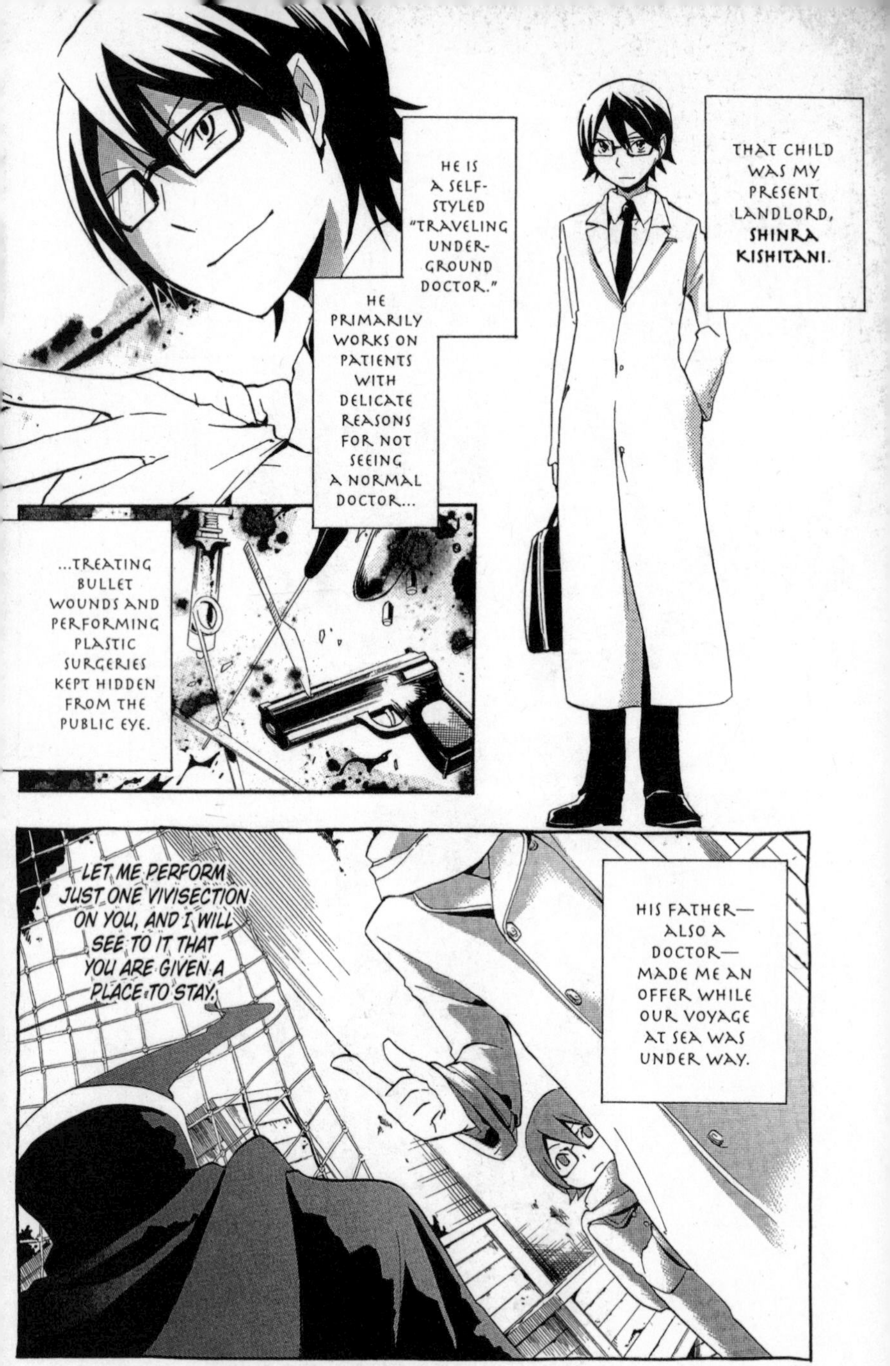
THAT CHILD WAS MY PRESENT LANDLORD, SHINRA KISHITANI.
HE IS A SELF-STYLED "TRAVELING UNDERGROUND DOCTOR."
HE PRIMARILY WORKS ON PATIENTS WITH DELICATE REASONS FOR NOT SEEING A NORMAL DOCTOR...
...TREATING BULLET WOUNDS AND PERFORMING PLASTIC SURGERIES KEPT HIDDEN FROM THE PUBLIC EYE.
HIS FATHER—ALSO A DOCTOR—MADE ME AN OFFER WHILE OUR VOYAGE AT SEA WAS UNDER WAY.
LET ME PERFORM JUST ONE VIVISECTION ON YOU, AND I WILL SEE TO IT THAT YOU ARE GIVEN A PLACE TO STAY.

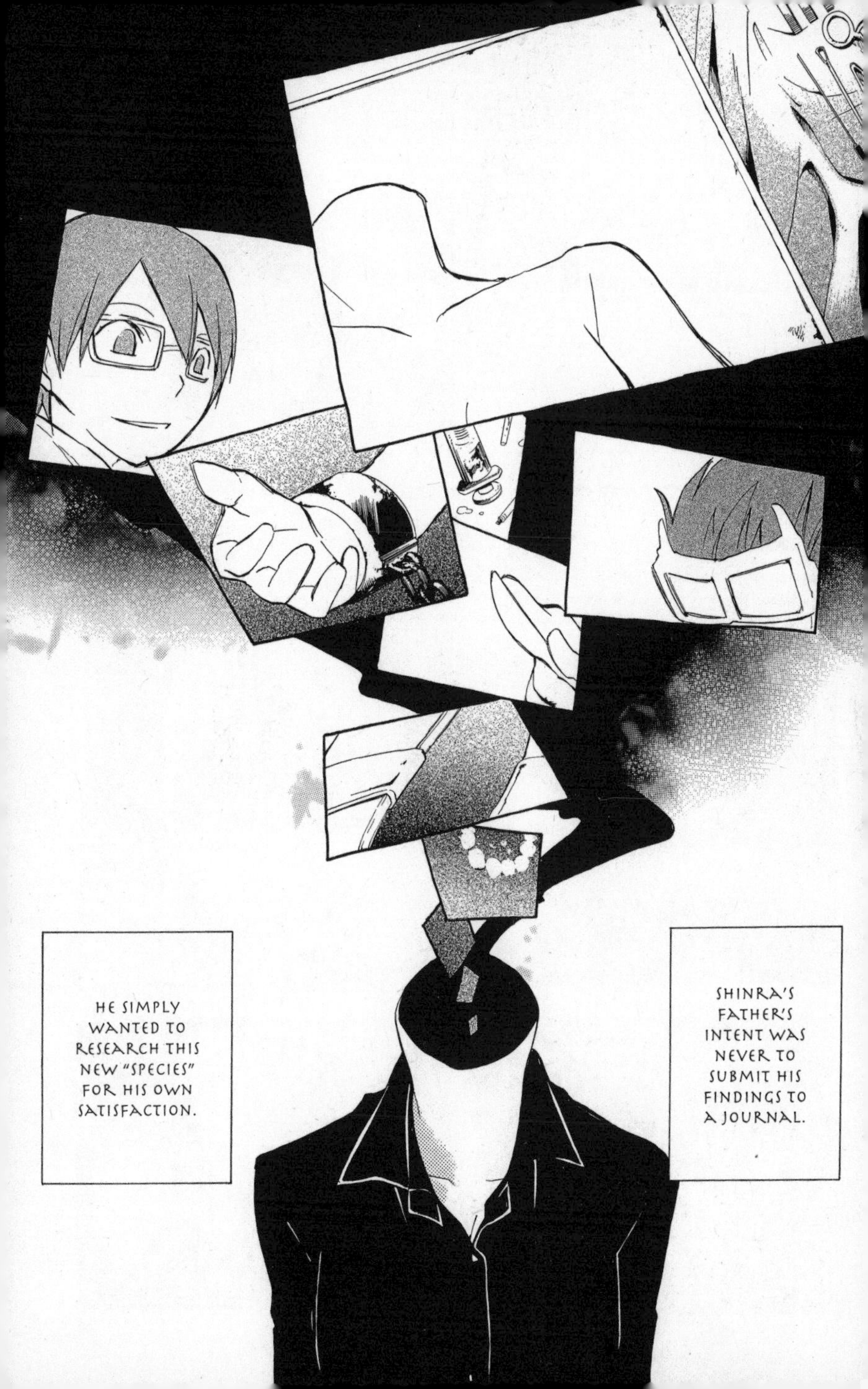
SHINRA'S FATHER'S INTENT WAS NEVER TO SUBMIT HIS FINDINGS TO A JOURNAL.
HE SIMPLY WANTED TO RESEARCH THIS NEW "SPECIES" FOR HIS OWN SATISFACTION.

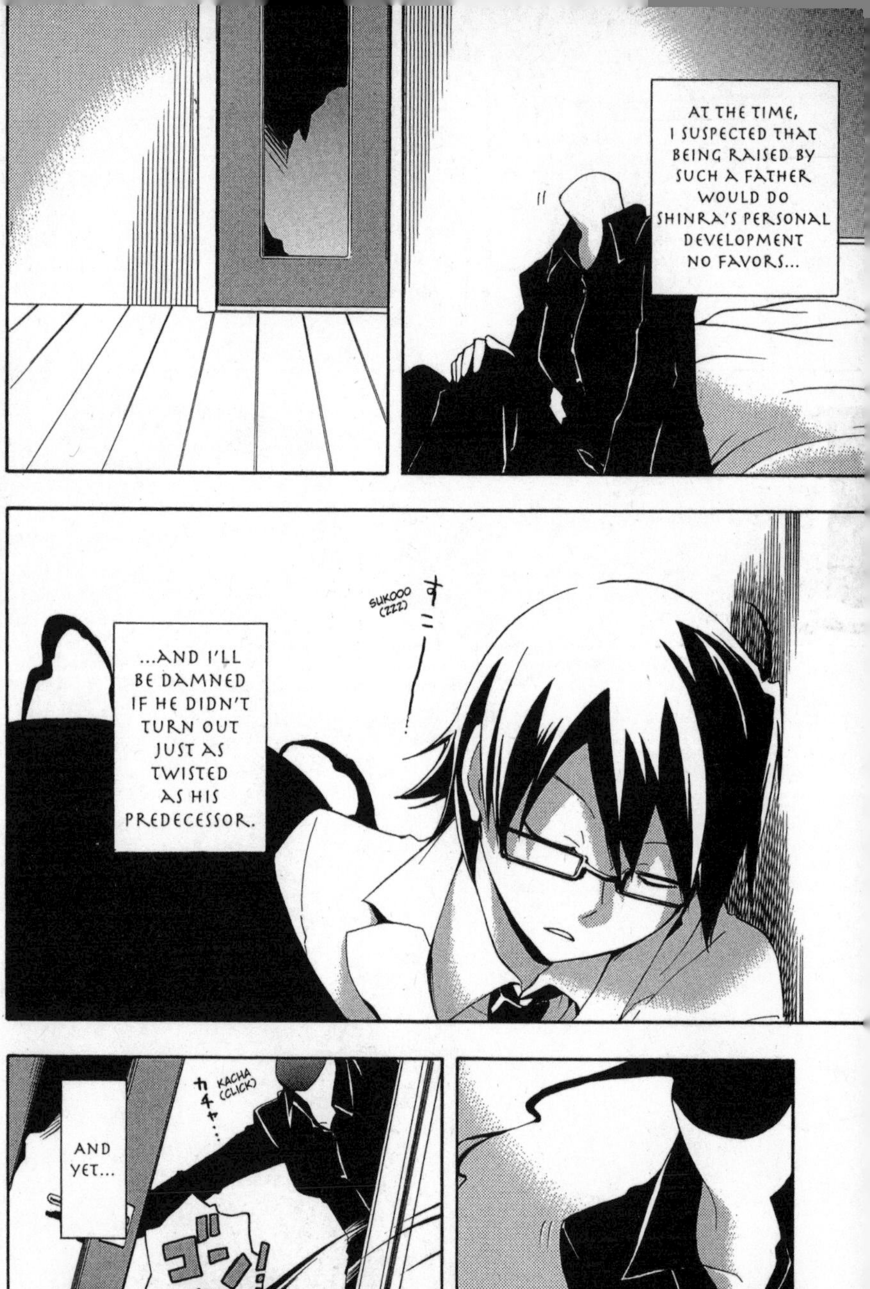
AT THE TIME, I SUSPECTED THAT BEING RAISED BY SUCH A FATHER WOULD DO SHINRA'S PERSONAL DEVELOPMENT NO FAVORS...
SUKOOO (ZZZ)
...AND I'LL BE DAMNED IF HE DIDN'T TURN OUT JUST AS TWISTED AS HIS PREDECESSOR.
KACHA (CLICK)
AND YET...
GON (GONK)

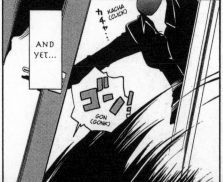

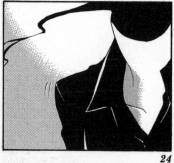

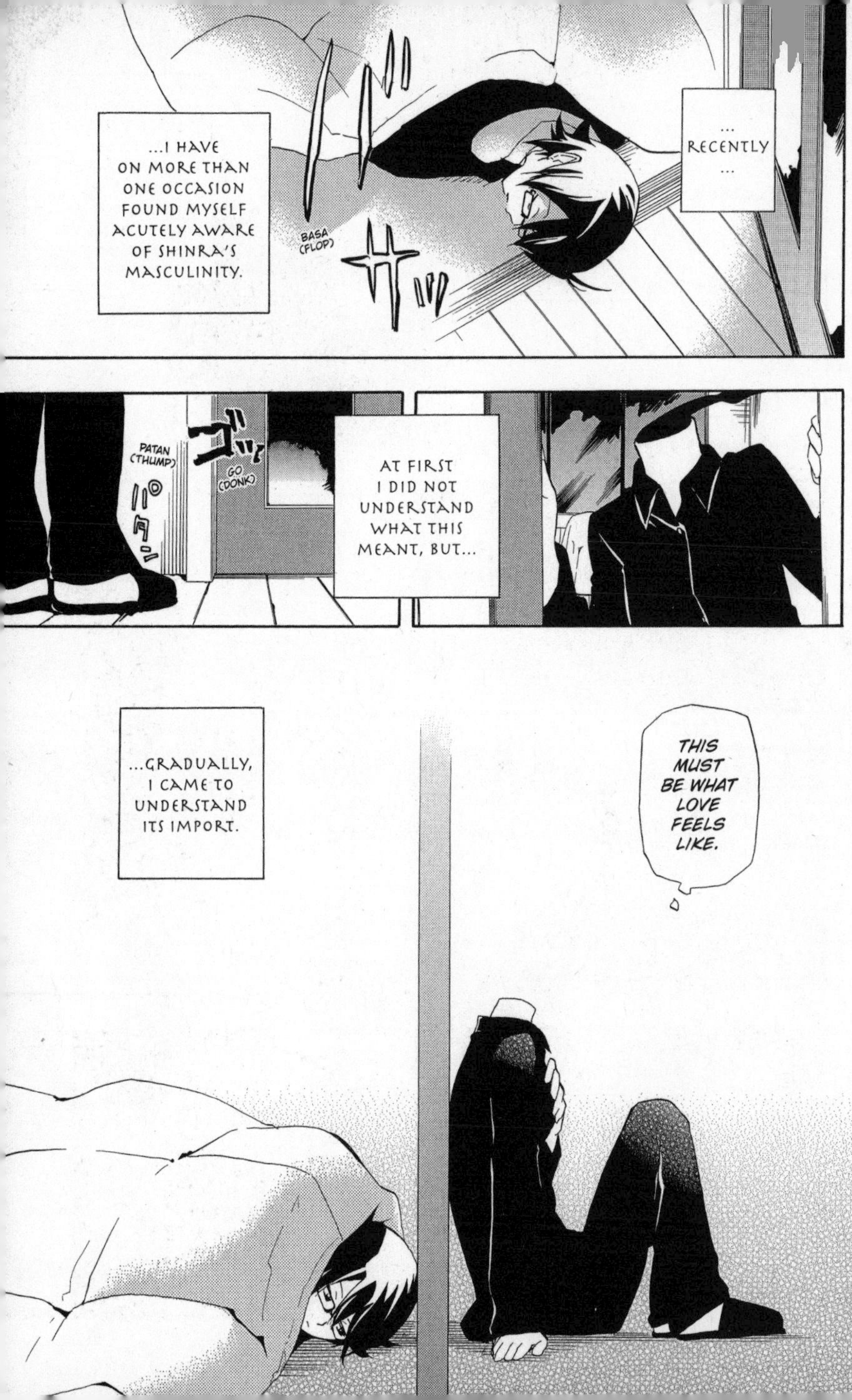
...RECENTLY...
...I HAVE ON MORE THAN ONE OCCASION FOUND MYSELF ACUTELY AWARE OF SHINRA'S MASCULINITY.
BASA (FLOP)
AT FIRST I DID NOT UNDERSTAND WHAT THIS MEANT, BUT...
GO (DONK)
PATAN (THUMP)
THIS MUST BE WHAT LOVE FEELS LIKE.
...GRADUALLY, I CAME TO UNDERSTAND ITS IMPORT.

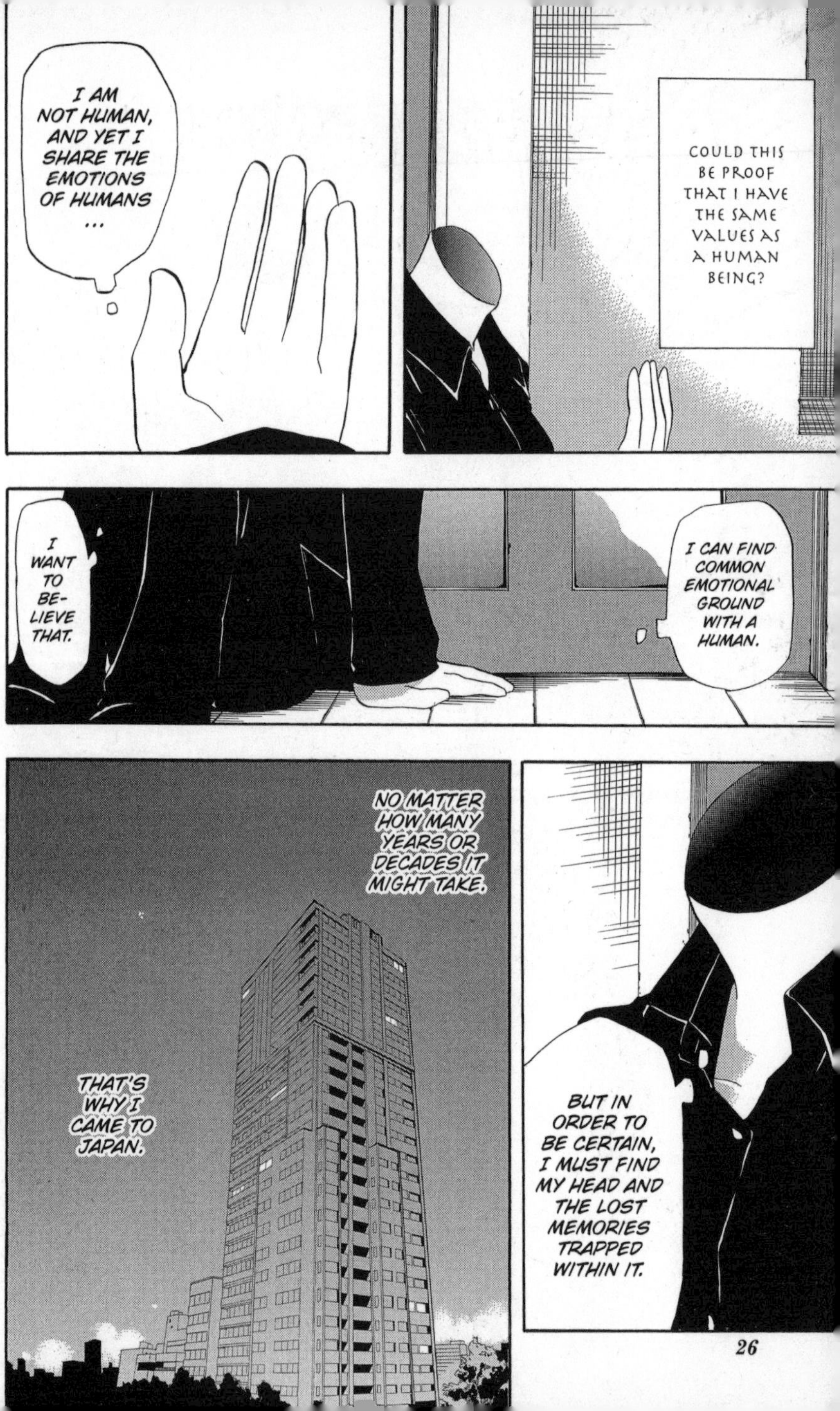
COULD THIS BE PROOF THAT I HAVE THE SAME VALUES AS A HUMAN BEING?
I AM NOT HUMAN, AND YET I SHARE THE EMOTIONS OF HUMANS ...
I CAN FIND COMMON EMOTIONAL GROUND WITH A HUMAN.
I WANT TO BE-LIEVE THAT.
BUT IN ORDER TO BE CERTAIN, I MUST FIND MY HEAD AND THE LOST MEMORIES TRAPPED WITHIN IT.
NO MATTER HOW MANY YEARS OR DECADES IT MIGHT TAKE.
THAT'S WHY I CAME TO JAPAN.

7: WAWAWAWAWAWAWA!!

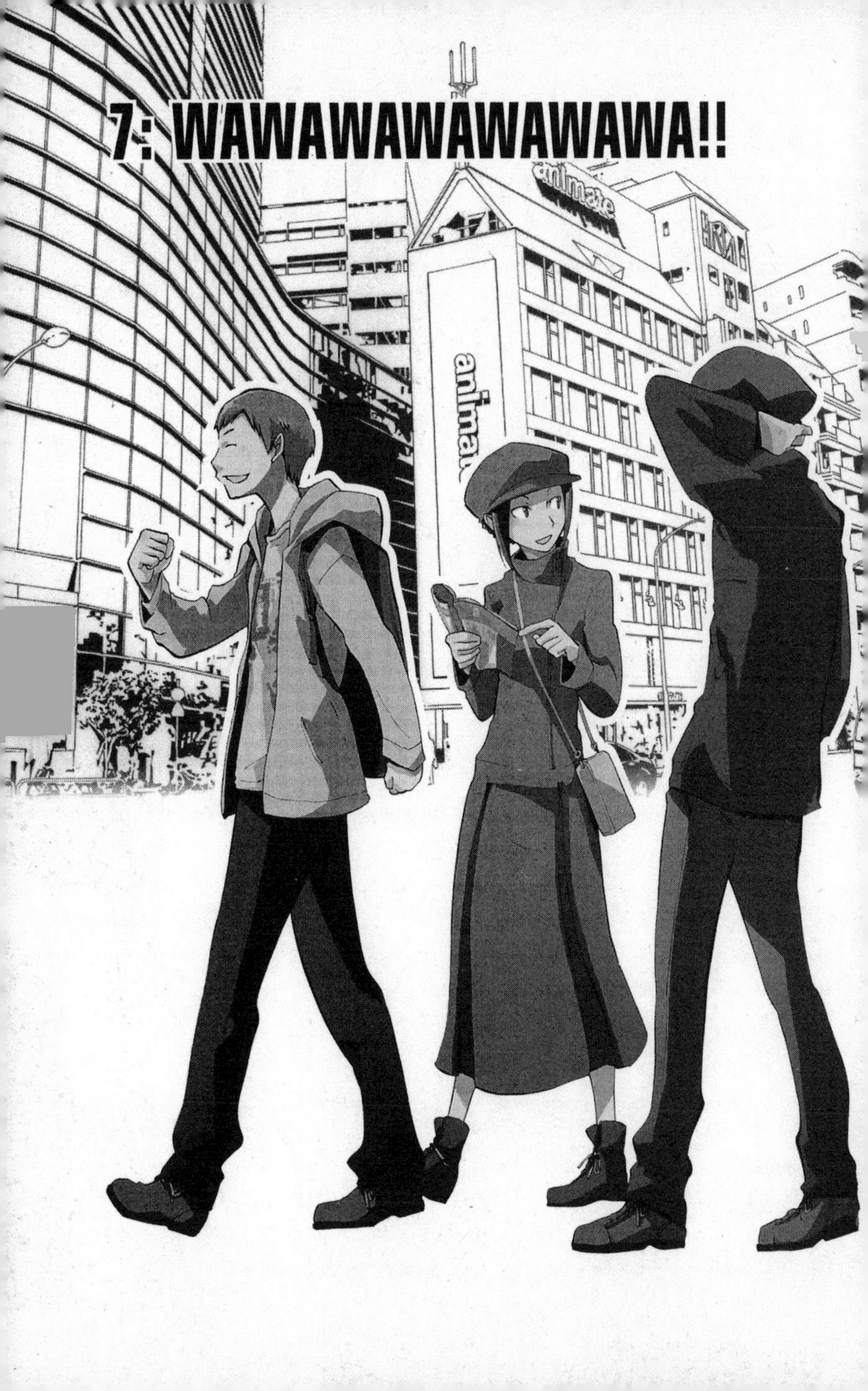

animate
animate

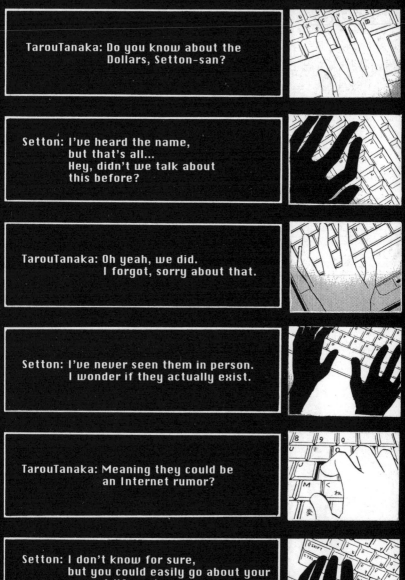

TarouTanaka: Do you know about the
                        Dollars, Setton-san?

Setton: I've heard the name,
              but that's all...
              Hey, didn't we talk about
              this before?

TarouTanaka: Oh yeah, we did.
                        I forgot, sorry about that.

Setton: I've never seen them in person.
              I wonder if they actually exist.

TarouTanaka: Meaning they could be
                        an Internet rumor?

Setton: I don't know for sure,
              but you could easily go about your
              normal life and never come across
              a team that you know for a fact
              exists.

—KANRA HAS ENTERED THE CHAT—

Kanra: Talking about the Dollars?
They do exist.
They even have a webpage
dedicated to them,
but you'll need a login and
password to see the page.

Setton: I wouldn't have any interest in
seeing it anyway.

Enter

TarouTanaka: Kanra-san, you really do
know everything!

Kanra: Well, it's all I'm good for.

TarouTanaka: Oh, can you tell me about
this Dotachin person?

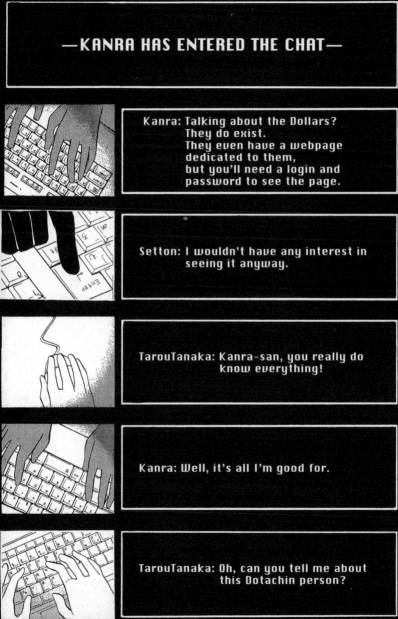

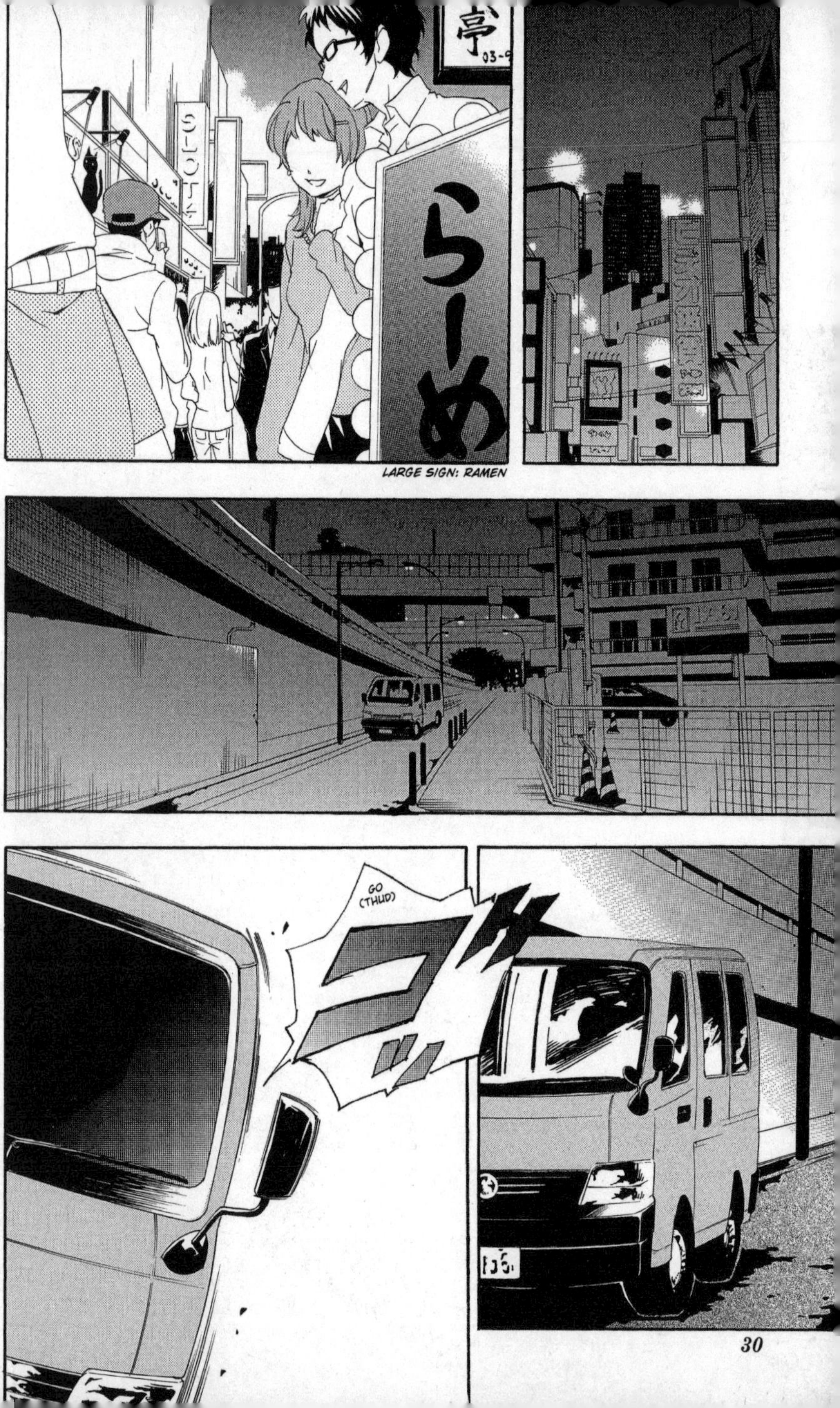
亭
らーめ
LARGE SIGN: RAMEN
GO
(THUD)

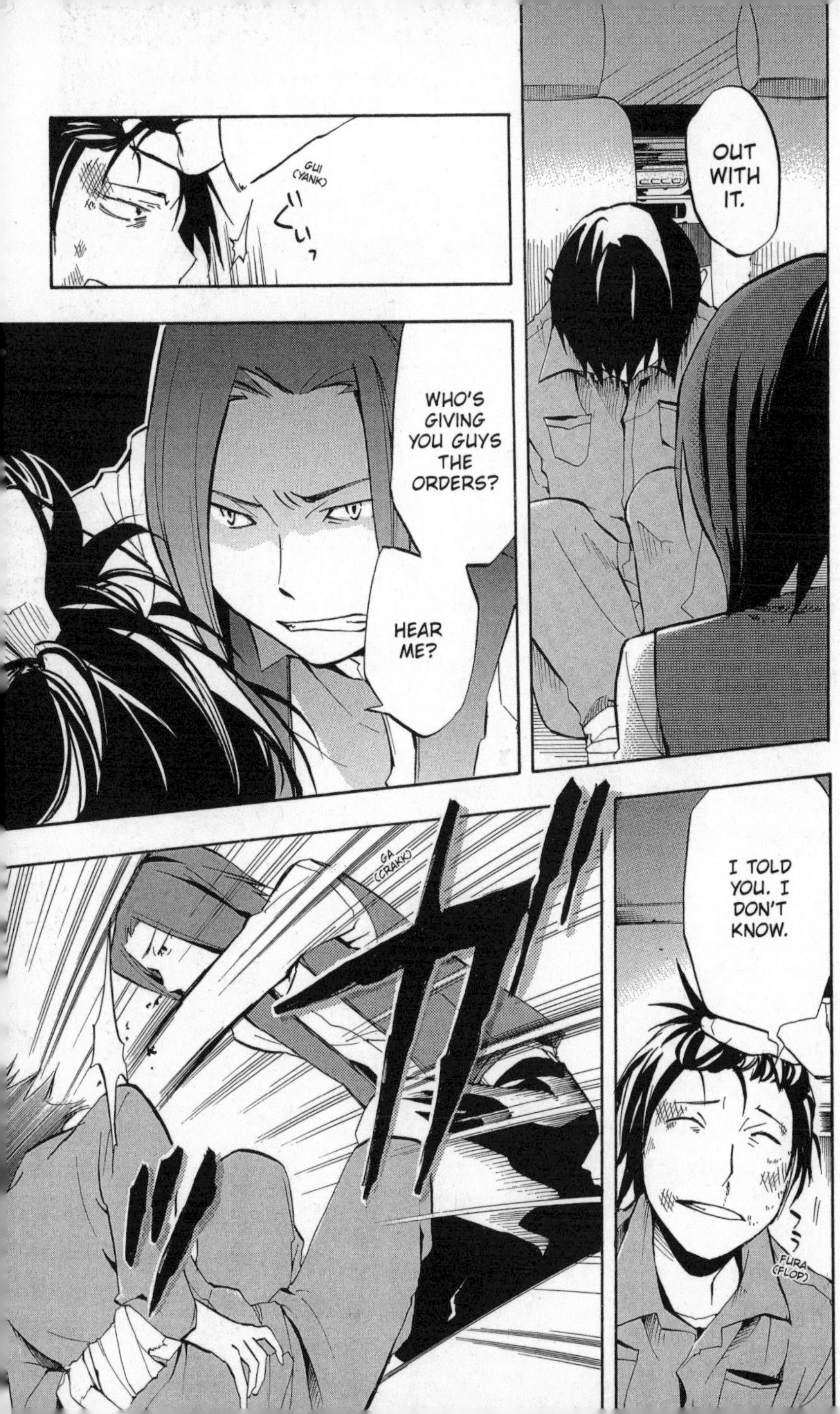
OUT WITH IT.
GUI (YANK)
WHO'S GIVING YOU GUYS THE ORDERS?
HEAR ME?
I TOLD YOU. I DON'T KNOW.
FURA (FLOP)
GA (CRAKK)

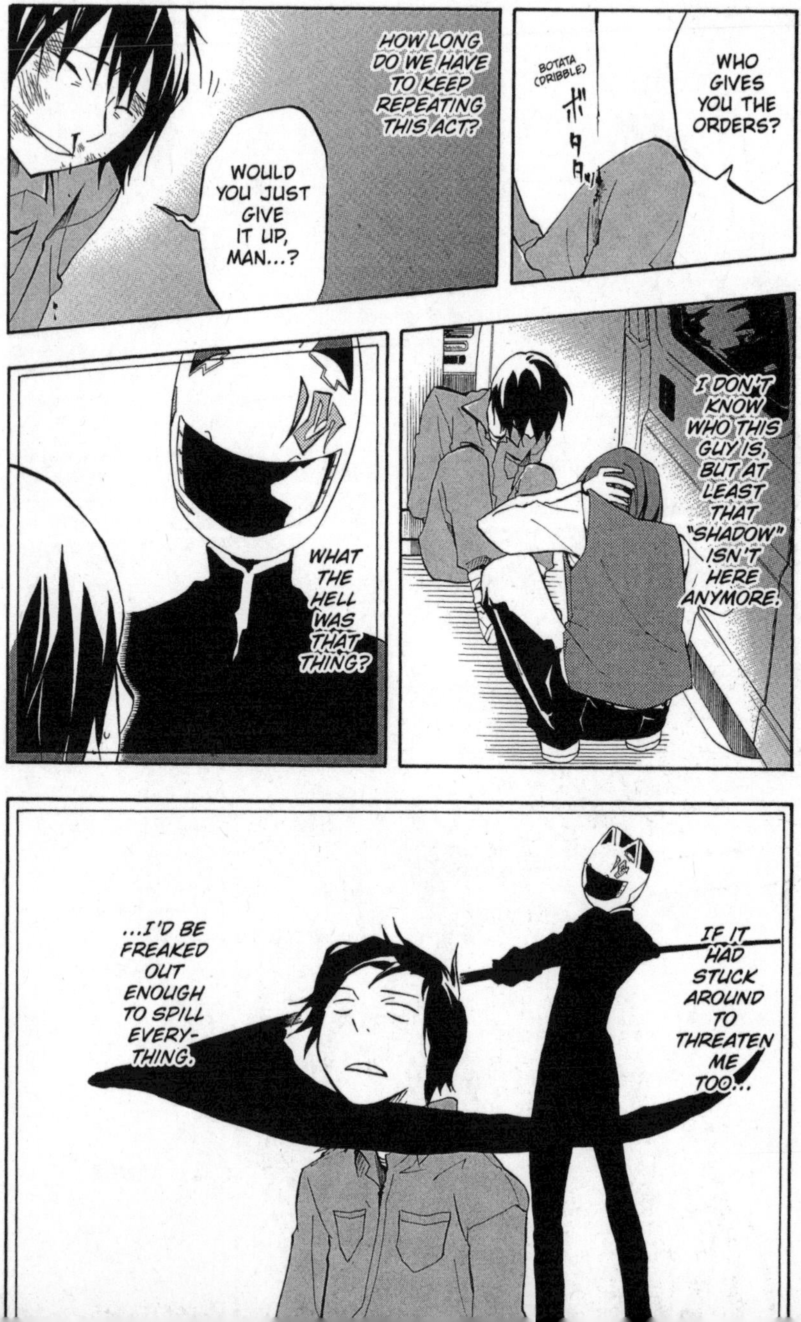
BOTATA (DRIBBLE)
ボタタッ
WHO GIVES YOU THE ORDERS?
HOW LONG DO WE HAVE TO KEEP REPEATING THIS ACT?
WOULD YOU JUST GIVE IT UP, MAN...?
I DON'T KNOW WHO THIS GUY IS, BUT AT LEAST THAT "SHADOW" ISN'T HERE ANYMORE.
WHAT THE HELL WAS THAT THING?
IF IT HAD STUCK AROUND TO THREATEN ME TOO...
...I'D BE FREAKED OUT ENOUGH TO SPILL EVERY-THING.

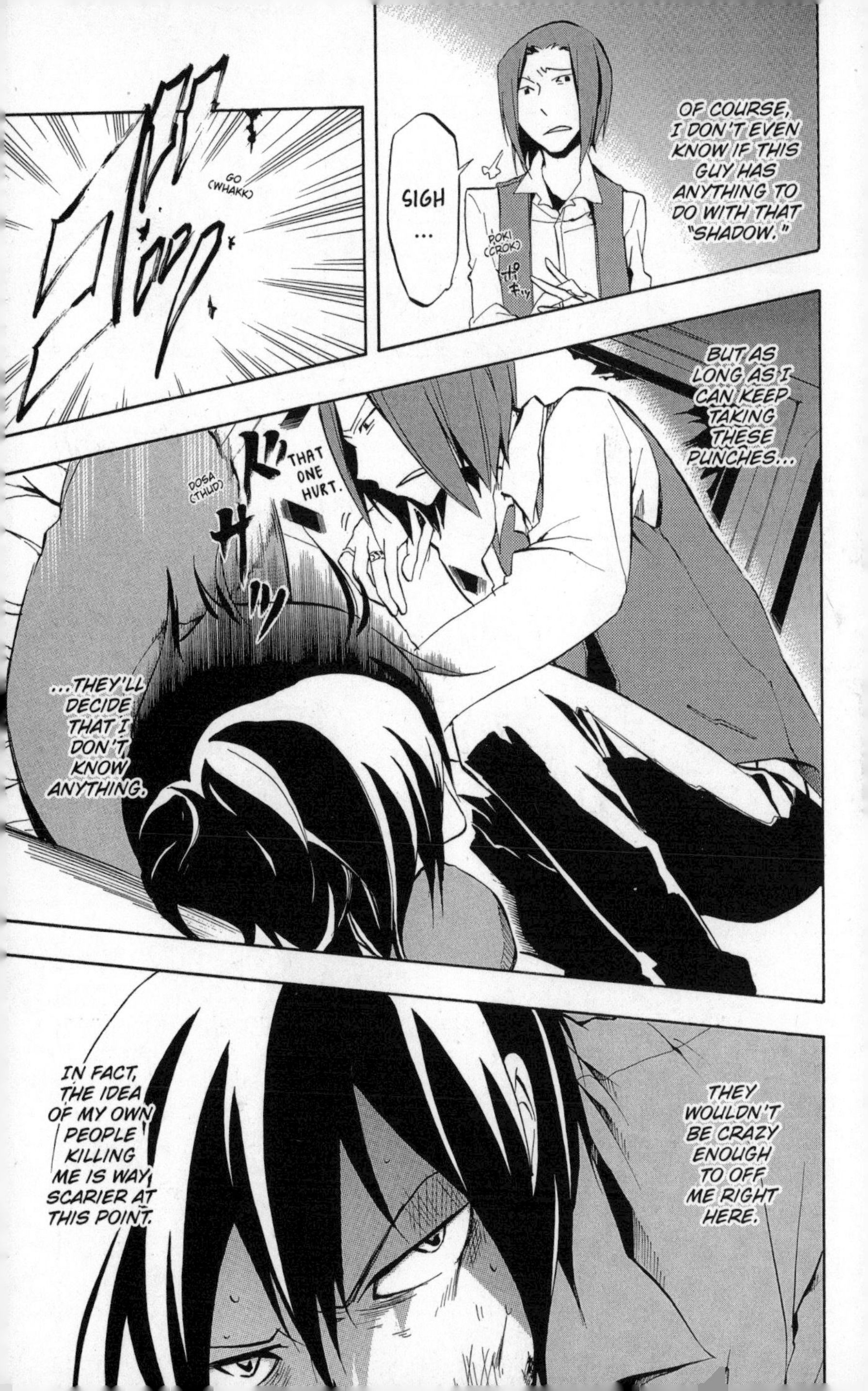
OF COURSE, I DON'T EVEN KNOW IF THIS GUY HAS ANYTHING TO DO WITH THAT "SHADOW."
SIGH ...
POKI (CROK)
GO (WHAKK)
BUT AS LONG AS I CAN KEEP TAKING THESE PUNCHES...
THAT ONE HURT.
DOSA (THUD)
...THEY'LL DECIDE THAT I DON'T KNOW ANYTHING.
THEY WOULDN'T BE CRAZY ENOUGH TO OFF ME RIGHT HERE.
IN FACT, THE IDEA OF MY OWN PEOPLE KILLING ME IS WAY SCARIER AT THIS POINT.

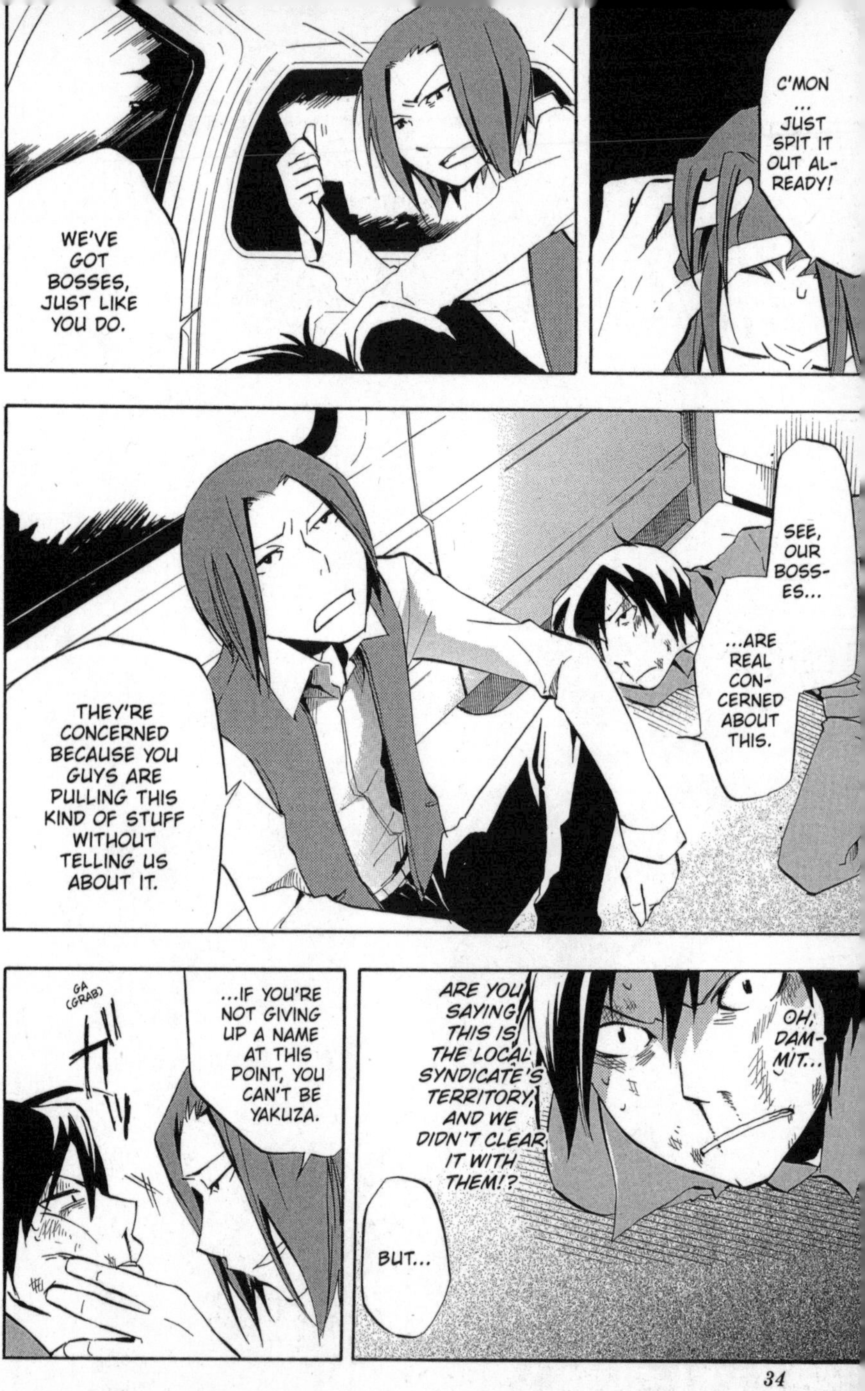
C'MON ... JUST SPIT IT OUT AL-READY!
WE'VE GOT BOSSES, JUST LIKE YOU DO.
SEE, OUR BOSS-ES...
...ARE REAL CON-CERNED ABOUT THIS.
THEY'RE CONCERNED BECAUSE YOU GUYS ARE PULLING THIS KIND OF STUFF WITHOUT TELLING US ABOUT IT.
OH, DAM-MIT...
ARE YOU SAYING THIS IS THE LOCAL SYNDICATE'S TERRITORY, AND WE DIDN'T CLEAR IT WITH THEM!?
BUT...
...IF YOU'RE NOT GIVING UP A NAME AT THIS POINT, YOU CAN'T BE YAKUZA.
GA (GRAB)

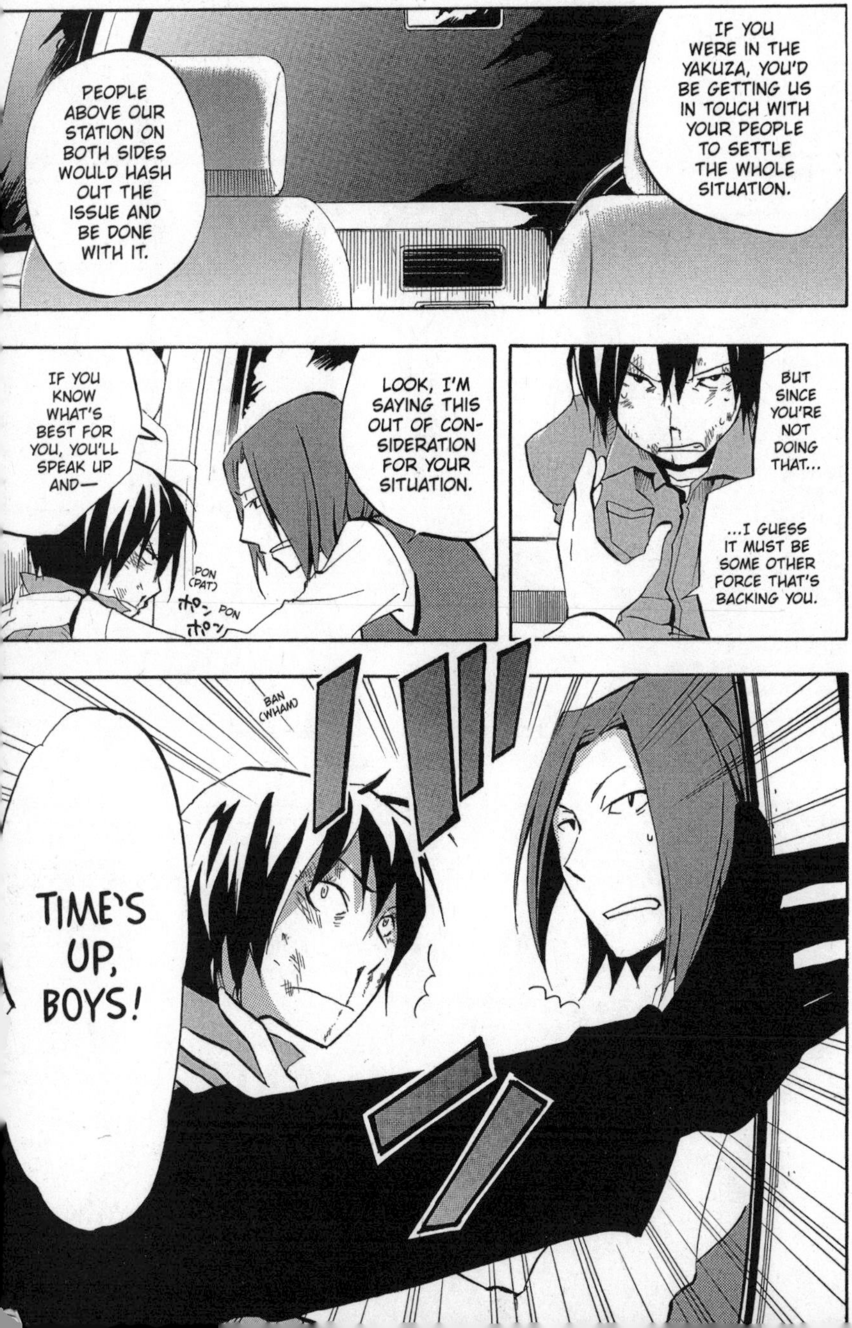
IF YOU WERE IN THE YAKUZA, YOU'D BE GETTING US IN TOUCH WITH YOUR PEOPLE TO SETTLE THE WHOLE SITUATION.
PEOPLE ABOVE OUR STATION ON BOTH SIDES WOULD HASH OUT THE ISSUE AND BE DONE WITH IT.
BUT SINCE YOU'RE NOT DOING THAT...
...I GUESS IT MUST BE SOME OTHER FORCE THAT'S BACKING YOU.
LOOK, I'M SAYING THIS OUT OF CONSIDERATION FOR YOUR SITUATION.
IF YOU KNOW WHAT'S BEST FOR YOU, YOU'LL SPEAK UP AND—
PON (PAT) PON
BAN (WHAM)
TIME'S UP, BOYS!

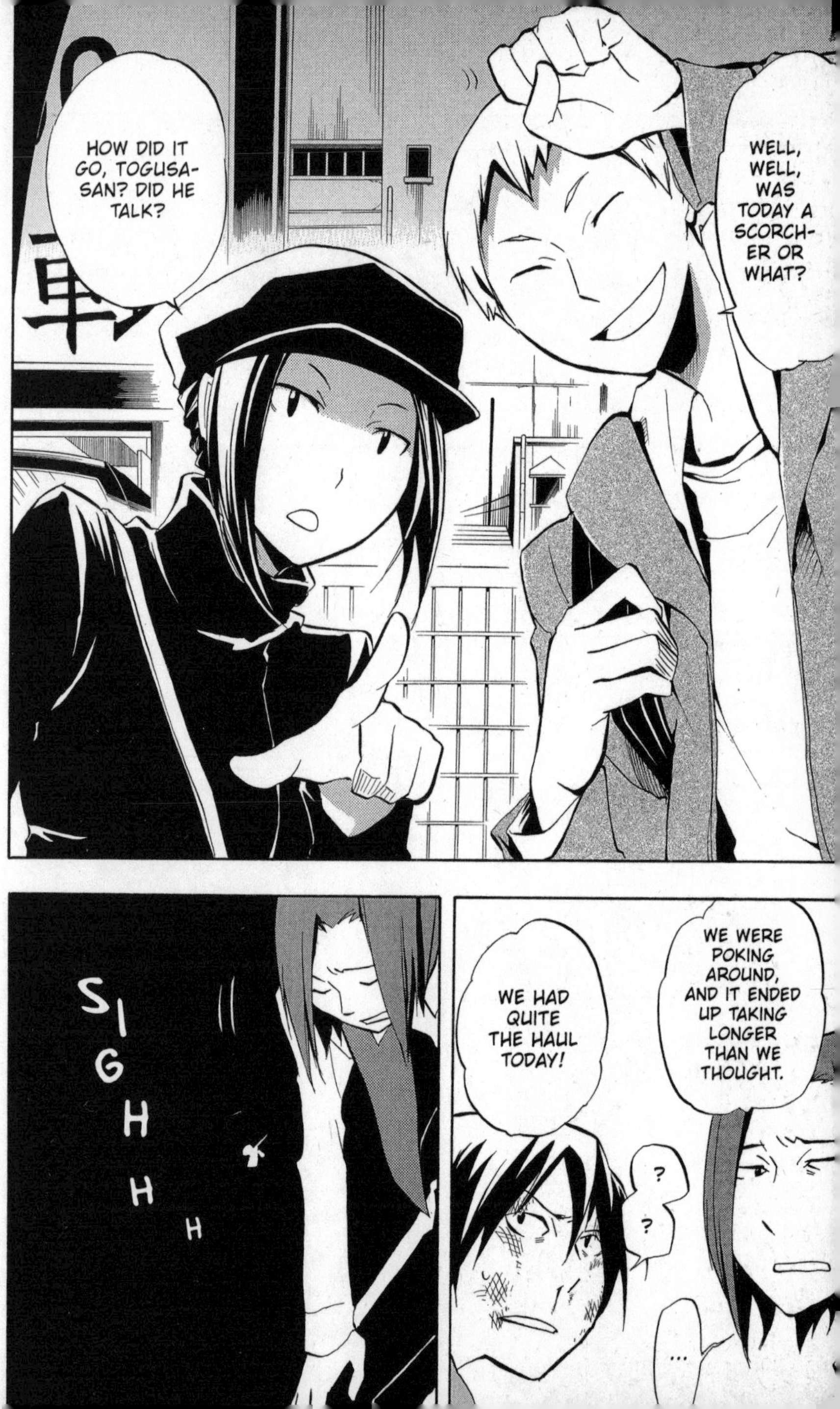
WELL, WELL, WAS TODAY A SCORCHER OR WHAT?
HOW DID IT GO, TOGUSA-SAN? DID HE TALK?
WE WERE POKING AROUND, AND IT ENDED UP TAKING LONGER THAN WE THOUGHT.
WE HAD QUITE THE HAUL TODAY!
?
?
...
SIGHHH

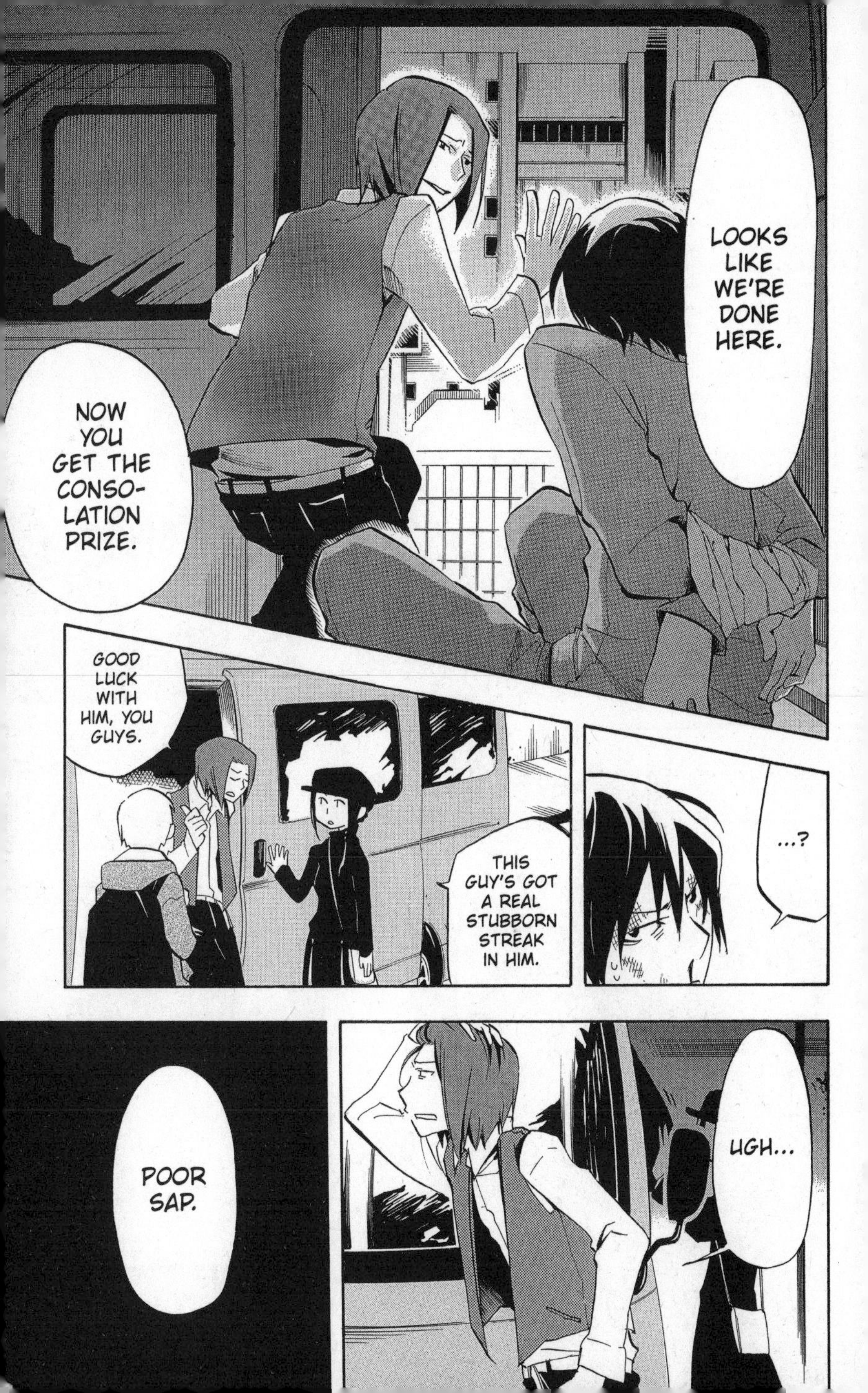

LOOKS LIKE WE'RE DONE HERE.
NOW YOU GET THE CONSO-LATION PRIZE.
...?
GOOD LUCK WITH HIM, YOU GUYS.
THIS GUY'S GOT A REAL STUBBORN STREAK IN HIM.
UGH...
POOR SAP.

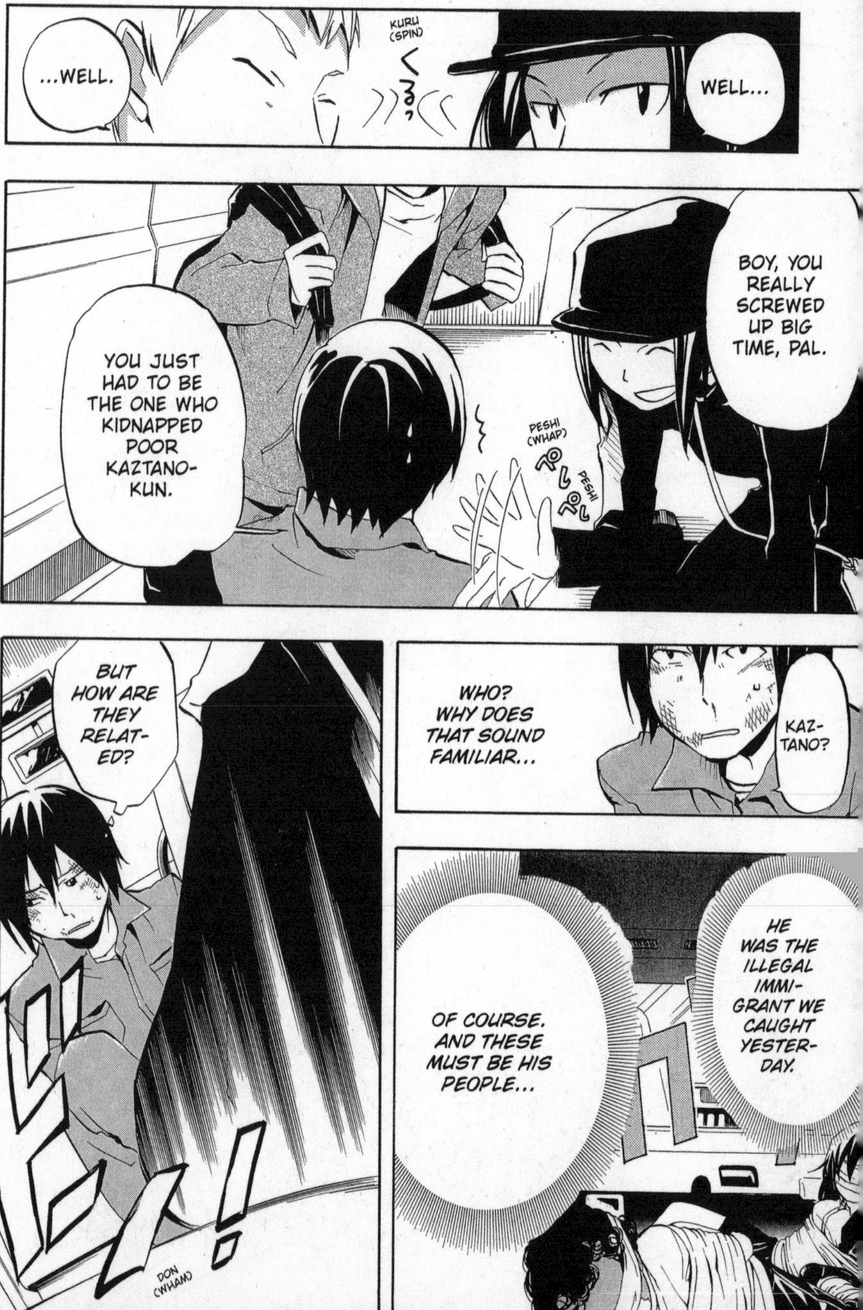
WELL...
KURU (SPIN)
...WELL.
BOY, YOU REALLY SCREWED UP BIG TIME, PAL.
PESHI (WHAP)
PESHI
YOU JUST HAD TO BE THE ONE WHO KIDNAPPED POOR KAZTANO-KUN.
KAZ-TANO?
WHO? WHY DOES THAT SOUND FAMILIAR...
HE WAS THE ILLEGAL IMMI-GRANT WE CAUGHT YESTER-DAY.
OF COURSE. AND THESE MUST BE HIS PEOPLE...
BUT HOW ARE THEY RELAT-ED?
DON (WHAM)

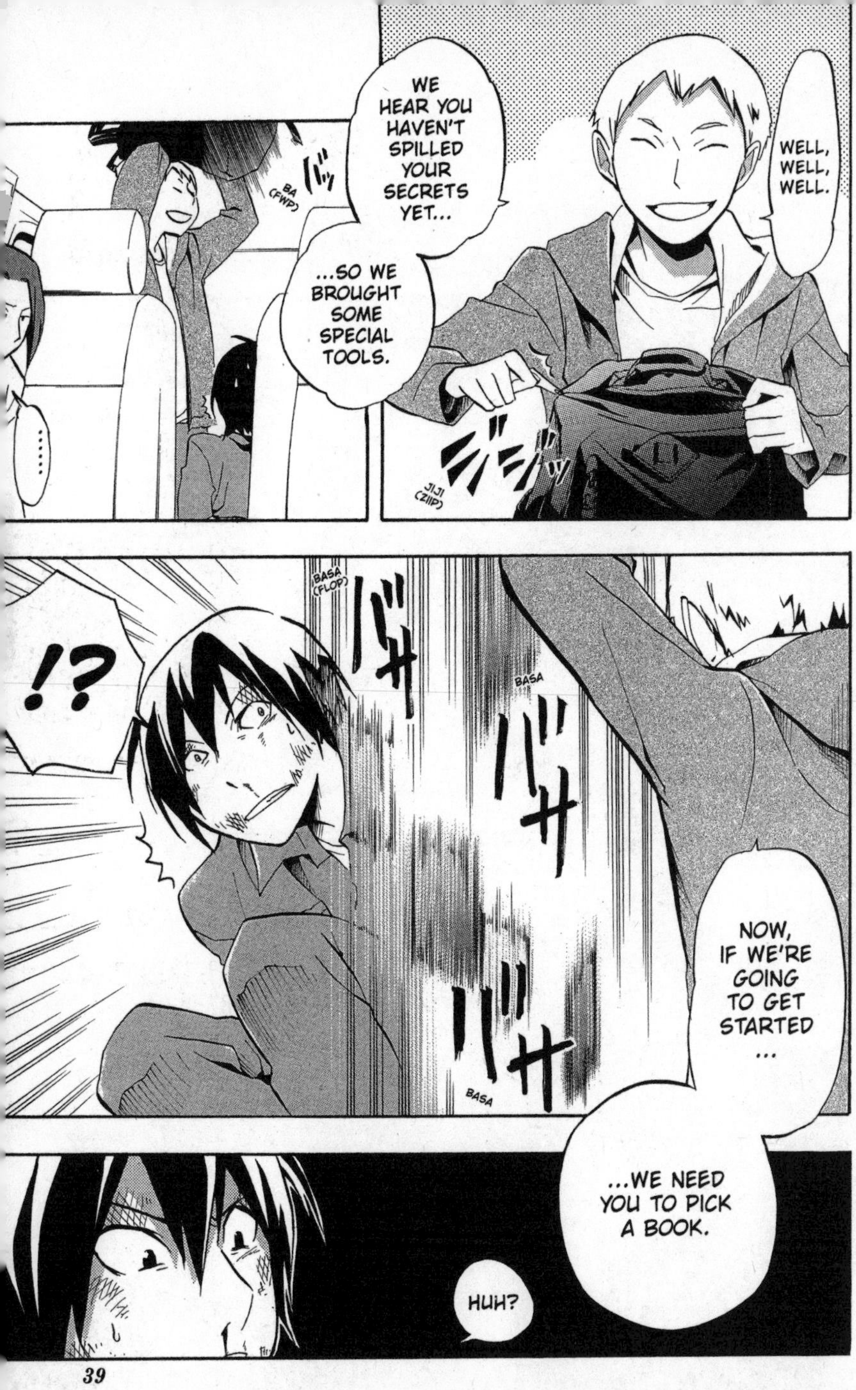
WELL, WELL, WELL.
WE HEAR YOU HAVEN'T SPILLED YOUR SECRETS YET...
...SO WE BROUGHT SOME SPECIAL TOOLS.
JIJI (ZIIP)
BA (FWP)
......
BASA (FLOP)
BASA
BASA
NOW, IF WE'RE GOING TO GET STARTED...
!?
...WE NEED YOU TO PICK A BOOK.
HUH?

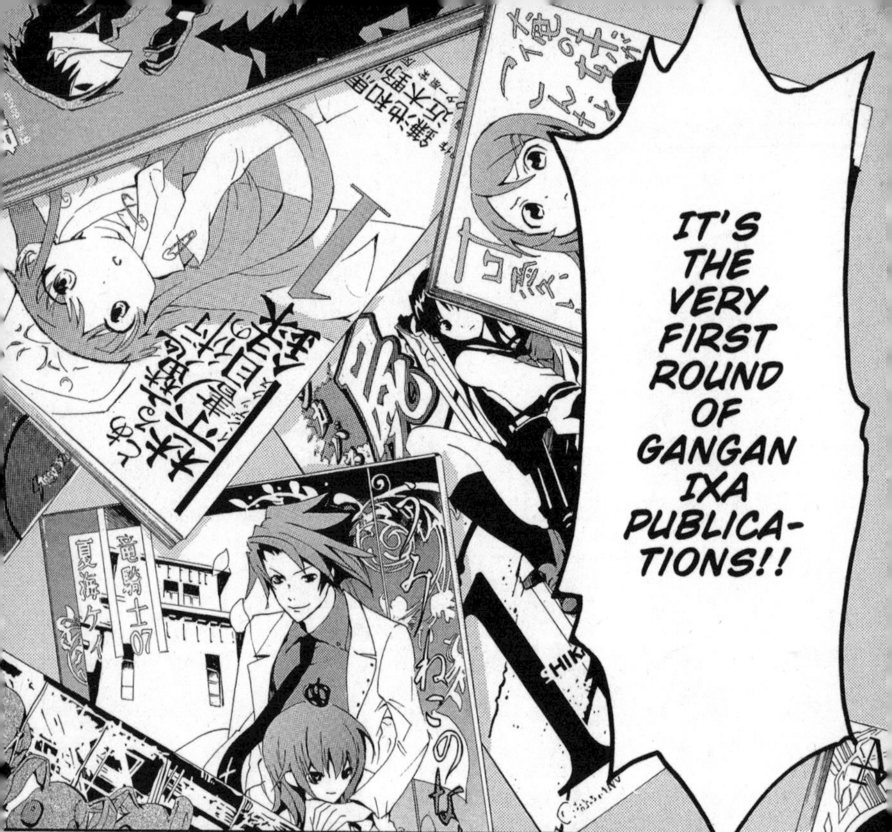
IT'S THE VERY FIRST ROUND OF GANGAN IXA PUBLICATIONS!!

BOOKS THIS PAGE (CLOCKWISE FROM TOP): DARKER THAN BLACK, A CERTAIN MAGICAL INDEX, OREIMO: MY LITTLE SISTER CAN'T BE THIS CUTE, SHIKABANE, UMINEKO, DOUBT

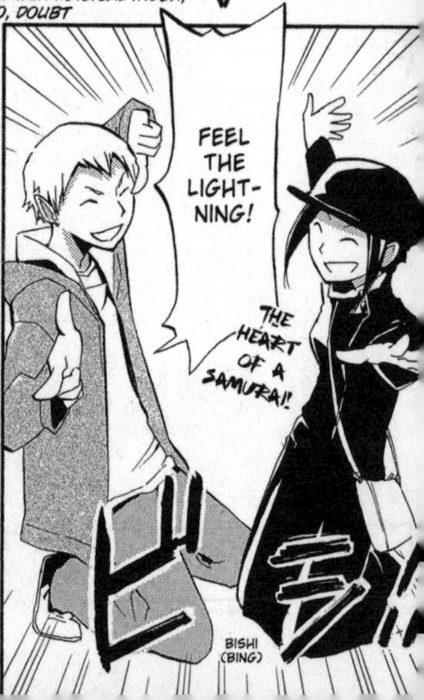
FEEL THE LIGHTNING!
THE HEART OF A SAMURAI!
BISHI (BING)

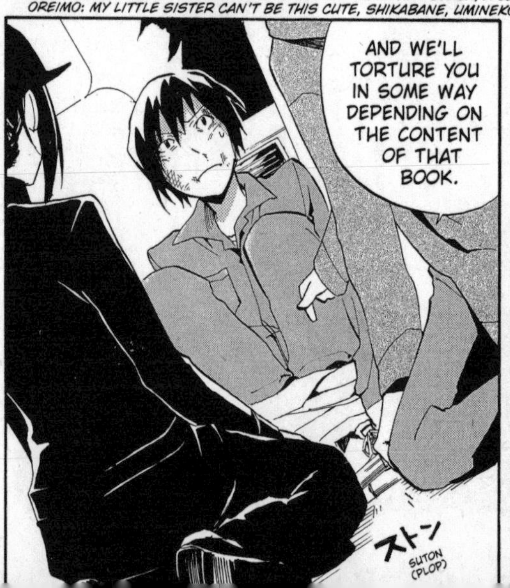
AND WE'LL TORTURE YOU IN SOME WAY DEPENDING ON THE CONTENT OF THAT BOOK.
ストン
SUTON (PLOP)

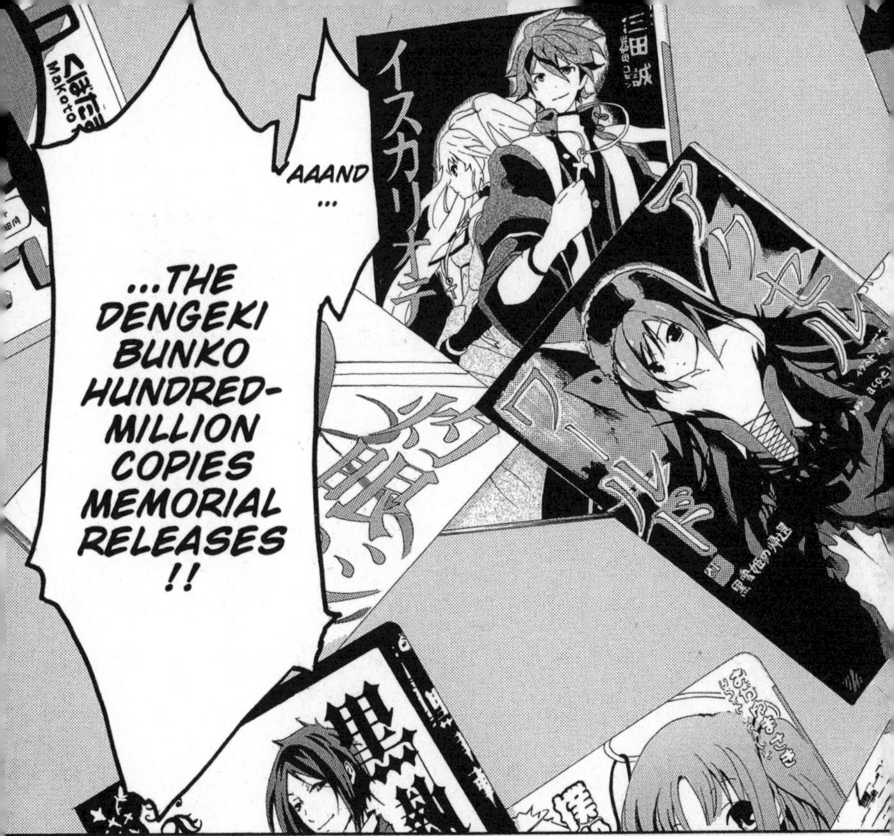
AAAND ...
...THE DENGEKI BUNKO HUNDRED-MILLION COPIES MEMORIAL RELEASES !!

BOOKS THIS PAGE (L-R): (TOP) ASTRO FIGHTER SUNRED, SHANA, ISCARIOT, ACCEL WORLD, (BOTTOM) BLACK BUTLER, BLUDGEONING ANGEL DOKURO-CHAN

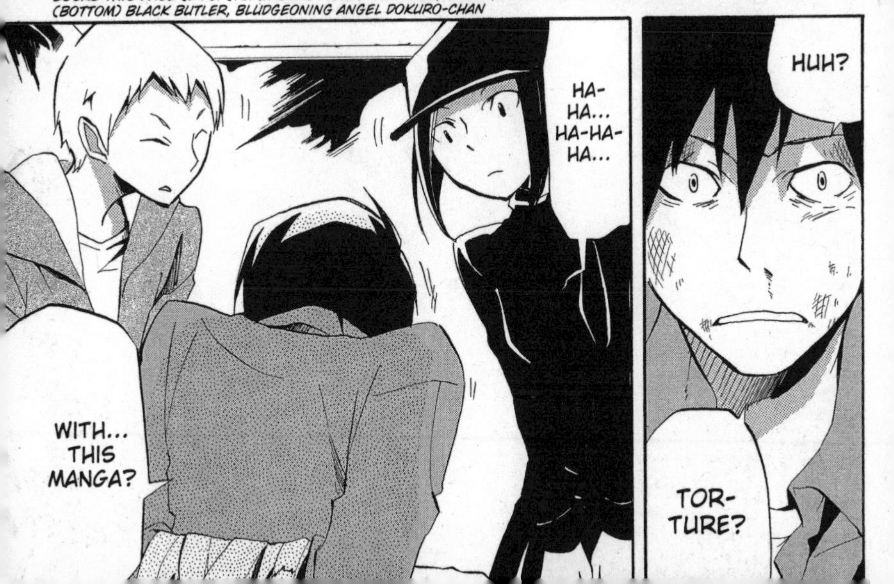
HUH?
TOR-TURE?
HA-HA... HA-HA-HA...
WITH... THIS MANGA?

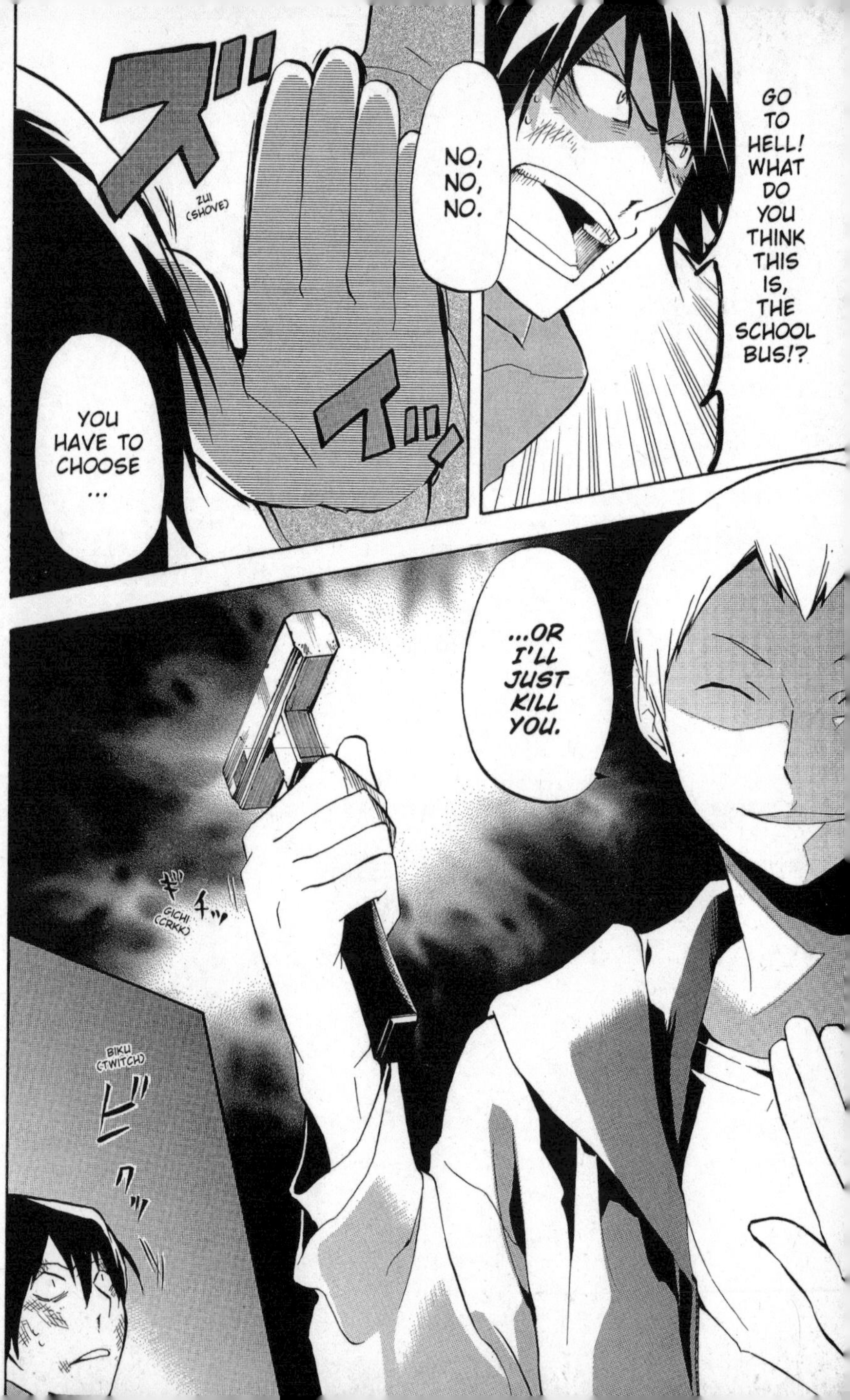
GO TO HELL! WHAT DO YOU THINK THIS IS, THE SCHOOL BUS!?
NO, NO, NO.
ZUI (SHOVE)
YOU HAVE TO CHOOSE ...
...OR I'LL JUST KILL YOU.
GICHI (CRKK)
BIKU (TWITCH)

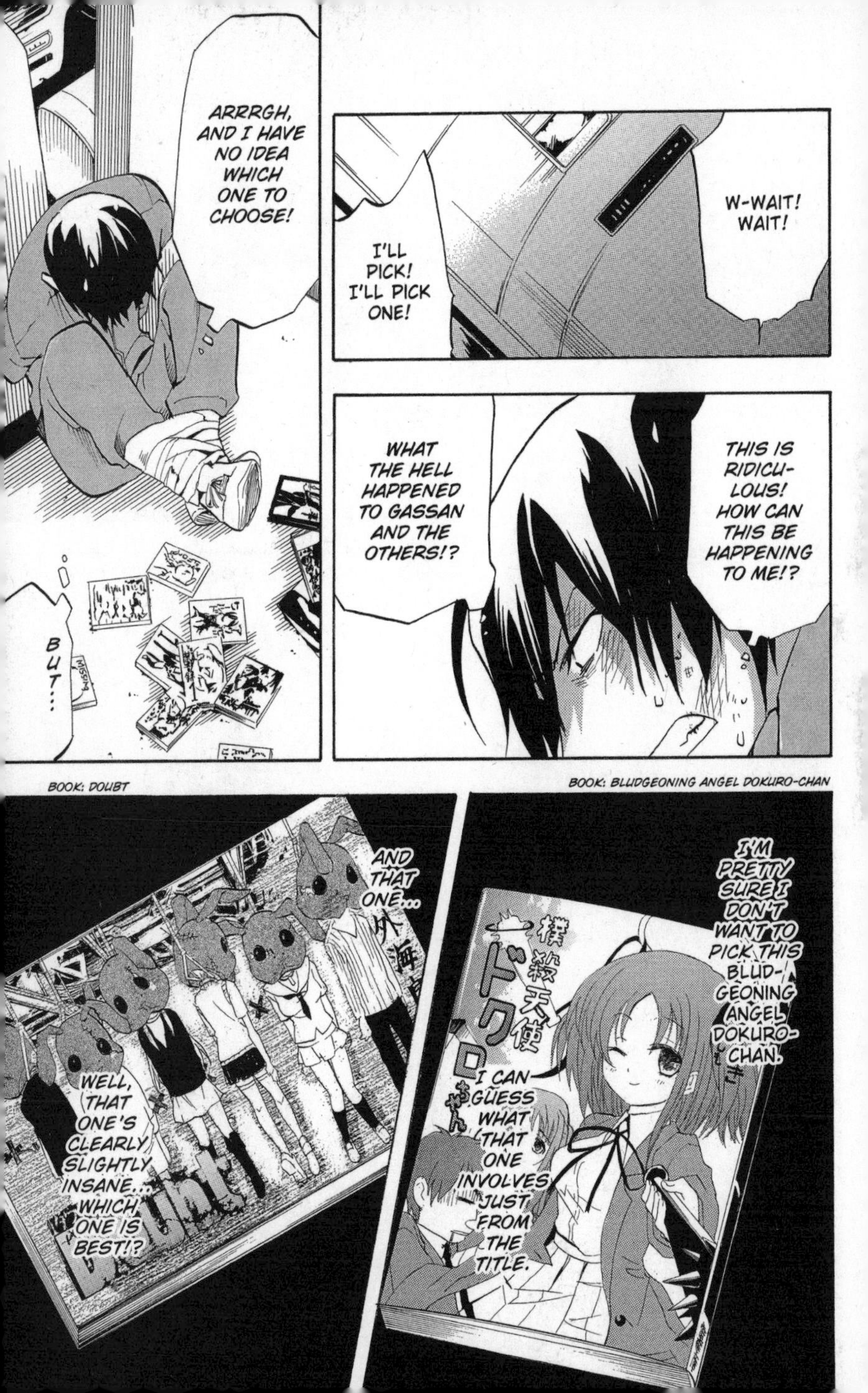
W-WAIT! WAIT!
I'LL PICK! I'LL PICK ONE!
THIS IS RIDICULOUS! HOW CAN THIS BE HAPPENING TO ME!?
WHAT THE HELL HAPPENED TO GASSAN AND THE OTHERS!?
ARRRGH, AND I HAVE NO IDEA WHICH ONE TO CHOOSE!
BUT...
BOOK: BLUDGEONING ANGEL DOKURO-CHAN
BOOK: DOUBT
I'M PRETTY SURE I DON'T WANT TO PICK THIS BLUDGEONING ANGEL DOKURO-CHAN.
撲殺天使ドクロちゃん
I CAN GUESS WHAT THAT ONE INVOLVES JUST FROM THE TITLE.
AND THAT ONE...
WELL, THAT ONE'S CLEARLY SLIGHTLY INSANE... WHICH ONE IS BEST!?

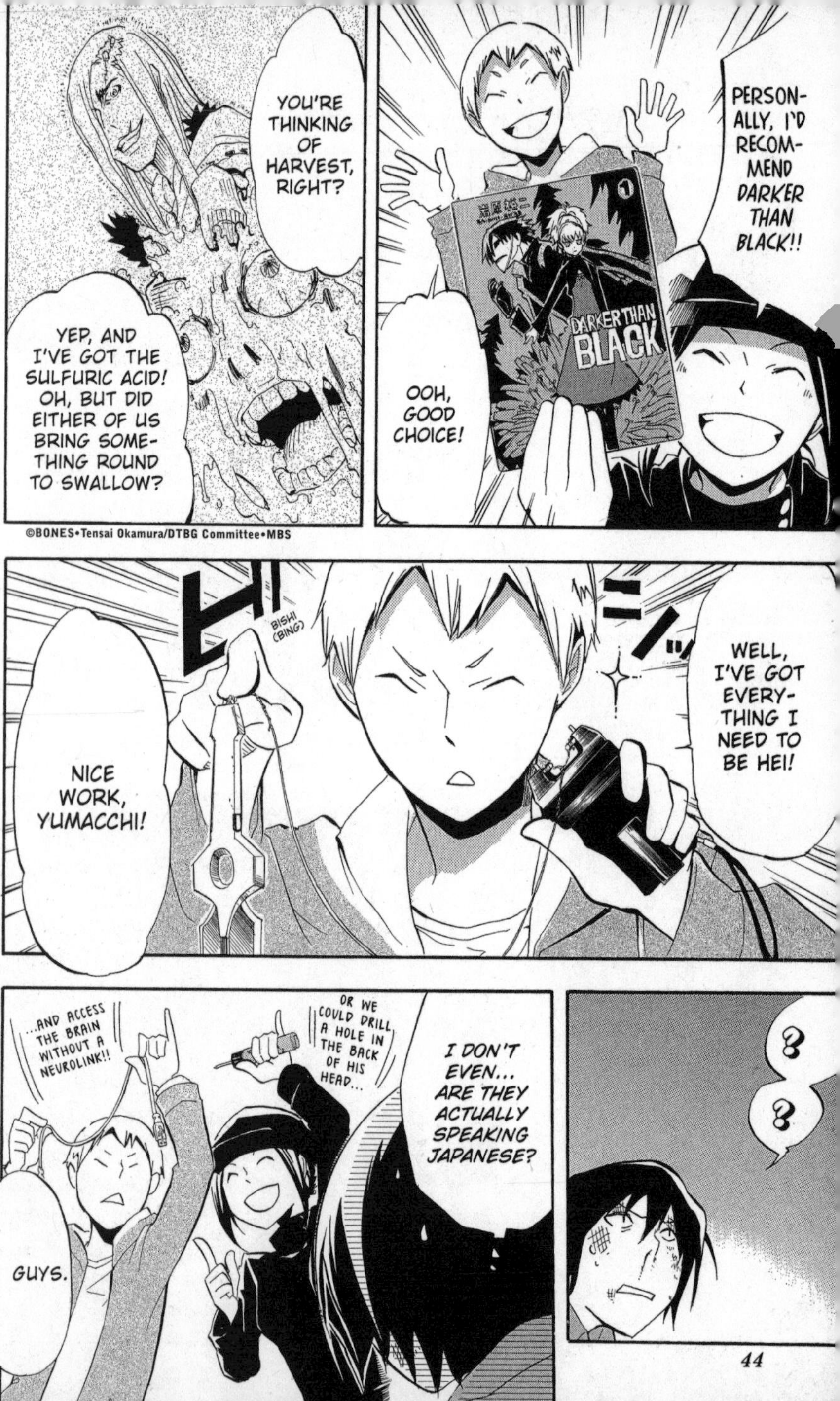
PERSONALLY, I'D RECOMMEND DARKER THAN BLACK!!
1
DARKER THAN BLACK
OOH, GOOD CHOICE!
YOU'RE THINKING OF HARVEST, RIGHT?
YEP, AND I'VE GOT THE SULFURIC ACID! OH, BUT DID EITHER OF US BRING SOMETHING ROUND TO SWALLOW?
WELL, I'VE GOT EVERYTHING I NEED TO BE HEI!
BISHI (BING)
NICE WORK, YUMACCHI!
?
?
I DON'T EVEN... ARE THEY ACTUALLY SPEAKING JAPANESE?
OR WE COULD DRILL A HOLE IN THE BACK OF HIS HEAD...
...AND ACCESS THE BRAIN WITHOUT A NEUROLINK!!
GUYS.

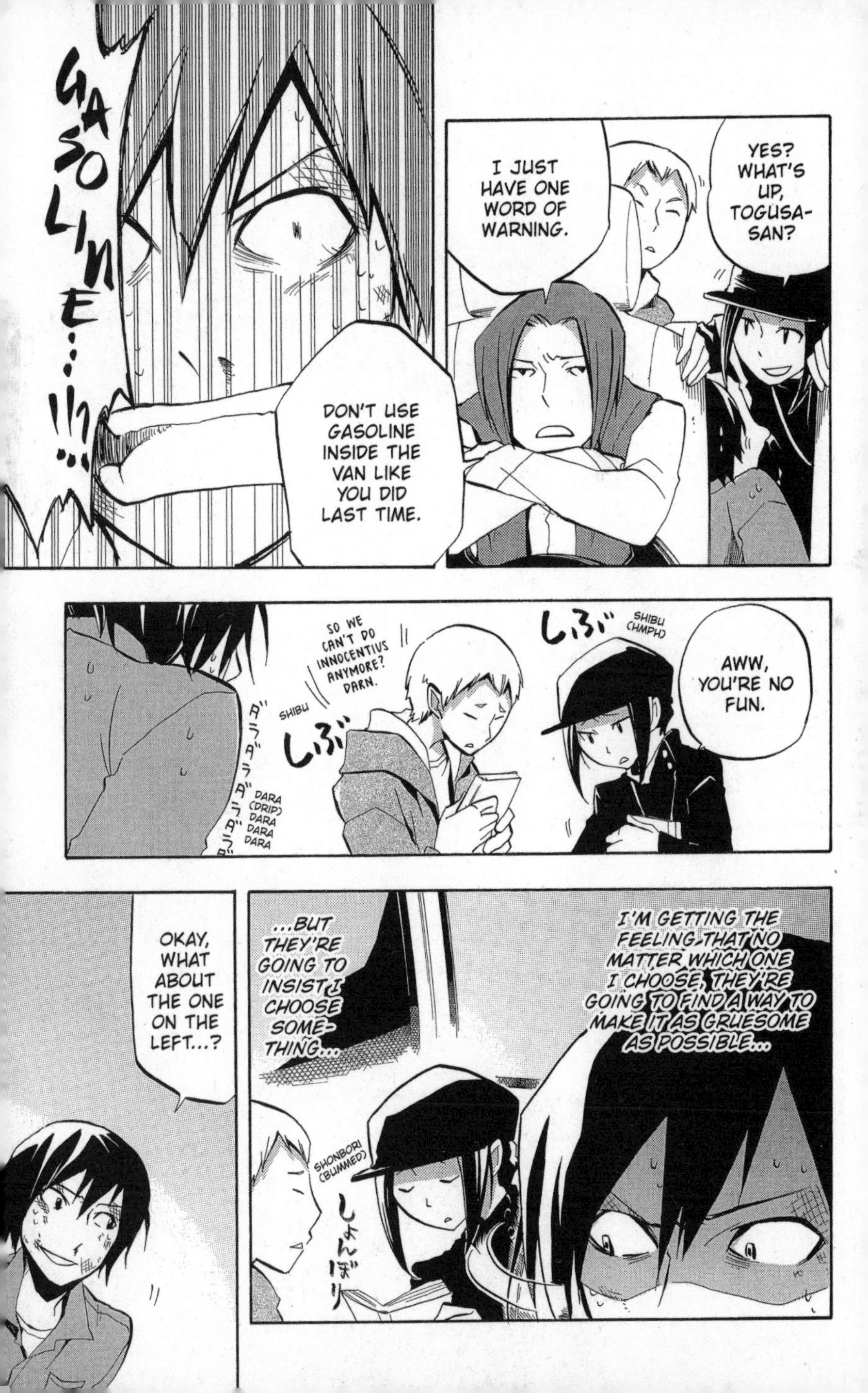
YES? WHAT'S UP, TOGUSA-SAN?
I JUST HAVE ONE WORD OF WARNING.
DON'T USE GASOLINE INSIDE THE VAN LIKE YOU DID LAST TIME.
GASOLINE...!!?!!
AWW, YOU'RE NO FUN.
しぶ
SHIBU (HMPH)
SO WE CAN'T DO INNOCENTIUS ANYMORE? DARN.
しぶ
SHIBU
ダラダラダラダラ
DARA (DRIP) DARA DARA DARA
I'M GETTING THE FEELING THAT NO MATTER WHICH ONE I CHOOSE, THEY'RE GOING TO FIND A WAY TO MAKE IT AS GRUESOME AS POSSIBLE...
...BUT THEY'RE GOING TO INSIST I CHOOSE SOME-THING...
しょんぼり
SHONBORI (BUMMED)
OKAY, WHAT ABOUT THE ONE ON THE LEFT...?

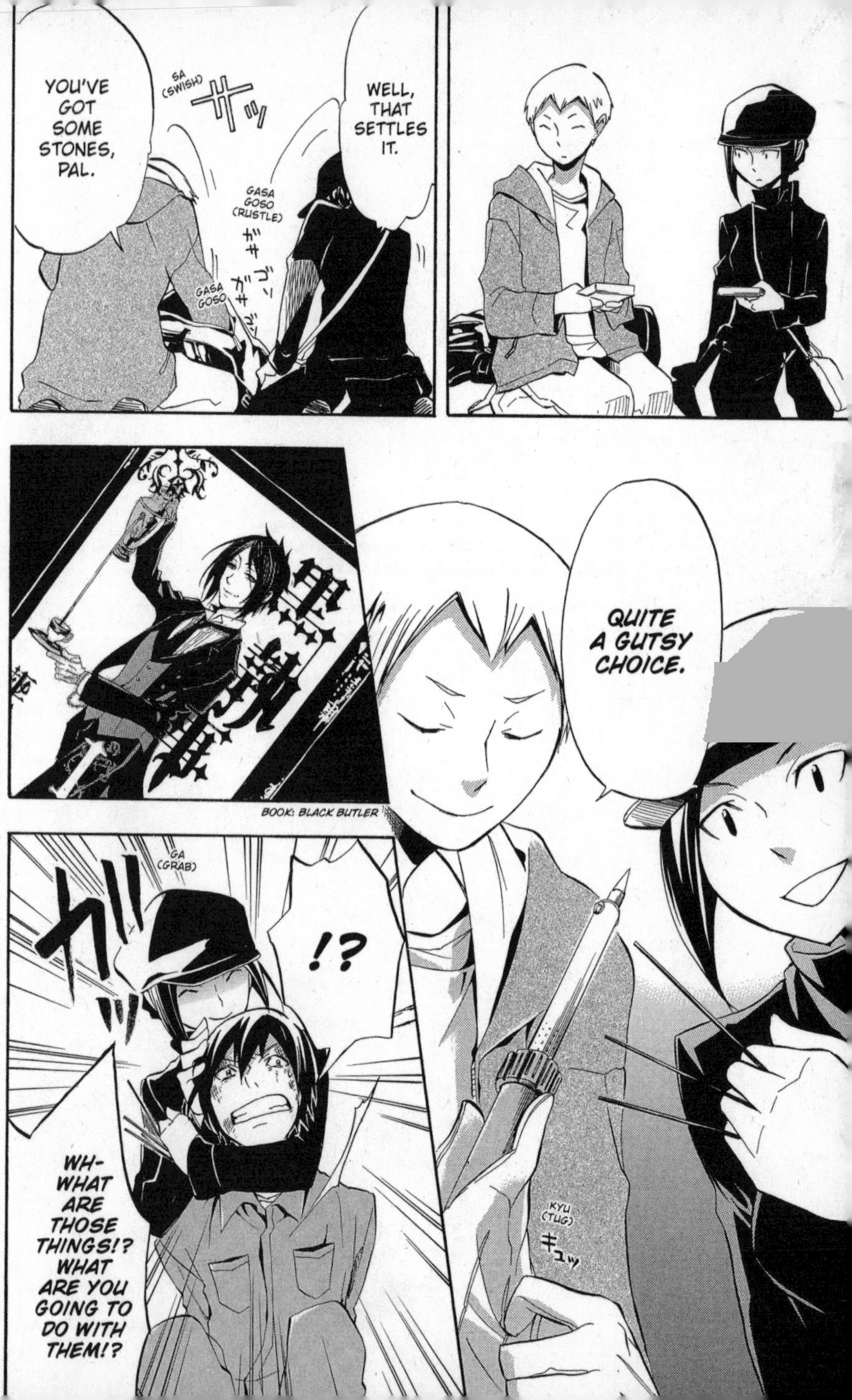
WELL, THAT SETTLES IT.
GASA GOSO (RUSTLE)
GASA GOSO
SA (SWISH)
YOU'VE GOT SOME STONES, PAL.
QUITE A GUTSY CHOICE.
BOOK: BLACK BUTLER
KYU (TUG)
!?
GA (GRAB)
WH- WHAT ARE THOSE THINGS!? WHAT ARE YOU GOING TO DO WITH THEM!?

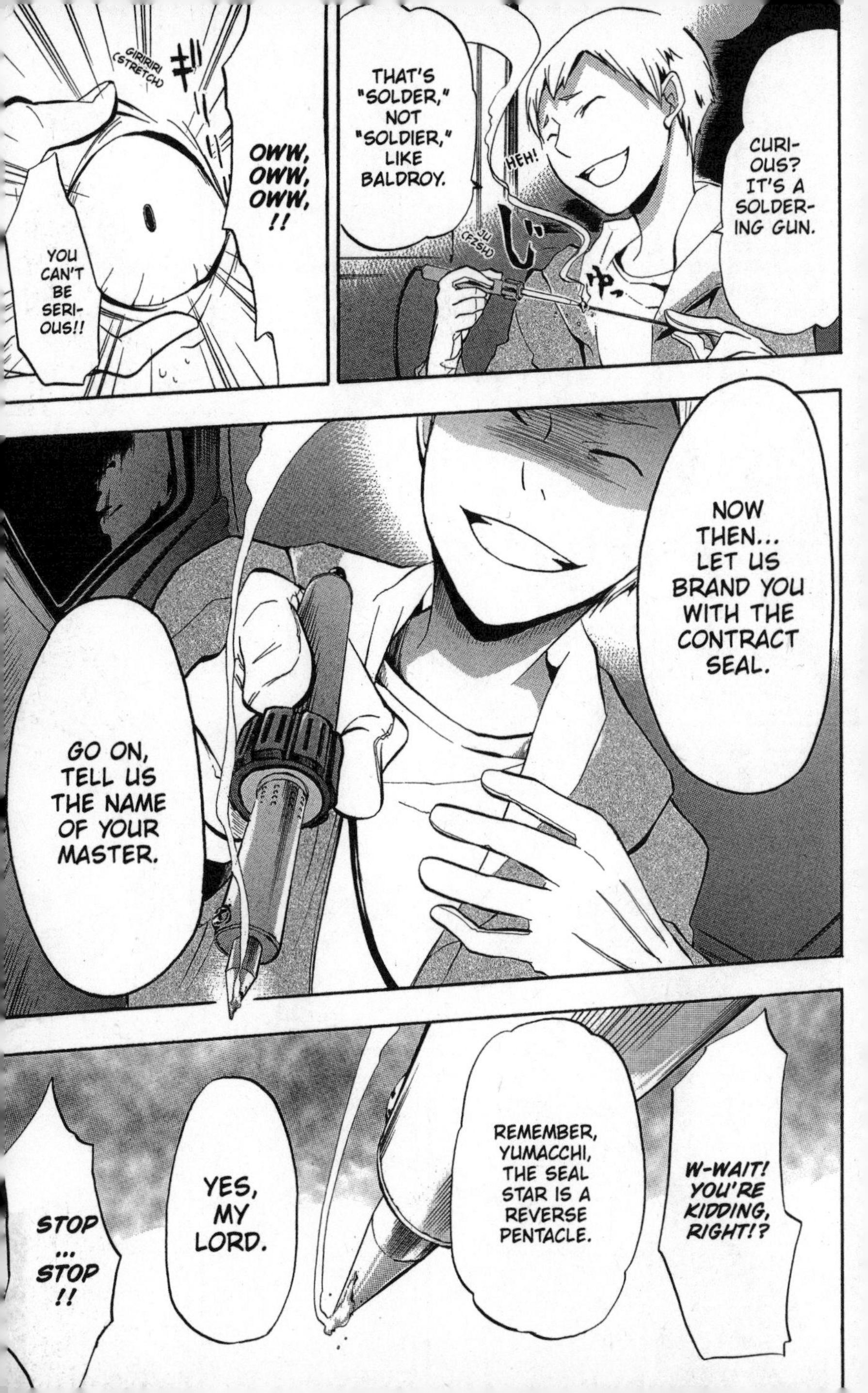
CURI-OUS? IT'S A SOLDER-ING GUN.
HEH!
JU (FZSH)
THAT'S "SOLDER," NOT "SOLDIER," LIKE BALDROY.
GIRIRIRI (STRETCH)
OWW, OWW, OWW, !!
YOU CAN'T BE SERI-OUS!!
NOW THEN... LET US BRAND YOU WITH THE CONTRACT SEAL.
GO ON, TELL US THE NAME OF YOUR MASTER.
W-WAIT! YOU'RE KIDDING, RIGHT!?
REMEMBER, YUMACCHI, THE SEAL STAR IS A REVERSE PENTACLE.
YES, MY LORD.
STOP ... STOP !!

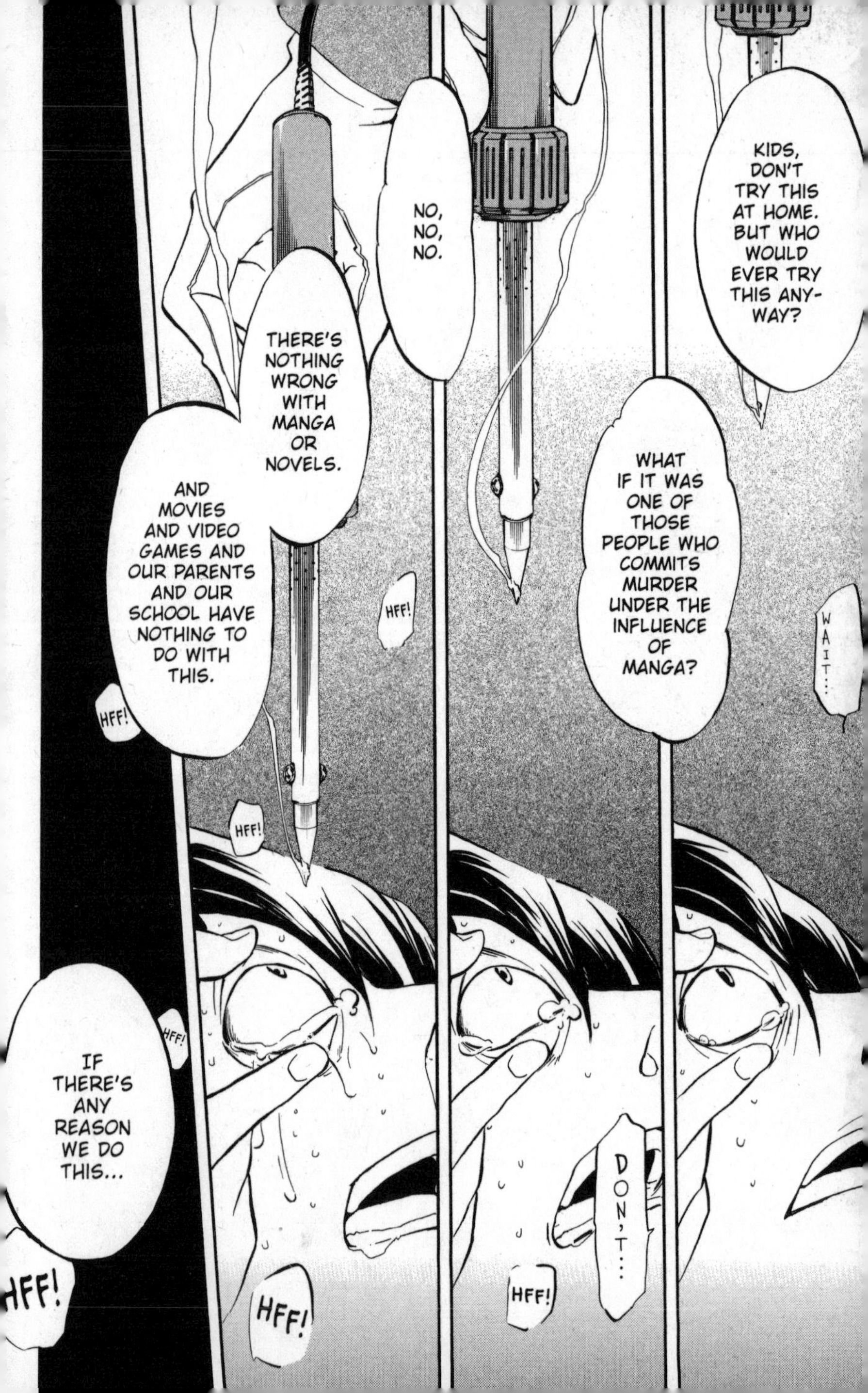
KIDS, DON'T TRY THIS AT HOME. BUT WHO WOULD EVER TRY THIS ANY-WAY?
WHAT IF IT WAS ONE OF THOSE PEOPLE WHO COMMITS MURDER UNDER THE INFLUENCE OF MANGA?
WAIT...
NO, NO, NO.
HFF!
DON'T...
HFF!
THERE'S NOTHING WRONG WITH MANGA OR NOVELS.
AND MOVIES AND VIDEO GAMES AND OUR PARENTS AND OUR SCHOOL HAVE NOTHING TO DO WITH THIS.
HFF!
HFF!
HFF!
IF THERE'S ANY REASON WE DO THIS...
HFF!
HFF!

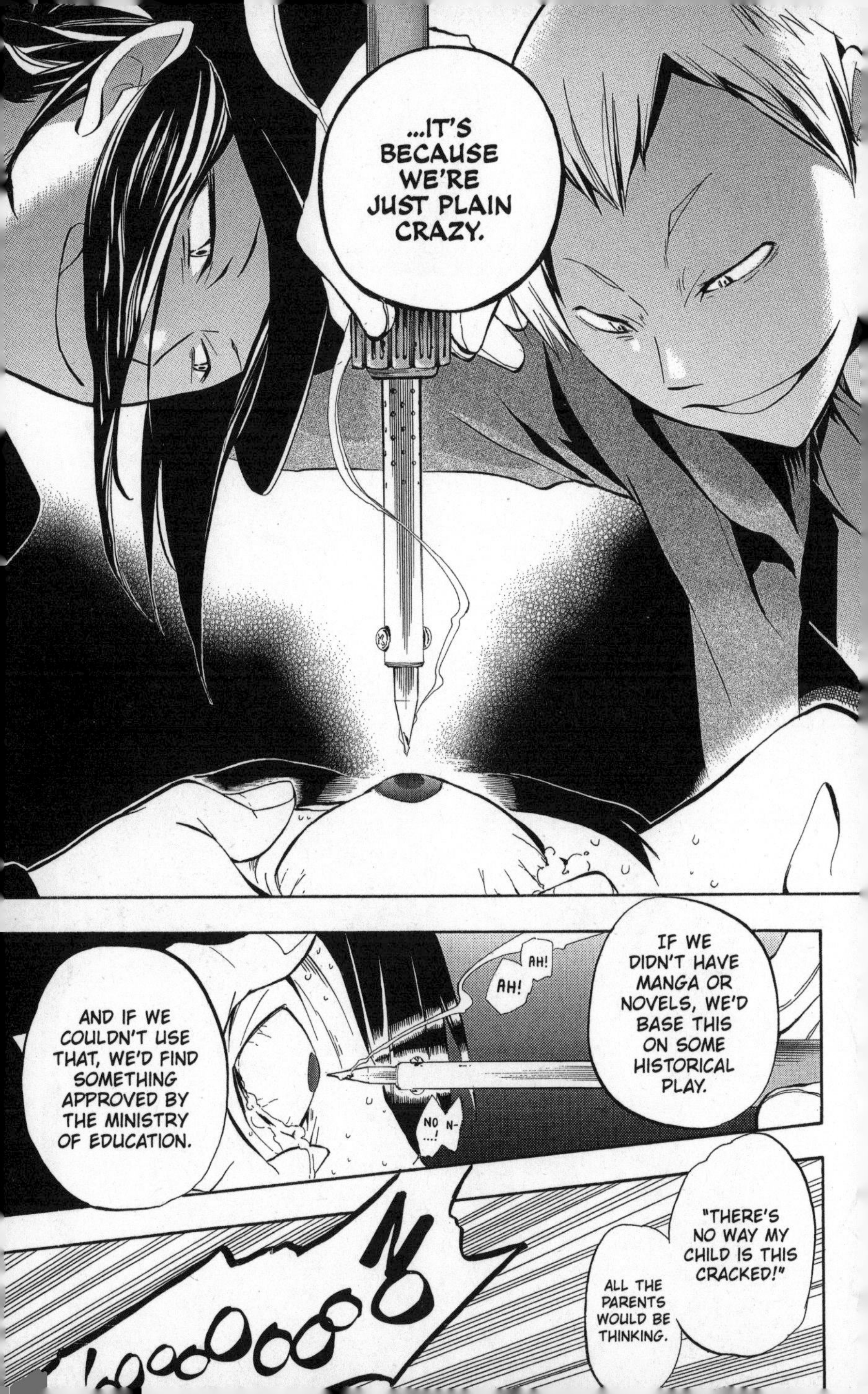
...IT'S BECAUSE WE'RE JUST PLAIN CRAZY.
IF WE DIDN'T HAVE MANGA OR NOVELS, WE'D BASE THIS ON SOME HISTORICAL PLAY.
AH!
AH!
NO N-...!
AND IF WE COULDN'T USE THAT, WE'D FIND SOMETHING APPROVED BY THE MINISTRY OF EDUCATION.
"THERE'S NO WAY MY CHILD IS THIS CRACKED!"
ALL THE PARENTS WOULD BE THINKING.
NOOOOOOOO

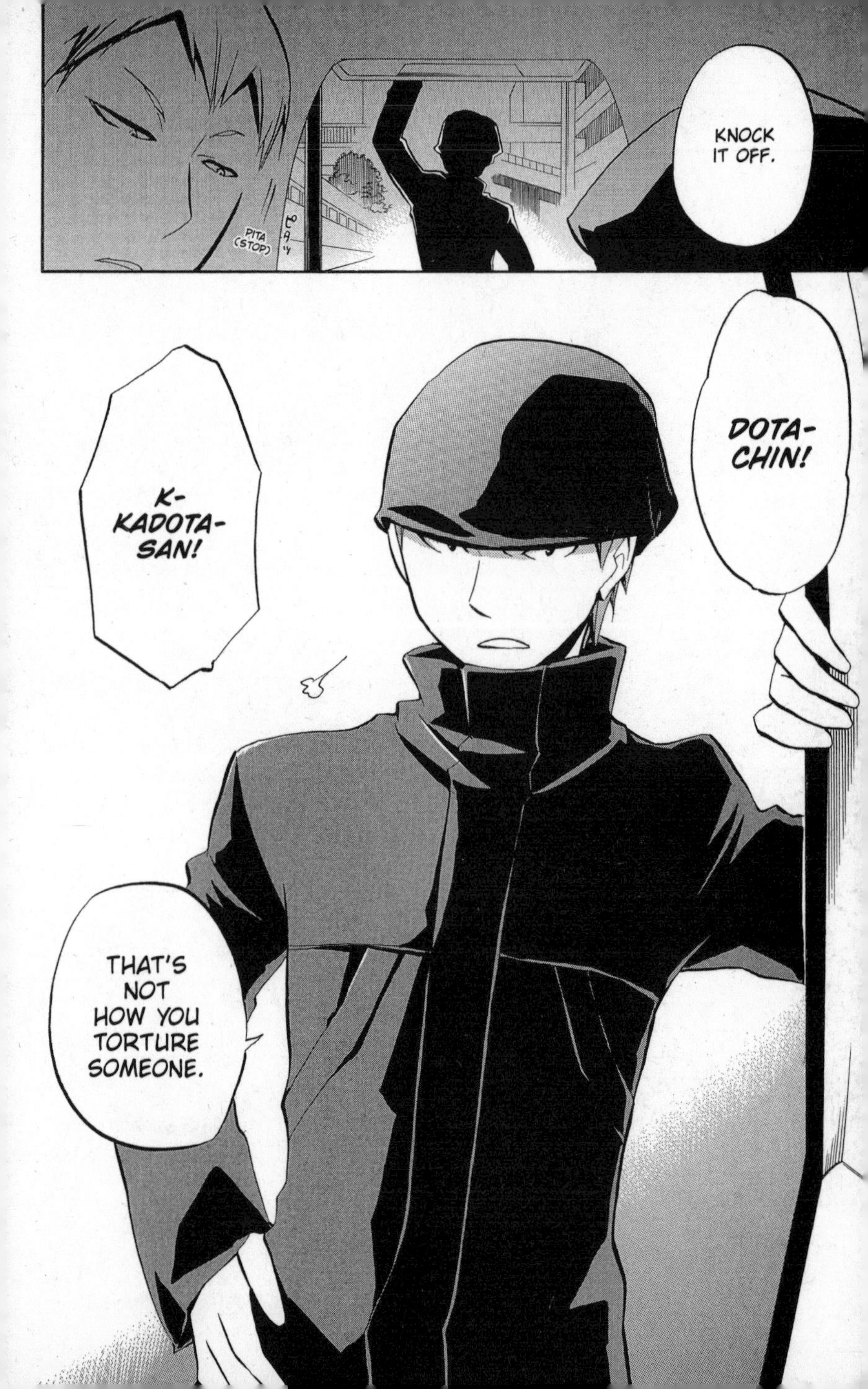
KNOCK IT OFF.
PITA (STOP)
DOTA-CHIN!
K-KADOTA-SAN!
THAT'S NOT HOW YOU TORTURE SOMEONE.

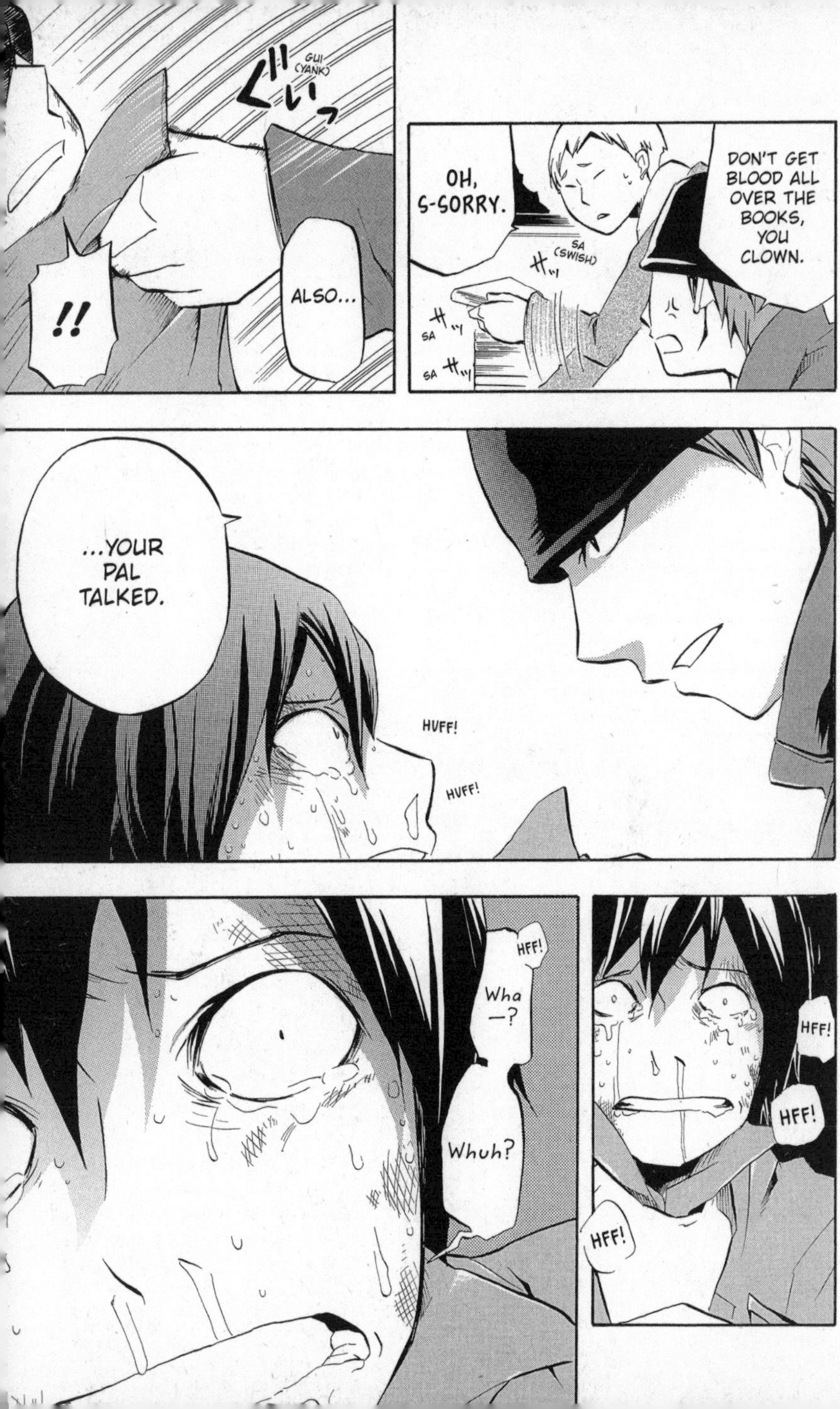
DON'T GET BLOOD ALL OVER THE BOOKS, YOU CLOWN.
OH, S-SORRY.
SA (SWISH)
SA
SA
GUI (YANK)
ALSO...
!!
...YOUR PAL TALKED.
HUFF!
HUFF!
HFF!
HFF!
HFF!
HFF!
Wha—?
Whuh?

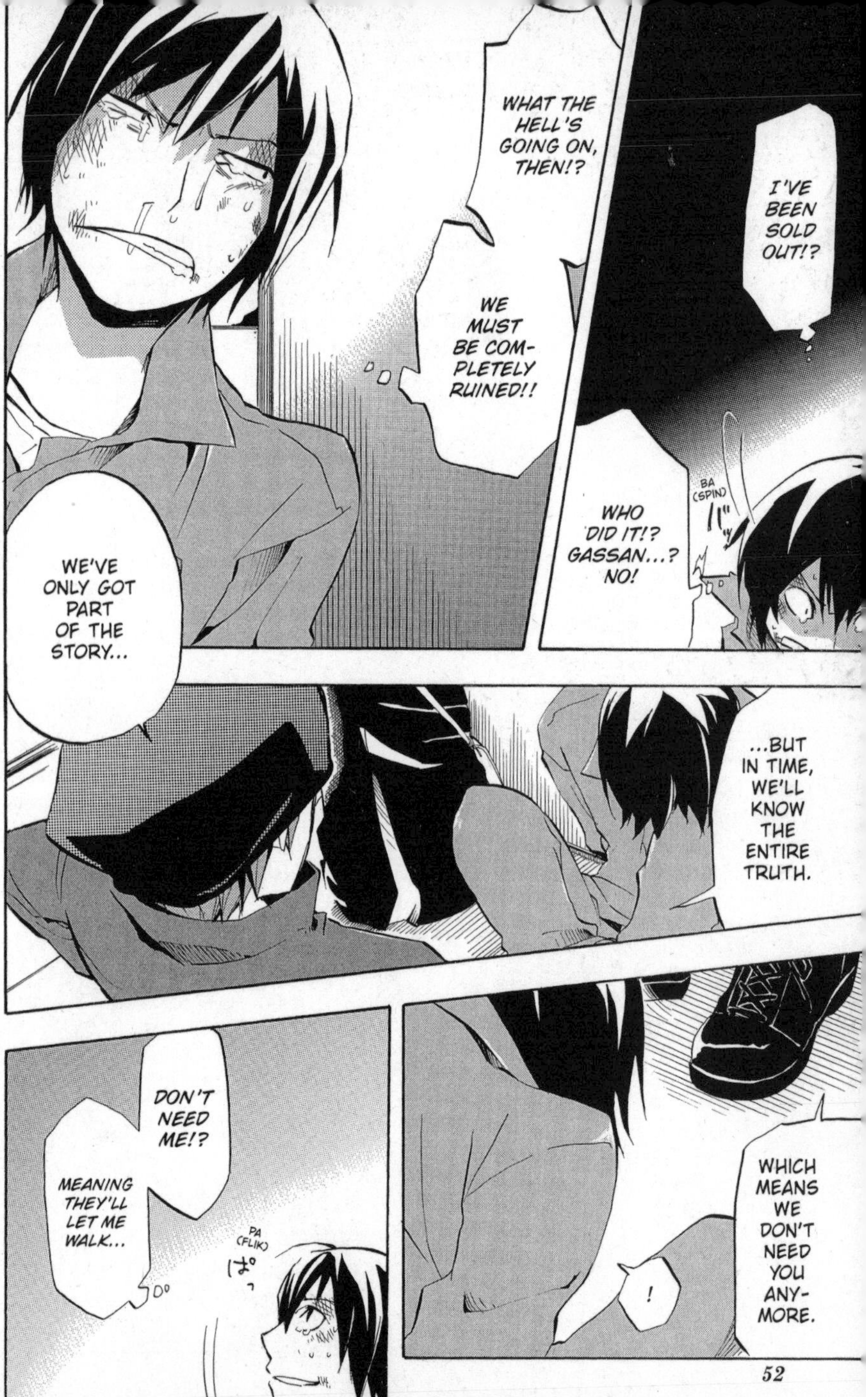
I'VE BEEN SOLD OUT!?
WHO DID IT!? GASSAN...? NO!
BA (SPIN)
WHAT THE HELL'S GOING ON, THEN!?
WE MUST BE COM-PLETELY RUINED!!
WE'VE ONLY GOT PART OF THE STORY...
...BUT IN TIME, WE'LL KNOW THE ENTIRE TRUTH.
WHICH MEANS WE DON'T NEED YOU ANY-MORE.
!
DON'T NEED ME!?
MEANING THEY'LL LET ME WALK...
PA (FLIK)
ぱっ

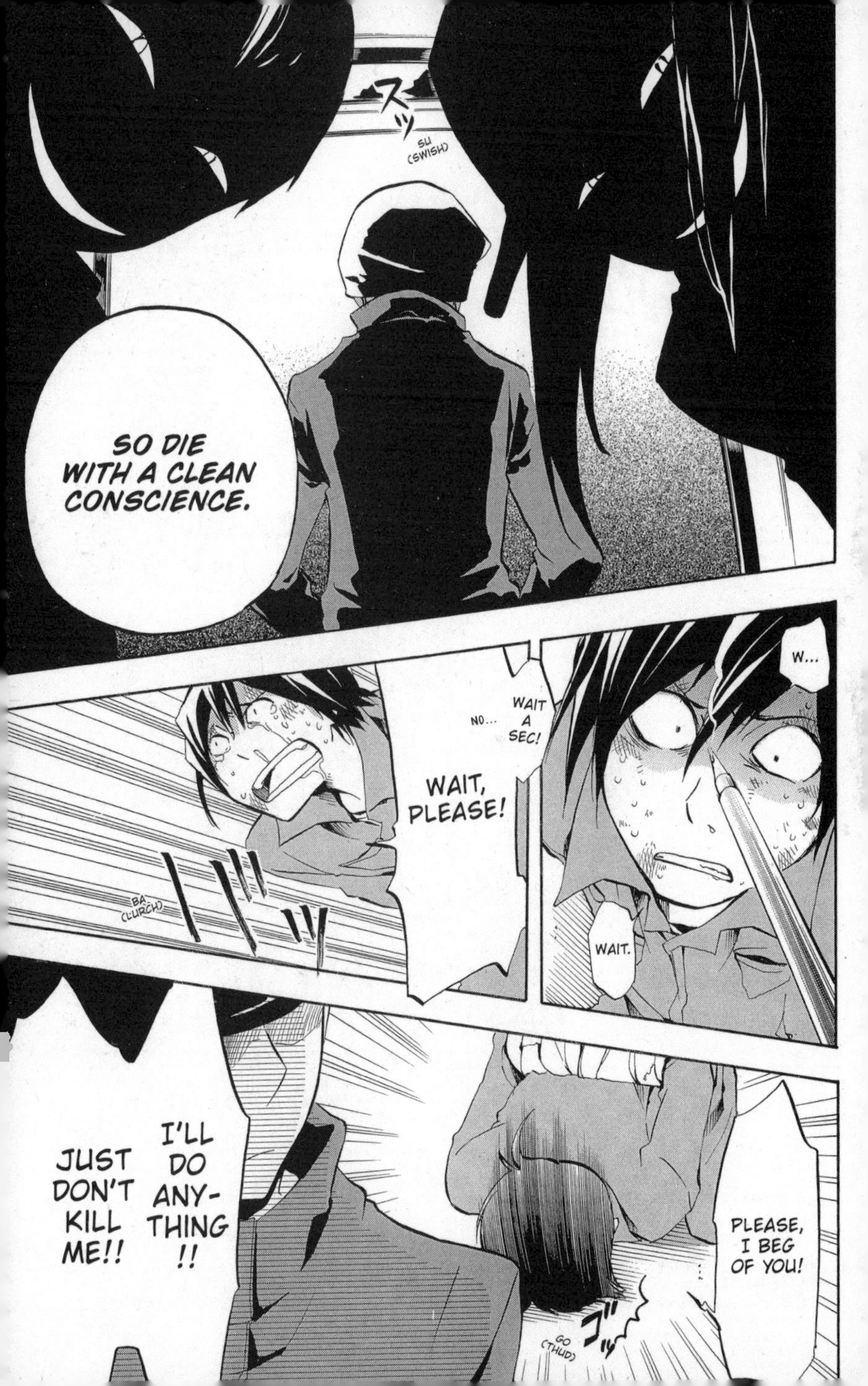
スッ
SU (SWISH)
SO DIE WITH A CLEAN CONSCIENCE.
W...
WAIT.
WAIT A SEC!
NO...
WAIT, PLEASE!
BA (LURCH)
PLEASE, I BEG OF YOU!
ゴッ
GO (THUD)
I'LL DO ANYTHING!!
JUST DON'T KILL ME!!

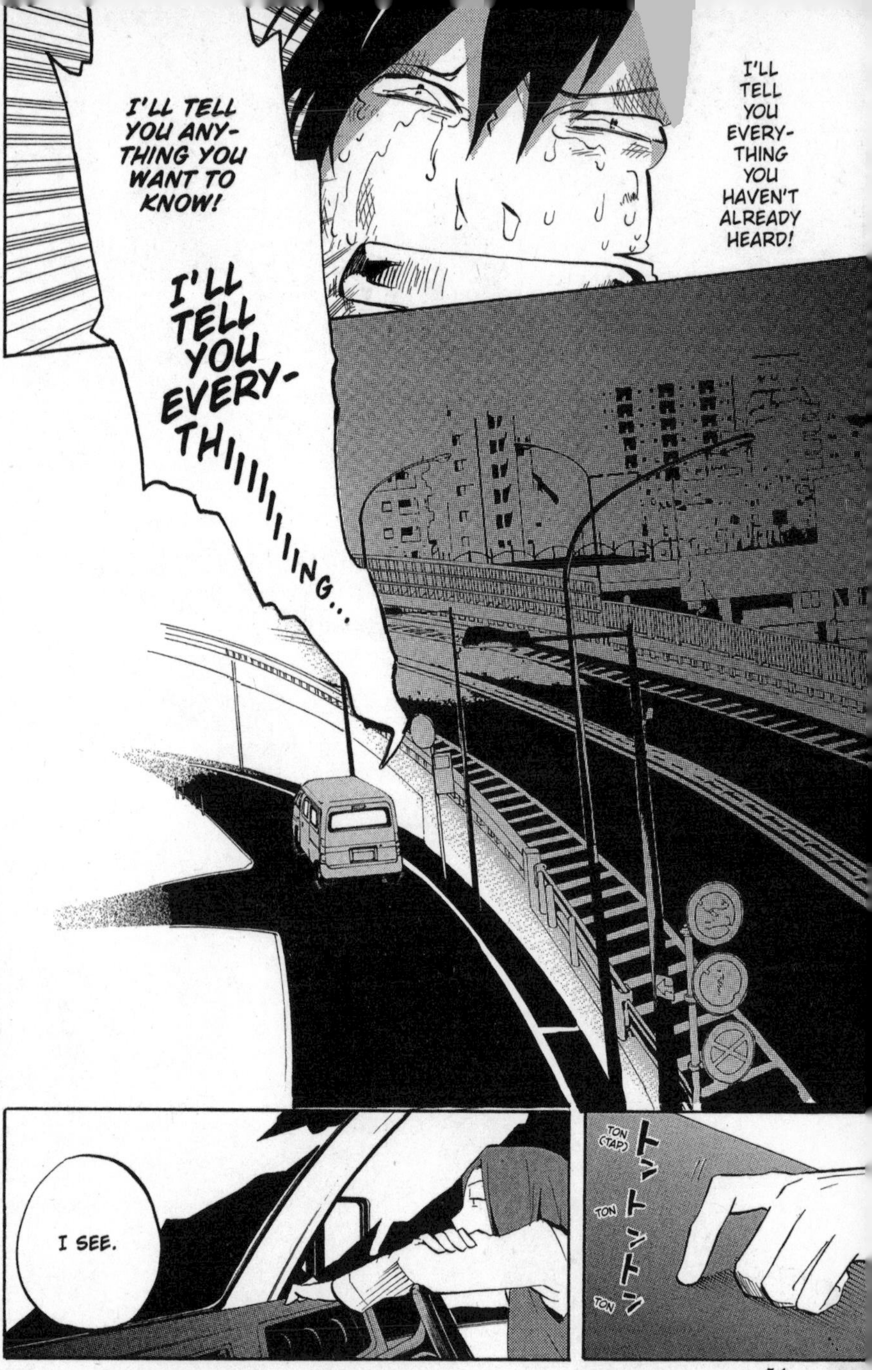
I'LL TELL YOU EVERYTHING YOU HAVEN'T ALREADY HEARD!
I'LL TELL YOU ANYTHING YOU WANT TO KNOW!
I'LL TELL YOU EVERYTHIIIIIIIIIING...
TON (TAP)
TON
TON
I SEE.

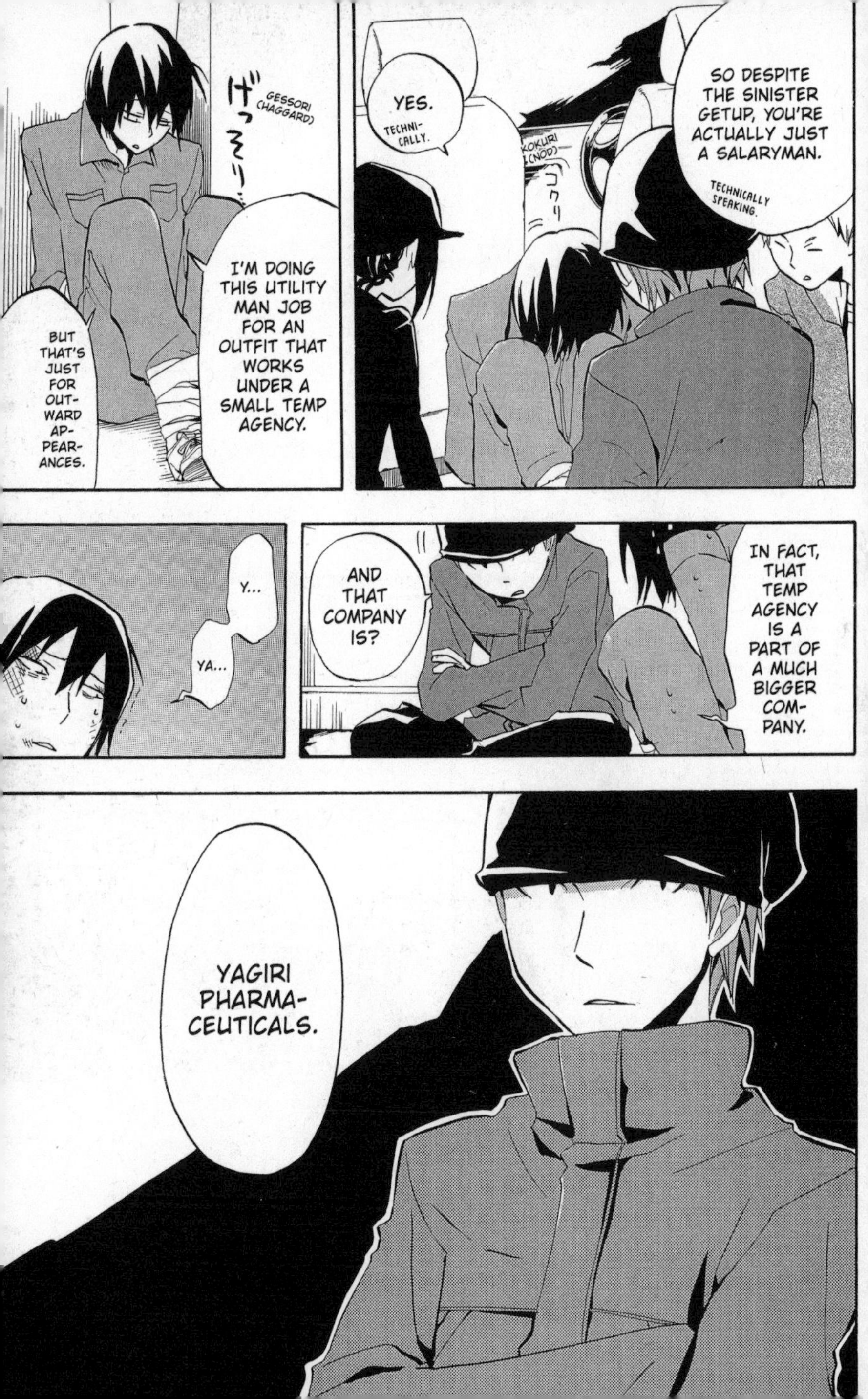
SO DESPITE THE SINISTER GETUP, YOU'RE ACTUALLY JUST A SALARYMAN.
TECHNICALLY SPEAKING.
コクリ
KOKURI (NOD)
YES.
TECHNI-CALLY.
げっそり
GESSORI (HAGGARD)
I'M DOING THIS UTILITY MAN JOB FOR AN OUTFIT THAT WORKS UNDER A SMALL TEMP AGENCY.
BUT THAT'S JUST FOR OUT-WARD AP-PEAR-ANCES.
IN FACT, THAT TEMP AGENCY IS A PART OF A MUCH BIGGER COM-PANY.
AND THAT COMPANY IS?
Y...
YA...
YAGIRI PHARMA-CEUTICALS.

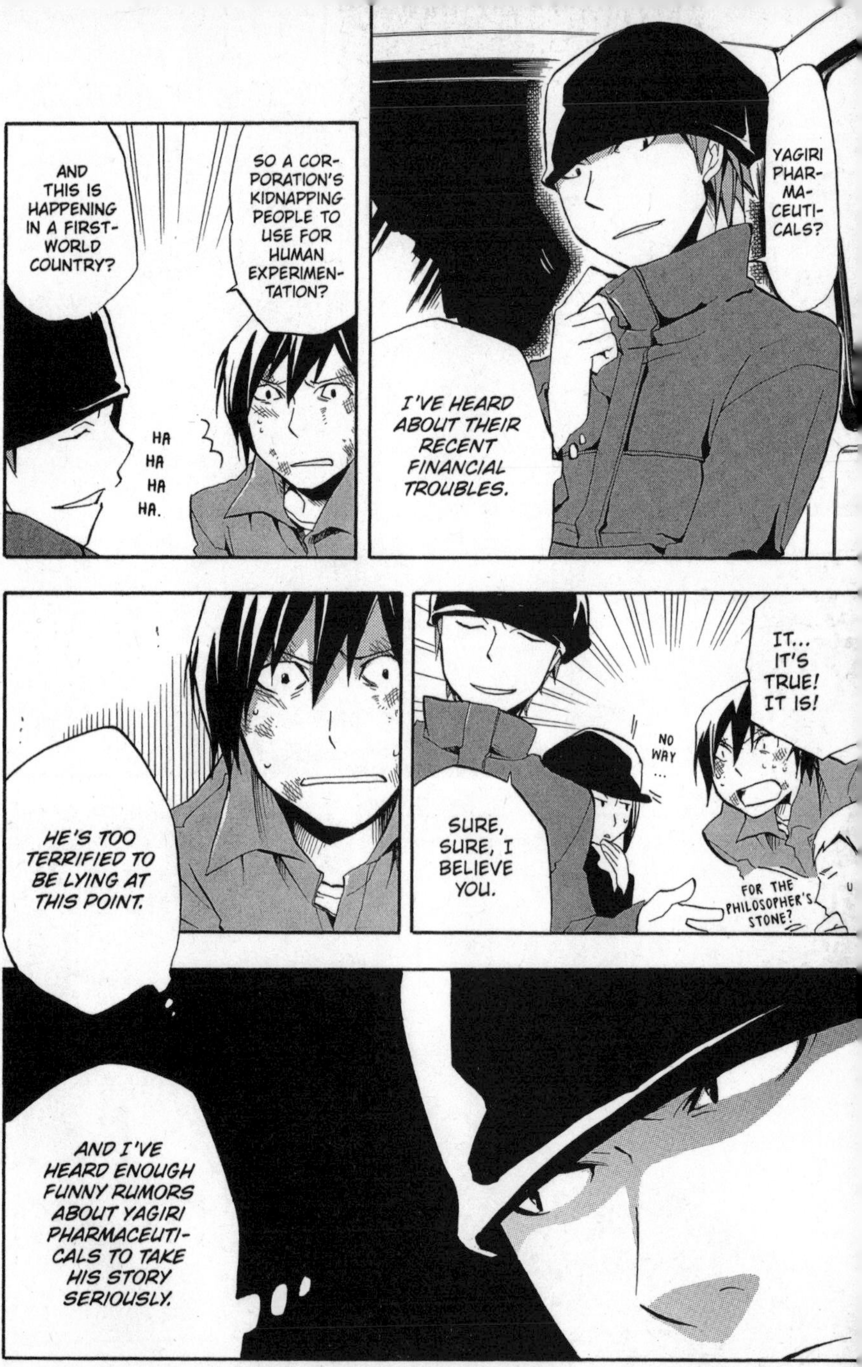
YAGIRI PHARMACEUTICALS?
I'VE HEARD ABOUT THEIR RECENT FINANCIAL TROUBLES.
SO A CORPORATION'S KIDNAPPING PEOPLE TO USE FOR HUMAN EXPERIMENTATION?
AND THIS IS HAPPENING IN A FIRST-WORLD COUNTRY?
HA HA HA HA.
IT... IT'S TRUE! IT IS!
NO WAY...
FOR THE PHILOSOPHER'S STONE?
SURE, SURE, I BELIEVE YOU.
HE'S TOO TERRIFIED TO BE LYING AT THIS POINT.
AND I'VE HEARD ENOUGH FUNNY RUMORS ABOUT YAGIRI PHARMACEUTICALS TO TAKE HIS STORY SERIOUSLY.

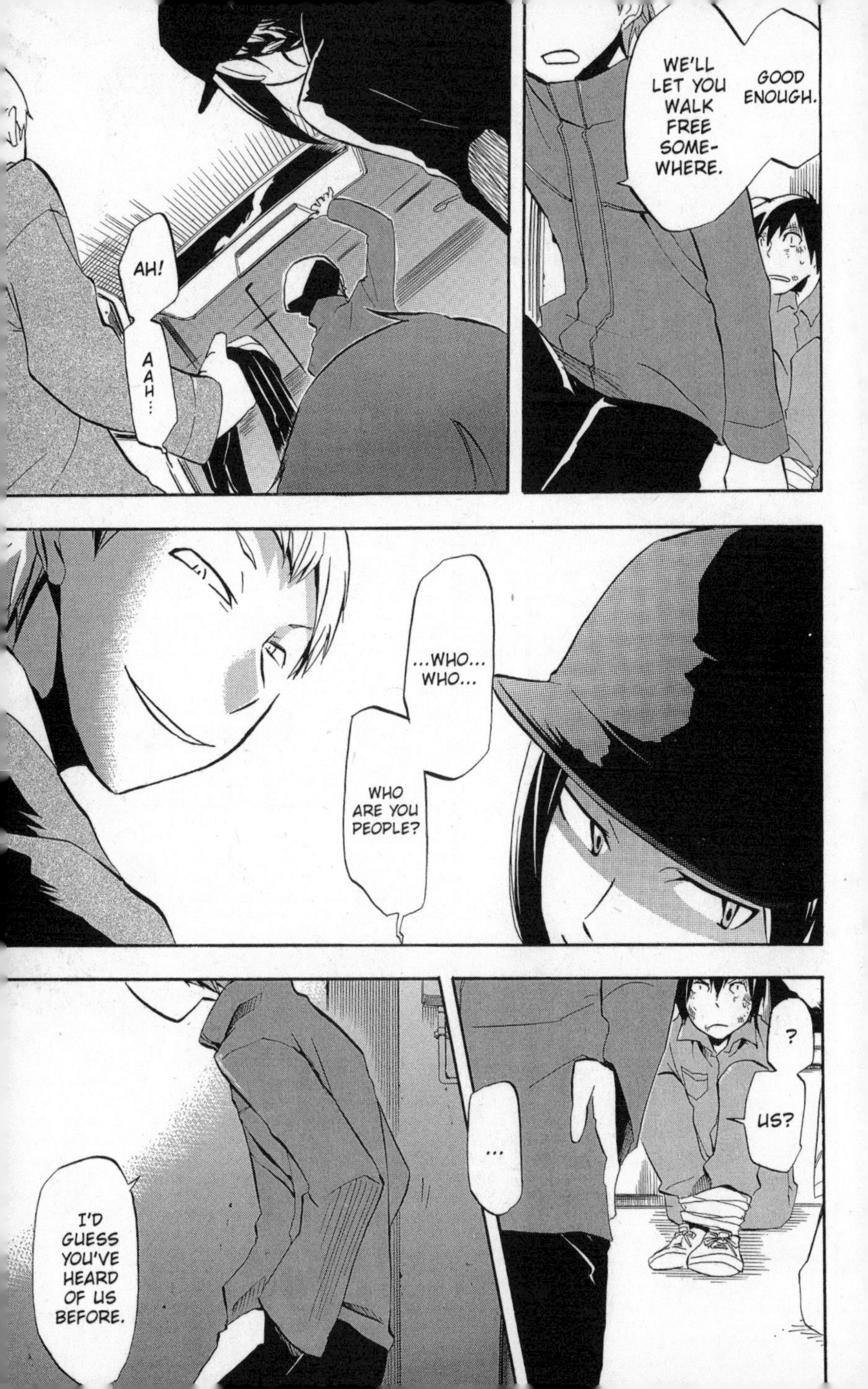
GOOD ENOUGH.
WE'LL LET YOU WALK FREE SOMEWHERE.
AH!
AAH...
...WHO... WHO...
WHO ARE YOU PEOPLE?
?
US?
...
I'D GUESS YOU'VE HEARD OF US BEFORE.

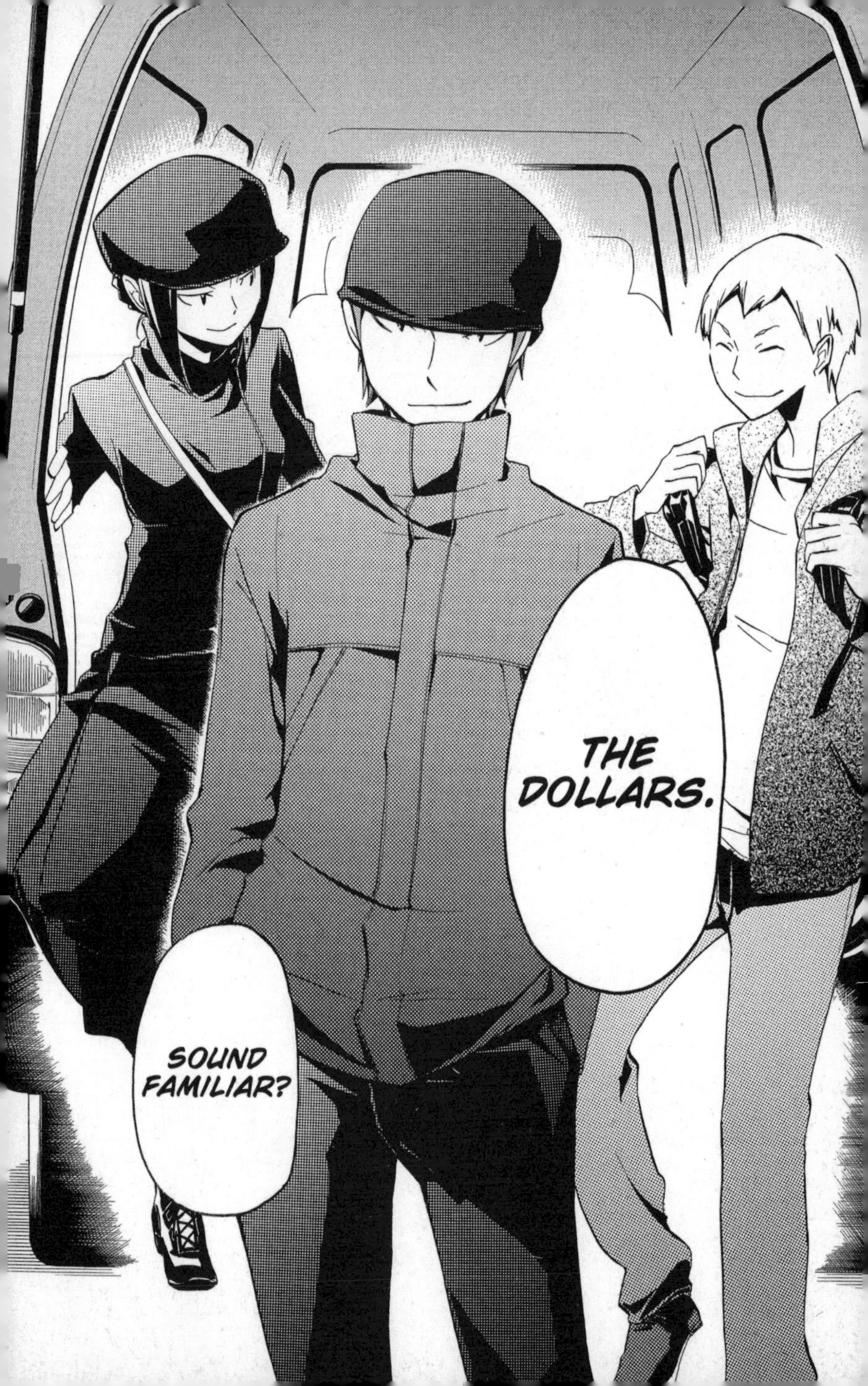
THE DOLLARS.
SOUND FAMILIAR?

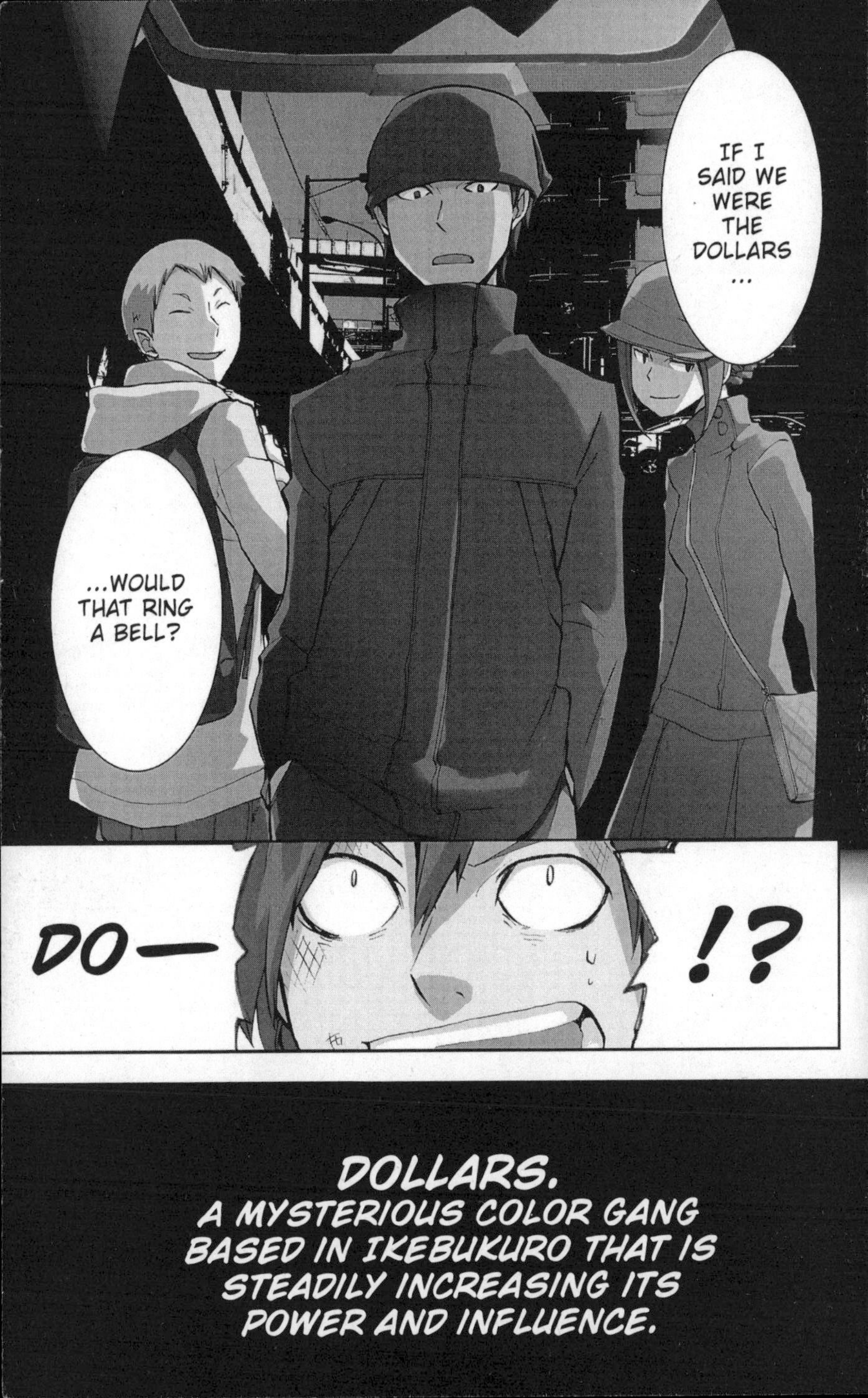
IF I SAID WE WERE THE DOLLARS ...
...WOULD THAT RING A BELL?
DO— !?
DOLLARS.
A MYSTERIOUS COLOR GANG BASED IN IKEBUKURO THAT IS STEADILY INCREASING ITS POWER AND INFLUENCE.

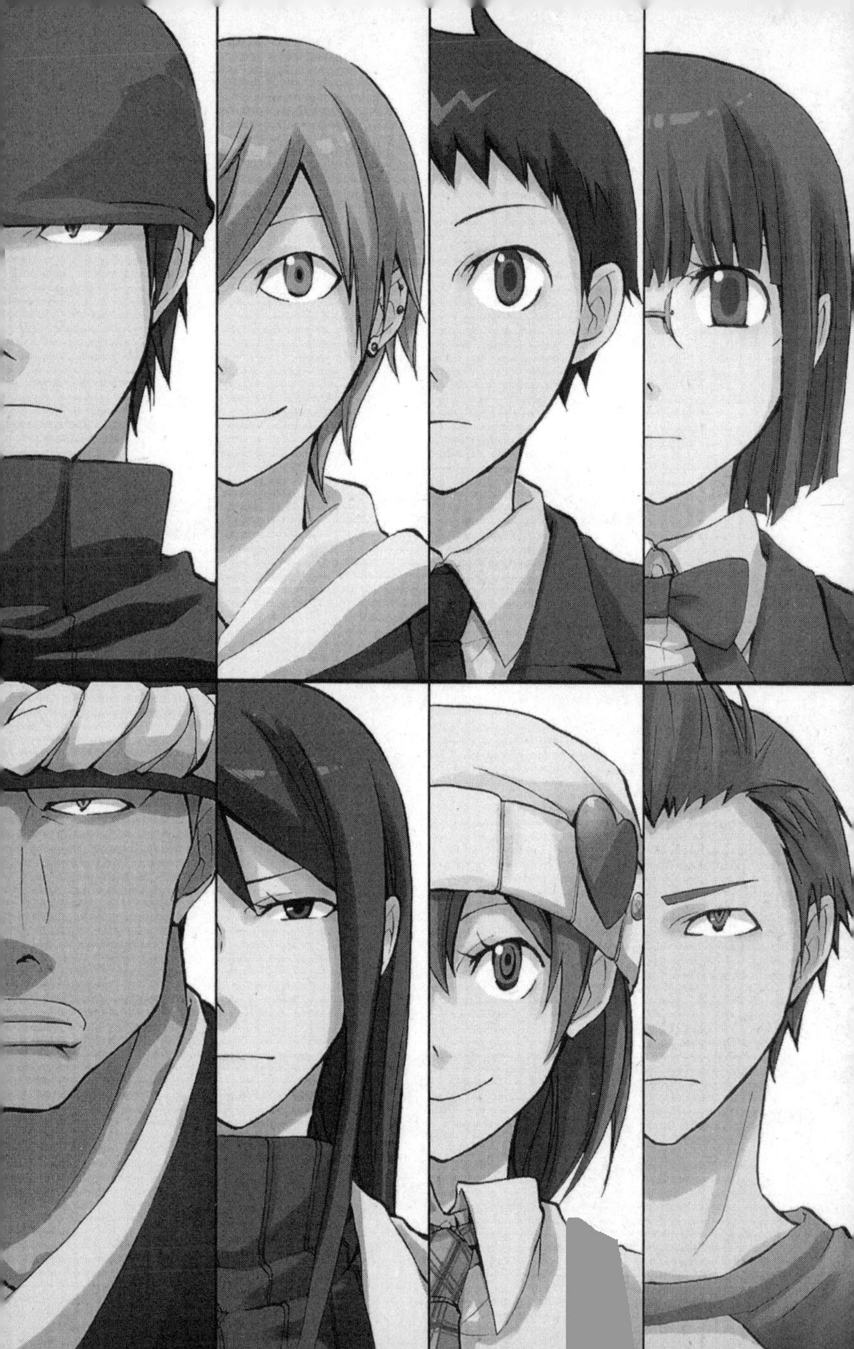

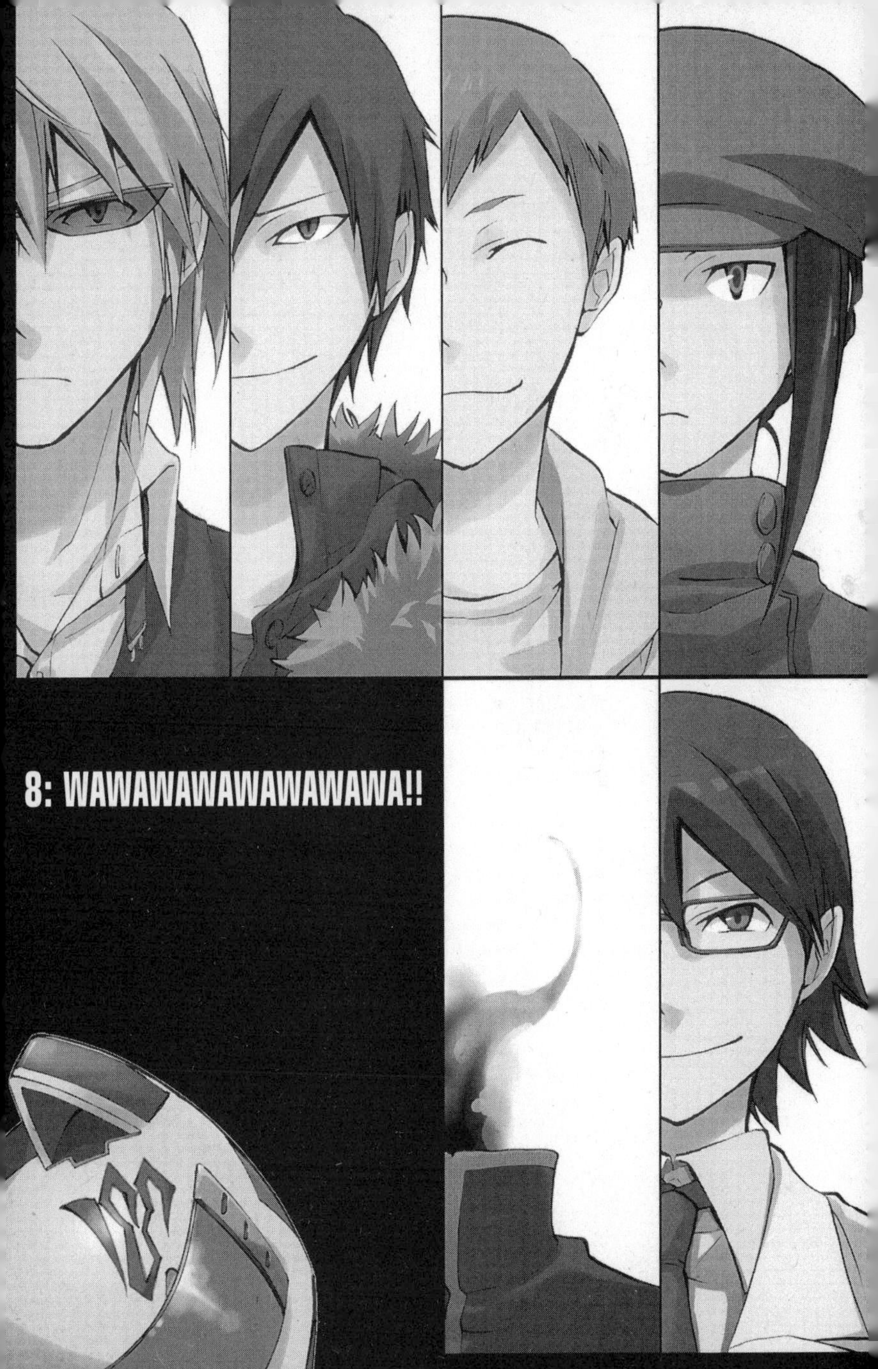
8: WAWAWAWAWAWAWAWA!!

DRRR!!

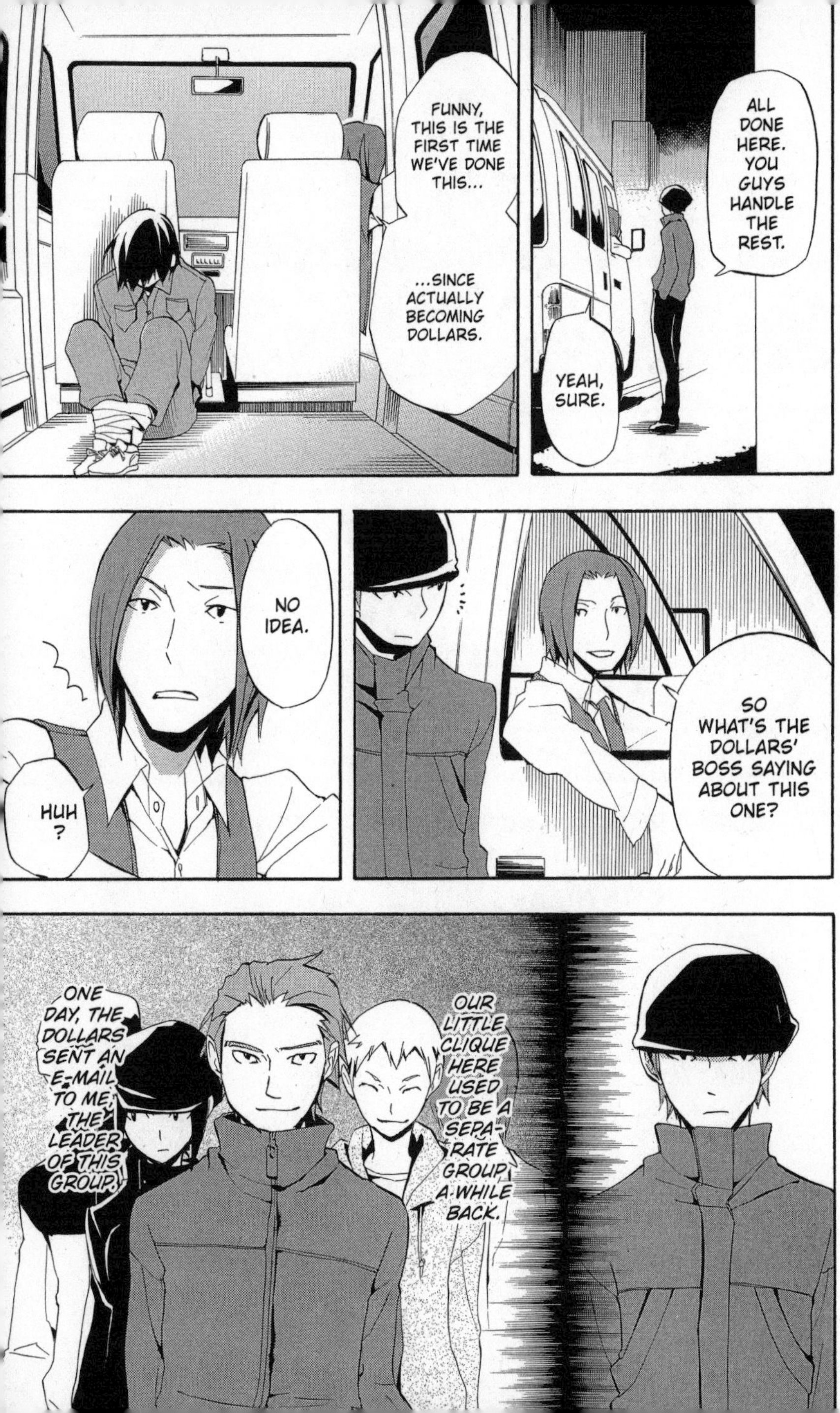
ALL DONE HERE. YOU GUYS HANDLE THE REST.
YEAH, SURE.
FUNNY, THIS IS THE FIRST TIME WE'VE DONE THIS...
...SINCE ACTUALLY BECOMING DOLLARS.
SO WHAT'S THE DOLLARS' BOSS SAYING ABOUT THIS ONE?
NO IDEA.
HUH?
OUR LITTLE CLIQUE HERE USED TO BE A SEPA-RATE GROUP A WHILE BACK.
ONE DAY, THE DOLLARS SENT AN E-MAIL TO ME, THE LEADER OF THIS GROUP.

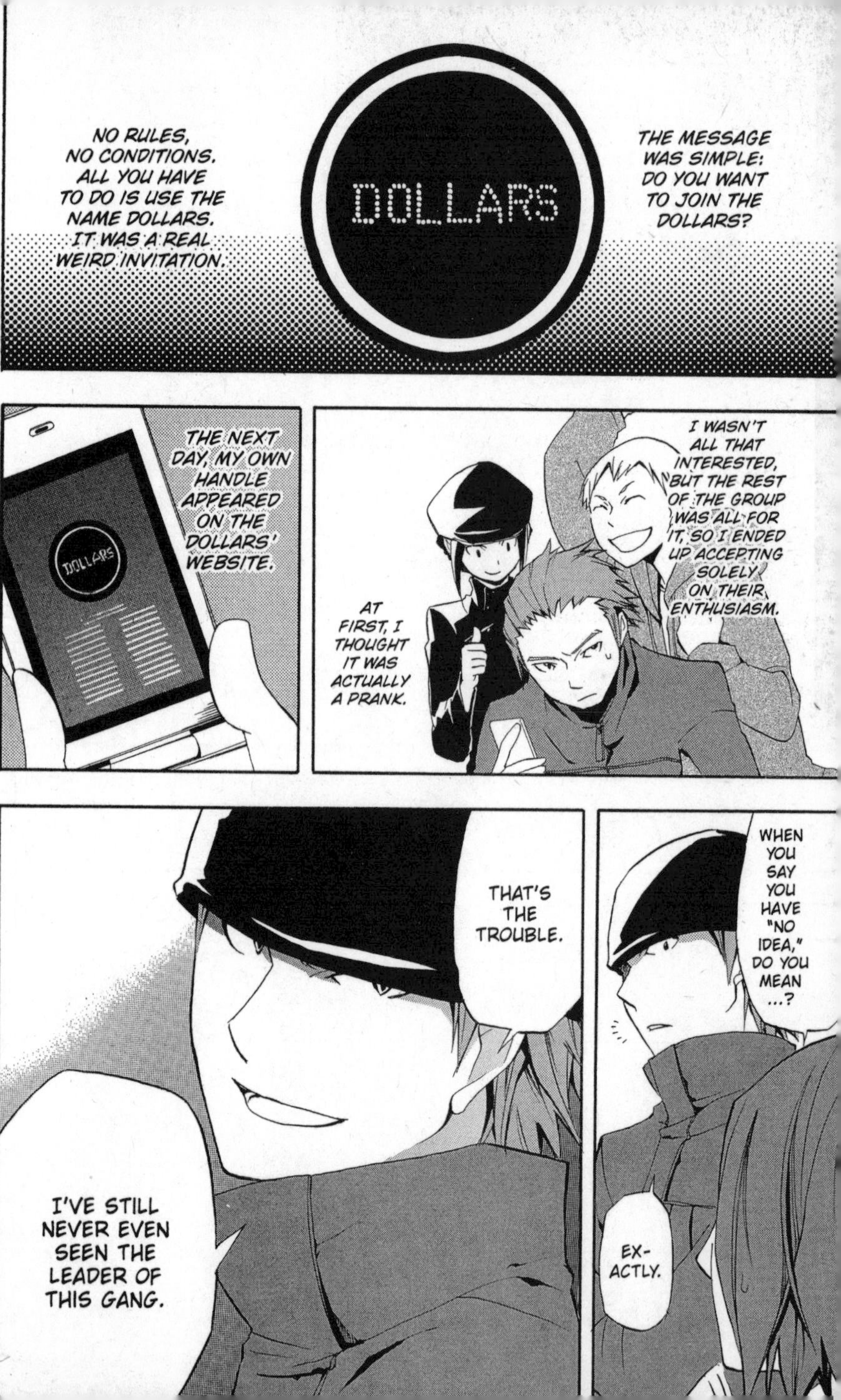
THE MESSAGE WAS SIMPLE: DO YOU WANT TO JOIN THE DOLLARS?
DOLLARS
NO RULES, NO CONDITIONS. ALL YOU HAVE TO DO IS USE THE NAME DOLLARS. IT WAS A REAL WEIRD INVITATION.
I WASN'T ALL THAT INTERESTED, BUT THE REST OF THE GROUP WAS ALL FOR IT, SO I ENDED UP ACCEPTING SOLELY ON THEIR ENTHUSIASM.
AT FIRST, I THOUGHT IT WAS ACTUALLY A PRANK.
THE NEXT DAY, MY OWN HANDLE APPEARED ON THE DOLLARS' WEBSITE.
DOLLARS
WHEN YOU SAY YOU HAVE "NO IDEA," DO YOU MEAN ...?
EX-ACTLY.
THAT'S THE TROUBLE.
I'VE STILL NEVER EVEN SEEN THE LEADER OF THIS GANG.

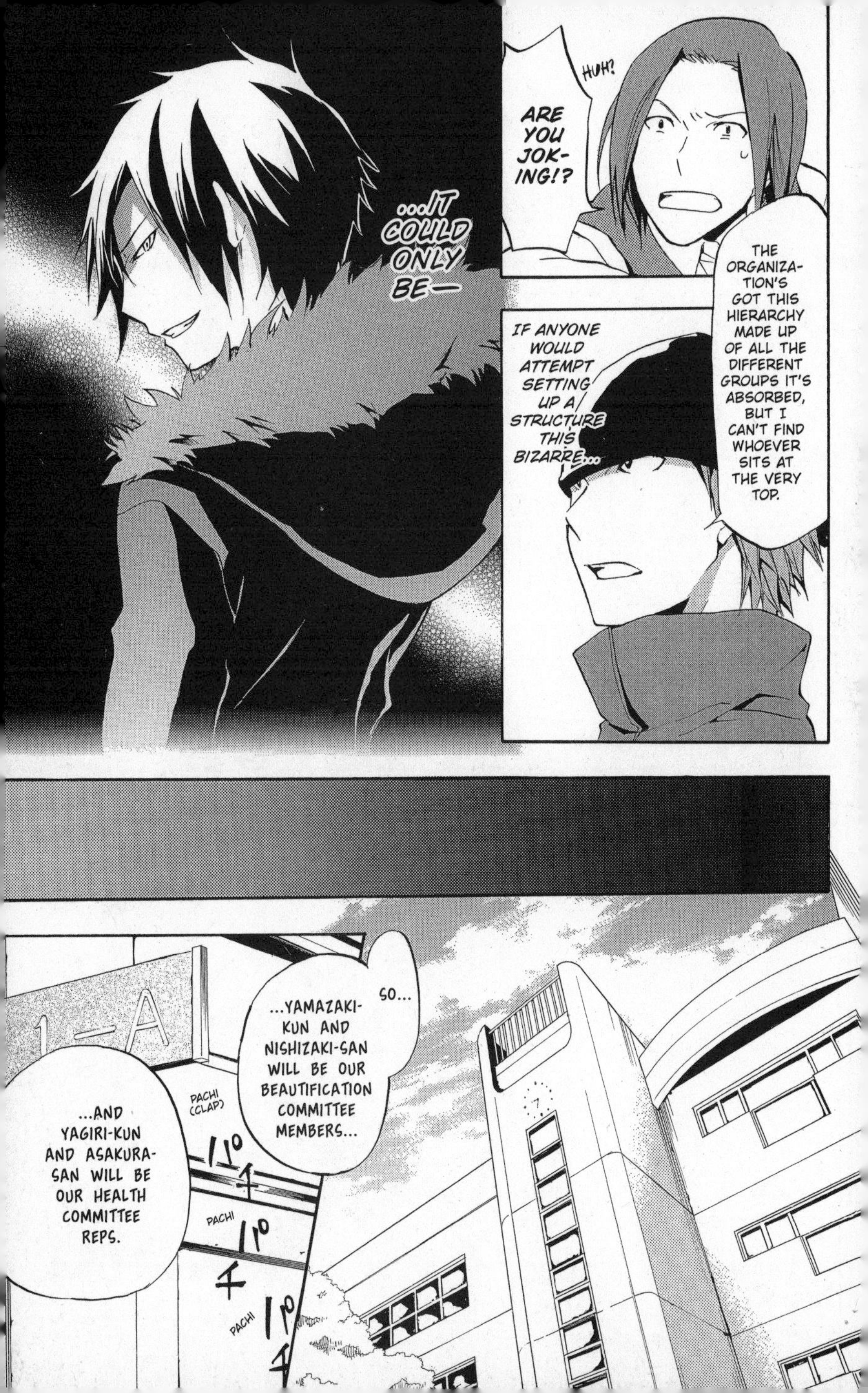
HUH?
ARE YOU JOK-ING!?
THE ORGANIZA-TION'S GOT THIS HIERARCHY MADE UP OF ALL THE DIFFERENT GROUPS IT'S ABSORBED, BUT I CAN'T FIND WHOEVER SITS AT THE VERY TOP.
IF ANYONE WOULD ATTEMPT SETTING UP A STRUCTURE THIS BIZARRE...
...IT COULD ONLY BE—
SO...
...YAMAZAKI-KUN AND NISHIZAKI-SAN WILL BE OUR BEAUTIFICATION COMMITTEE MEMBERS...
PACHI (CLAP)
PACHI
PACHI
...AND YAGIRI-KUN AND ASAKURA-SAN WILL BE OUR HEALTH COMMITTEE REPS.
1-A

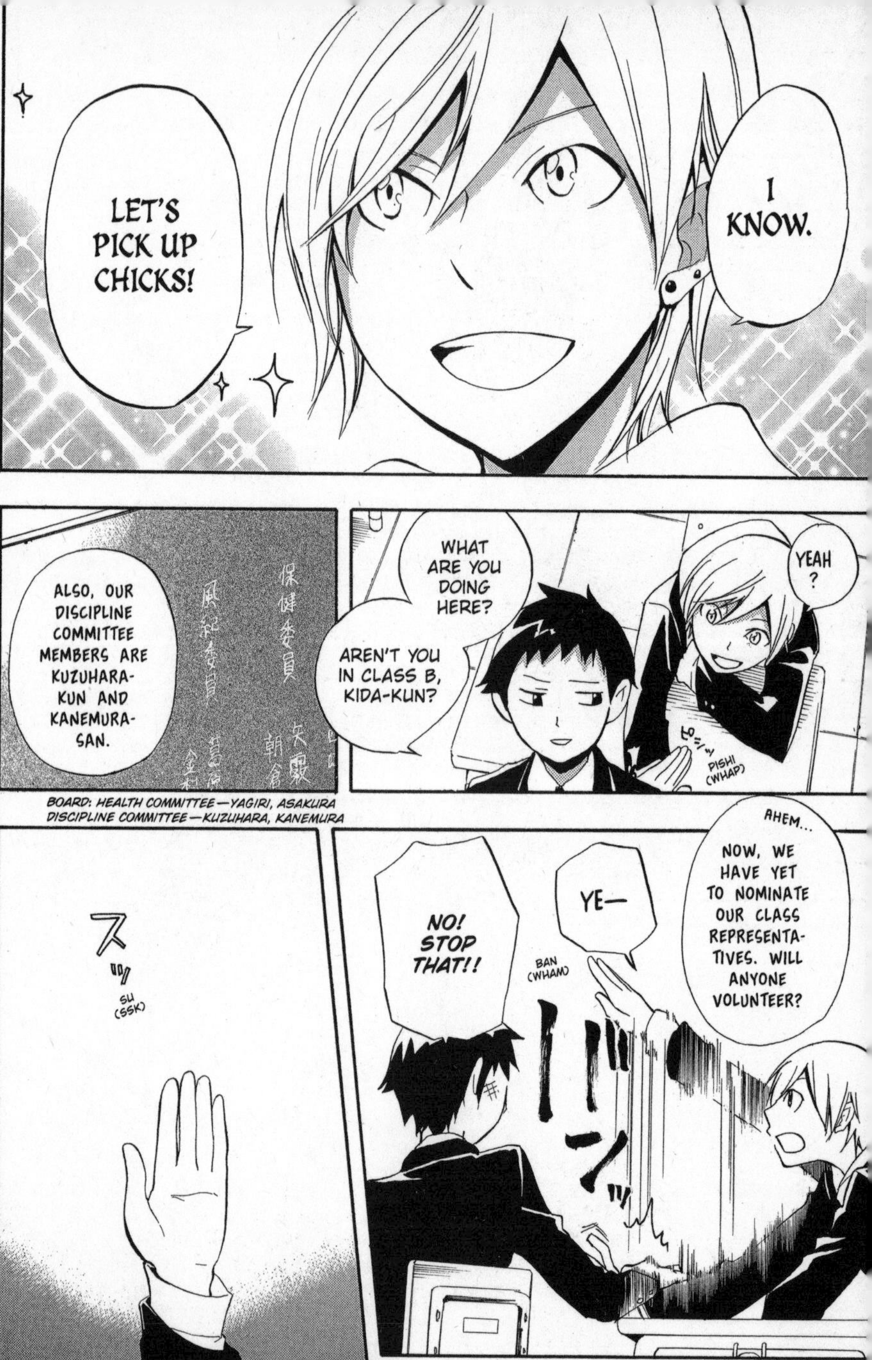
I KNOW.
LET'S PICK UP CHICKS!
YEAH?
WHAT ARE YOU DOING HERE?
AREN'T YOU IN CLASS B, KIDA-KUN?
PISHI (WHAP)
ALSO, OUR DISCIPLINE COMMITTEE MEMBERS ARE KUZUHARA-KUN AND KANEMURA-SAN.
BOARD: HEALTH COMMITTEE—YAGIRI, ASAKURA
DISCIPLINE COMMITTEE—KUZUHARA, KANEMURA
AHEM...
NOW, WE HAVE YET TO NOMINATE OUR CLASS REPRESENTATIVES. WILL ANYONE VOLUNTEER?
YE—
BAN (WHAM)
NO! STOP THAT!!
SU (SSK)

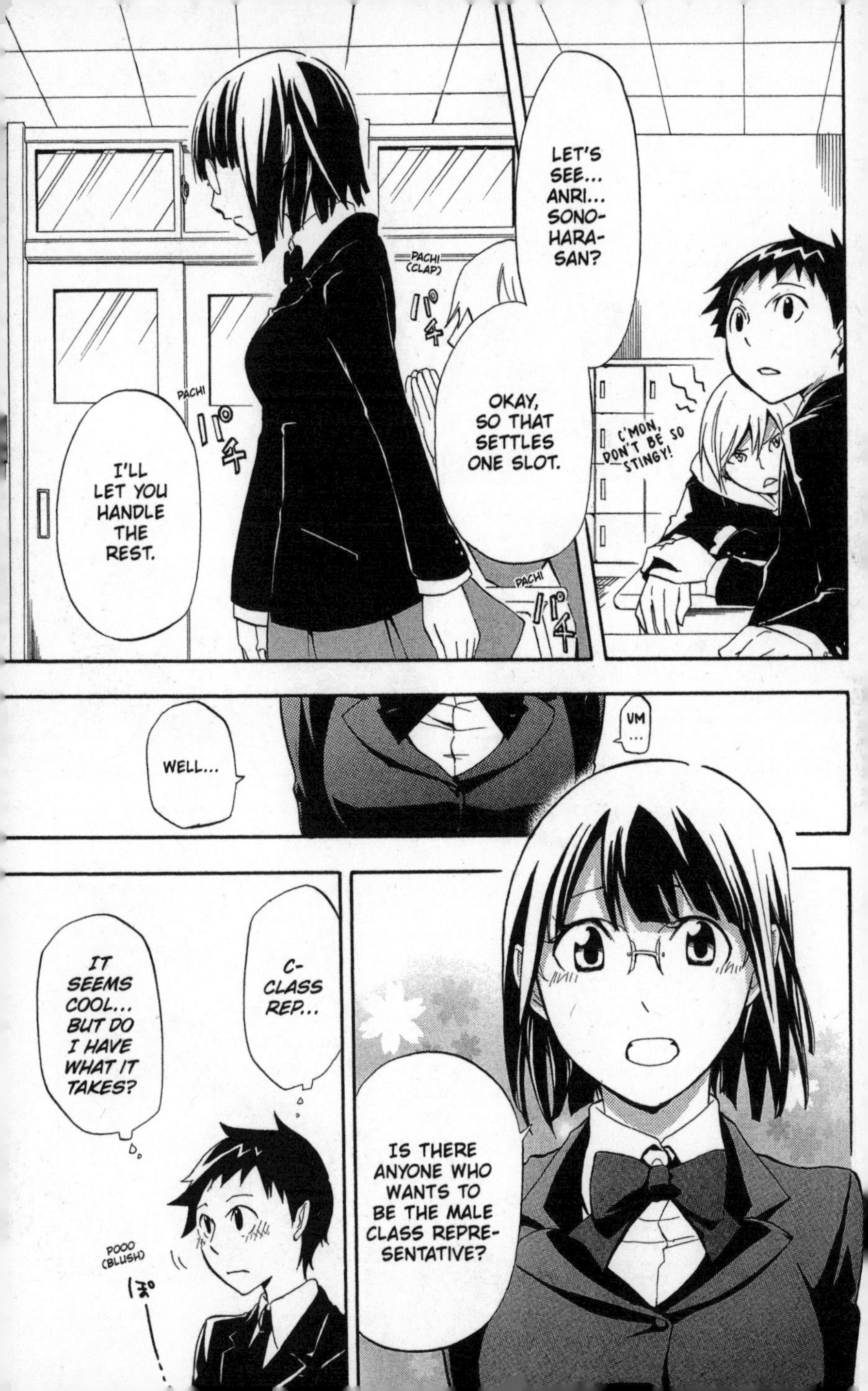
LET'S SEE... ANRI... SONOHARA-SAN?
C'MON, DON'T BE SO STINGY!
PACHI (CLAP)
パチ
OKAY, SO THAT SETTLES ONE SLOT.
PACHI
パチ
PACHI
パチ
I'LL LET YOU HANDLE THE REST.
UM...
WELL...
IS THERE ANYONE WHO WANTS TO BE THE MALE CLASS REPRESENTATIVE?
C-CLASS REP...
IT SEEMS COOL... BUT DO I HAVE WHAT IT TAKES?
POOO (BLUSH)
ぽー

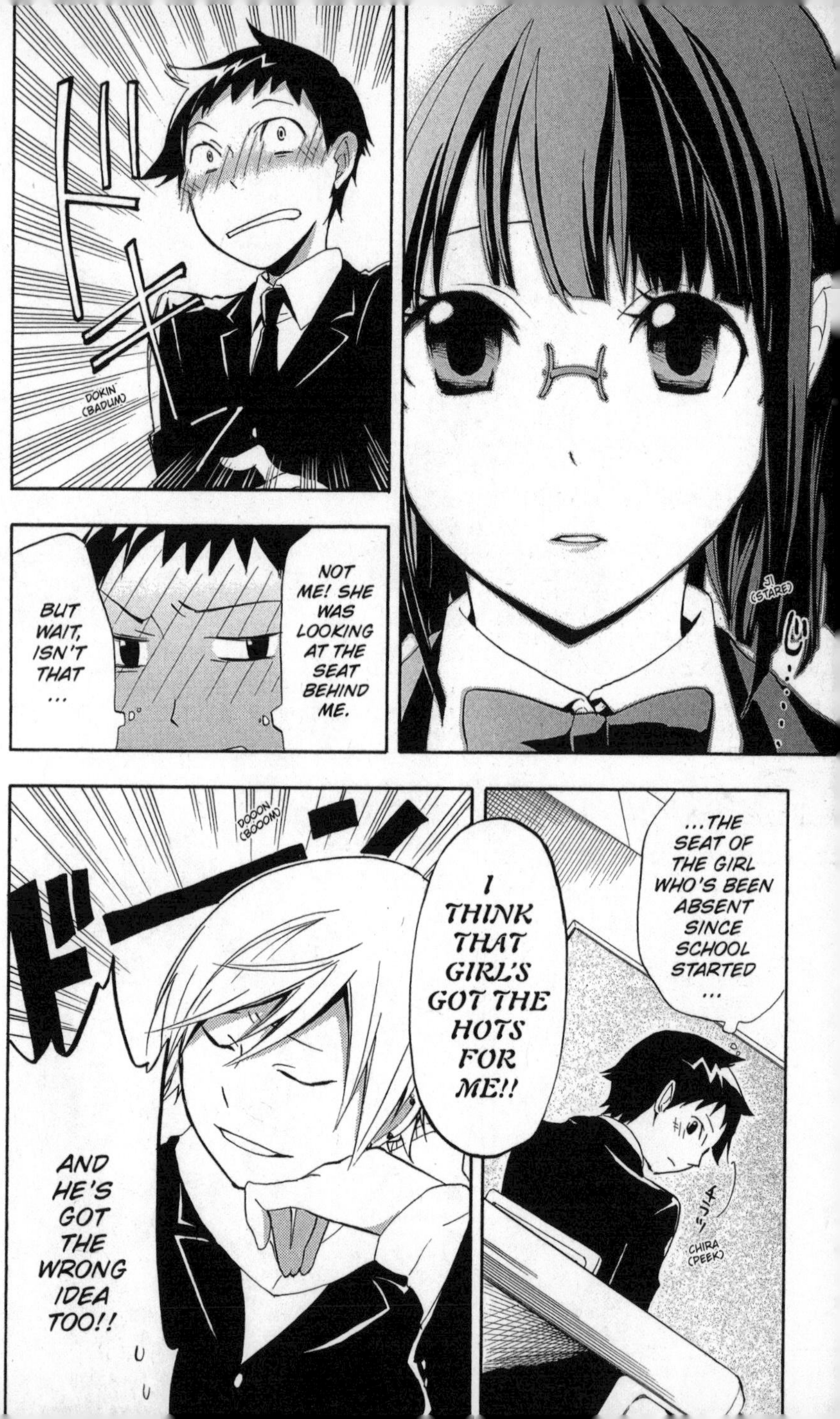
JI (STARE)
DOKIN (BADUM)
NOT ME! SHE WAS LOOKING AT THE SEAT BEHIND ME.
BUT WAIT, ISN'T THAT ...
...THE SEAT OF THE GIRL WHO'S BEEN ABSENT SINCE SCHOOL STARTED ...
CHIRA (PEEK)
I THINK THAT GIRL'S GOT THE HOTS FOR ME!!
DOOON (BOOOM)
AND HE'S GOT THE WRONG IDEA TOO!!

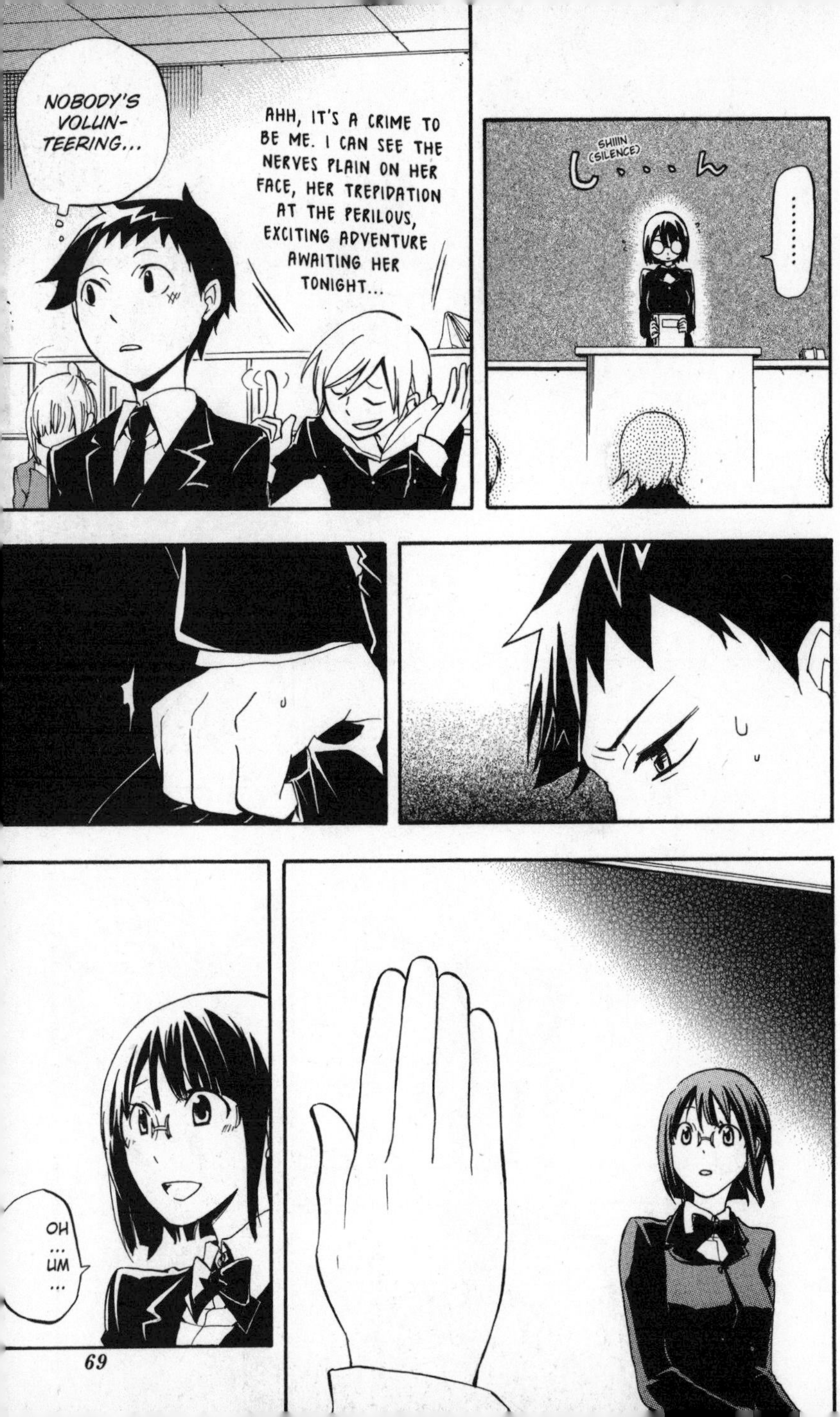
SHIIIN (SILENCE)
......
AHH, IT'S A CRIME TO BE ME. I CAN SEE THE NERVES PLAIN ON HER FACE, HER TREPIDATION AT THE PERILOUS, EXCITING ADVENTURE AWAITING HER TONIGHT...
NOBODY'S VOLUN-TEERING...
OH ... UM ...

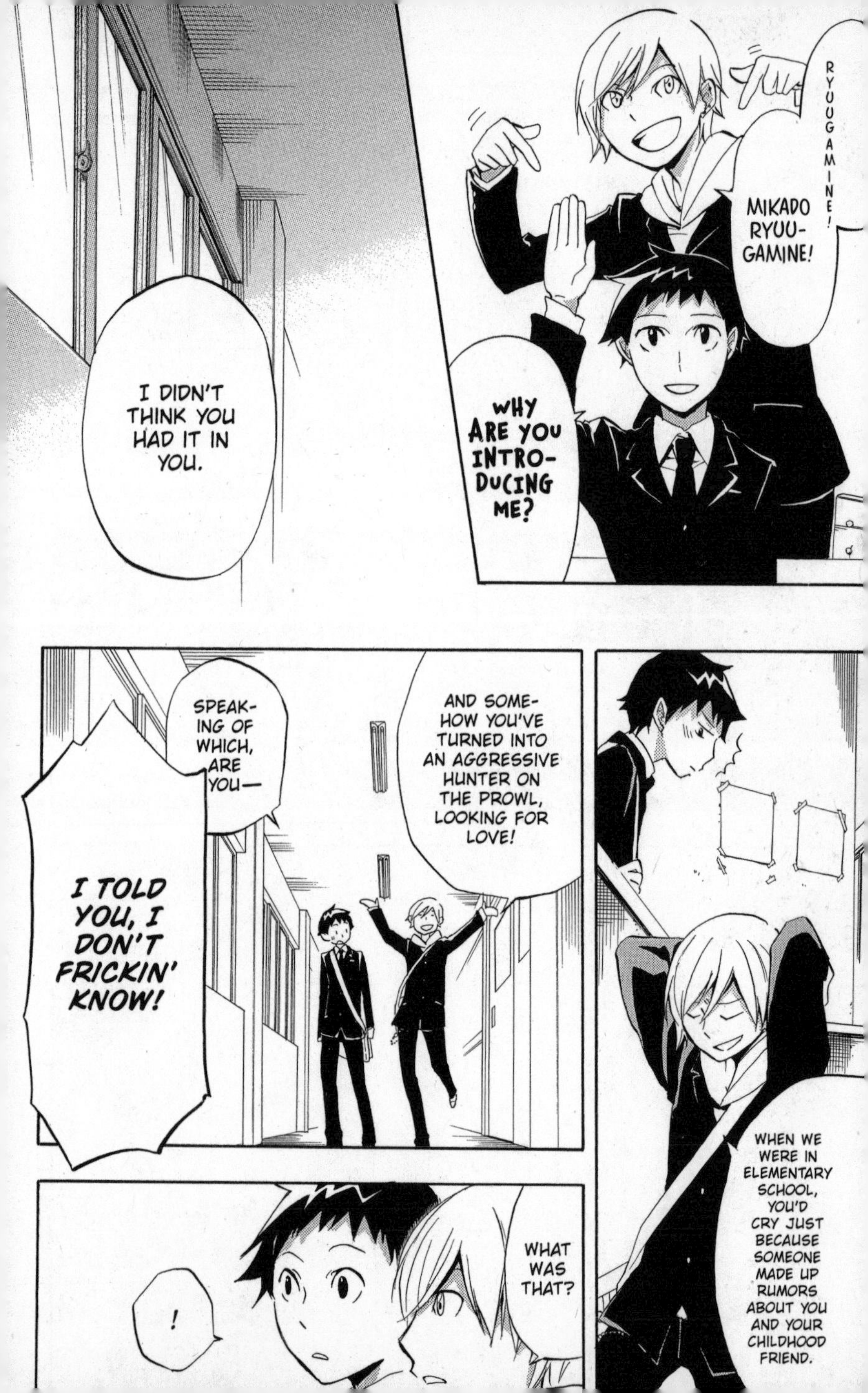
RYUUGAMINE!
MIKADO RYUU-GAMINE!
WHY ARE YOU INTRO-DUCING ME?
I DIDN'T THINK YOU HAD IT IN YOU.
WHEN WE WERE IN ELEMENTARY SCHOOL, YOU'D CRY JUST BECAUSE SOMEONE MADE UP RUMORS ABOUT YOU AND YOUR CHILDHOOD FRIEND.
AND SOME-HOW YOU'VE TURNED INTO AN AGGRESSIVE HUNTER ON THE PROWL, LOOKING FOR LOVE!
SPEAK-ING OF WHICH, ARE YOU—
I TOLD YOU, I DON'T FRICKIN' KNOW!
WHAT WAS THAT?
!

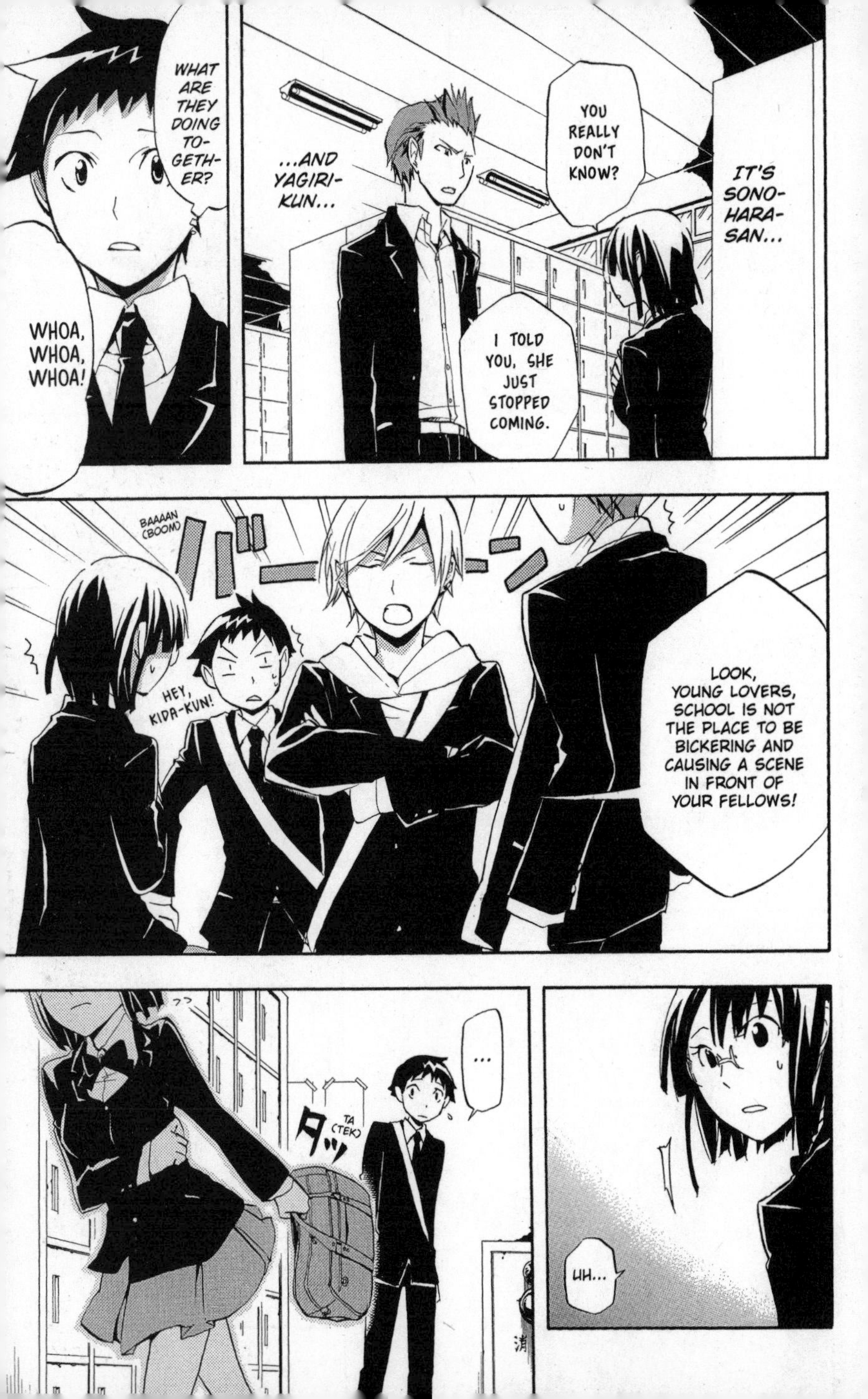
IT'S SONO-HARA-SAN...
YOU REALLY DON'T KNOW?
...AND YAGIRI-KUN...
I TOLD YOU, SHE JUST STOPPED COMING.
WHAT ARE THEY DOING TO-GETH-ER?
WHOA, WHOA, WHOA!
LOOK, YOUNG LOVERS, SCHOOL IS NOT THE PLACE TO BE BICKERING AND CAUSING A SCENE IN FRONT OF YOUR FELLOWS!
BAAAAN (BOOM)
HEY, KIDA-KUN!
UH...
...
TA (TEK)

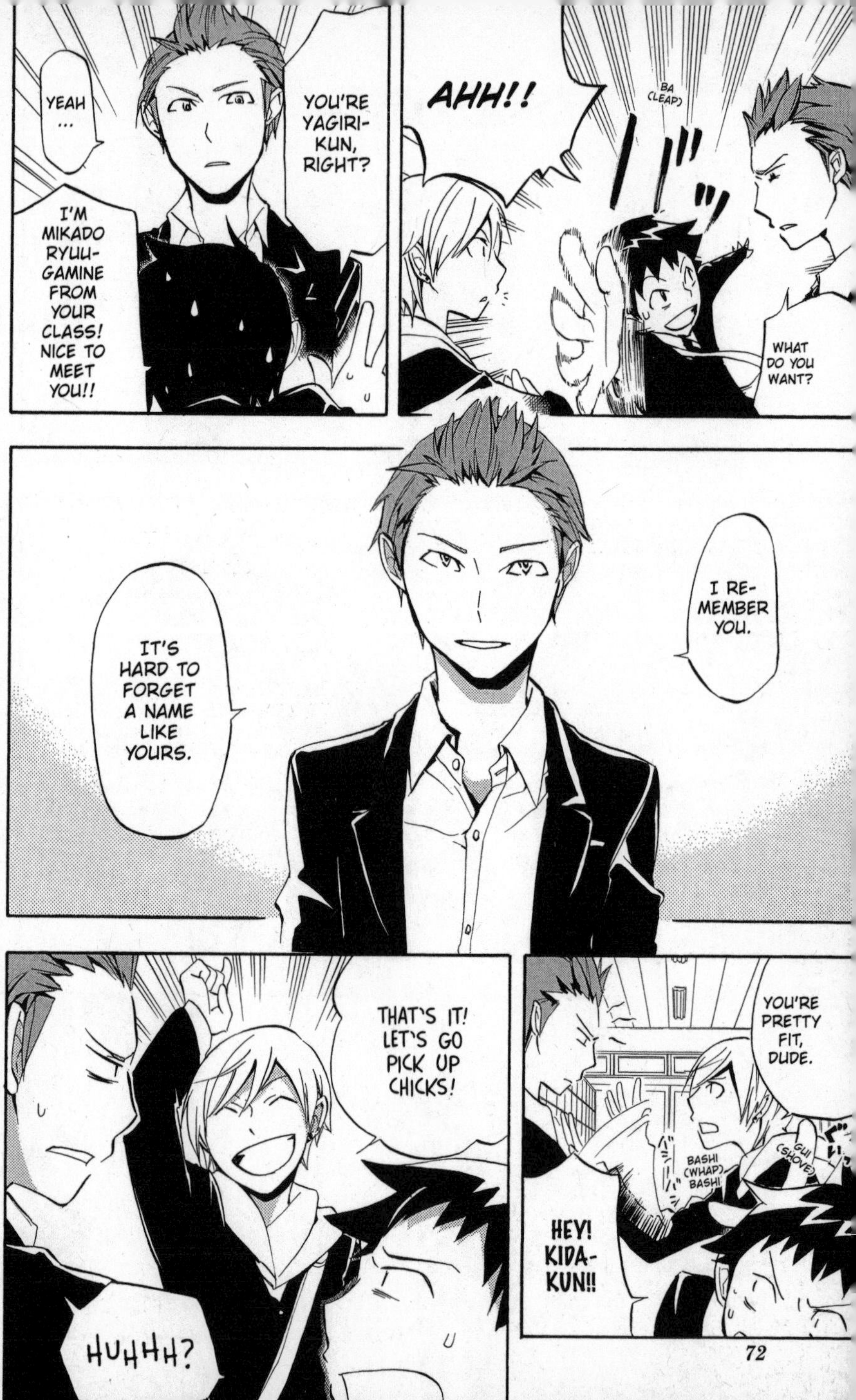
BA (LEAP)
AHH!!
WHAT DO YOU WANT?
YOU'RE YAGIRI-KUN, RIGHT?
YEAH ...
I'M MIKADO RYUU-GAMINE FROM YOUR CLASS! NICE TO MEET YOU!!
I RE-MEMBER YOU.
IT'S HARD TO FORGET A NAME LIKE YOURS.
YOU'RE PRETTY FIT, DUDE.
GUI (SHOVE)
BASHI (WHAP) BASHI
HEY! KIDA-KUN!!
THAT'S IT! LET'S GO PICK UP CHICKS!
HUHHH?

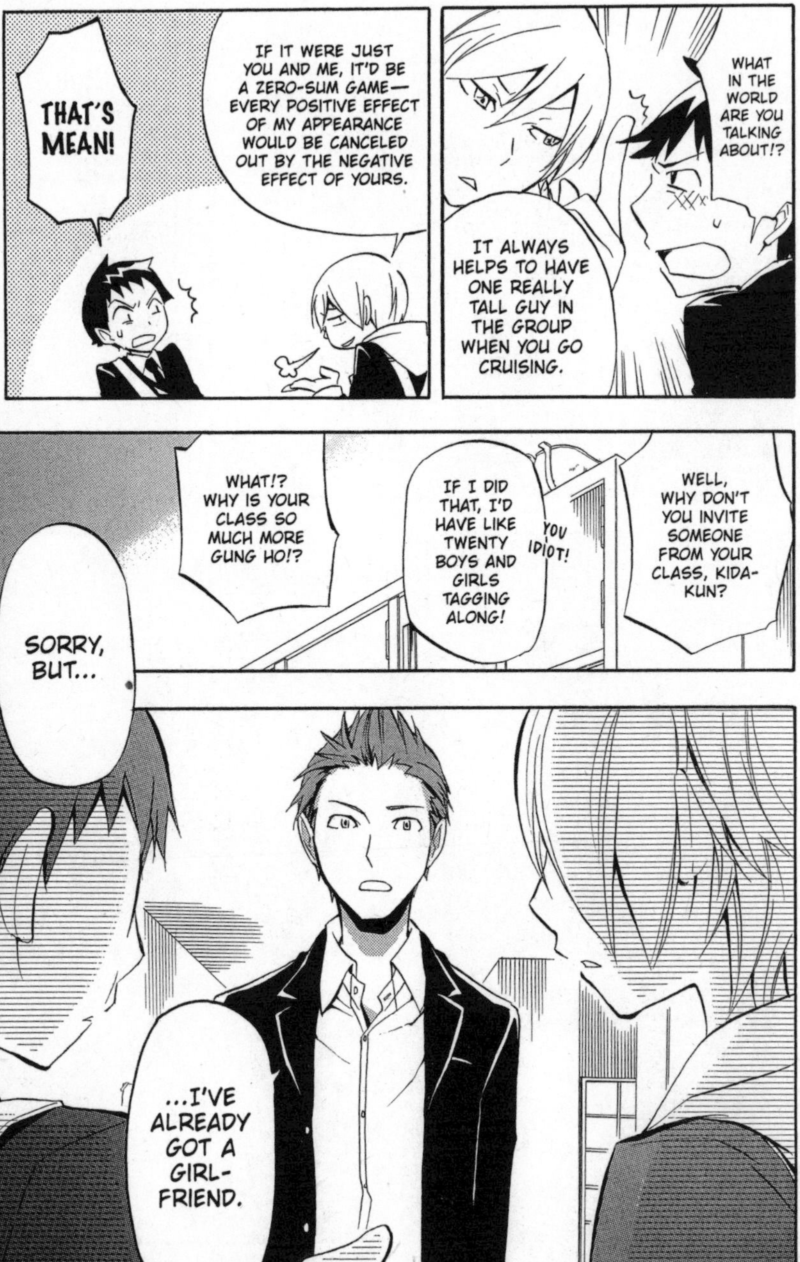
WHAT IN THE WORLD ARE YOU TALKING ABOUT!?
IT ALWAYS HELPS TO HAVE ONE REALLY TALL GUY IN THE GROUP WHEN YOU GO CRUISING.
IF IT WERE JUST YOU AND ME, IT'D BE A ZERO-SUM GAME—EVERY POSITIVE EFFECT OF MY APPEARANCE WOULD BE CANCELED OUT BY THE NEGATIVE EFFECT OF YOURS.
THAT'S MEAN!
WELL, WHY DON'T YOU INVITE SOMEONE FROM YOUR CLASS, KIDA-KUN?
YOU IDIOT!
IF I DID THAT, I'D HAVE LIKE TWENTY BOYS AND GIRLS TAGGING ALONG!
WHAT!? WHY IS YOUR CLASS SO MUCH MORE GUNG HO!?
SORRY, BUT...
...I'VE ALREADY GOT A GIRL-FRIEND.

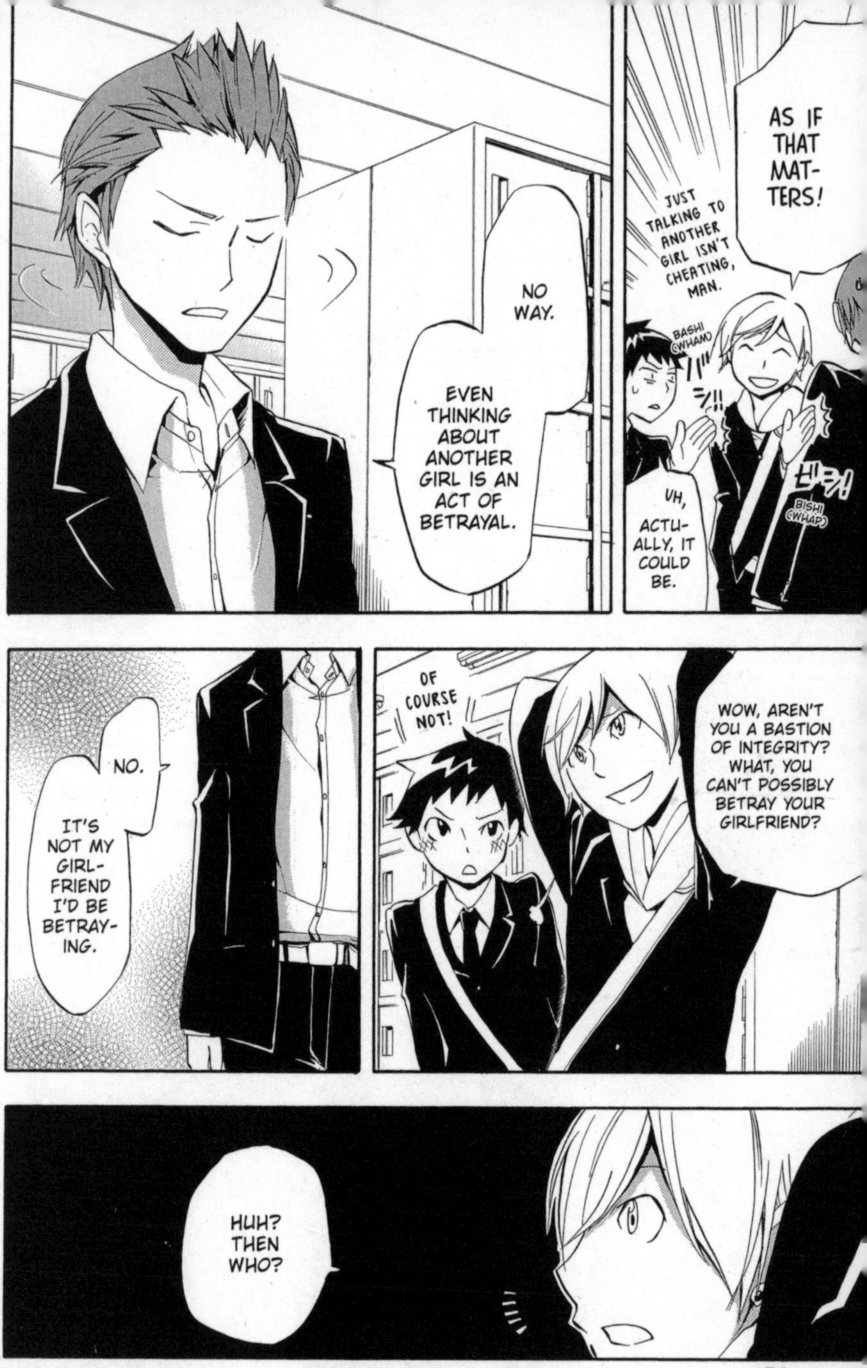
AS IF THAT MAT-TERS!
JUST TALKING TO ANOTHER GIRL ISN'T CHEATING, MAN.
BISHI (WHAP)
BASHI (WHAM)
UH, ACTU-ALLY, IT COULD BE.
NO WAY.
EVEN THINKING ABOUT ANOTHER GIRL IS AN ACT OF BETRAYAL.
WOW, AREN'T YOU A BASTION OF INTEGRITY? WHAT, YOU CAN'T POSSIBLY BETRAY YOUR GIRLFRIEND?
OF COURSE NOT!
NO.
IT'S NOT MY GIRL-FRIEND I'D BE BETRAY-ING.
HUH? THEN WHO?

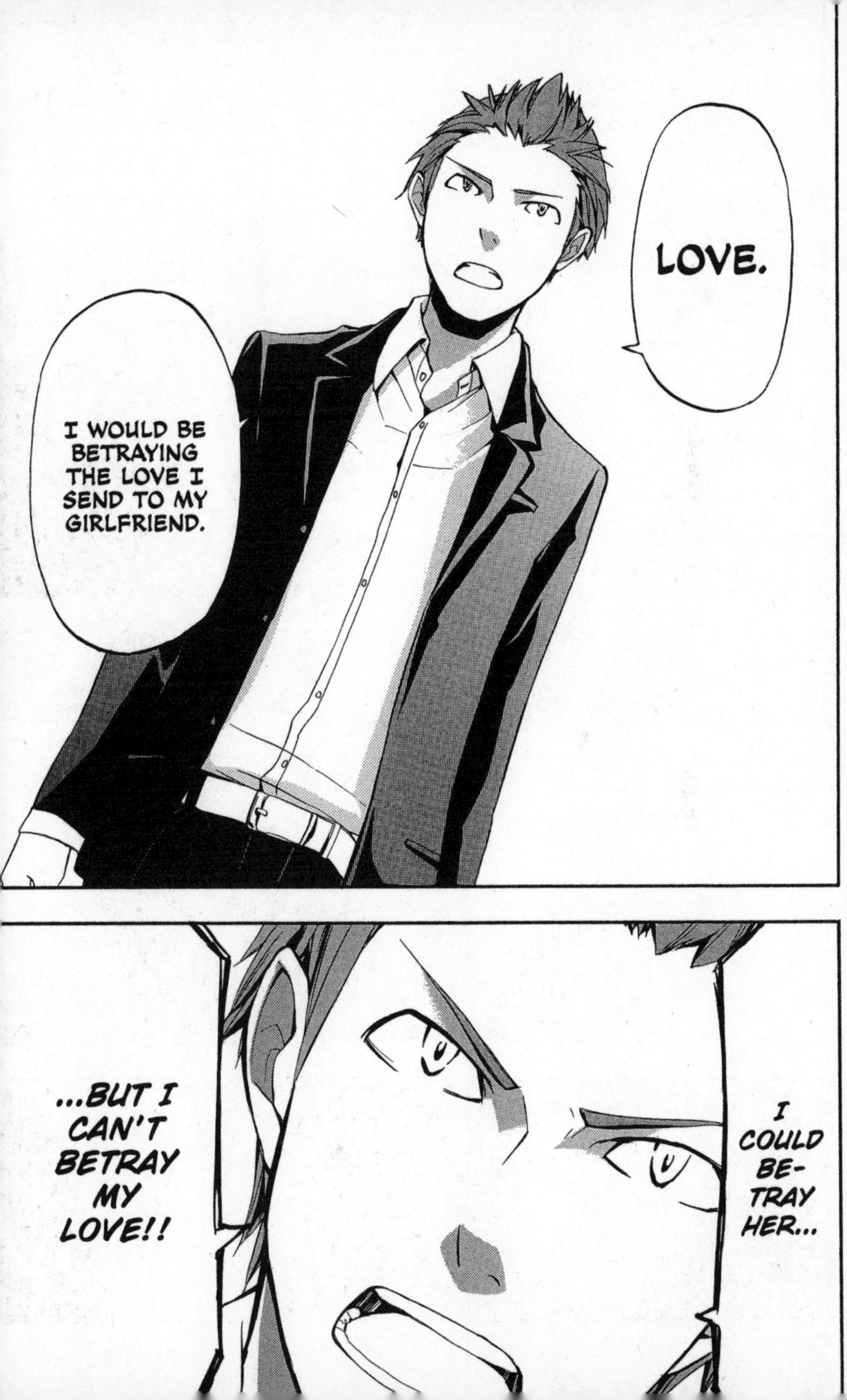
LOVE.
I WOULD BE BETRAYING THE LOVE I SEND TO MY GIRLFRIEND.
I COULD BE-TRAY HER...
...BUT I CAN'T BETRAY MY LOVE!!

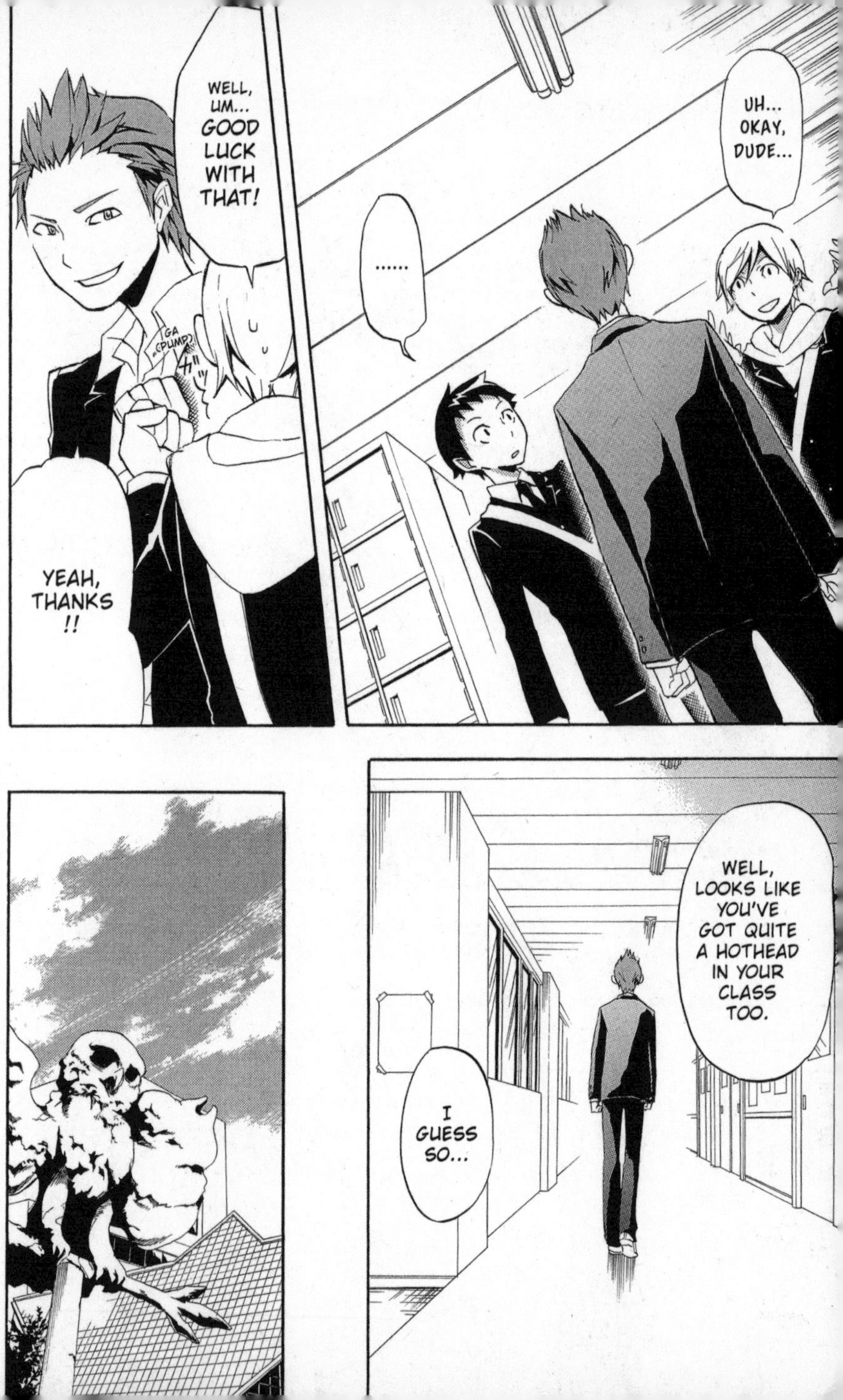
UH... OKAY, DUDE...
......
WELL, UM... GOOD LUCK WITH THAT!
GA (PUMP)
YEAH, THANKS !!
WELL, LOOKS LIKE YOU'VE GOT QUITE A HOTHEAD IN YOUR CLASS TOO.
I GUESS SO...

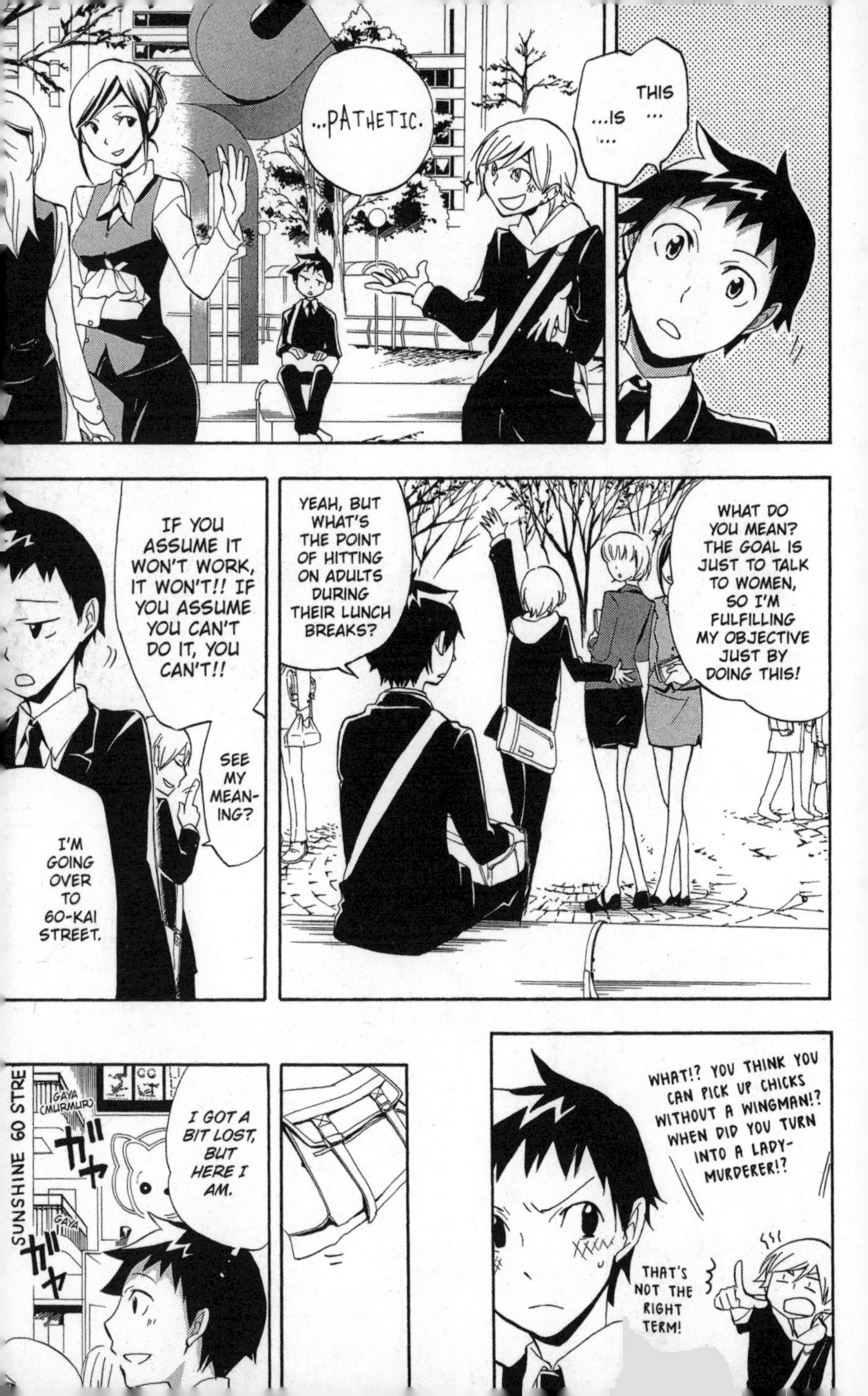

THIS ... ...IS ...
...PATHETIC.
YEAH, BUT WHAT'S THE POINT OF HITTING ON ADULTS DURING THEIR LUNCH BREAKS?
WHAT DO YOU MEAN? THE GOAL IS JUST TO TALK TO WOMEN, SO I'M FULFILLING MY OBJECTIVE JUST BY DOING THIS!
IF YOU ASSUME IT WON'T WORK, IT WON'T!! IF YOU ASSUME YOU CAN'T DO IT, YOU CAN'T!!
SEE MY MEANING?
I'M GOING OVER TO 60-KAI STREET.
WHAT!? YOU THINK YOU CAN PICK UP CHICKS WITHOUT A WINGMAN!? WHEN DID YOU TURN INTO A LADY-MURDERER!?
THAT'S NOT THE RIGHT TERM!
I GOT A BIT LOST, BUT HERE I AM.
SUNSHINE 60 STRE
GAYA (MURMUR)
ガヤ
GAYA
ガヤ

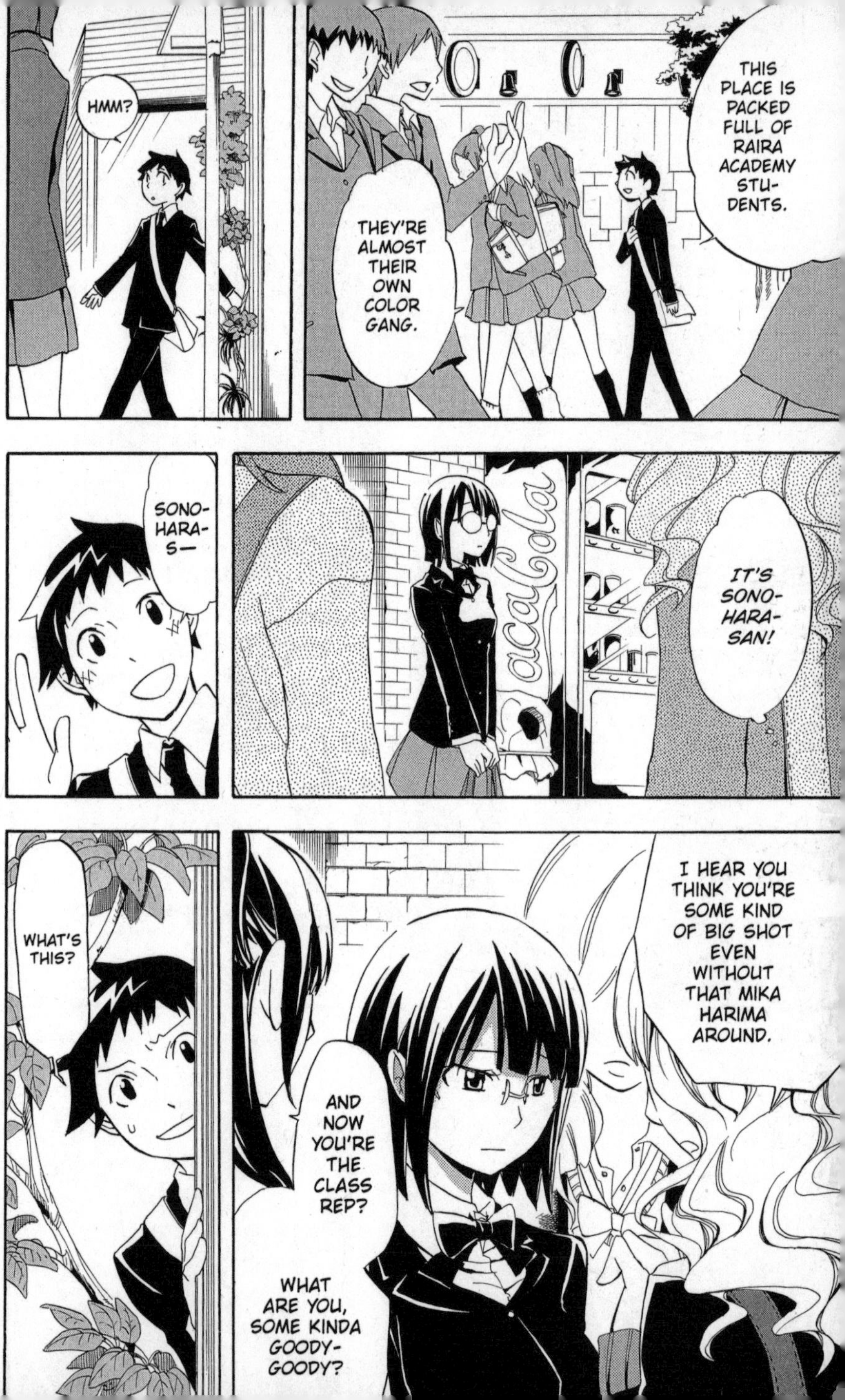
THIS PLACE IS PACKED FULL OF RAIRA ACADEMY STU-DENTS.
THEY'RE ALMOST THEIR OWN COLOR GANG.
HMM?
IT'S SONO-HARA-SAN!
SONO-HARA-S—
I HEAR YOU THINK YOU'RE SOME KIND OF BIG SHOT EVEN WITHOUT THAT MIKA HARIMA AROUND.
AND NOW YOU'RE THE CLASS REP?
WHAT ARE YOU, SOME KINDA GOODY-GOODY?
WHAT'S THIS?

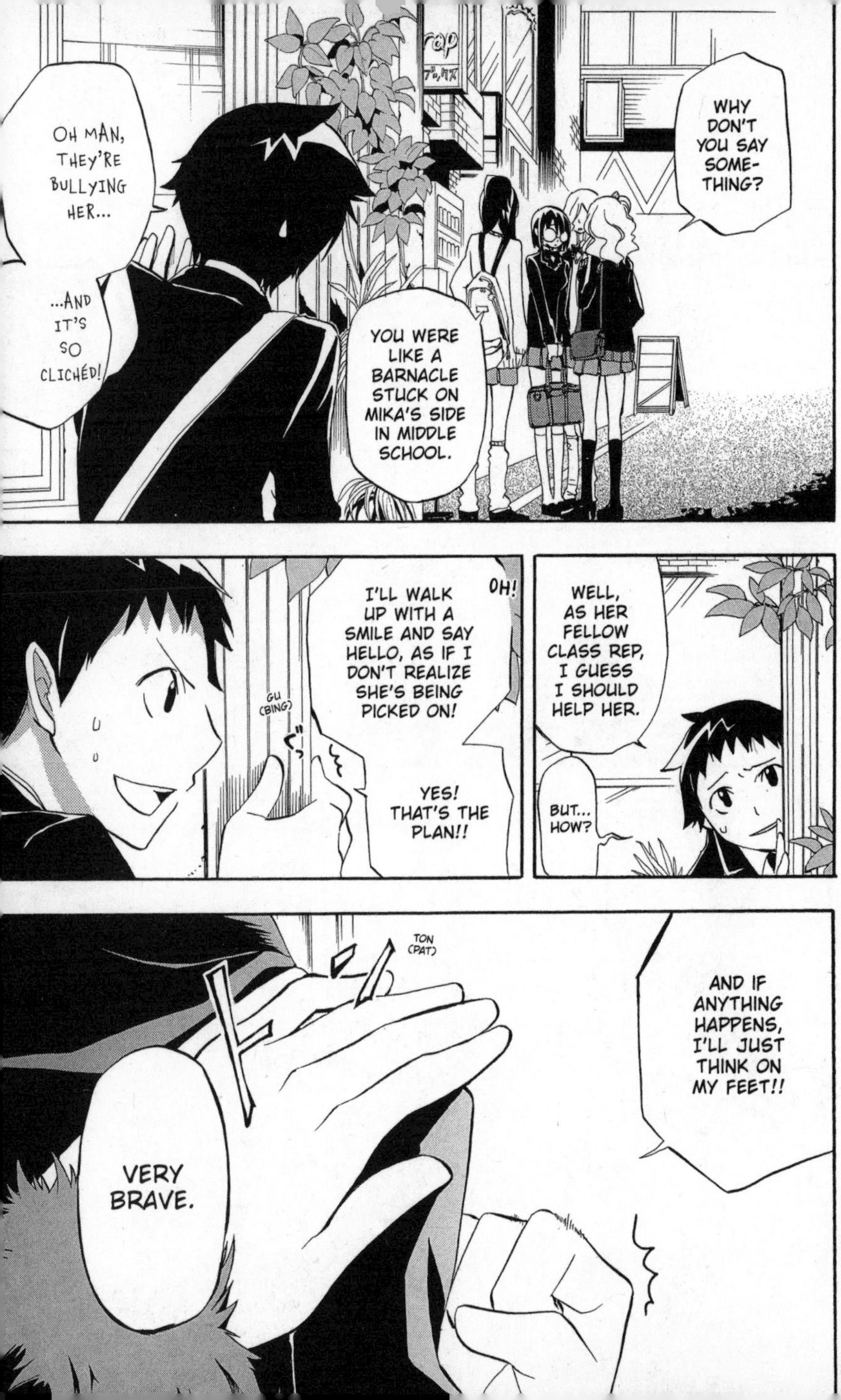
WHY DON'T YOU SAY SOME-THING?
YOU WERE LIKE A BARNACLE STUCK ON MIKA'S SIDE IN MIDDLE SCHOOL.
OH MAN, THEY'RE BULLYING HER...
...AND IT'S SO CLICHÉD!
WELL, AS HER FELLOW CLASS REP, I GUESS I SHOULD HELP HER.
BUT... HOW?
OH!
I'LL WALK UP WITH A SMILE AND SAY HELLO, AS IF I DON'T REALIZE SHE'S BEING PICKED ON!
YES! THAT'S THE PLAN!!
GU (BING)
AND IF ANYTHING HAPPENS, I'LL JUST THINK ON MY FEET!!
TON (PAT)
VERY BRAVE.

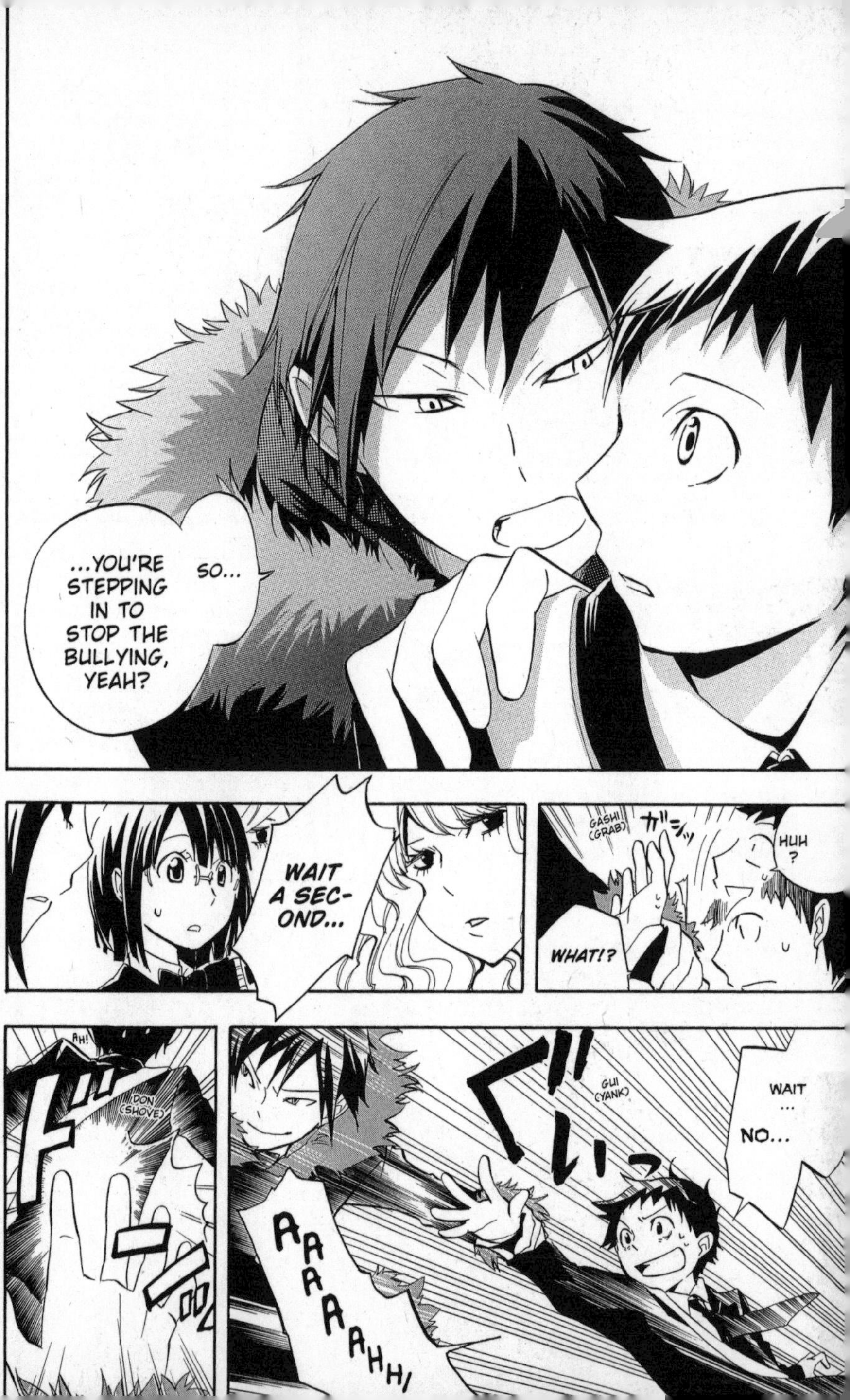
SO...
...YOU'RE STEPPING IN TO STOP THE BULLYING, YEAH?
GASHI (GRAB)
HUH?
WHAT!?
WAIT A SEC-OND...
GUI (YANK)
WAIT ... NO...
AAAAAHH!
AH!
DON (SHOVE)

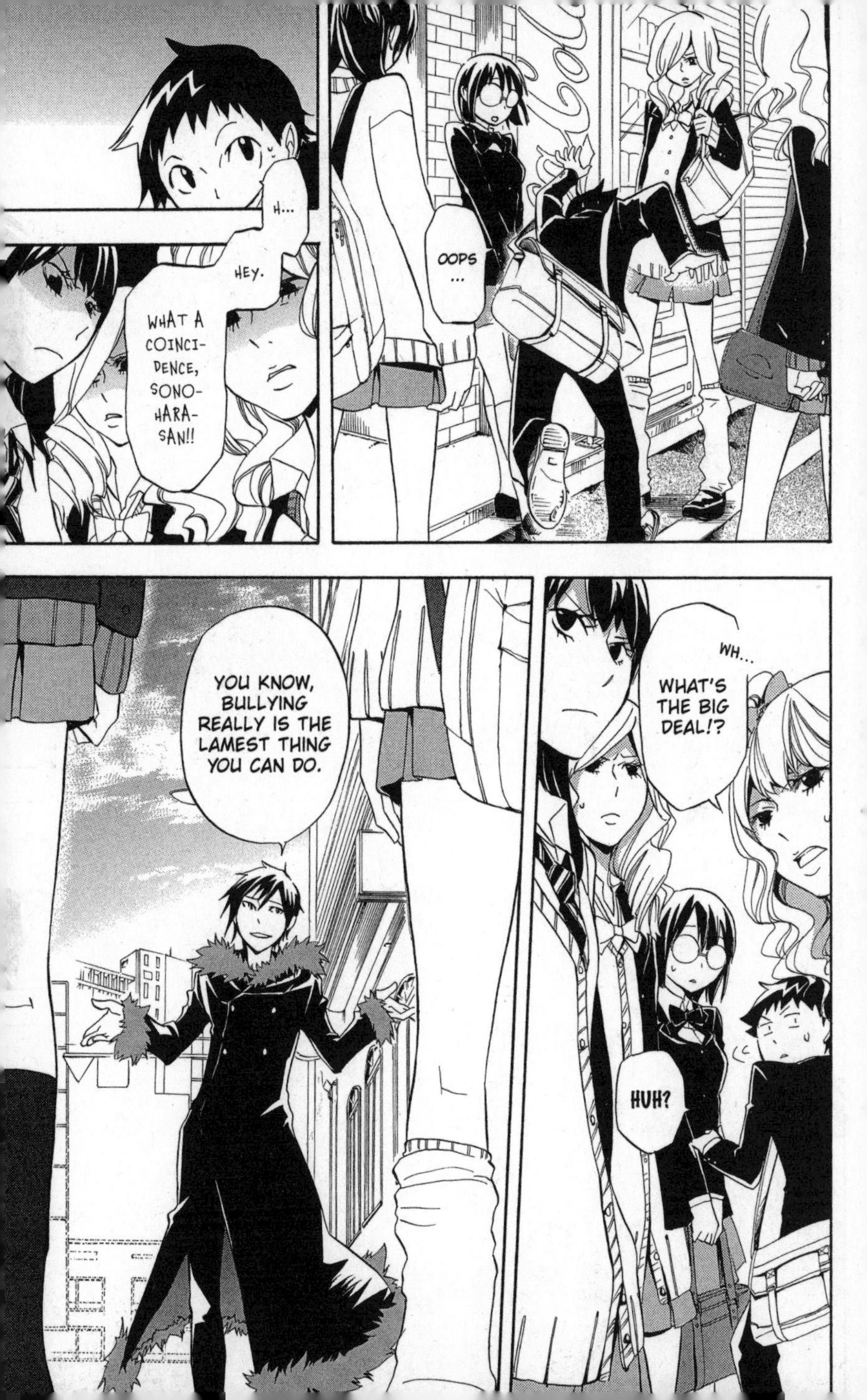
OOPS...
H...
HEY.
WHAT A COINCIDENCE, SONOHARA-SAN!!
WH... WHAT'S THE BIG DEAL!?
HUH?
YOU KNOW, BULLYING REALLY IS THE LAMEST THING YOU CAN DO.

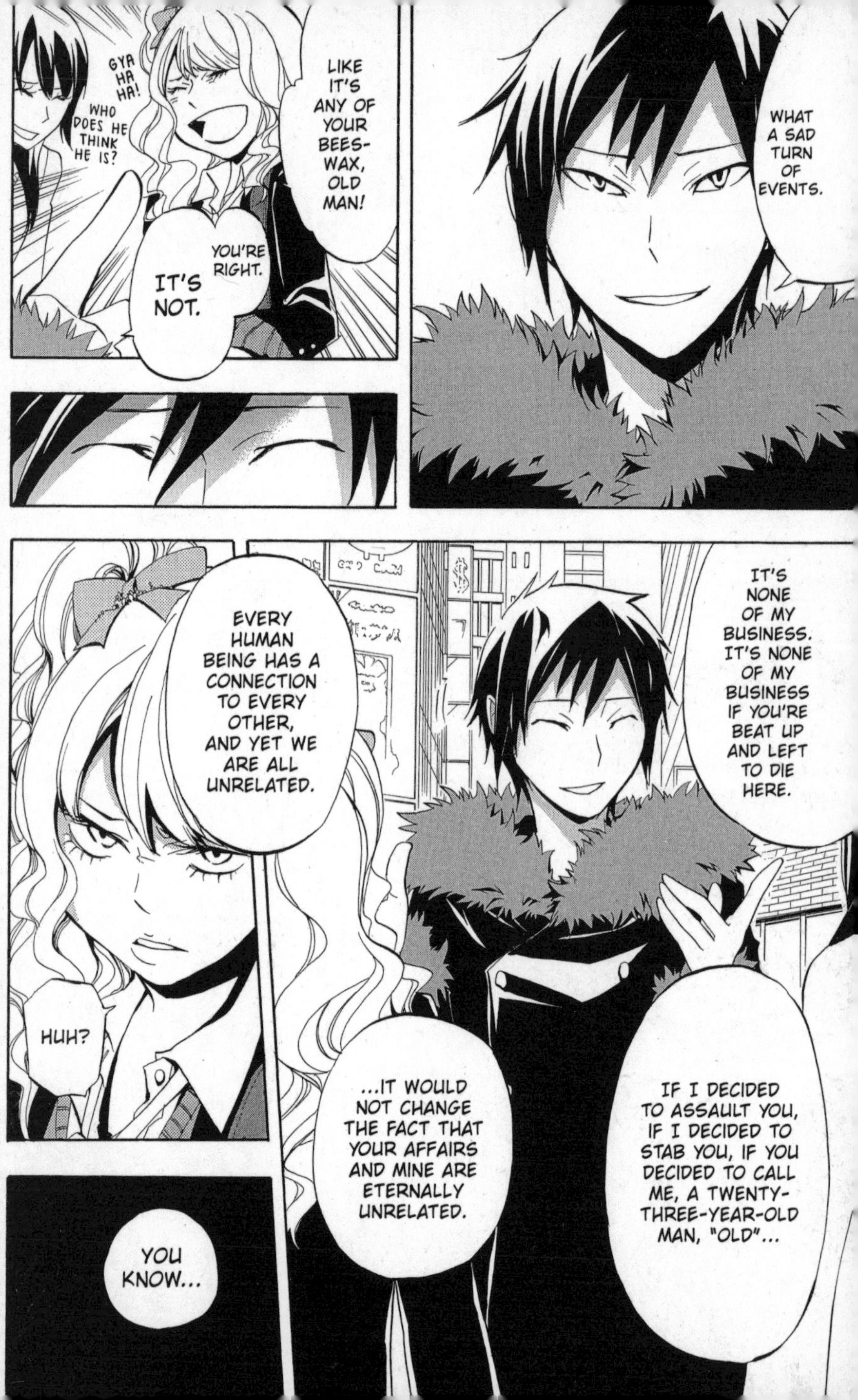
WHAT A SAD TURN OF EVENTS.
LIKE IT'S ANY OF YOUR BEES-WAX, OLD MAN!
GYA HA HA!
WHO DOES HE THINK HE IS?
YOU'RE RIGHT.
IT'S NOT.
IT'S NONE OF MY BUSINESS. IT'S NONE OF MY BUSINESS IF YOU'RE BEAT UP AND LEFT TO DIE HERE.
IF I DECIDED TO ASSAULT YOU, IF I DECIDED TO STAB YOU, IF YOU DECIDED TO CALL ME, A TWENTY-THREE-YEAR-OLD MAN, "OLD"...
...IT WOULD NOT CHANGE THE FACT THAT YOUR AFFAIRS AND MINE ARE ETERNALLY UNRELATED.
HUH?
YOU KNOW...
EVERY HUMAN BEING HAS A CONNECTION TO EVERY OTHER, AND YET WE ARE ALL UNRELATED.

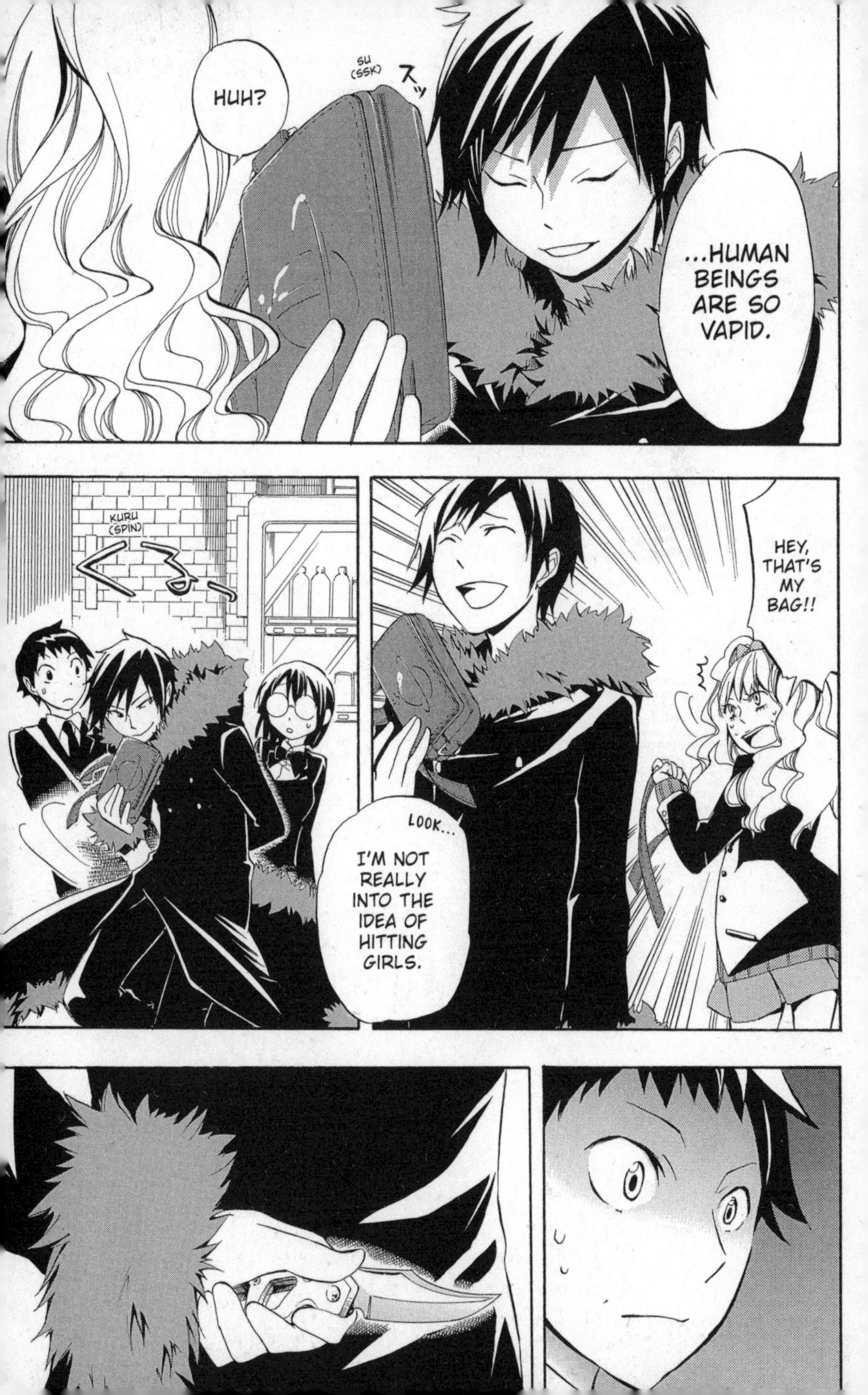
...HUMAN BEINGS ARE SO VAPID.
SU (SSK)
HUH?
HEY, THAT'S MY BAG!!
LOOK...
I'M NOT REALLY INTO THE IDEA OF HITTING GIRLS.
KURU (SPIN)

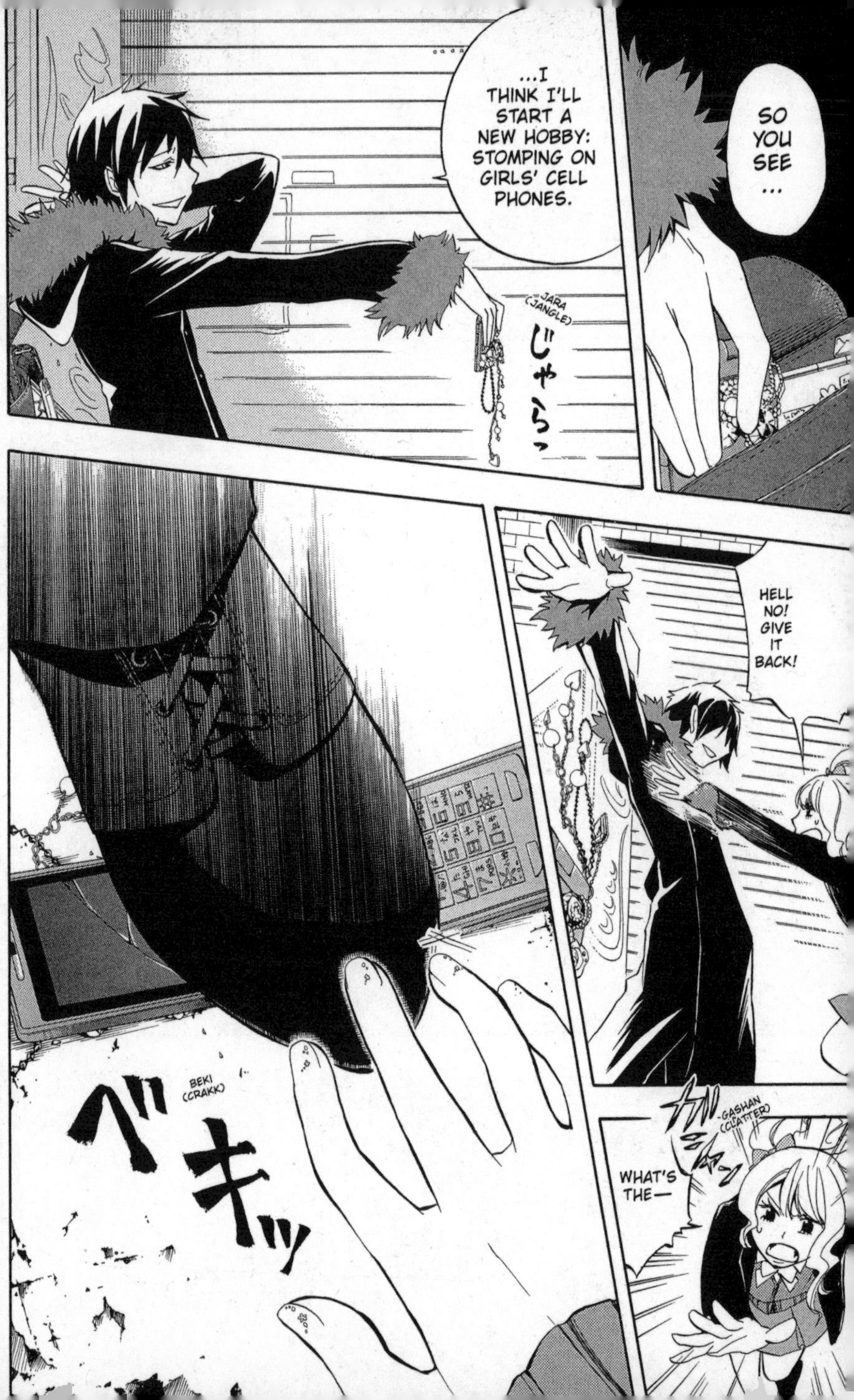
SO YOU SEE...
...I THINK I'LL START A NEW HOBBY: STOMPING ON GIRLS' CELL PHONES.
JARA (JANGLE)
じゃらっ
HELL NO! GIVE IT BACK!
GASHAN (CLATTER)
WHAT'S THE—
BEKI (CRAKK)
ベキッ

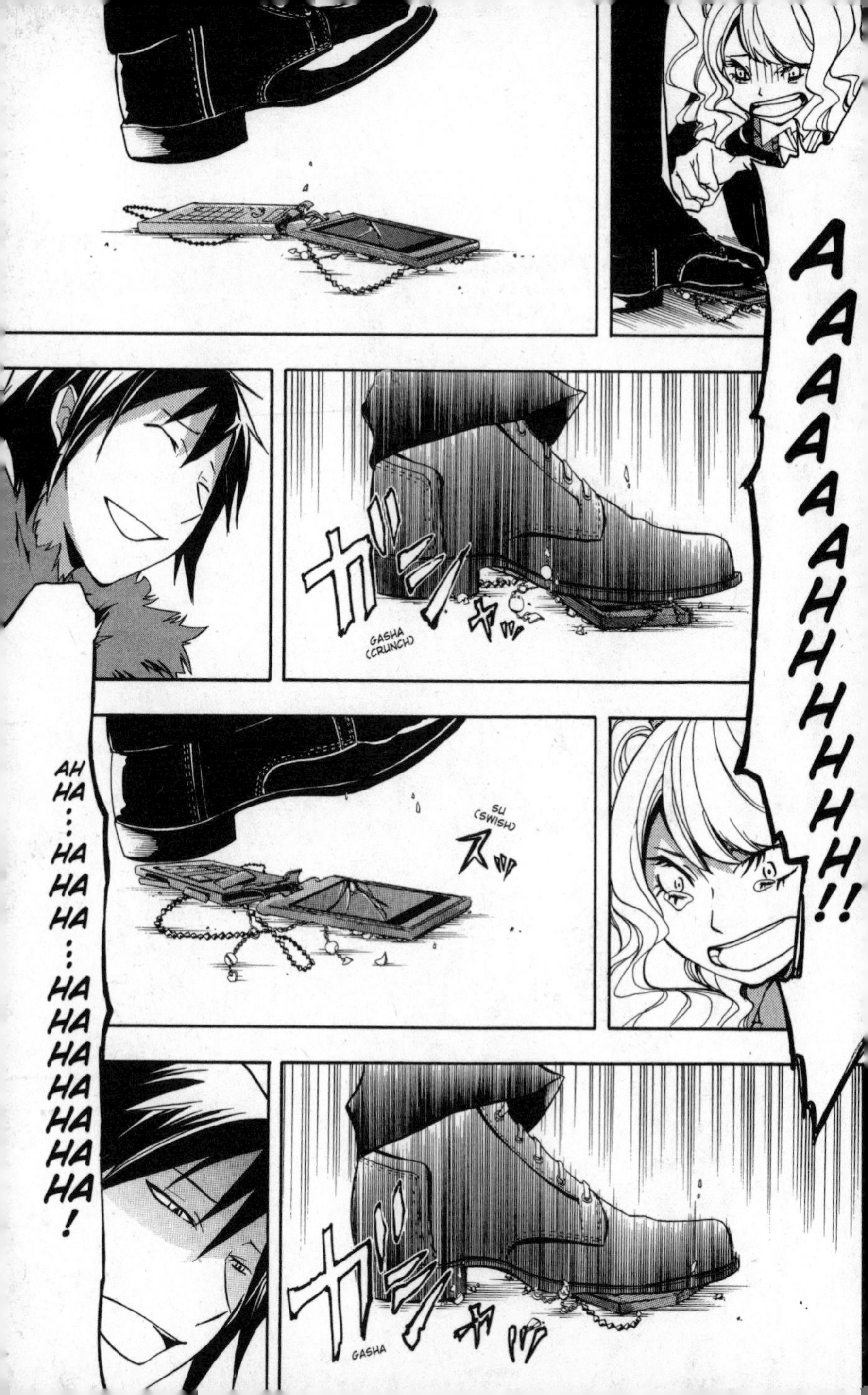
AAAAAAHHHHHH!!
GASHA (CRUNCH)
SU (SWISH)
AH HA... HA HA HA... HA HA HA HA HA HA HA!
GASHA

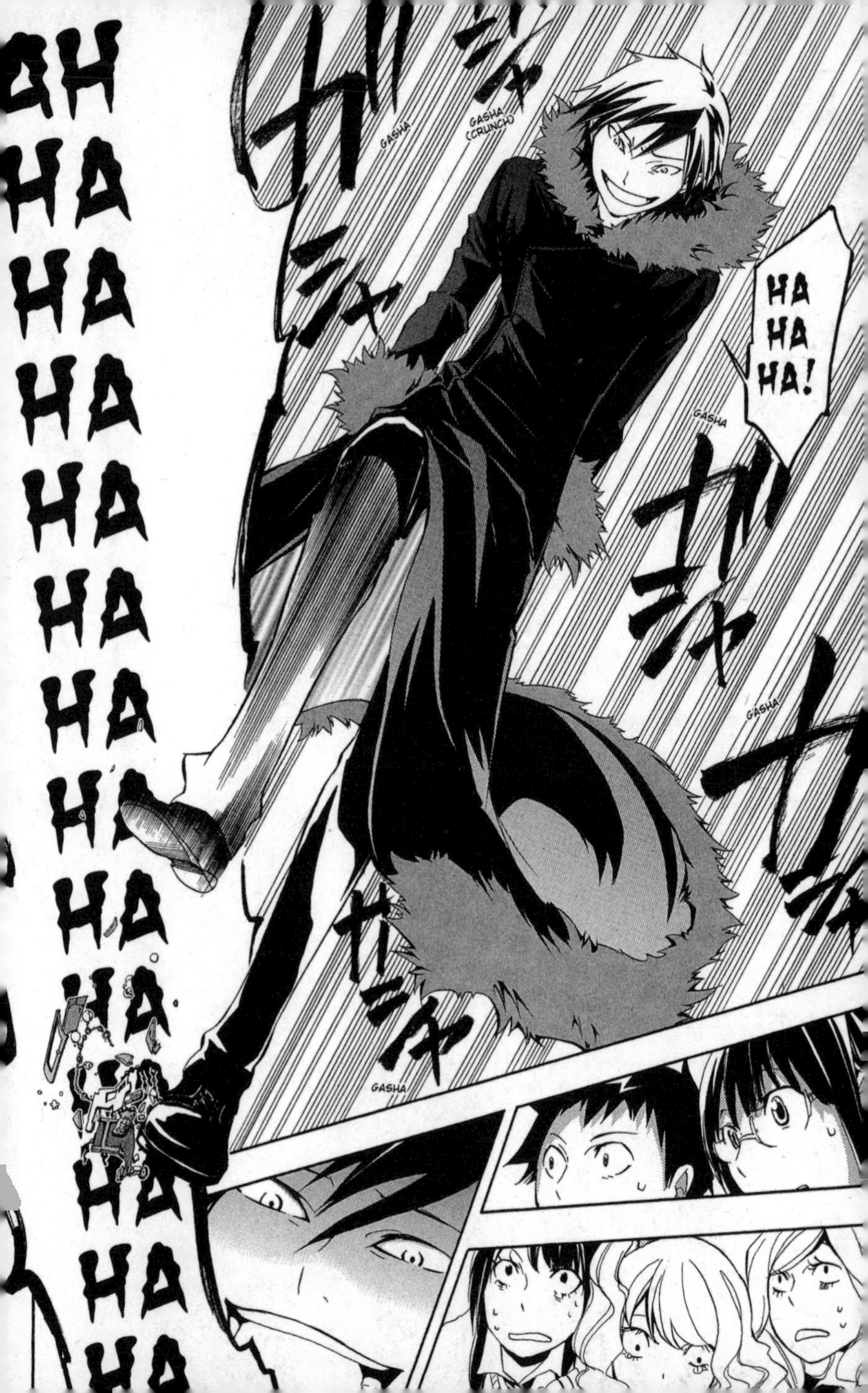
GASHA (CRUNCH)
GASHA
HA HA HA!
GASHA
GASHA
GASHA
AH HA HA HA HA HA HA HA HA HA HA HA HA HA

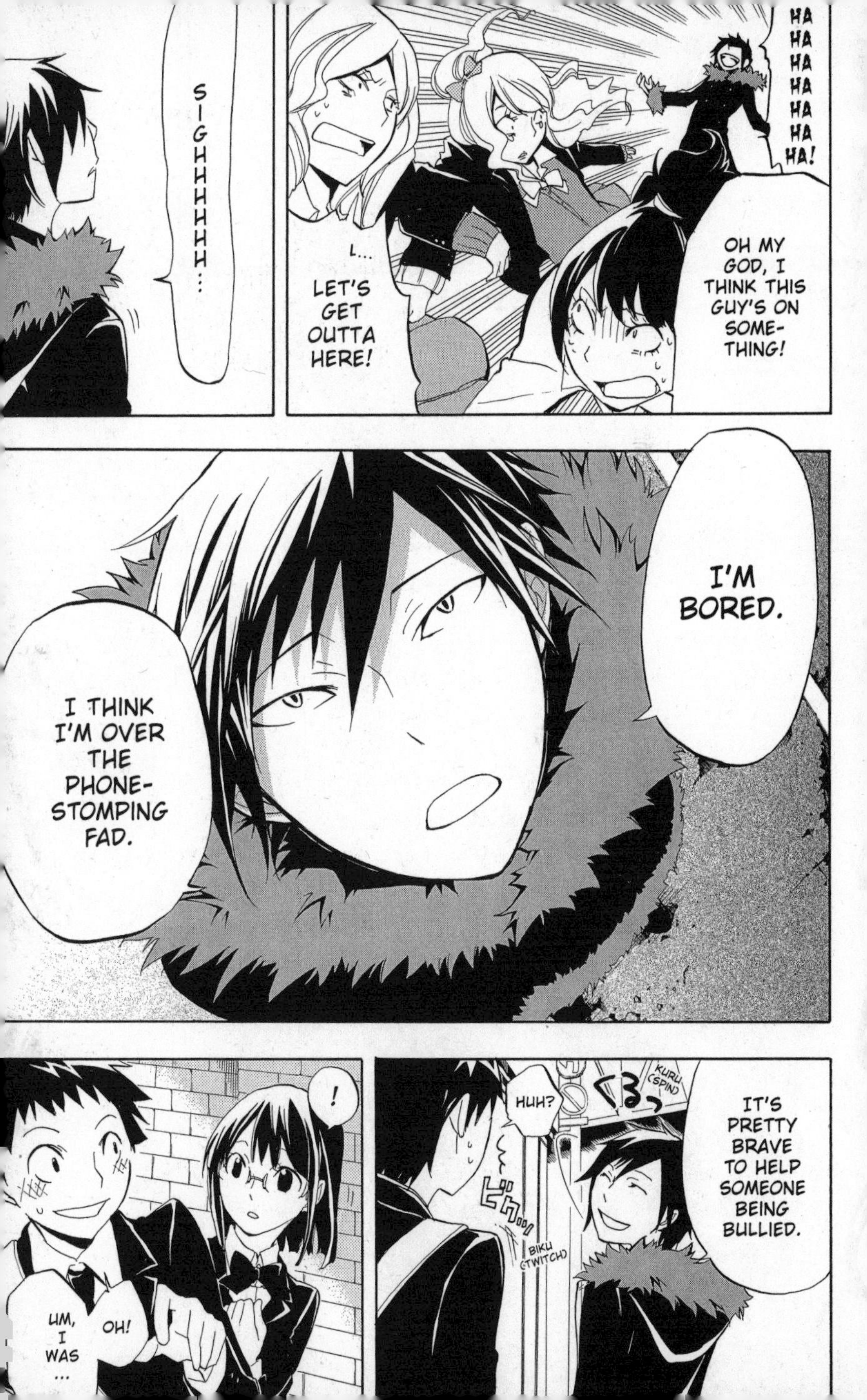
HA HA HA HA HA HA HA!
OH MY GOD, I THINK THIS GUY'S ON SOME-THING!
I... LET'S GET OUTTA HERE!
SIGHHHHHHH...
I'M BORED.
I THINK I'M OVER THE PHONE-STOMPING FAD.
IT'S PRETTY BRAVE TO HELP SOMEONE BEING BULLIED.
KURU (SPIN)
HUH?
BIKU (TWITCH)
!
OH!
UM, I WAS ...

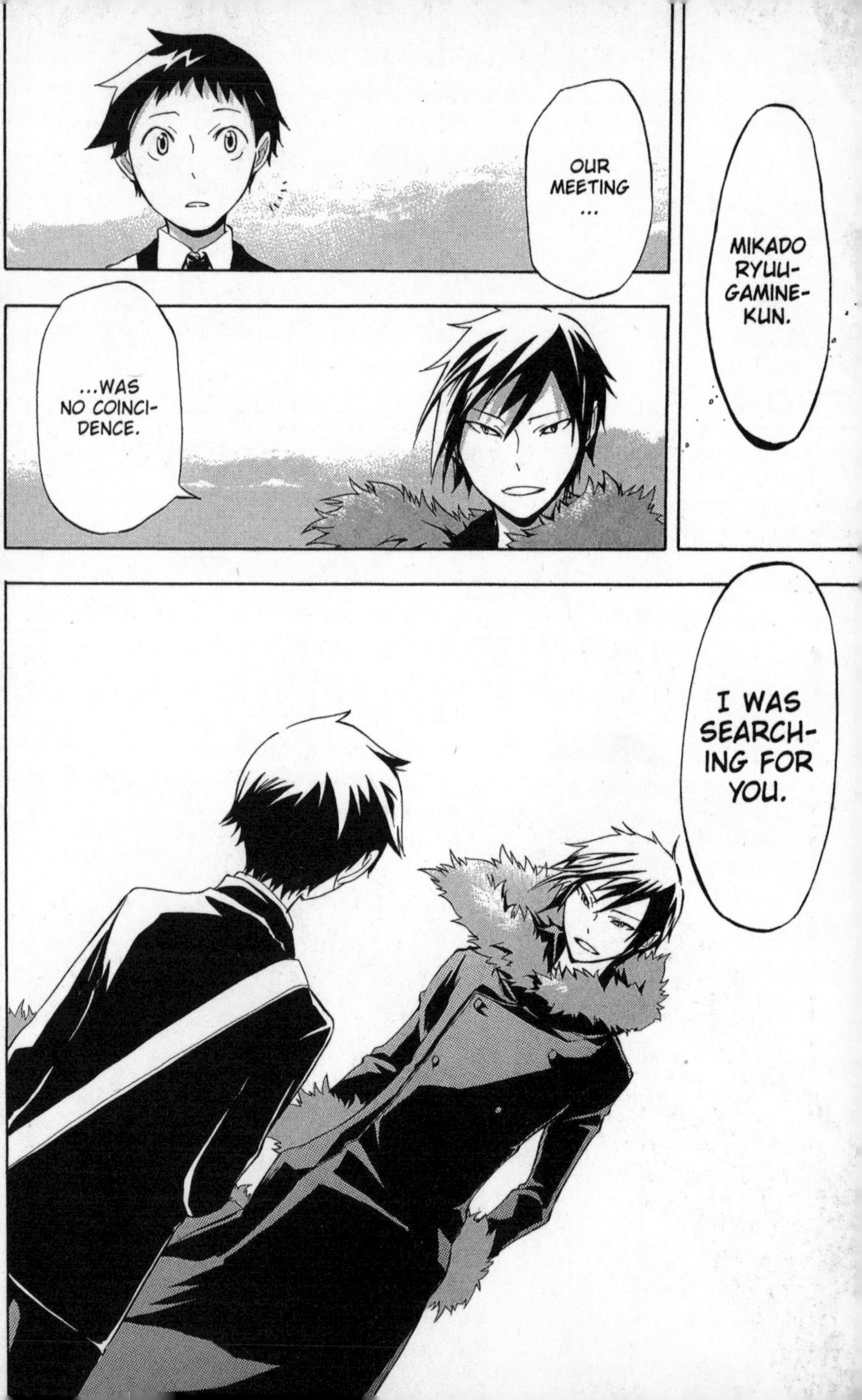
MIKADO RYUU-GAMINE-KUN.
OUR MEETING ...
...WAS NO COINCI-DENCE.
I WAS SEARCH-ING FOR YOU.

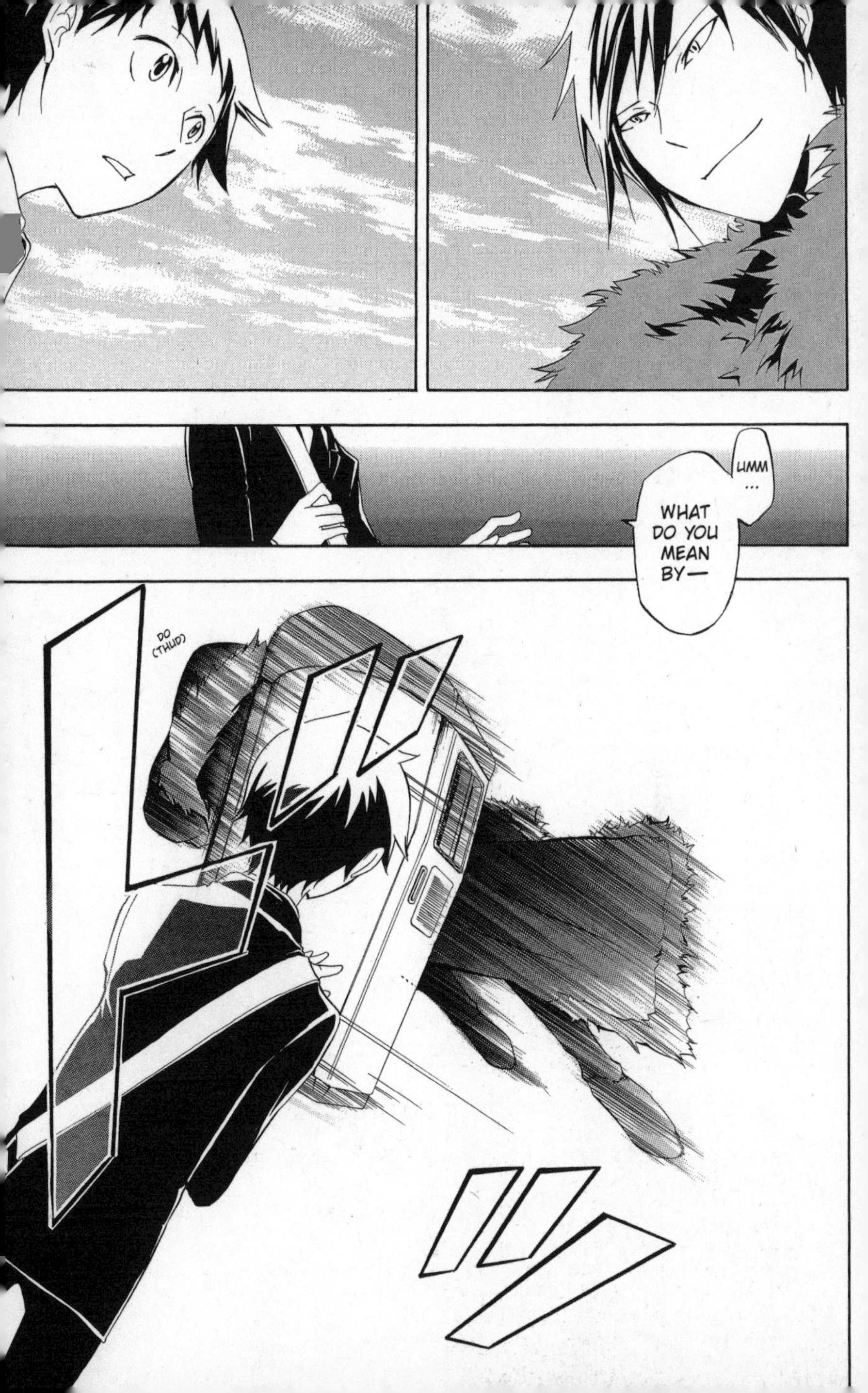
UMM...
WHAT DO YOU MEAN BY—
DO
(THUD)

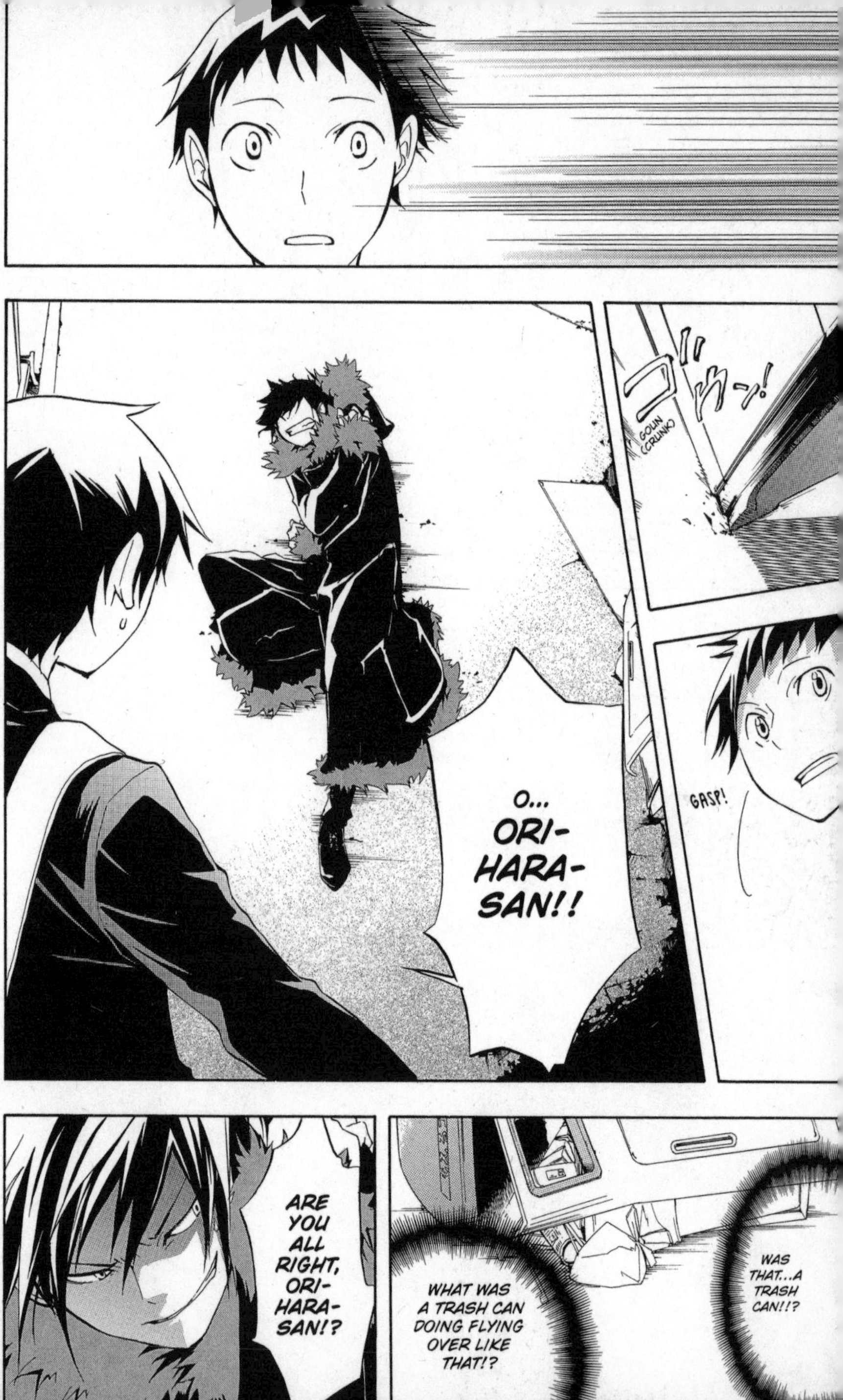
GOUN (CRUNK)
GASP!
O... ORI-HARA-SAN!!
WAS THAT...A TRASH CAN!?
WHAT WAS A TRASH CAN DOING FLYING OVER LIKE THAT!?
ARE YOU ALL RIGHT, ORI-HARA-SAN!?

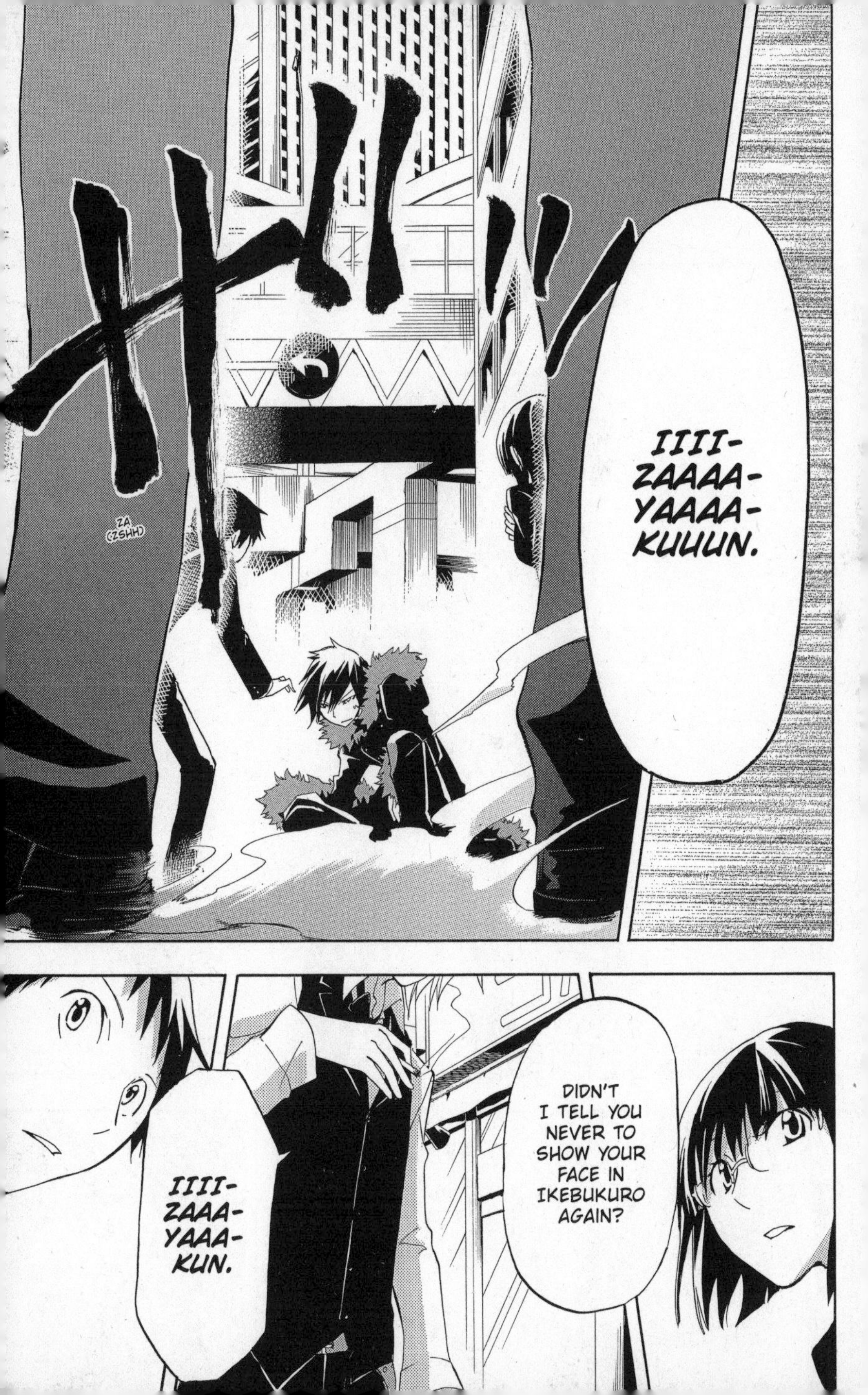
IIII-ZAAAA-YAAAA-KUUUN.
ZA (ZSHH)
DIDN'T I TELL YOU NEVER TO SHOW YOUR FACE IN IKEBUKURO AGAIN?
IIII-ZAAA-YAAA-KUN.

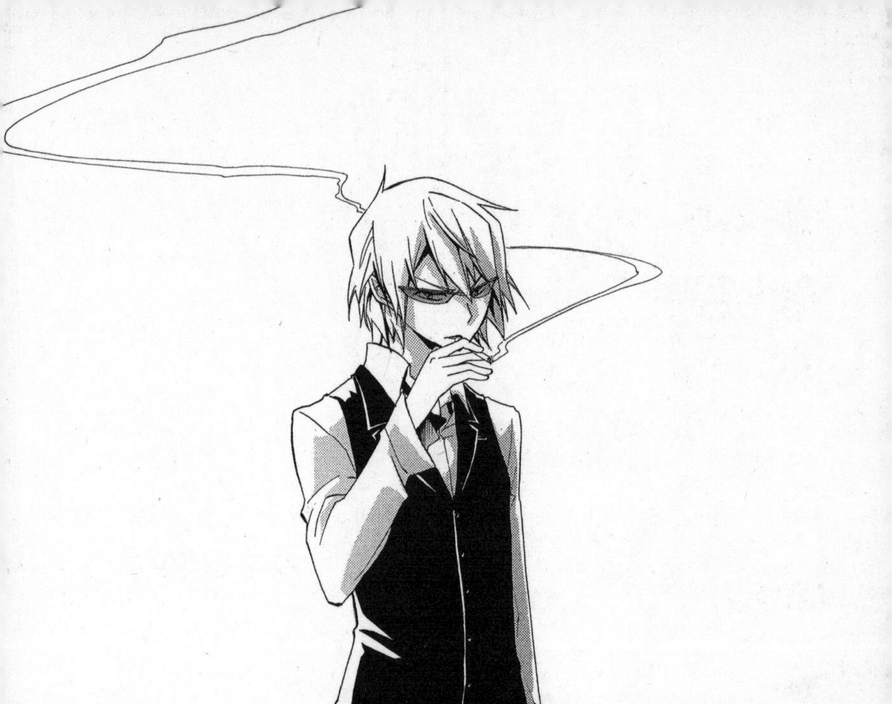

カン

LABELS: BOTTLES / CANS

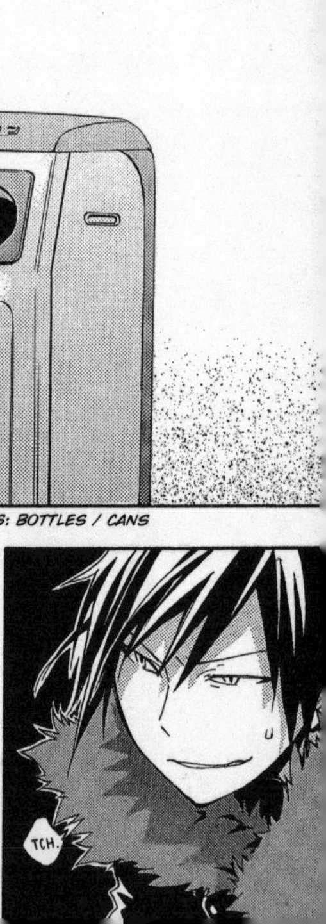

TCH.

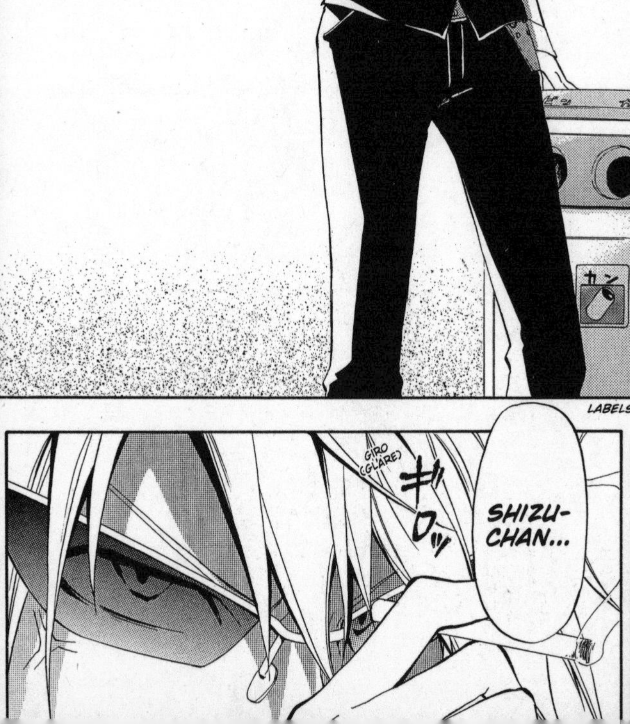

GIRO (GLARE)
ギロッ
SHIZU-CHAN...

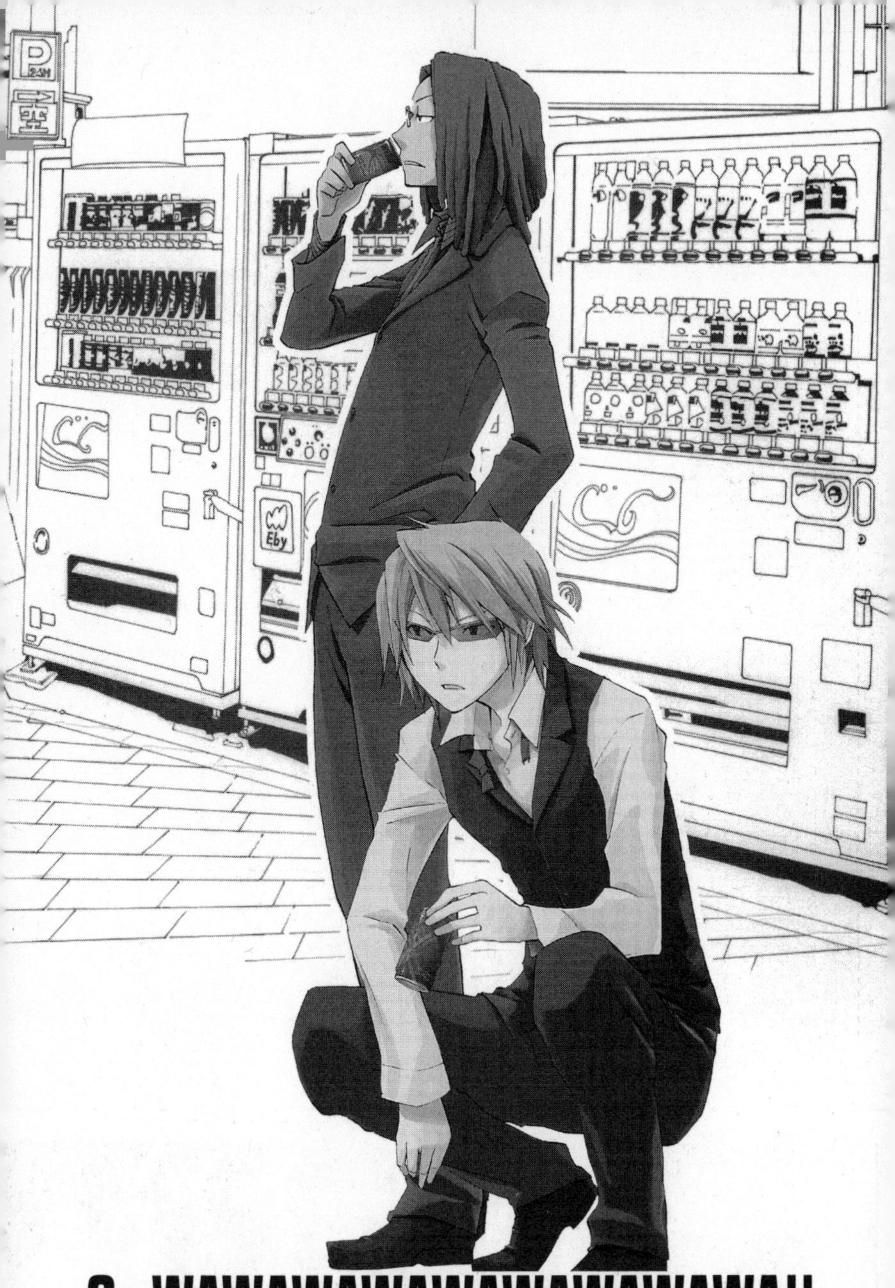
P
Eby

9: WAWAWAWAWAWAWAWAWAWA!!

DRRR!!

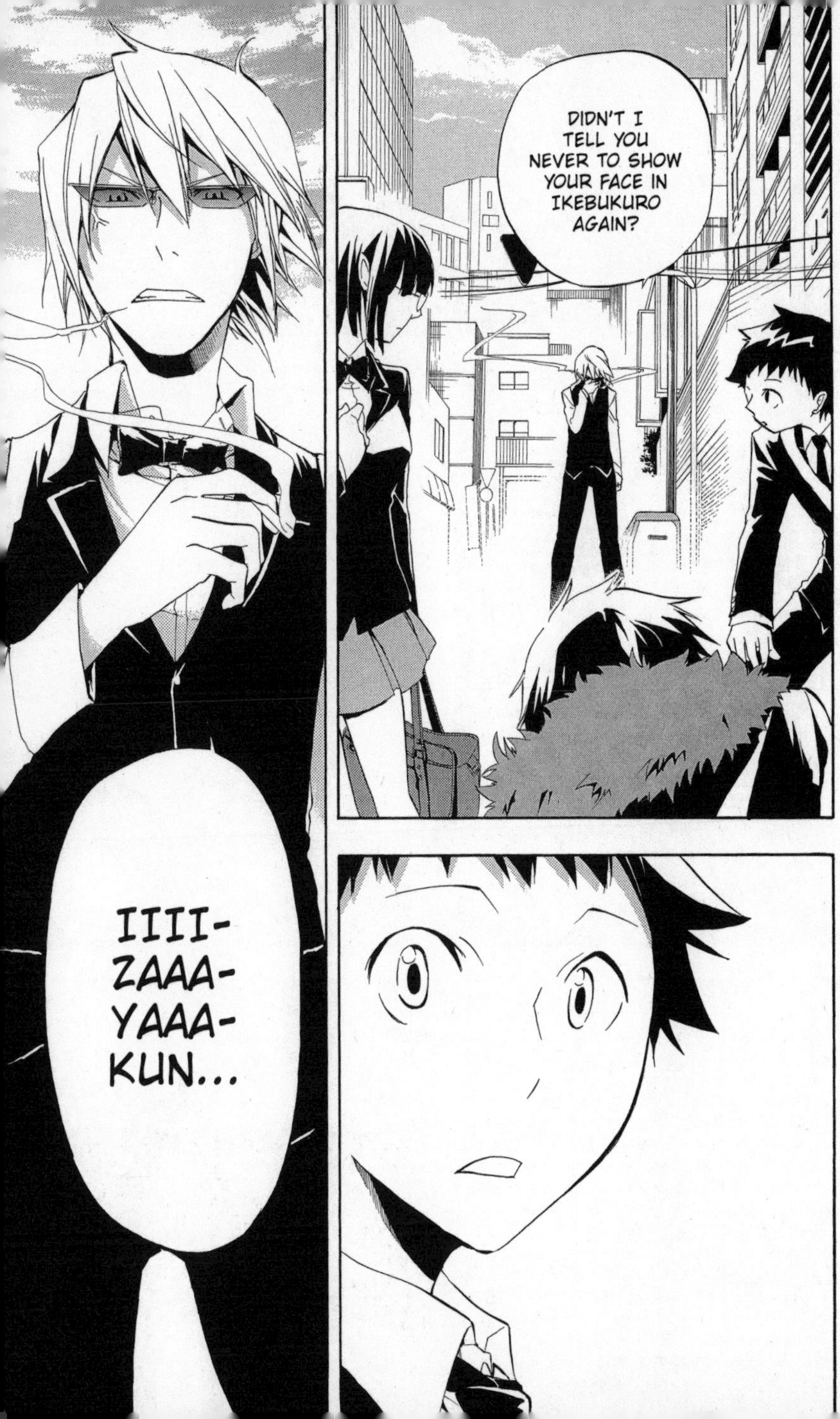
DIDN'T I TELL YOU NEVER TO SHOW YOUR FACE IN IKEBUKURO AGAIN?
IIII-ZAAA-YAAA-KUN...

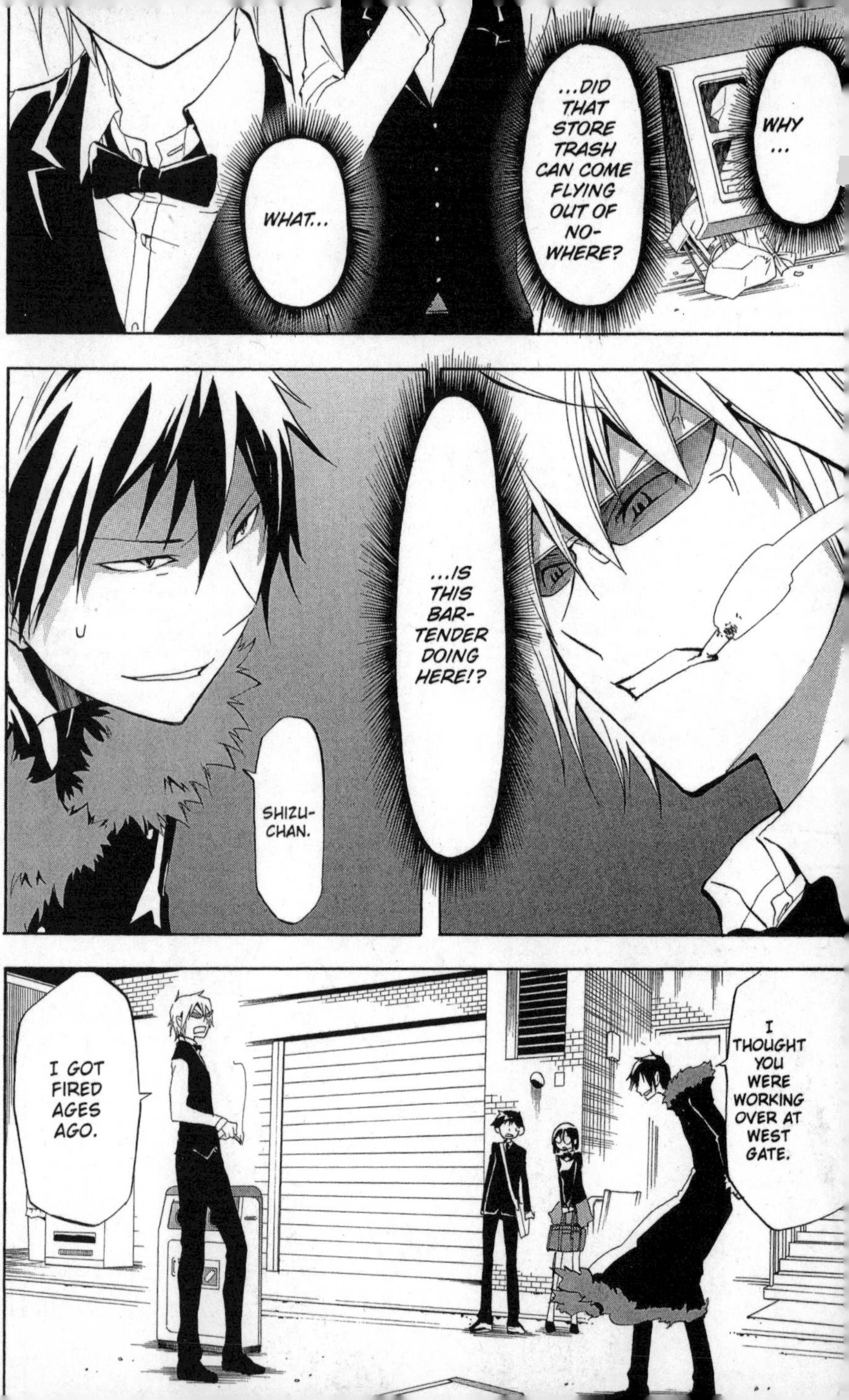
WHY...
...DID THAT STORE TRASH CAN COME FLYING OUT OF NO-WHERE?
WHAT...
...IS THIS BAR-TENDER DOING HERE!?
SHIZU-CHAN.
I THOUGHT YOU WERE WORKING OVER AT WEST GATE.
I GOT FIRED AGES AGO.

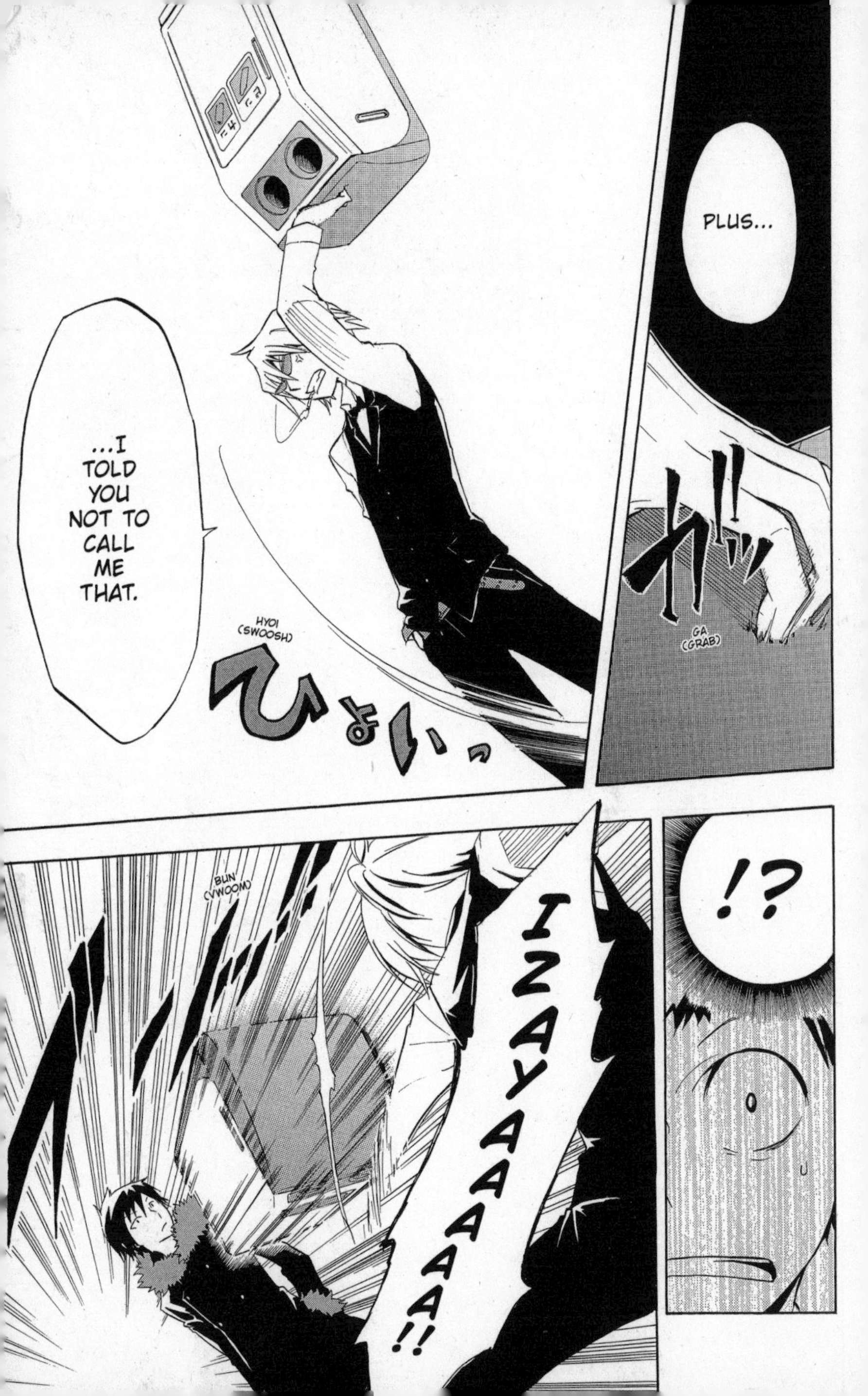
PLUS...
ガッ
GA (GRAB)
...I TOLD YOU NOT TO CALL ME THAT.
ひょいっ
HYOI (SWOOSH)
!?
IZAYAAAAAAA!!
BUN (VWOOM)

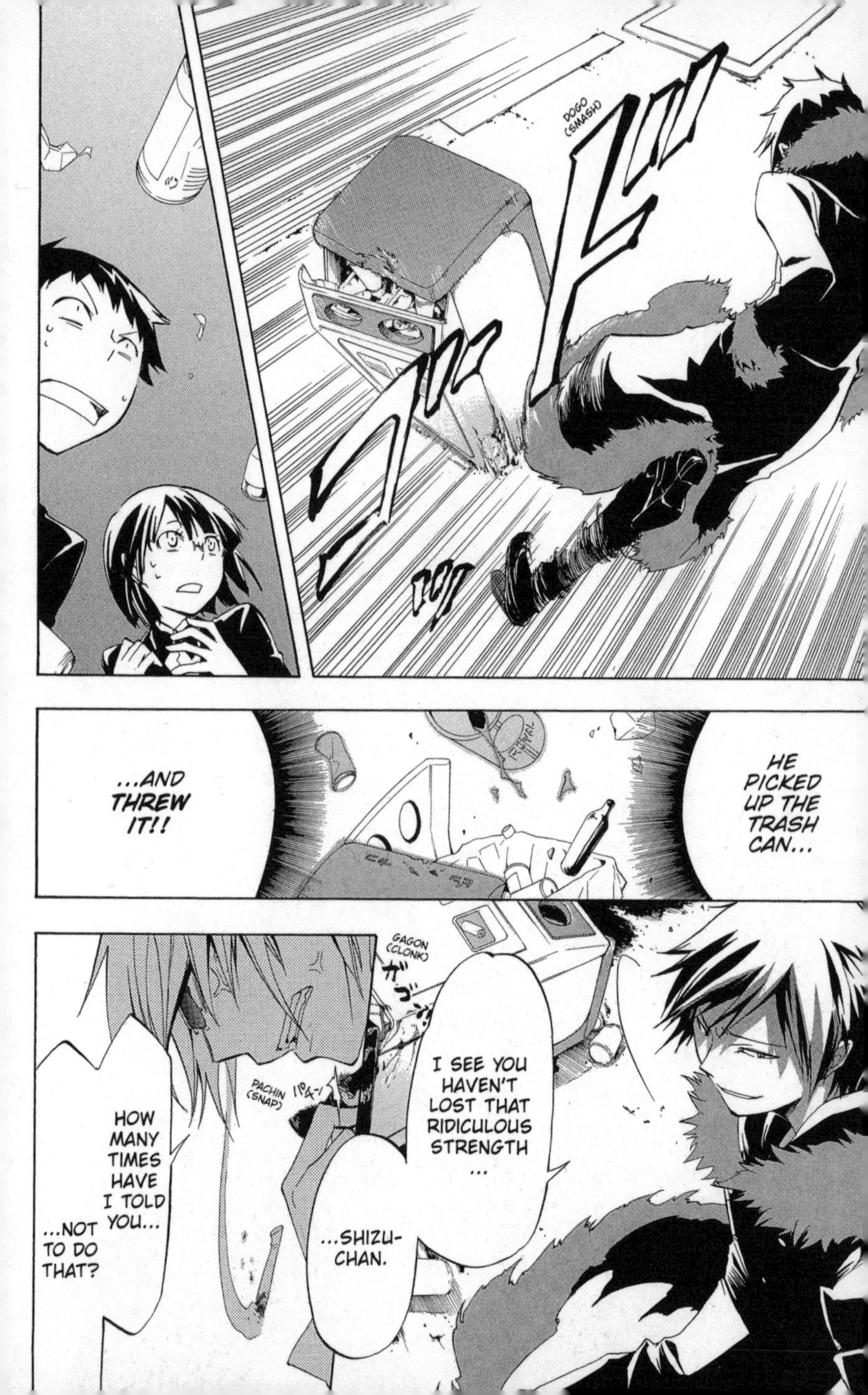
DOGO (SMASH)
HE PICKED UP THE TRASH CAN...
...AND THREW IT!!
GAGON (CLONK)
I SEE YOU HAVEN'T LOST THAT RIDICULOUS STRENGTH ...
PACHIN (SNAP)
...SHIZU-CHAN.
HOW MANY TIMES HAVE I TOLD YOU...
...NOT TO DO THAT?

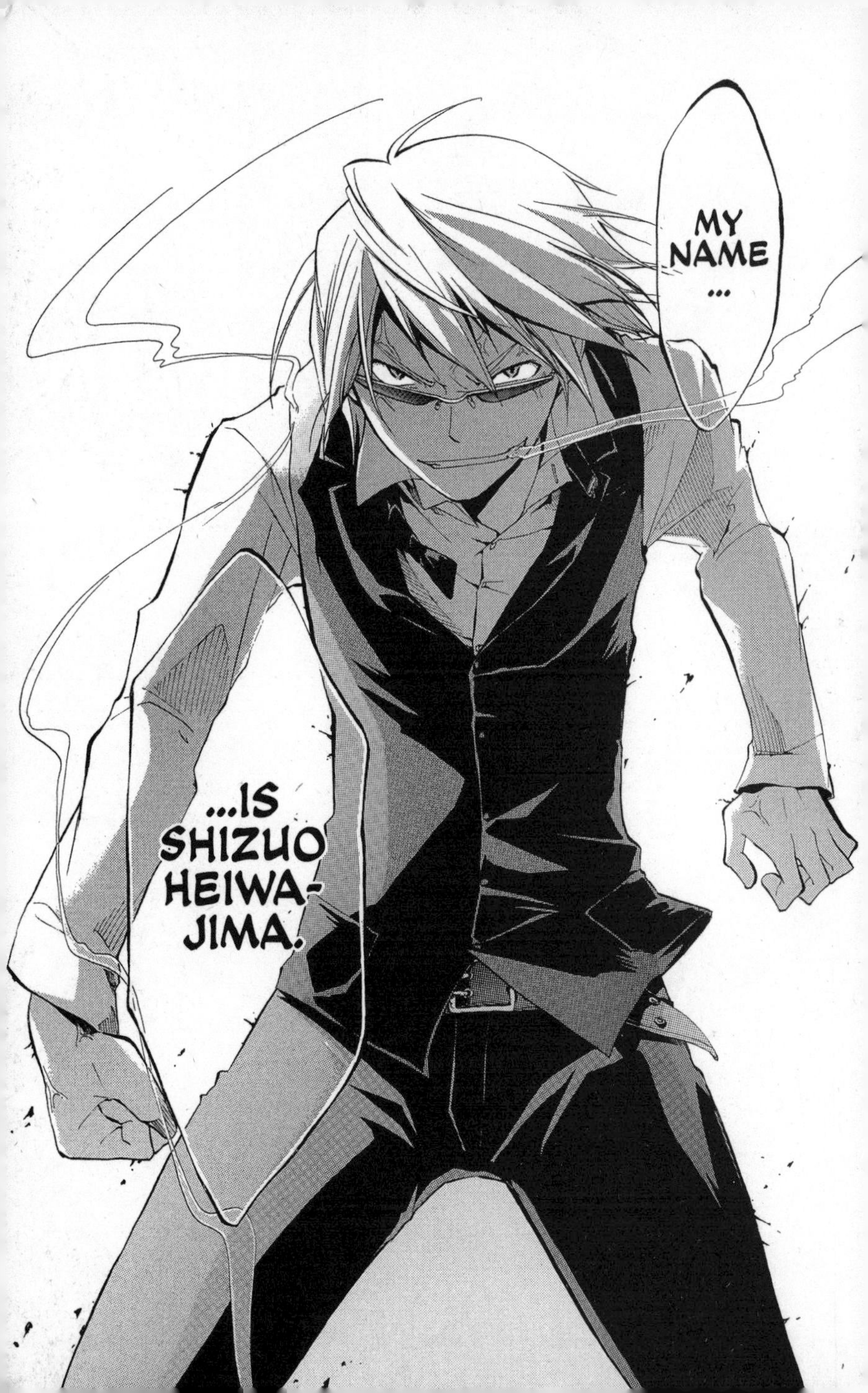
MY NAME ...
...IS SHIZUO HEIWA-JIMA.

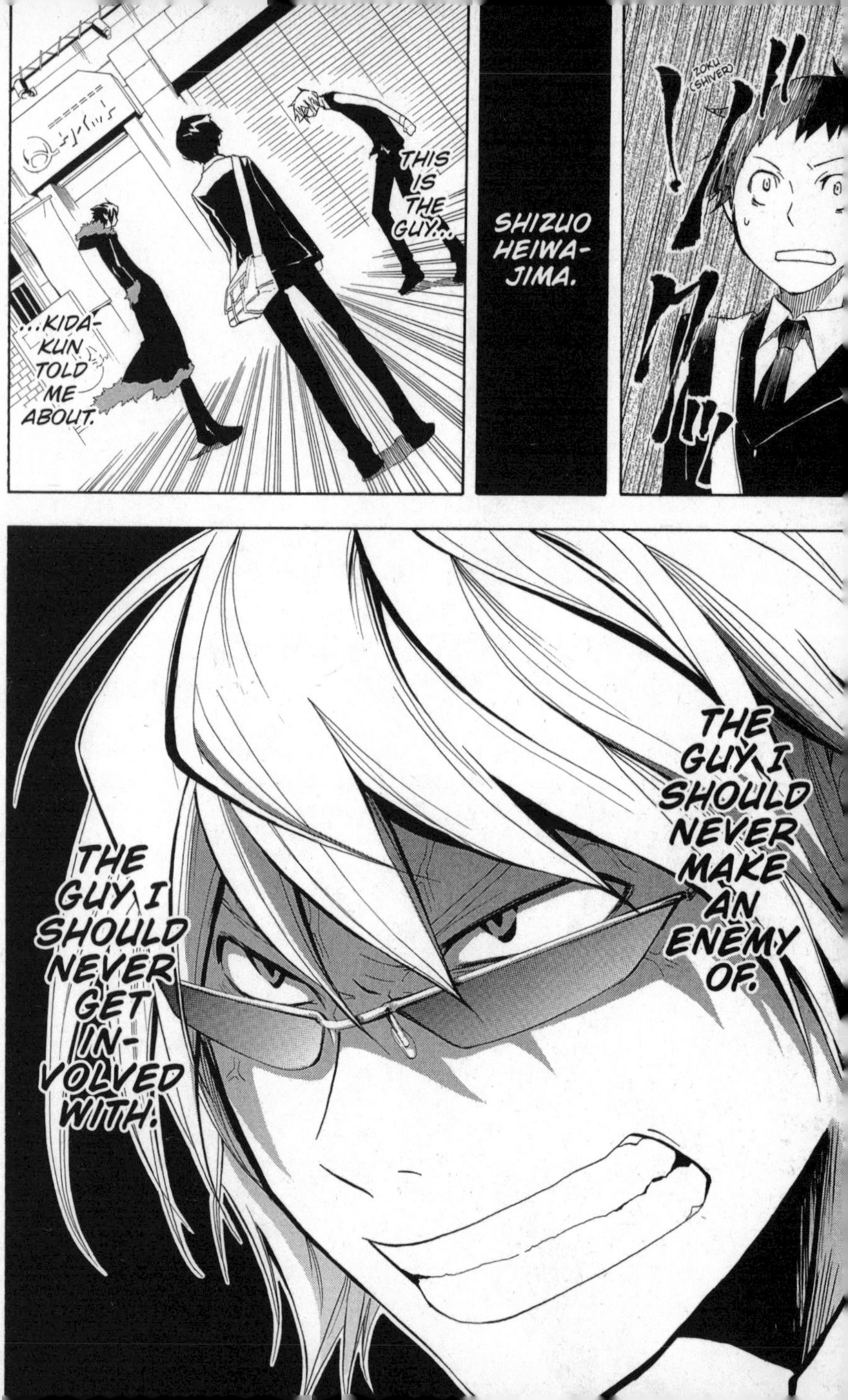
ZOKU (SHIVER)
SHIZUO HEIWA-JIMA.
THIS IS THE GUY...
...KIDA-KUN TOLD ME ABOUT.
THE GUY I SHOULD NEVER MAKE AN ENEMY OF.
THE GUY I SHOULD NEVER GET IN-VOLVED WITH.

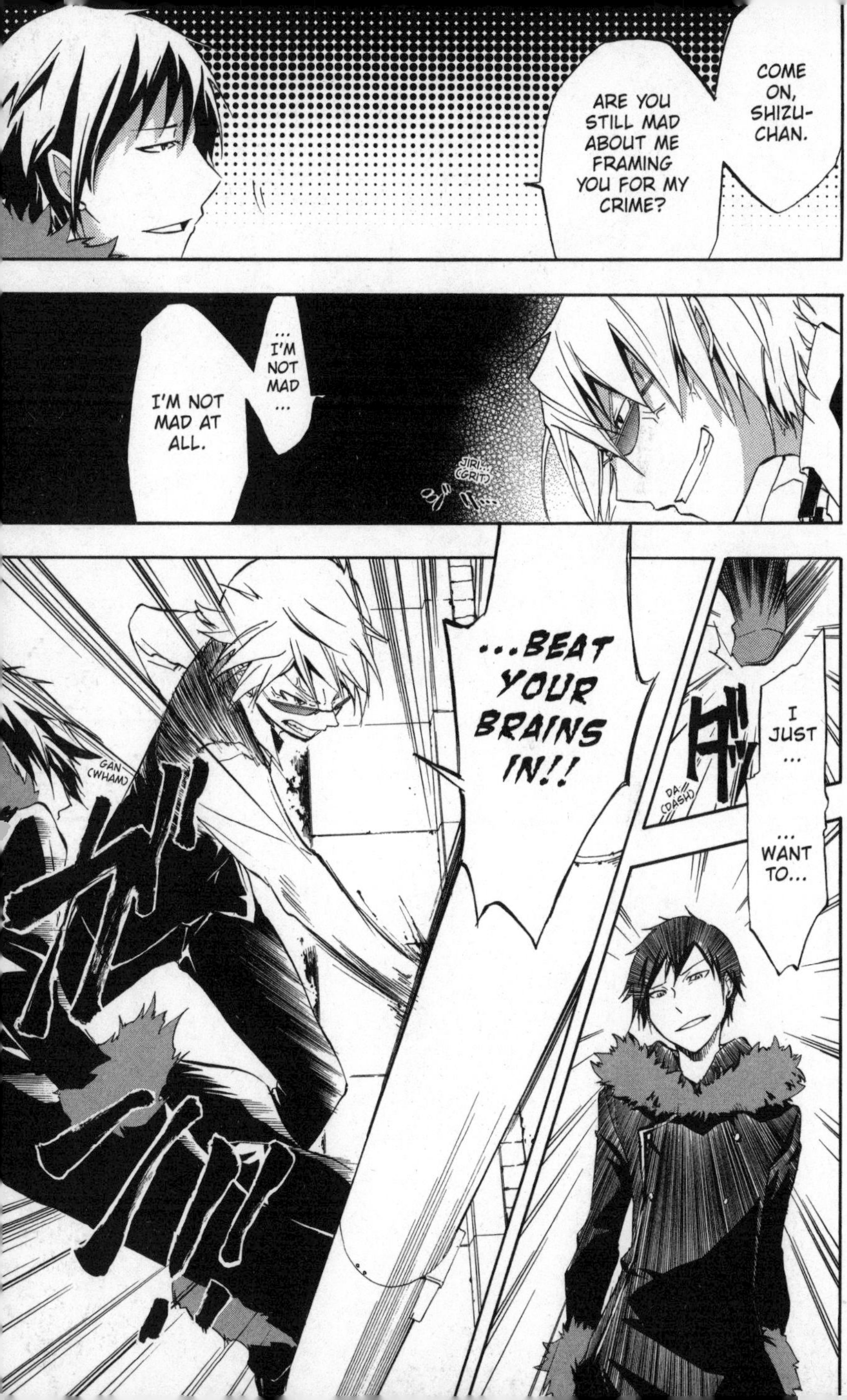
COME ON, SHIZU-CHAN.
ARE YOU STILL MAD ABOUT ME FRAMING YOU FOR MY CRIME?
...I'M NOT MAD...
I'M NOT MAD AT ALL.
JIRI... (GRIT)
I JUST...
DA (DASH)
...WANT TO...
...BEAT YOUR BRAINS IN!!
GAN (WHAM)

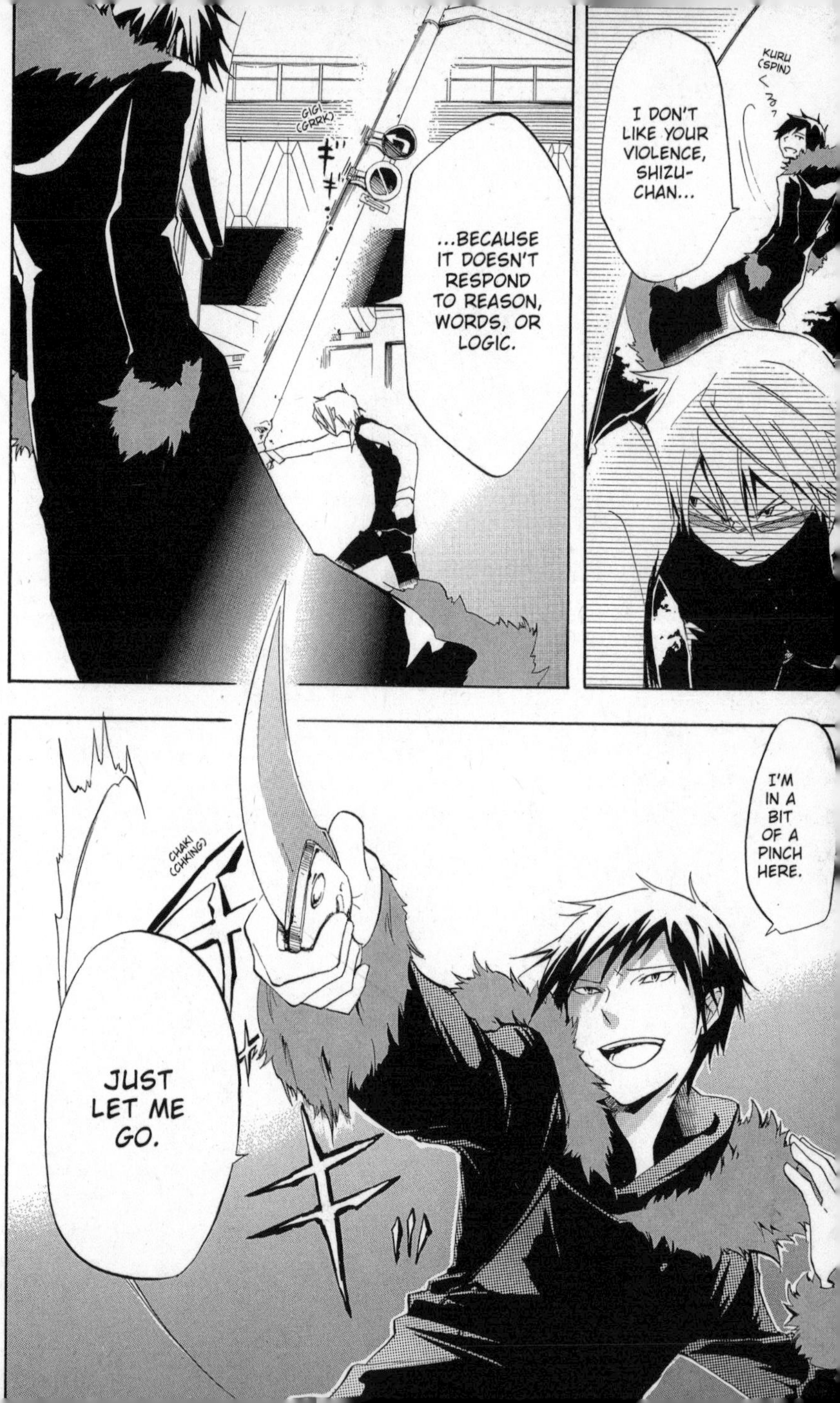
KURU (SPIN)
I DON'T LIKE YOUR VIOLENCE, SHIZU-CHAN...
GIGI (GRRK)
...BECAUSE IT DOESN'T RESPOND TO REASON, WORDS, OR LOGIC.
I'M IN A BIT OF A PINCH HERE.
CHAKI (CHKING)
JUST LET ME GO.

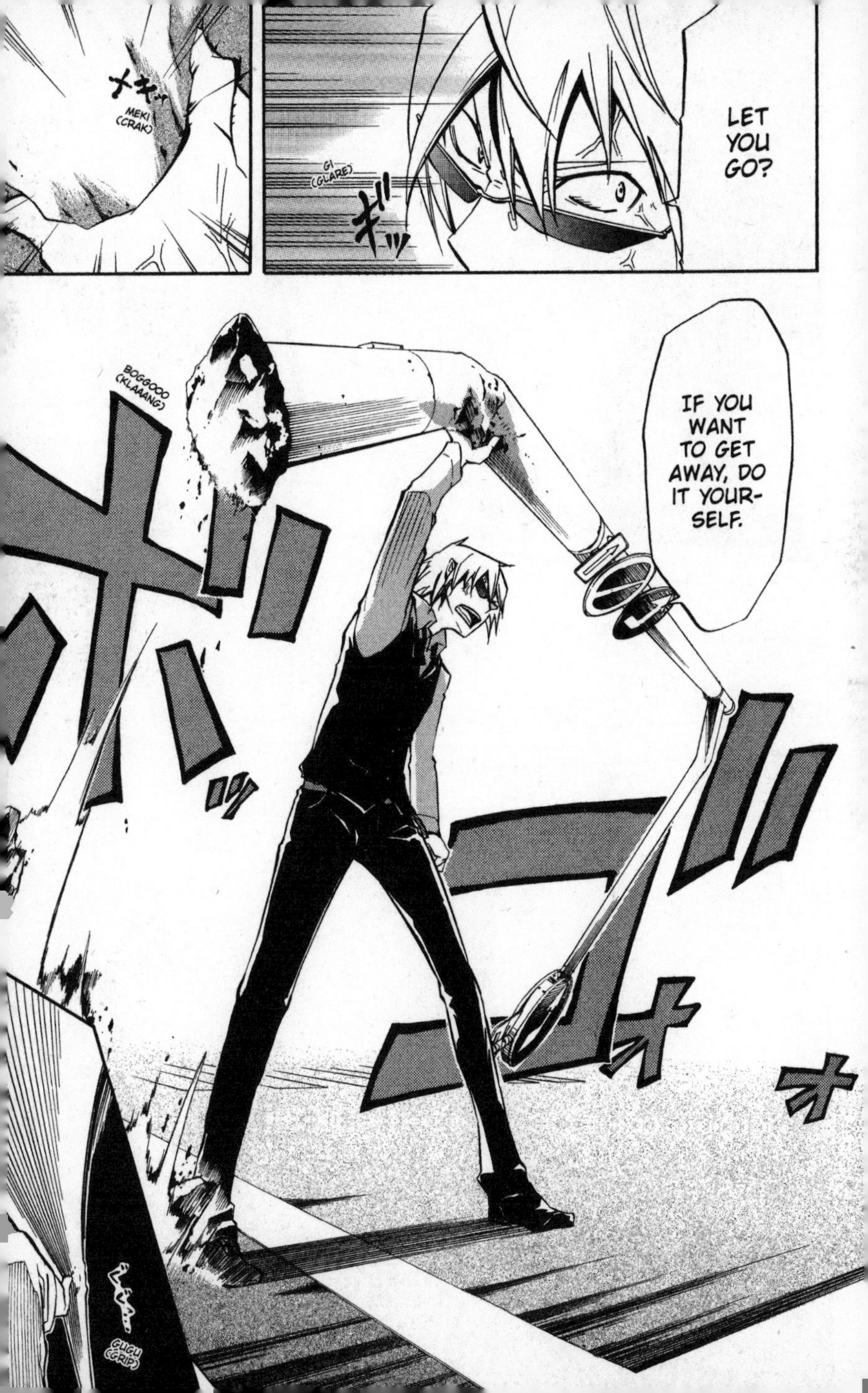
LET YOU GO?
GI (GLARE)
MEKI (CRAK)
IF YOU WANT TO GET AWAY, DO IT YOUR-SELF.
BOGGOOO (KLAAANG)
GUGU (GRIP)

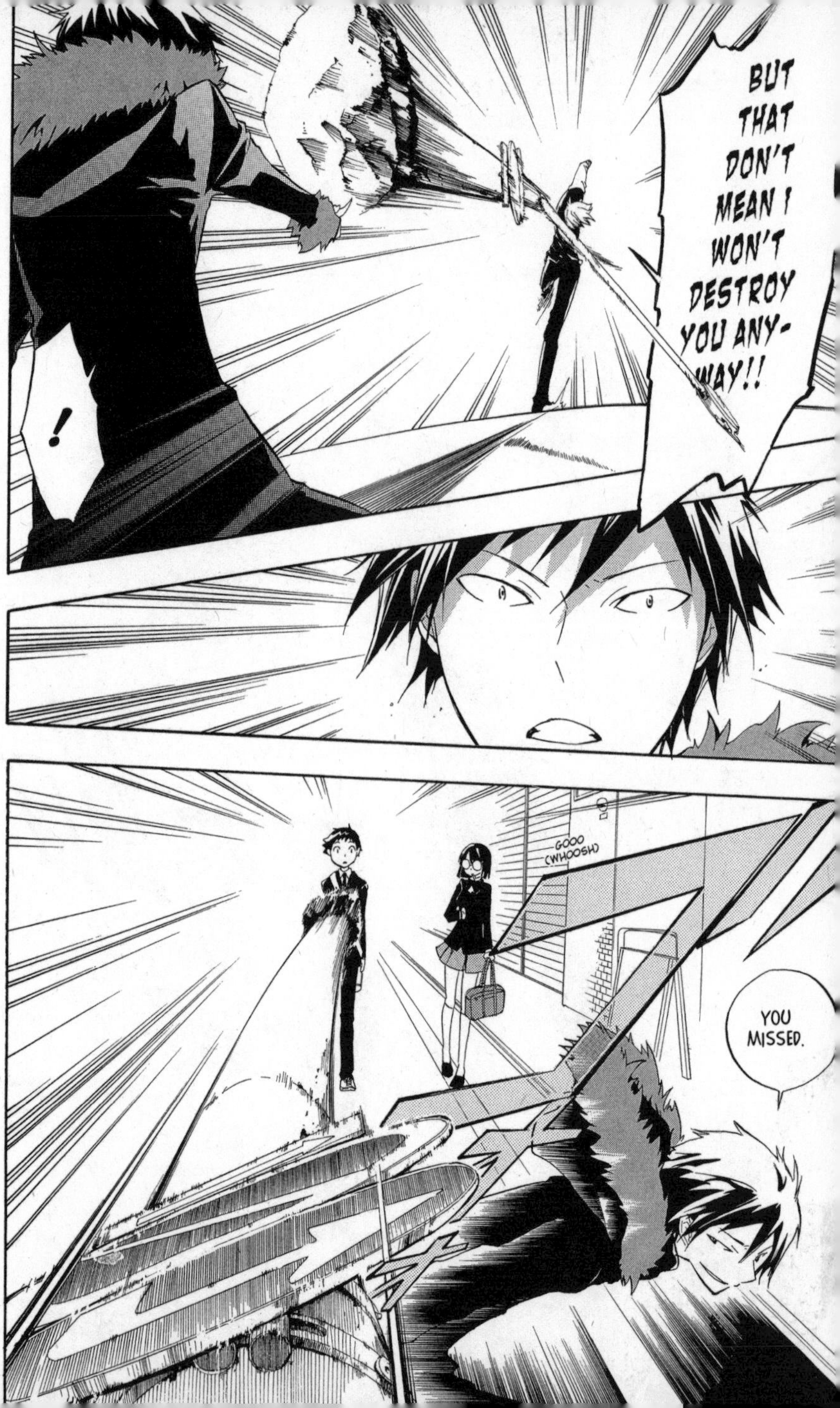
BUT THAT DON'T MEAN I WON'T DESTROY YOU ANY-WAY!!
!
GOOO (WHOOSH)
YOU MISSED.

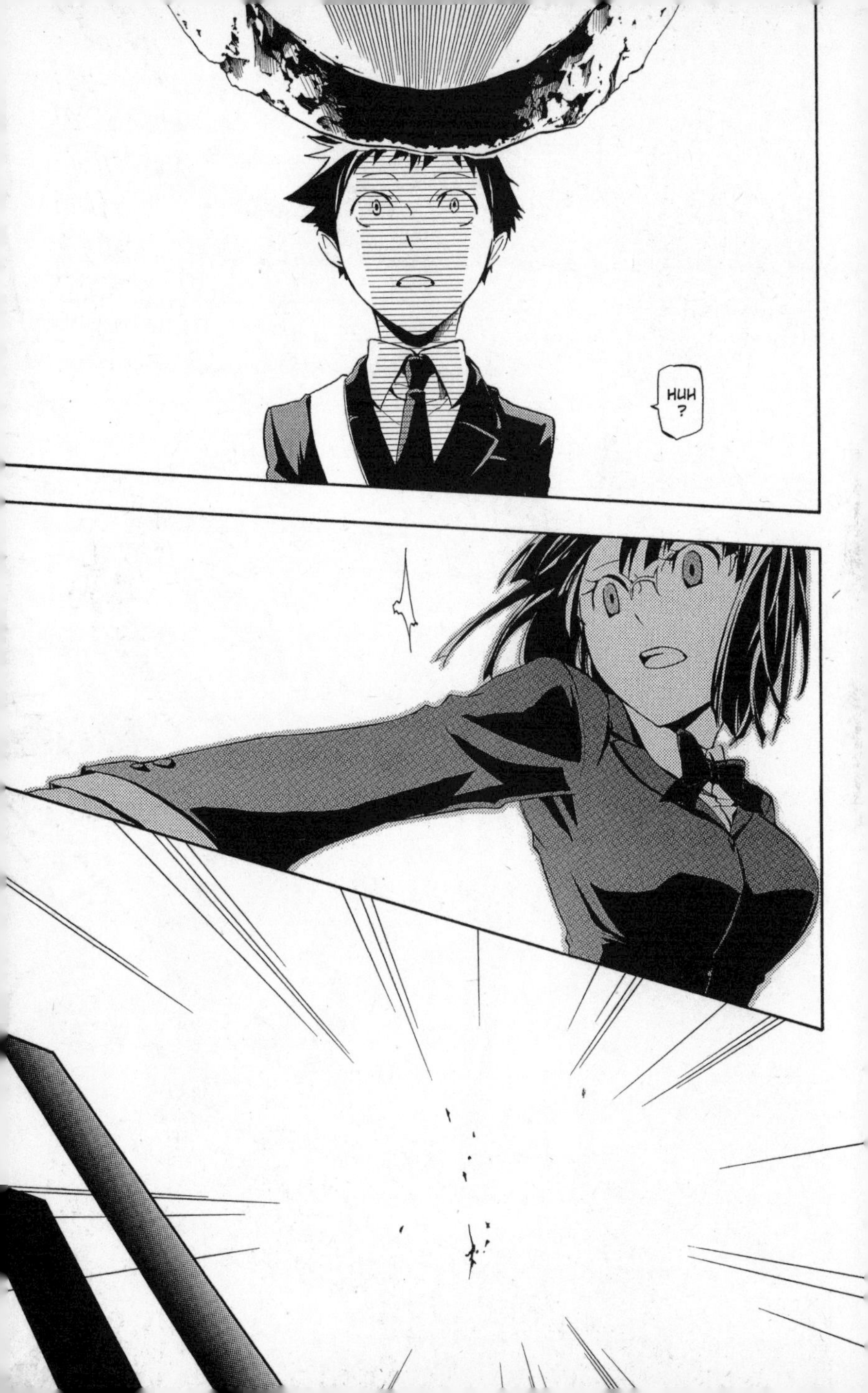
HUH
?

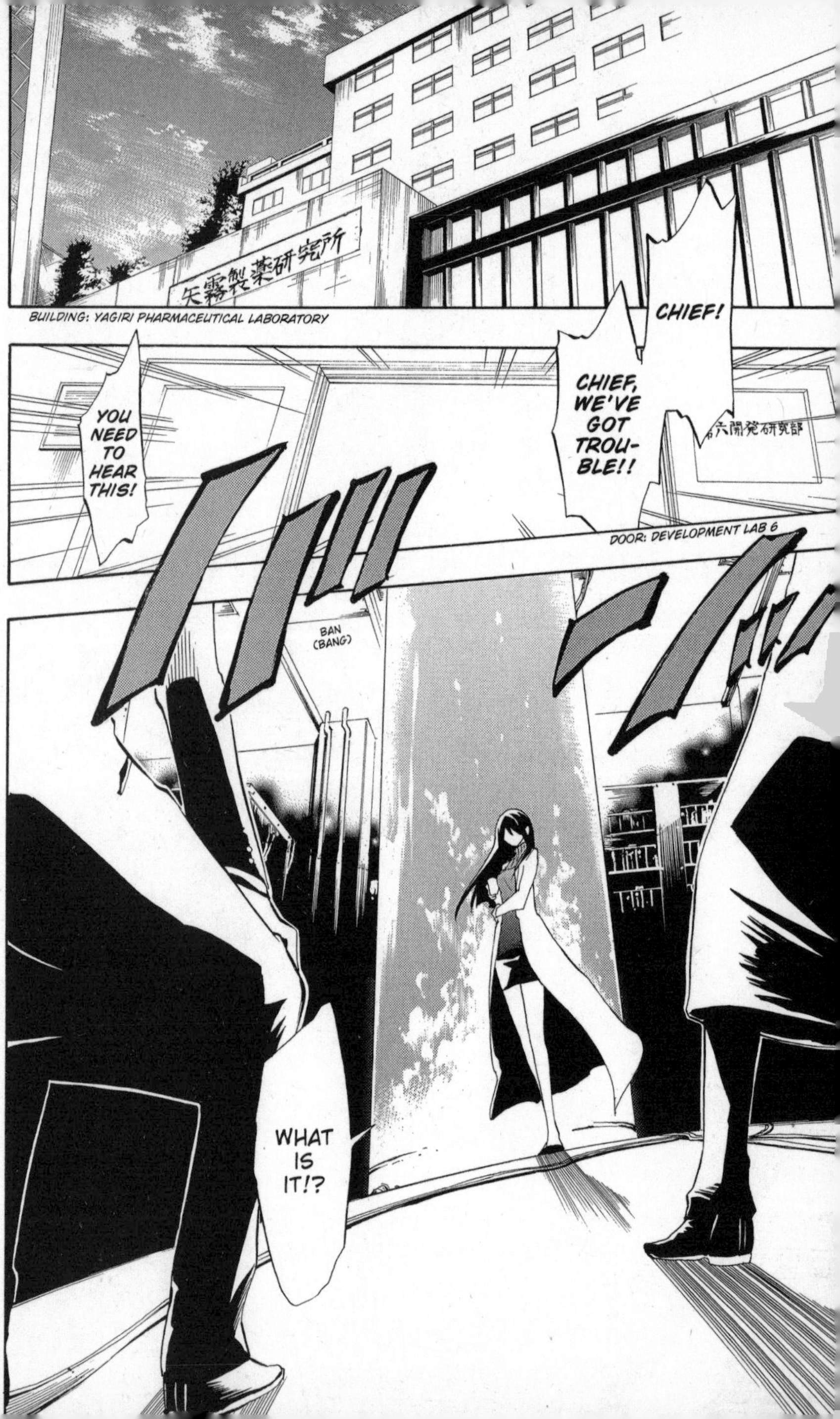
矢霧製薬研究所
BUILDING: YAGIRI PHARMACEUTICAL LABORATORY
CHIEF!
CHIEF, WE'VE GOT TROUBLE!!
六開発研究部
DOOR: DEVELOPMENT LAB 6
YOU NEED TO HEAR THIS!
BAN (BANG)
WHAT IS IT!?

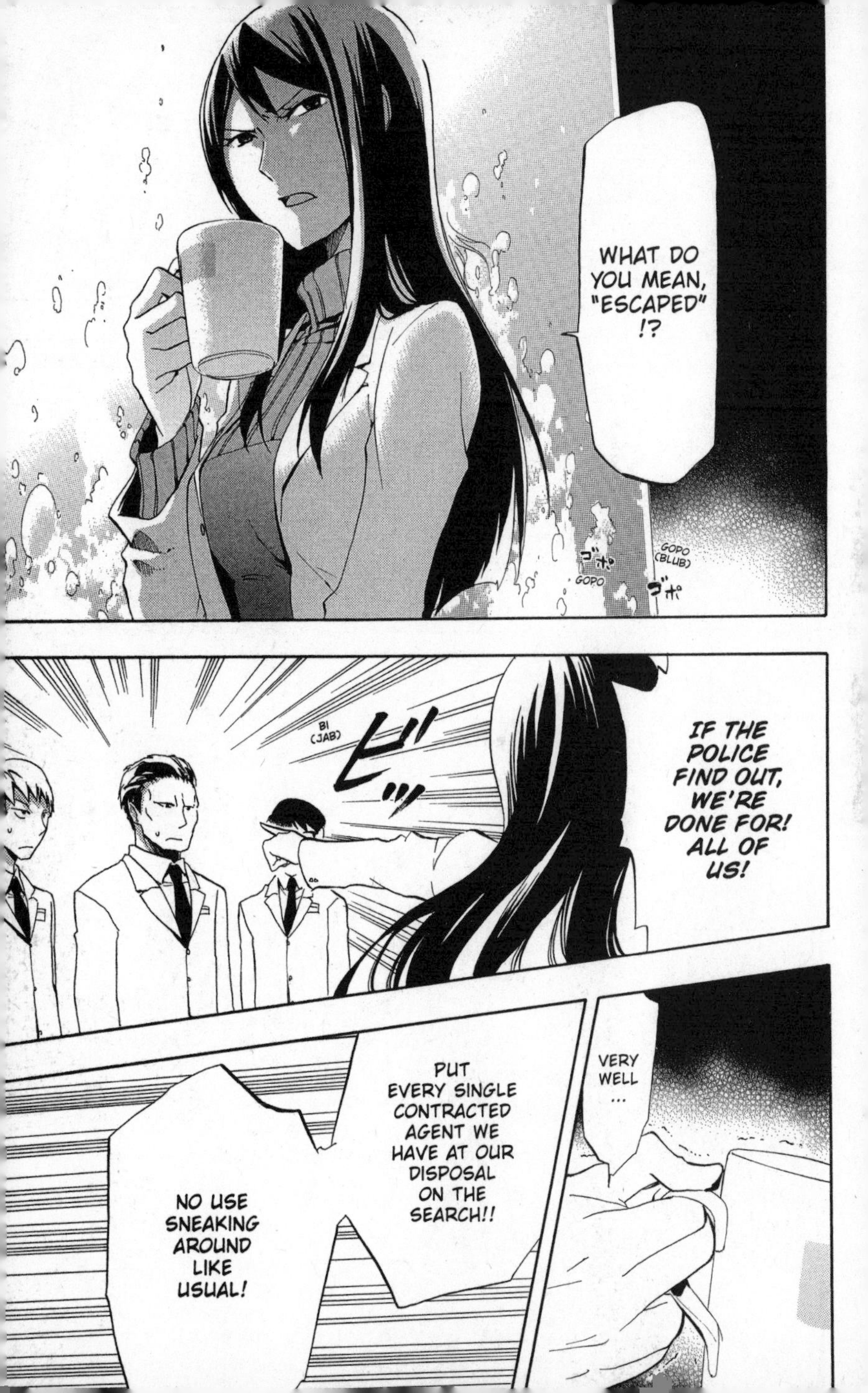

WHAT DO YOU MEAN, "ESCAPED" !?
GOPO (BLUB)
ゴポ
GOPO
ゴポ
IF THE POLICE FIND OUT, WE'RE DONE FOR! ALL OF US!
BI (JAB)
ビッ
VERY WELL ...
PUT EVERY SINGLE CONTRACTED AGENT WE HAVE AT OUR DISPOSAL ON THE SEARCH!!
NO USE SNEAKING AROUND LIKE USUAL!

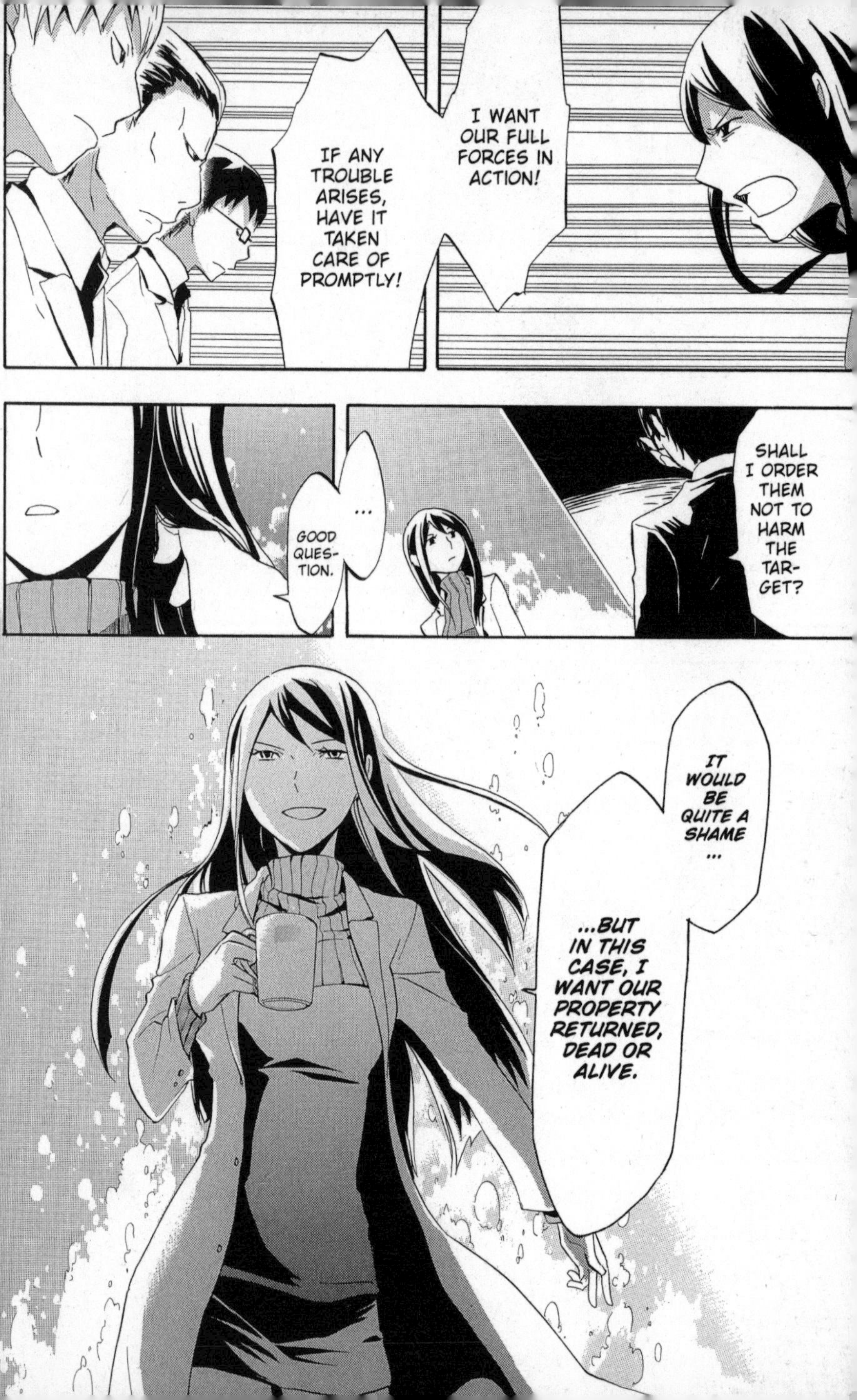
I WANT OUR FULL FORCES IN ACTION!
IF ANY TROUBLE ARISES, HAVE IT TAKEN CARE OF PROMPTLY!
SHALL I ORDER THEM NOT TO HARM THE TARGET?
...
GOOD QUES-TION.
IT WOULD BE QUITE A SHAME...
...BUT IN THIS CASE, I WANT OUR PROPERTY RETURNED, DEAD OR ALIVE.

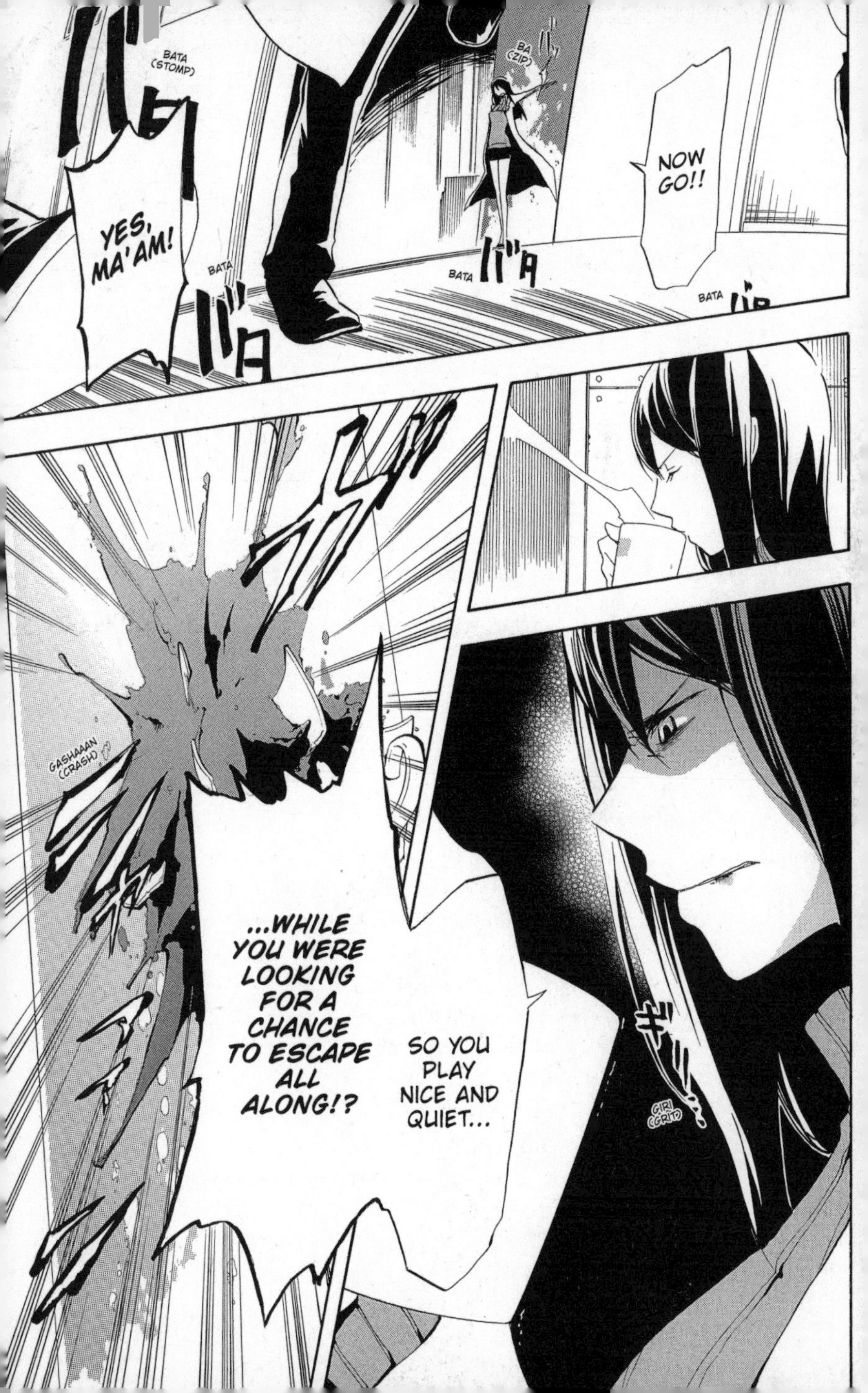
NOW GO!!
BA (ZIP)
BATA
BATA
BATA
BATA (STOMP)
YES, MA'AM!
BATA
GASHAAAN (CRASH)
SO YOU PLAY NICE AND QUIET...
...WHILE YOU WERE LOOKING FOR A CHANCE TO ESCAPE ALL ALONG!?
GIRI (GRIT)

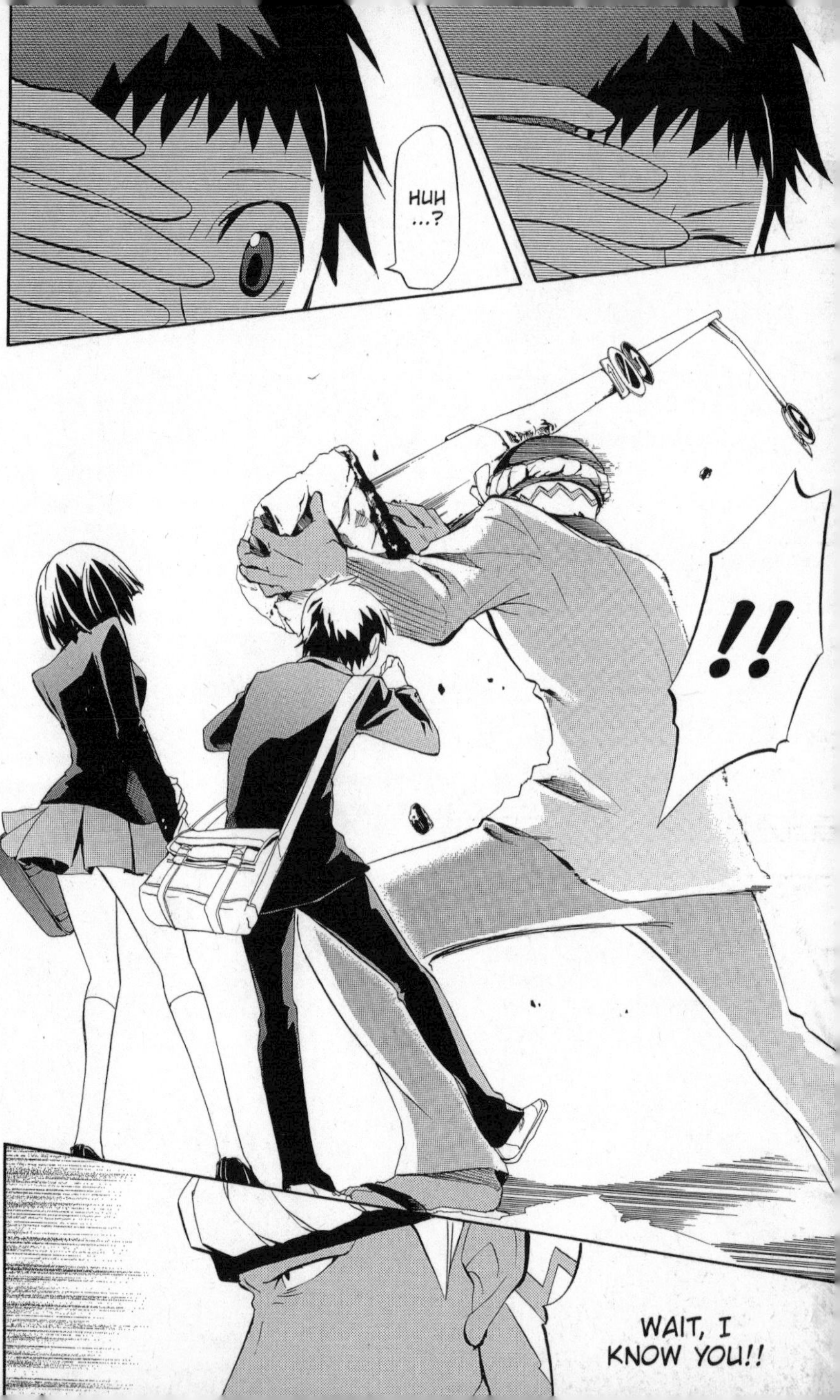
HUH ...?
!!
WAIT, I KNOW YOU!!

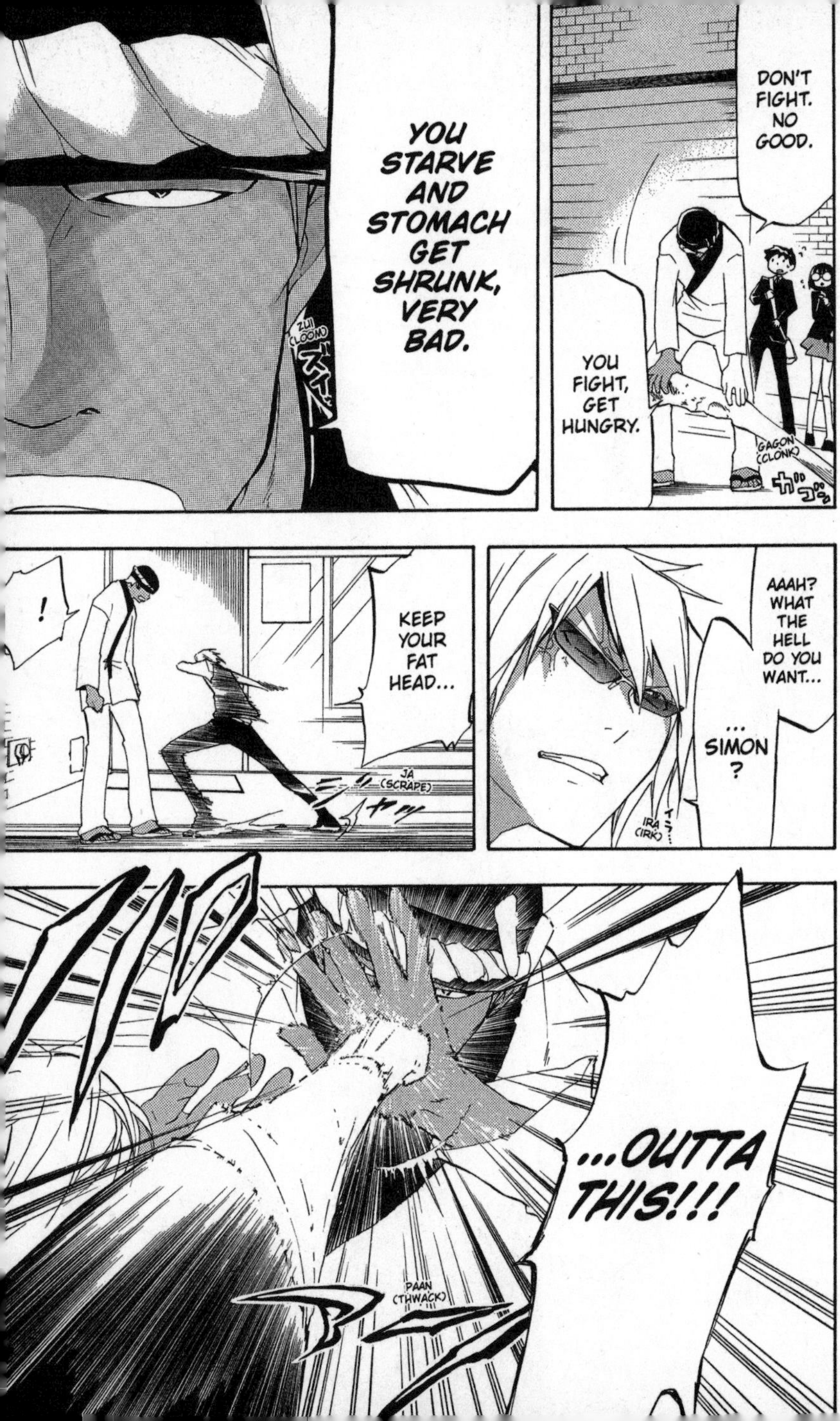
DON'T FIGHT. NO GOOD.
YOU FIGHT, GET HUNGRY.
GAGON (CLONK)
YOU STARVE AND STOMACH GET SHRUNK, VERY BAD.
ZUI (LOOM)
AAAH? WHAT THE HELL DO YOU WANT...
...SIMON?
IRA (IRK)
KEEP YOUR FAT HEAD...
!
JA (SCRAPE)
...OUTTA THIS!!!
PAAN (THWACK)

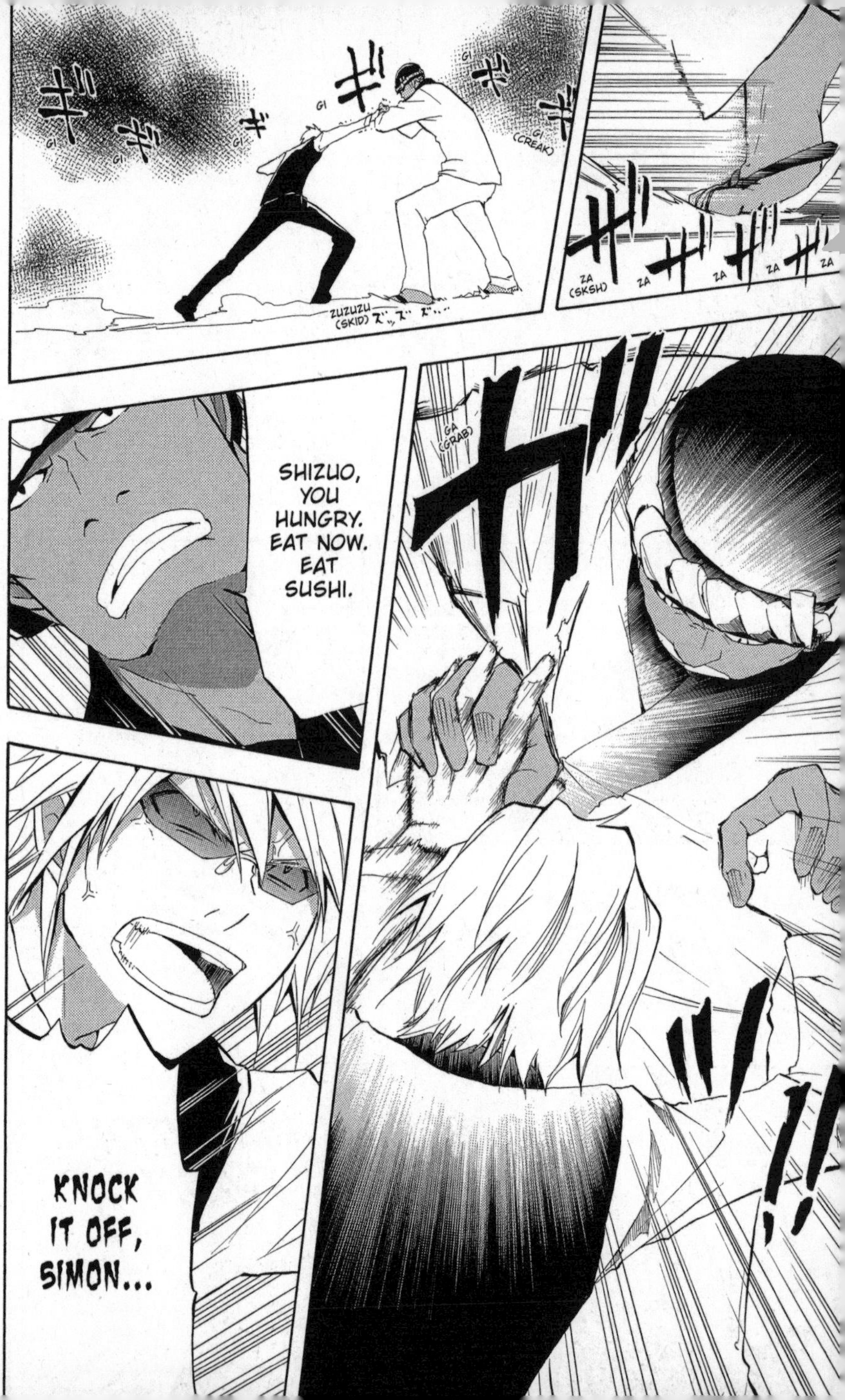

ZA (SKSH)
ZA
ZA
ZA
ZA
GI
GI (CREAK)
GI
GI
GI
GI
ZUZUZU (SKID)
GA (GRAB)
SHIZUO, YOU HUNGRY. EAT NOW. EAT SUSHI.
KNOCK IT OFF, SIMON...

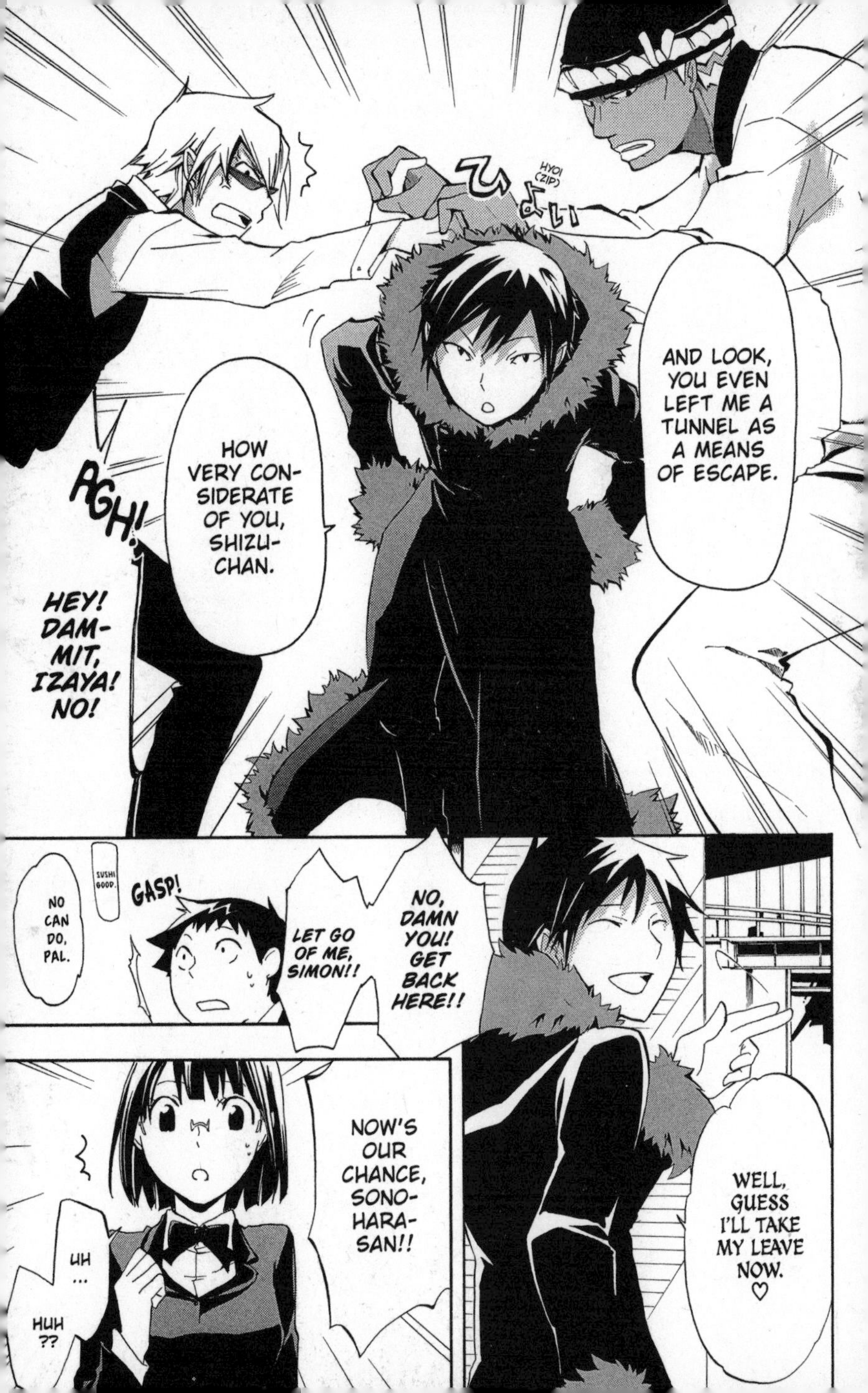
HYOI (ZIP)
AND LOOK, YOU EVEN LEFT ME A TUNNEL AS A MEANS OF ESCAPE.
HOW VERY CON-SIDERATE OF YOU, SHIZU-CHAN.
AGH!
HEY! DAM-MIT, IZAYA! NO!
WELL, GUESS I'LL TAKE MY LEAVE NOW. ♡
NO, DAMN YOU! GET BACK HERE!!
LET GO OF ME, SIMON!!
GASP!
SUSHI GOOD.
NO CAN DO, PAL.
NOW'S OUR CHANCE, SONO-HARA-SAN!!
UH...
HUH??

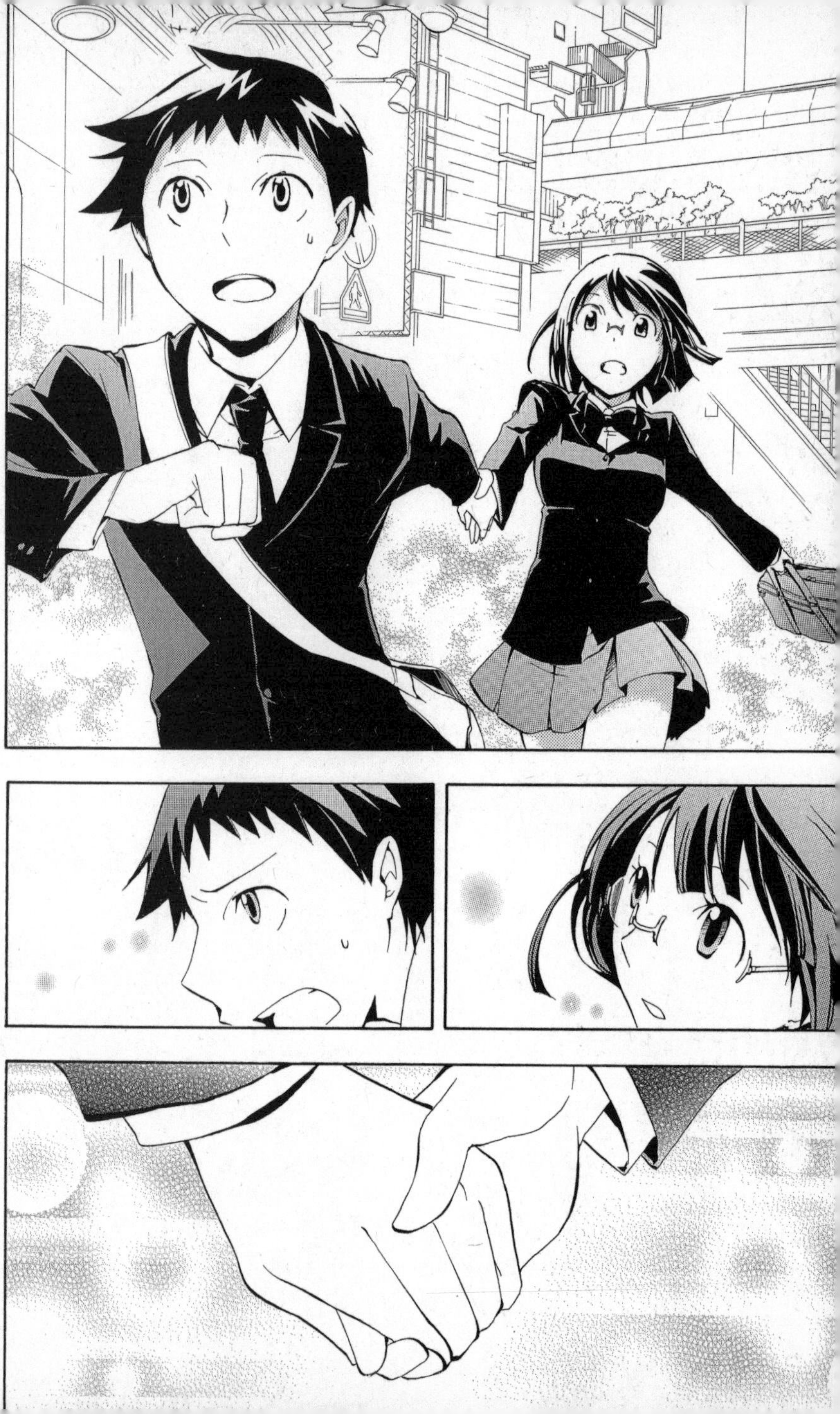

10: WAWAWAWAWAWAWAWAWAWAWA!!

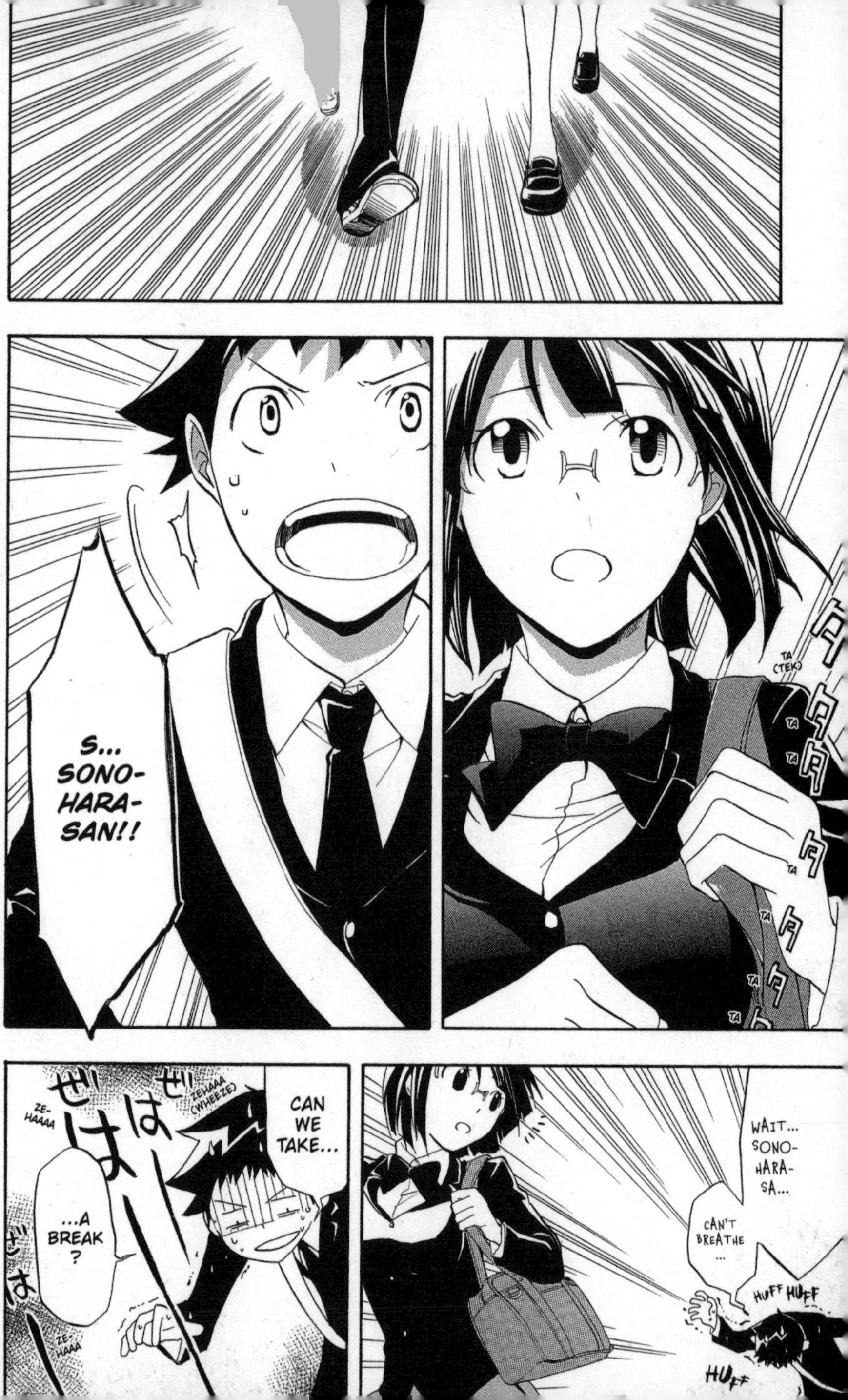
TA (TEK)
TA
TA
TA
TA
TA
TA
S... SONO-HARA-SAN!!
WAIT... SONO-HARA-SA...
CAN'T BREATHE...
HUFF HUFF
HUFF
ZEHAAA (WHEEZE)
CAN WE TAKE...
ZE-HAAAA
...A BREAK?
ZE-HAAA

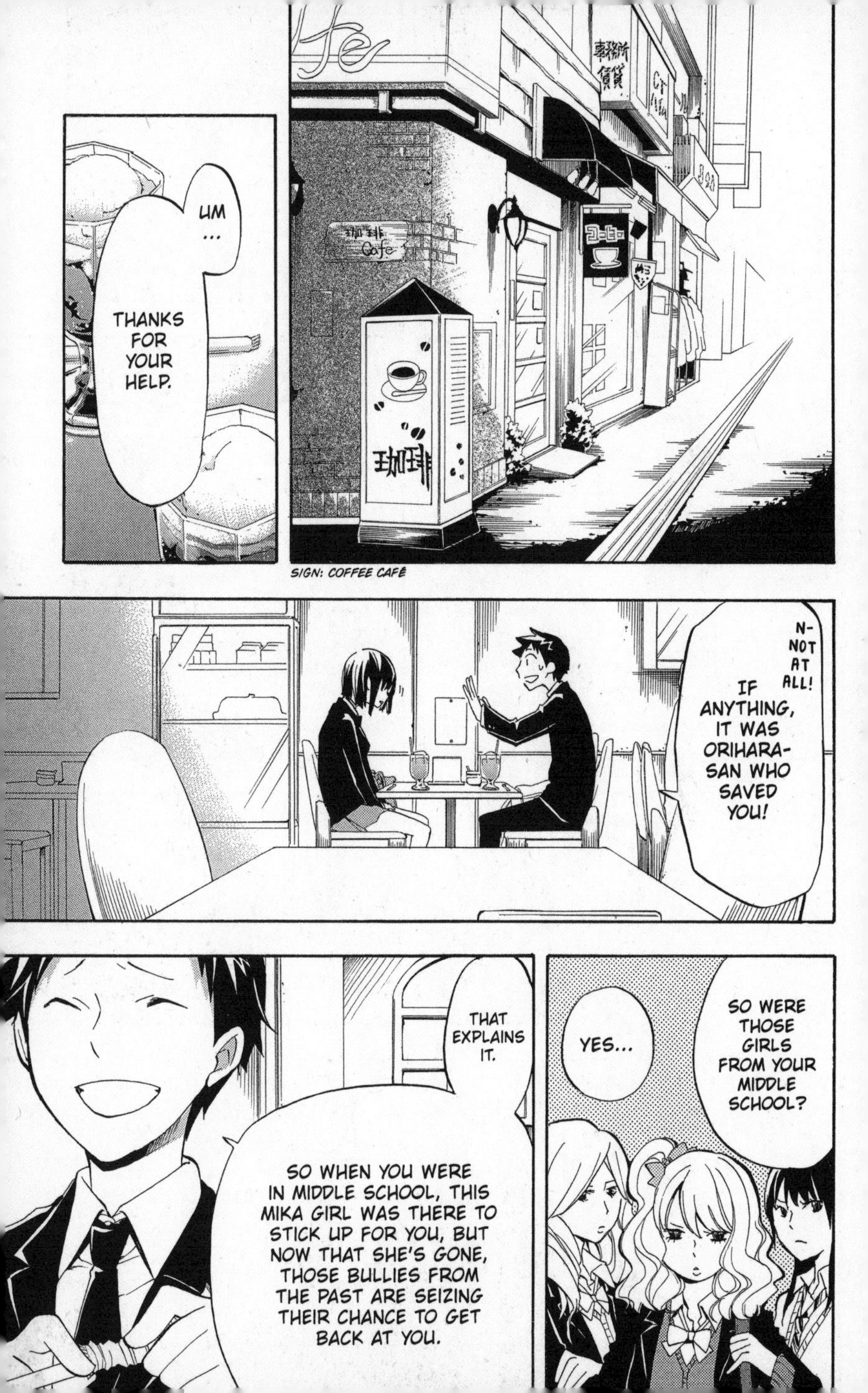
SIGN: COFFEE CAFÉ
UM...
THANKS FOR YOUR HELP.
N-NOT AT ALL!
IF ANYTHING, IT WAS ORIHARA-SAN WHO SAVED YOU!
SO WERE THOSE GIRLS FROM YOUR MIDDLE SCHOOL?
YES...
THAT EXPLAINS IT.
SO WHEN YOU WERE IN MIDDLE SCHOOL, THIS MIKA GIRL WAS THERE TO STICK UP FOR YOU, BUT NOW THAT SHE'S GONE, THOSE BULLIES FROM THE PAST ARE SEIZING THEIR CHANCE TO GET BACK AT YOU.

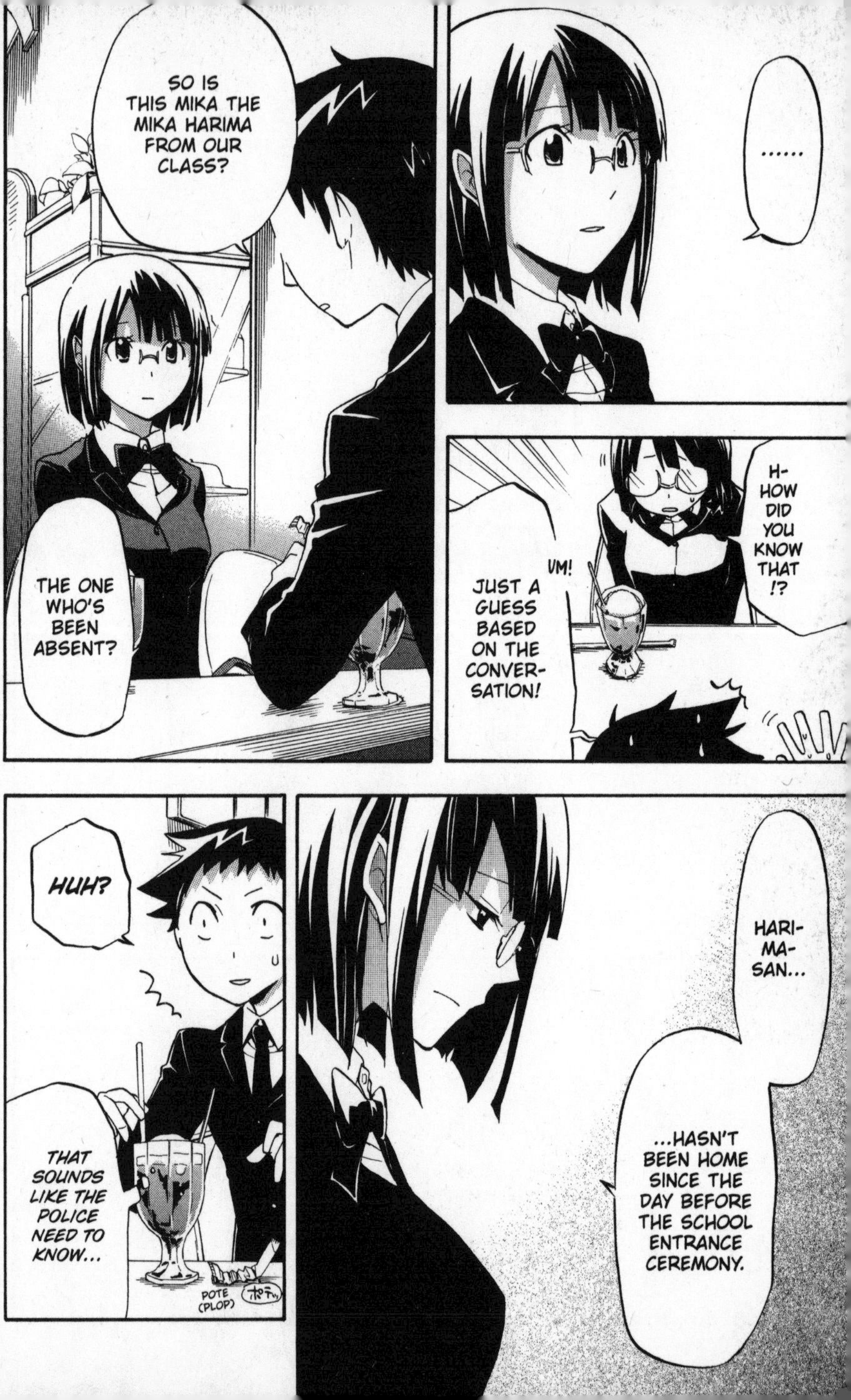
......
H-HOW DID YOU KNOW THAT!?
UM!
JUST A GUESS BASED ON THE CONVERSATION!
SO IS THIS MIKA THE MIKA HARIMA FROM OUR CLASS?
THE ONE WHO'S BEEN ABSENT?
HARI-MA-SAN...
...HASN'T BEEN HOME SINCE THE DAY BEFORE THE SCHOOL ENTRANCE CEREMONY.
HUH?
THAT SOUNDS LIKE THE POLICE NEED TO KNOW...
POTE (PLOP)
ポテッ

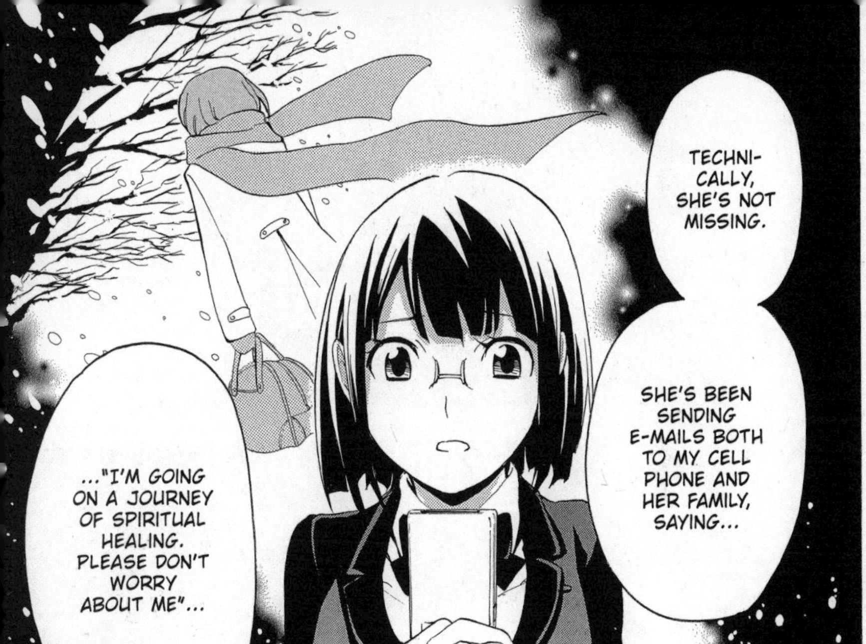
TECHNI-
CALLY,
SHE'S NOT
MISSING.
SHE'S BEEN SENDING E-MAILS BOTH TO MY CELL PHONE AND HER FAMILY, SAYING...
..."I'M GOING ON A JOURNEY OF SPIRITUAL HEALING. PLEASE DON'T WORRY ABOUT ME"...
...OR "I'M AT □□ STATION NOW." THINGS LIKE THAT.

SIGN: □□ STATION

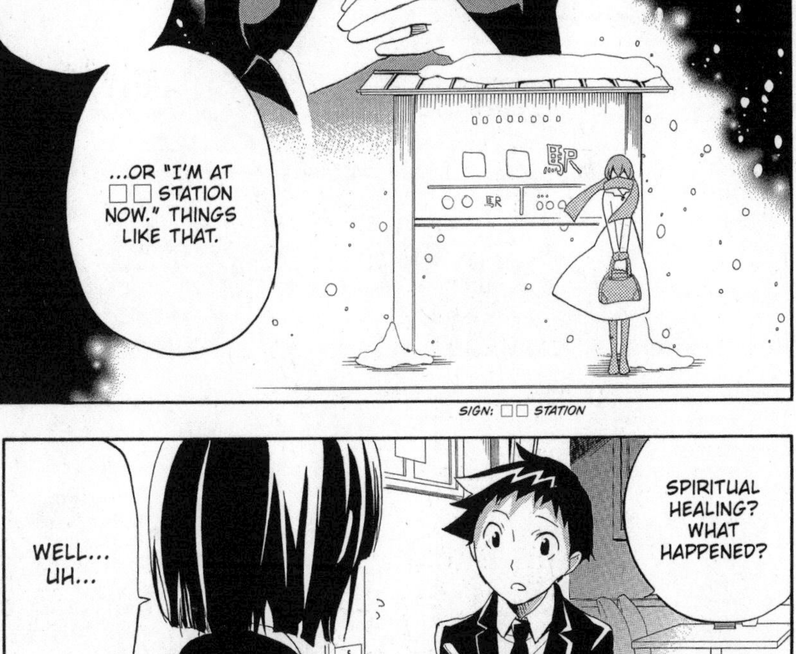
SPIRITUAL HEALING? WHAT HAPPENED?
WELL... UH...

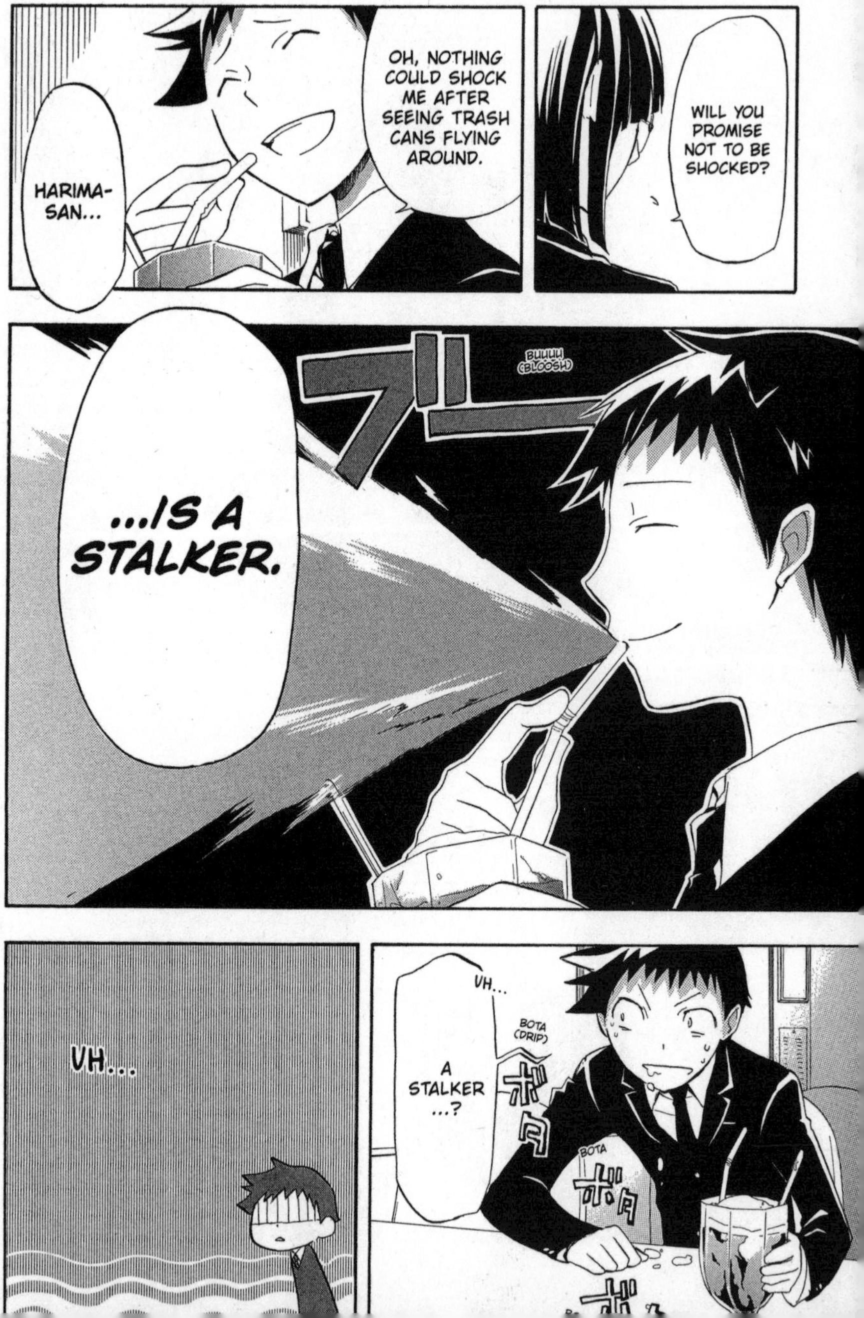

WILL YOU PROMISE NOT TO BE SHOCKED?
OH, NOTHING COULD SHOCK ME AFTER SEEING TRASH CANS FLYING AROUND.
HARIMA-SAN...
BUUUU (BLOOSH)
...IS A STALKER.
UH...
BOTA (DRIP)
A STALKER ...?
BOTA
UH...

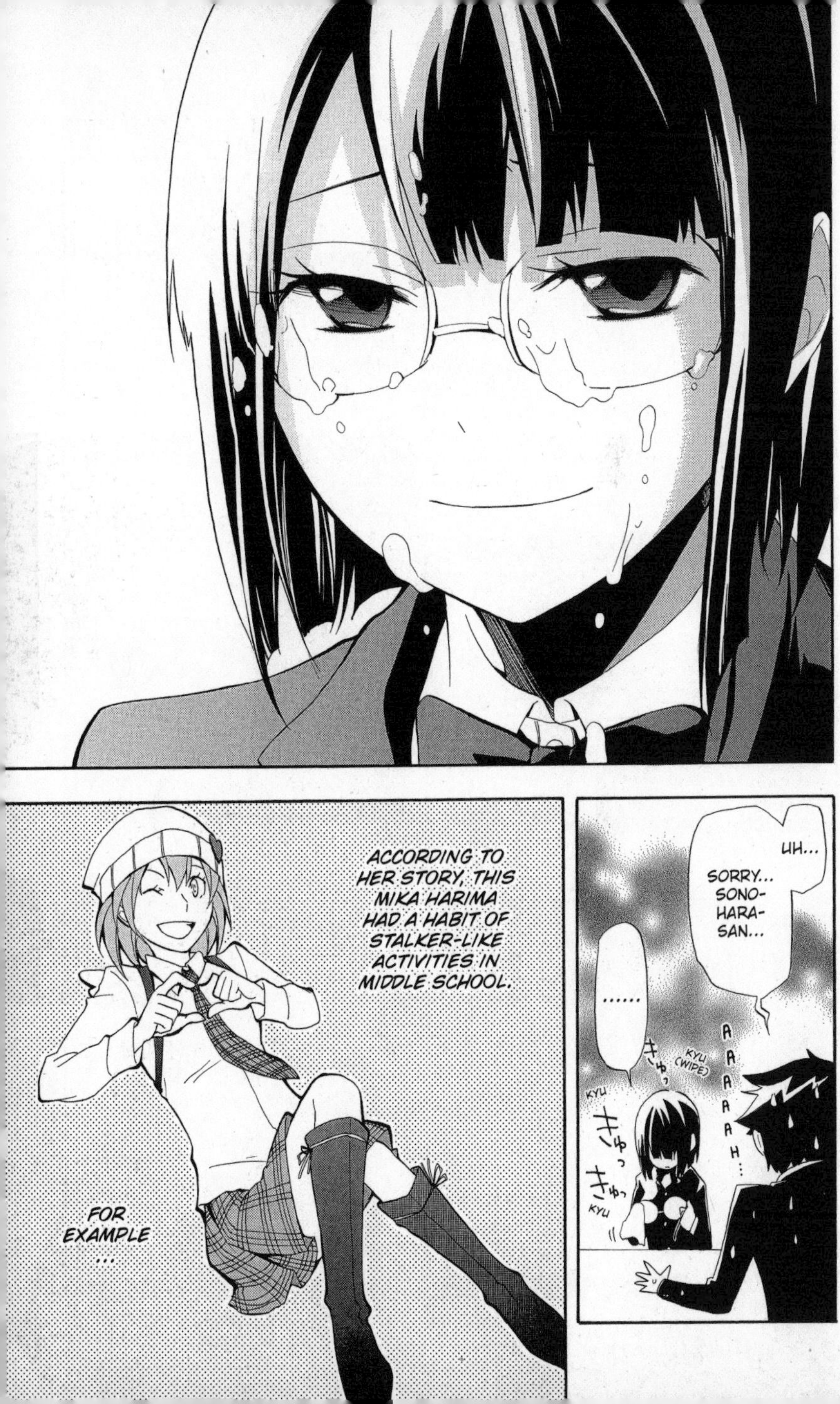
UH...
SORRY... SONO-HARA-SAN...
......
KYU (WIPE)
AAAAAAH...
KYU
KYU
ACCORDING TO HER STORY, THIS MIKA HARIMA HAD A HABIT OF STALKER-LIKE ACTIVITIES IN MIDDLE SCHOOL.
FOR EXAMPLE ...

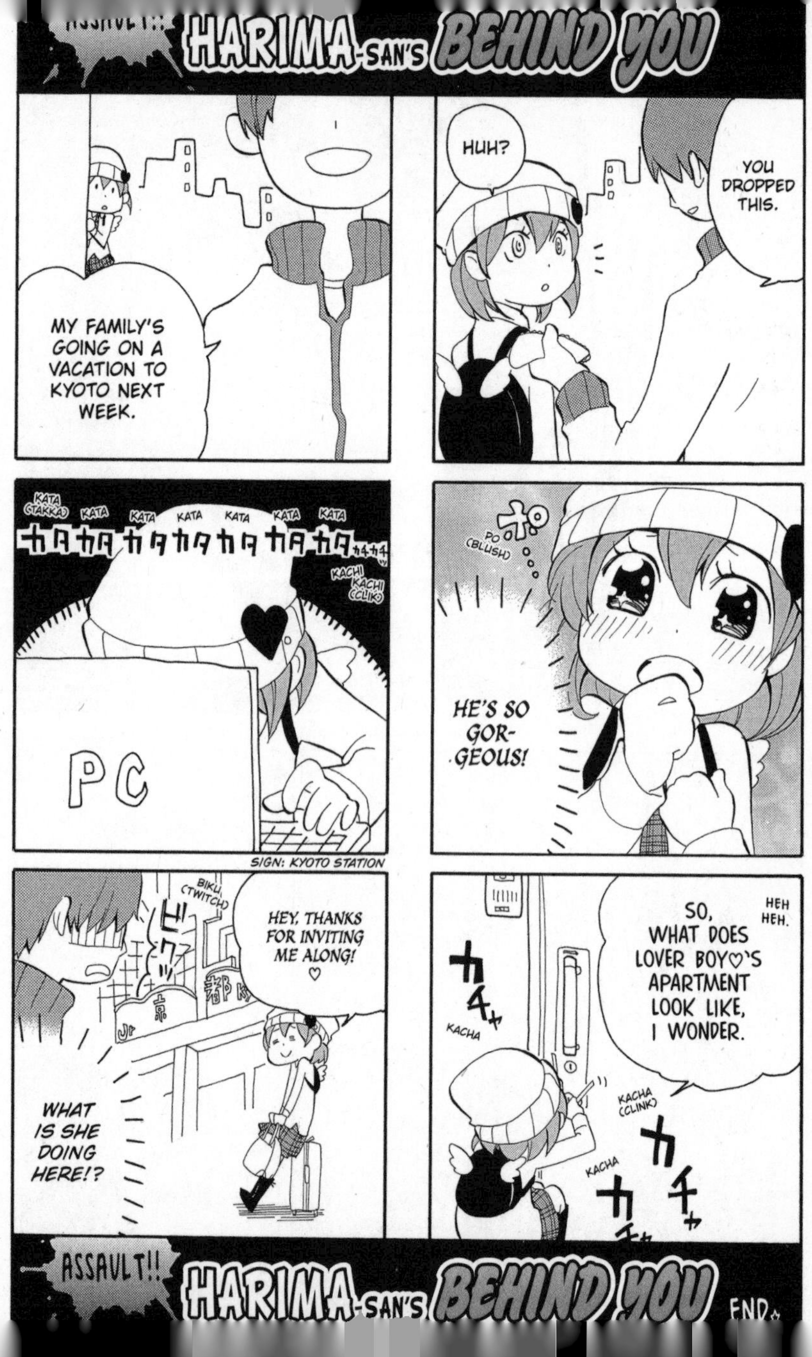
HARIMA-SAN'S BEHIND YOU
HUH?
YOU DROPPED THIS.
MY FAMILY'S GOING ON A VACATION TO KYOTO NEXT WEEK.
PO (BLUSH)
HE'S SO GOR-GEOUS!
KATA (TAKKA) KATA KATA KATA KATA KATA KATA
KACHI KACHI (CLIK)
PC
HEH HEH.
SO, WHAT DOES LOVER BOY♡'S APARTMENT LOOK LIKE, I WONDER.
KACHA
KACHA (CLINK)
KACHA
SIGN: KYOTO STATION
BIKU (TWITCH)
HEY, THANKS FOR INVITING ME ALONG! ♡
WHAT IS SHE DOING HERE!?
ASSAULT!!
HARIMA-SAN'S BEHIND YOU
END☆

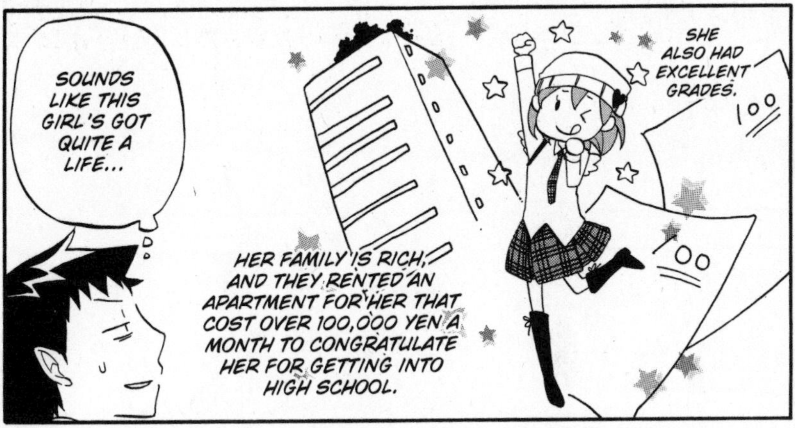
SHE ALSO HAD EXCELLENT GRADES.
100
100
HER FAMILY IS RICH, AND THEY RENTED AN APARTMENT FOR HER THAT COST OVER 100,000 YEN A MONTH TO CONGRATULATE HER FOR GETTING INTO HIGH SCHOOL.
SOUNDS LIKE THIS GIRL'S GOT QUITE A LIFE...

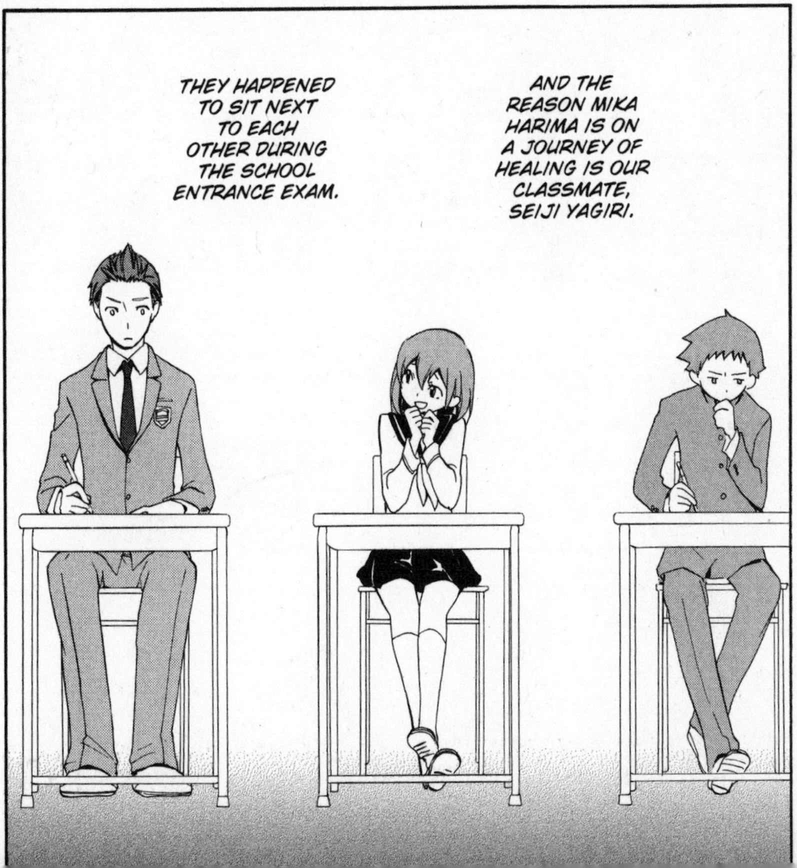
AND THE REASON MIKA HARIMA IS ON A JOURNEY OF HEALING IS OUR CLASSMATE, SEIJI YAGIRI.
THEY HAPPENED TO SIT NEXT TO EACH OTHER DURING THE SCHOOL ENTRANCE EXAM.

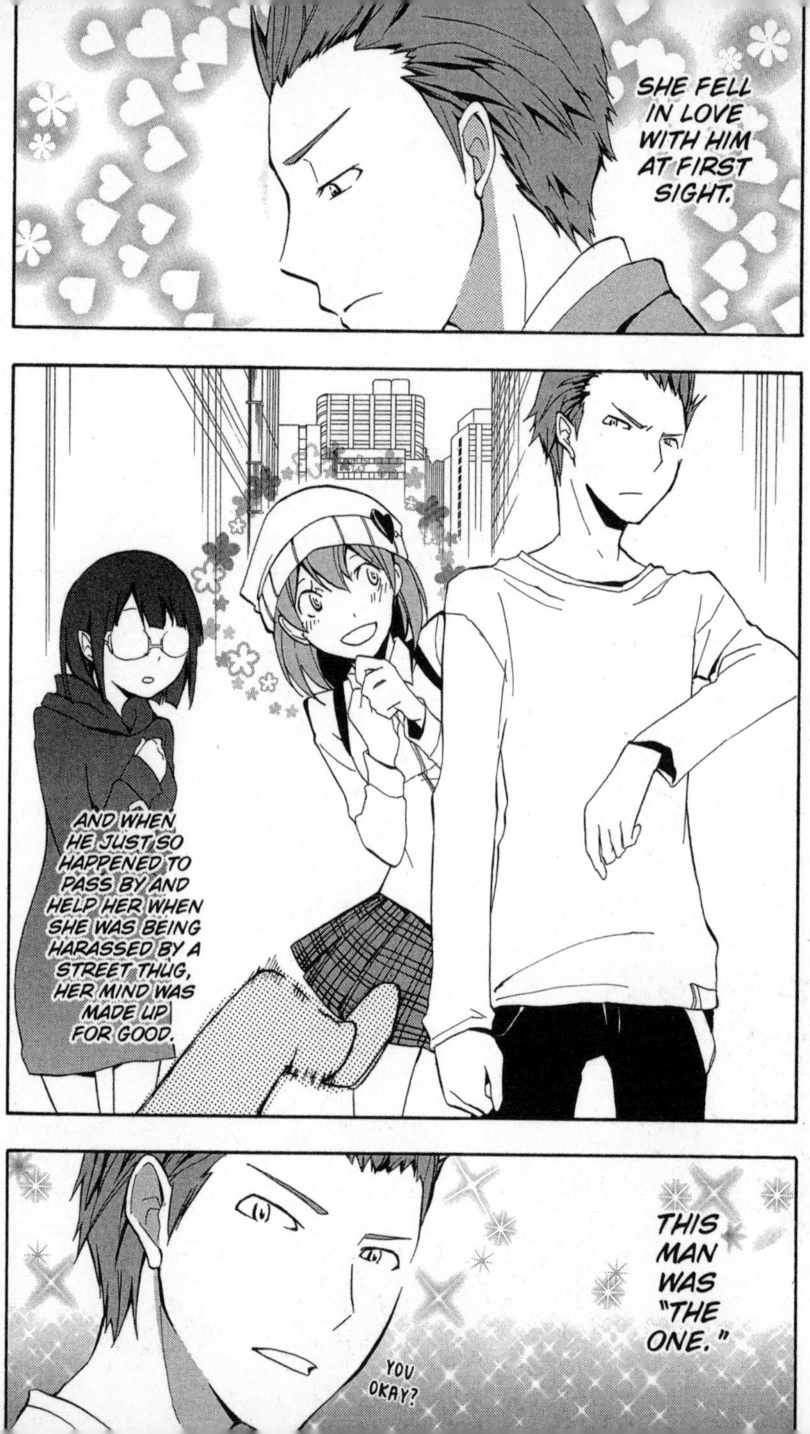
SHE FELL IN LOVE WITH HIM AT FIRST SIGHT.
AND WHEN HE JUST SO HAPPENED TO PASS BY AND HELP HER WHEN SHE WAS BEING HARASSED BY A STREET THUG, HER MIND WAS MADE UP FOR GOOD.
THIS MAN WAS "THE ONE."
YOU OKAY?

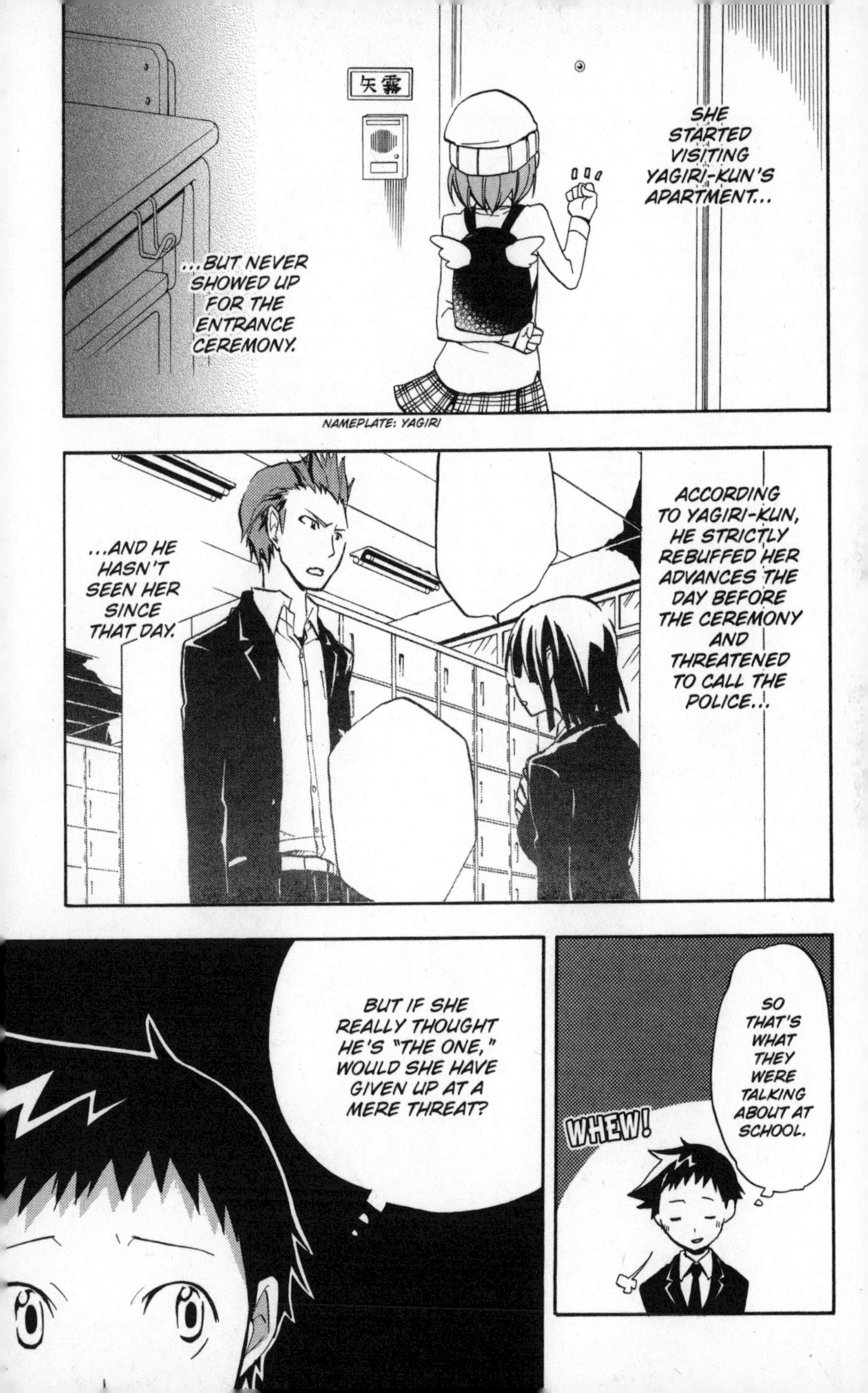
矢霧
SHE STARTED VISITING YAGIRI-KUN'S APARTMENT...
...BUT NEVER SHOWED UP FOR THE ENTRANCE CEREMONY.
NAMEPLATE: YAGIRI
ACCORDING TO YAGIRI-KUN, HE STRICTLY REBUFFED HER ADVANCES THE DAY BEFORE THE CEREMONY AND THREATENED TO CALL THE POLICE...
...AND HE HASN'T SEEN HER SINCE THAT DAY.
SO THAT'S WHAT THEY WERE TALKING ABOUT AT SCHOOL.
WHEW!
BUT IF SHE REALLY THOUGHT HE'S "THE ONE," WOULD SHE HAVE GIVEN UP AT A MERE THREAT?

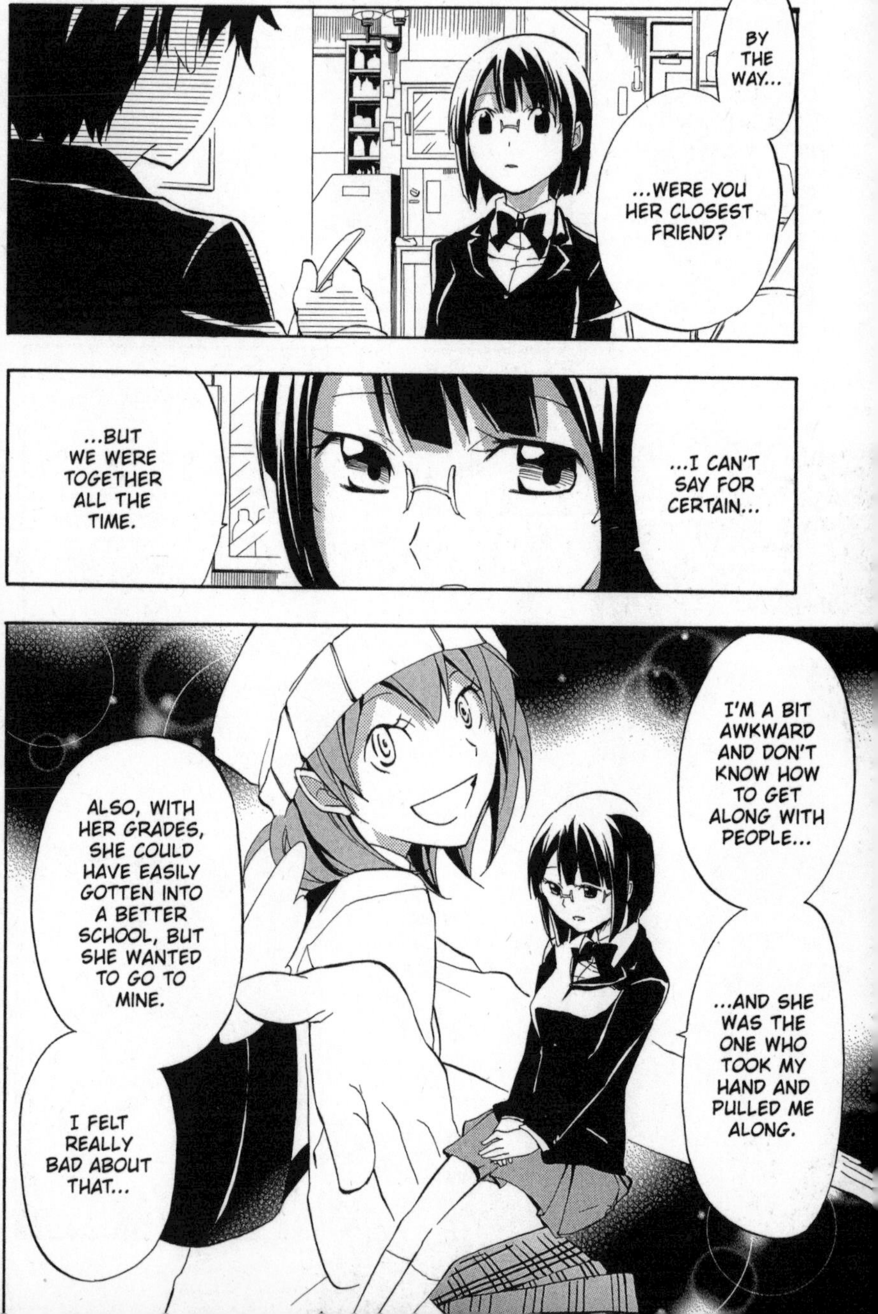
BY THE WAY...
...WERE YOU HER CLOSEST FRIEND?
...I CAN'T SAY FOR CERTAIN...
...BUT WE WERE TOGETHER ALL THE TIME.
I'M A BIT AWKWARD AND DON'T KNOW HOW TO GET ALONG WITH PEOPLE...
...AND SHE WAS THE ONE WHO TOOK MY HAND AND PULLED ME ALONG.
ALSO, WITH HER GRADES, SHE COULD HAVE EASILY GOTTEN INTO A BETTER SCHOOL, BUT SHE WANTED TO GO TO MINE.
I FELT REALLY BAD ABOUT THAT...

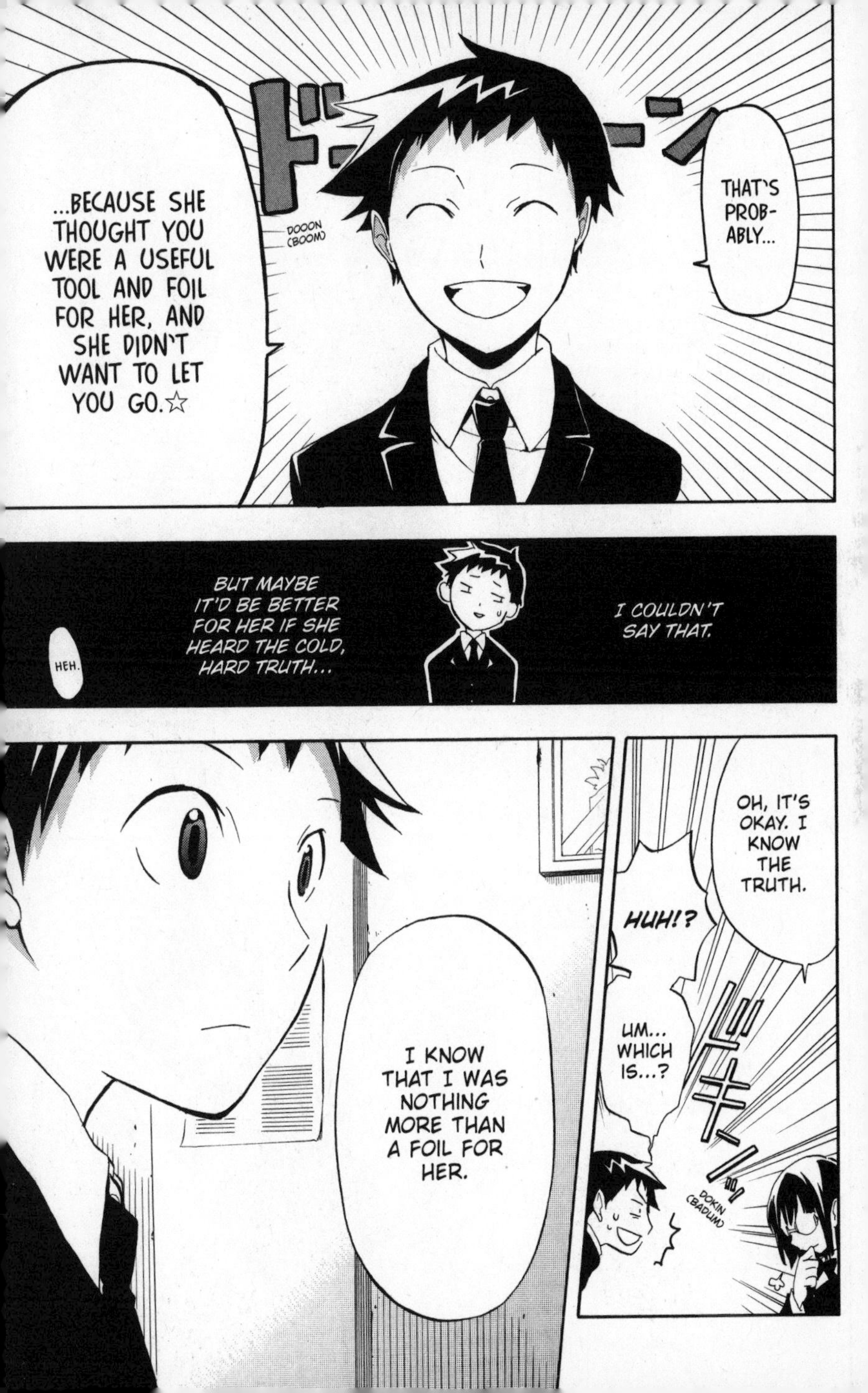
THAT'S PROB-ABLY...
DOOON (BOOM)
...BECAUSE SHE THOUGHT YOU WERE A USEFUL TOOL AND FOIL FOR HER, AND SHE DIDN'T WANT TO LET YOU GO.☆
I COULDN'T SAY THAT.
BUT MAYBE IT'D BE BETTER FOR HER IF SHE HEARD THE COLD, HARD TRUTH...
HEH.
OH, IT'S OKAY. I KNOW THE TRUTH.
HUH!?
UM... WHICH IS...?
DOKIN (BADUM)
I KNOW THAT I WAS NOTHING MORE THAN A FOIL FOR HER.

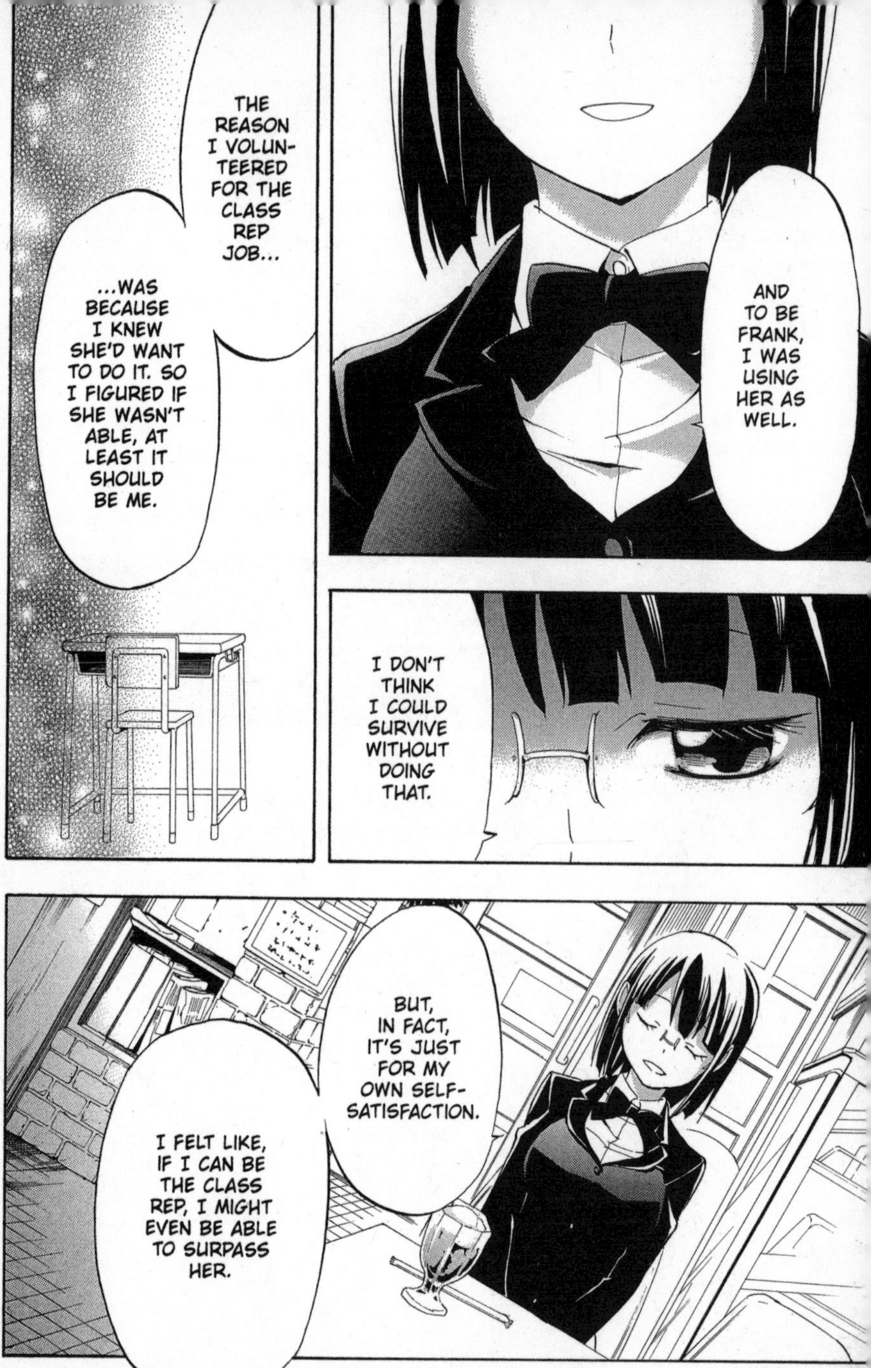
THE REASON I VOLUNTEERED FOR THE CLASS REP JOB...
...WAS BECAUSE I KNEW SHE'D WANT TO DO IT. SO I FIGURED IF SHE WASN'T ABLE, AT LEAST IT SHOULD BE ME.
AND TO BE FRANK, I WAS USING HER AS WELL.
I DON'T THINK I COULD SURVIVE WITHOUT DOING THAT.
BUT, IN FACT, IT'S JUST FOR MY OWN SELF-SATISFACTION.
I FELT LIKE, IF I CAN BE THE CLASS REP, I MIGHT EVEN BE ABLE TO SURPASS HER.

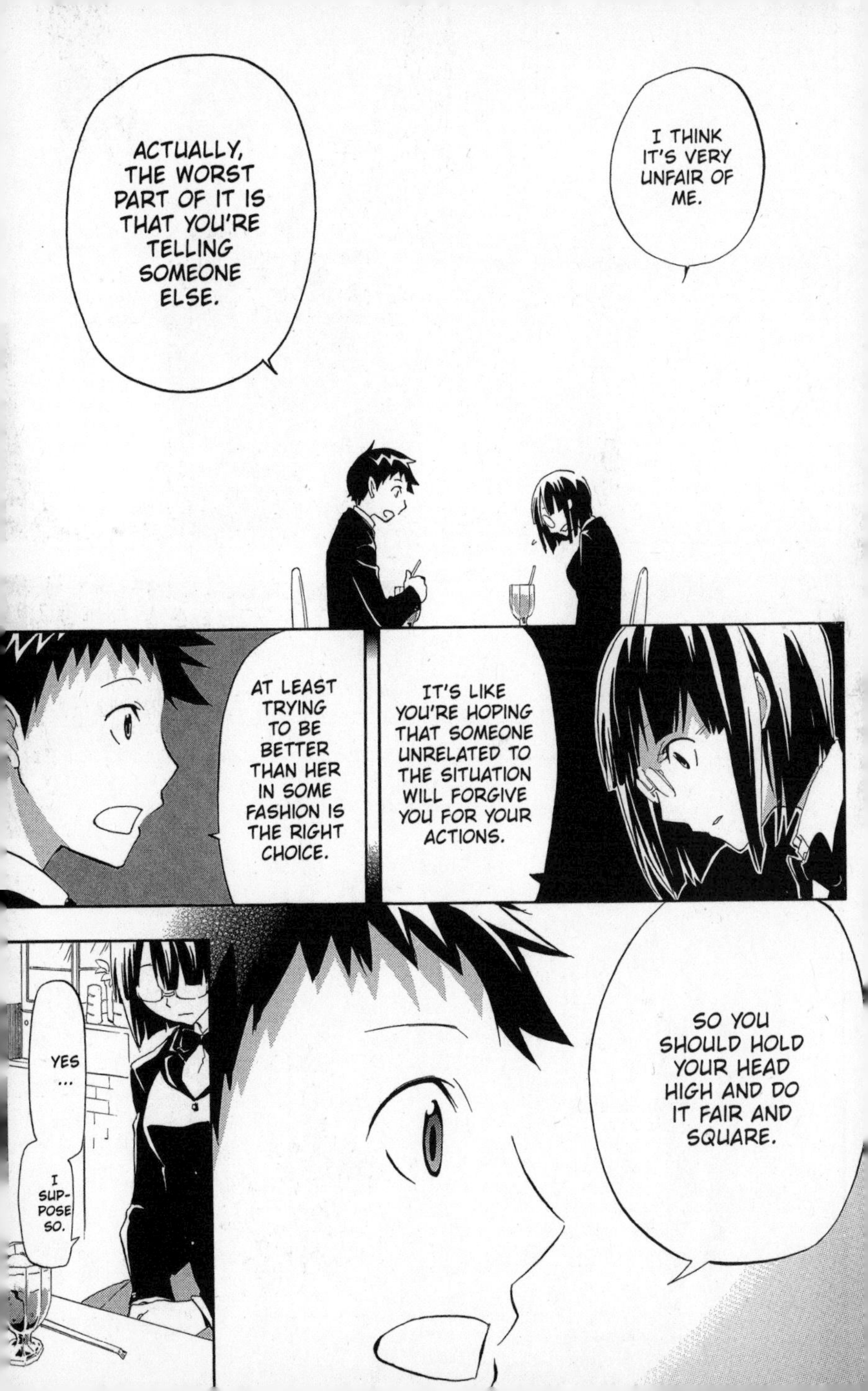
I THINK IT'S VERY UNFAIR OF ME.
ACTUALLY, THE WORST PART OF IT IS THAT YOU'RE TELLING SOMEONE ELSE.
IT'S LIKE YOU'RE HOPING THAT SOMEONE UNRELATED TO THE SITUATION WILL FORGIVE YOU FOR YOUR ACTIONS.
AT LEAST TRYING TO BE BETTER THAN HER IN SOME FASHION IS THE RIGHT CHOICE.
SO YOU SHOULD HOLD YOUR HEAD HIGH AND DO IT FAIR AND SQUARE.
YES ...
I SUP-POSE SO.

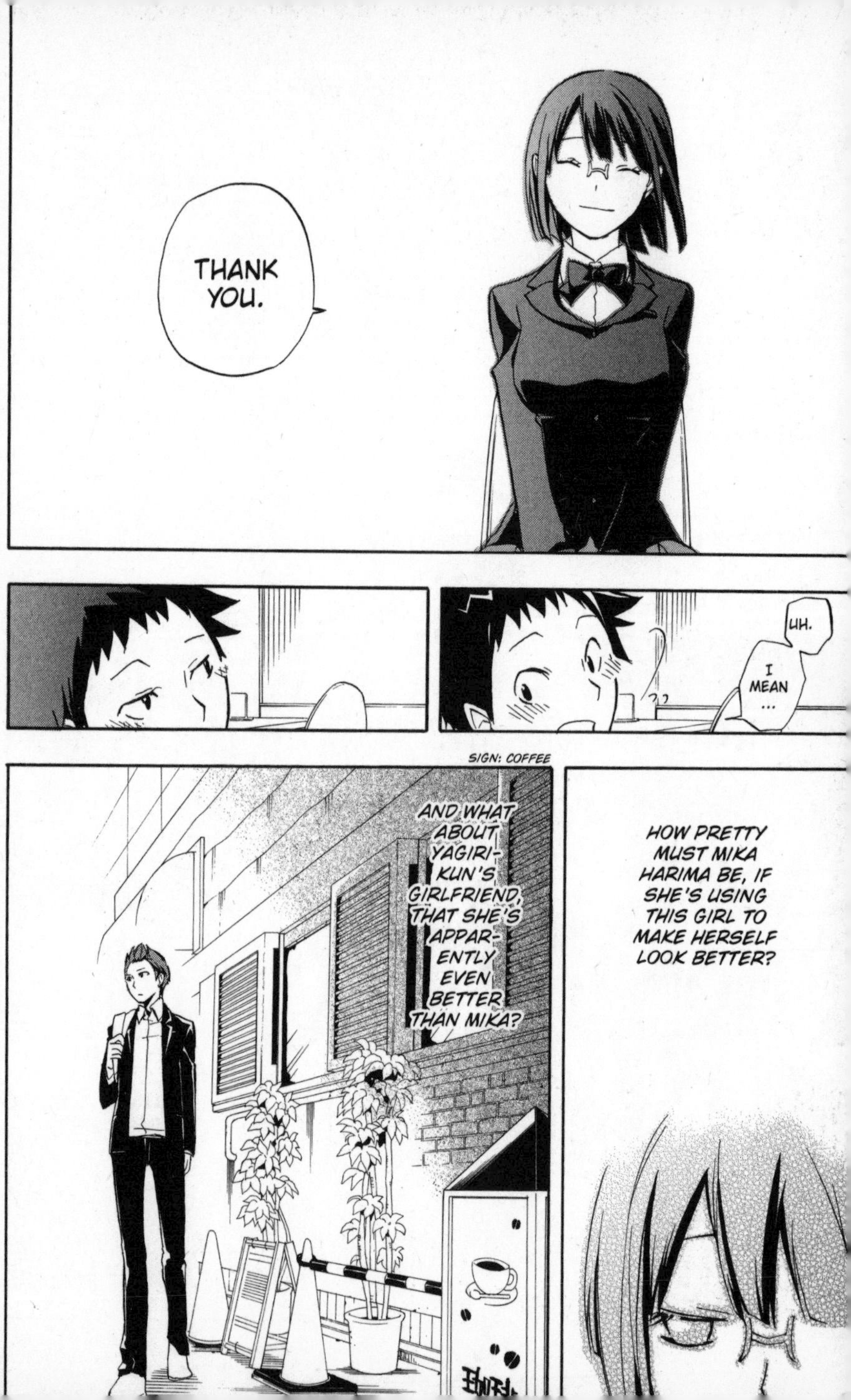
THANK YOU.
UH.
I MEAN ...
HOW PRETTY MUST MIKA HARIMA BE, IF SHE'S USING THIS GIRL TO MAKE HERSELF LOOK BETTER?
SIGN: COFFEE
AND WHAT ABOUT YAGIRI-KUN'S GIRLFRIEND, THAT SHE'S APPARENTLY EVEN BETTER THAN MIKA?

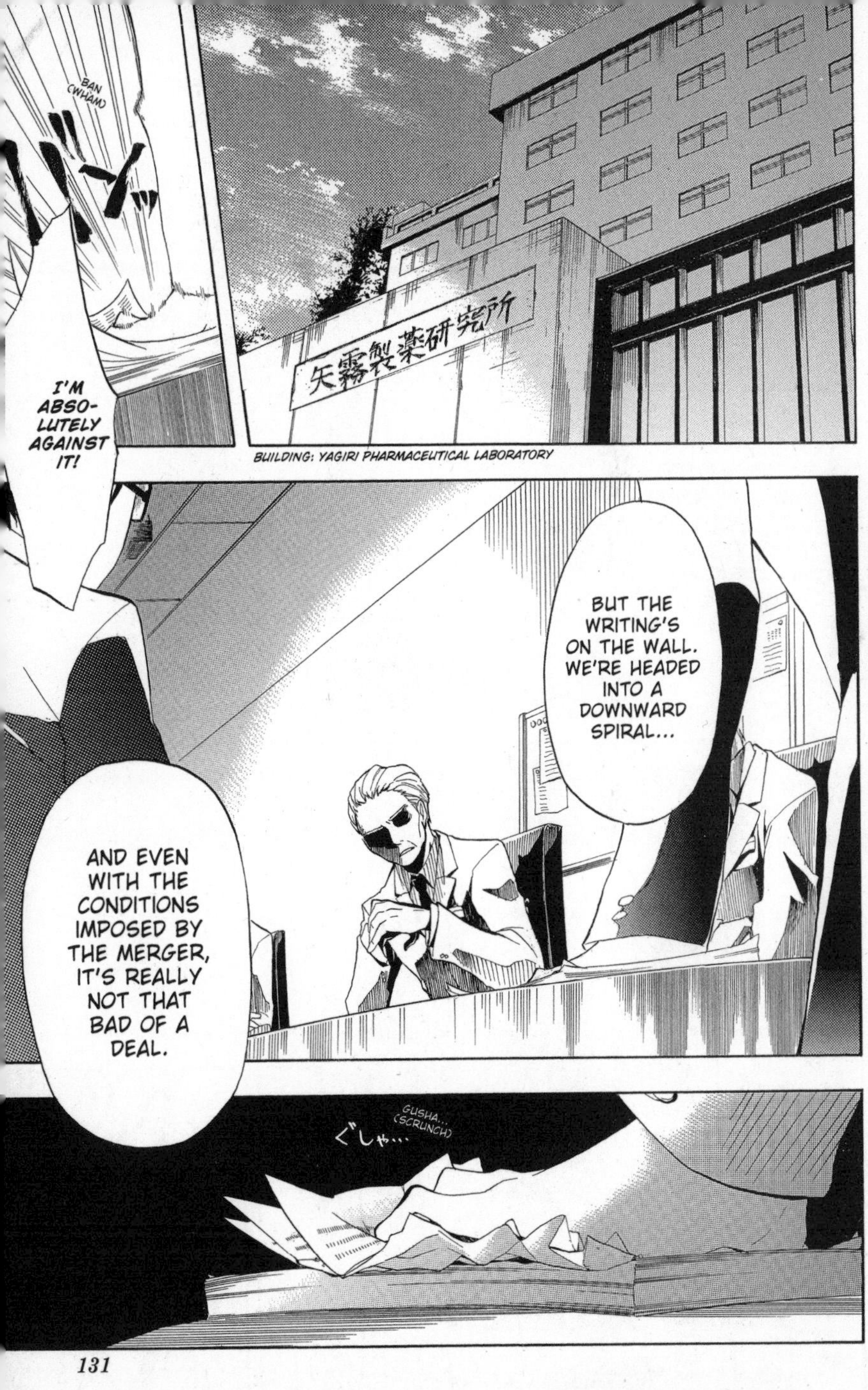
矢霧製薬研究所
BUILDING: YAGIRI PHARMACEUTICAL LABORATORY
BAN (WHAM)
I'M ABSOLUTELY AGAINST IT!
BUT THE WRITING'S ON THE WALL. WE'RE HEADED INTO A DOWNWARD SPIRAL...
AND EVEN WITH THE CONDITIONS IMPOSED BY THE MERGER, IT'S REALLY NOT THAT BAD OF A DEAL.
ぐしゃ…
GUSHA... (SCRUNCH)

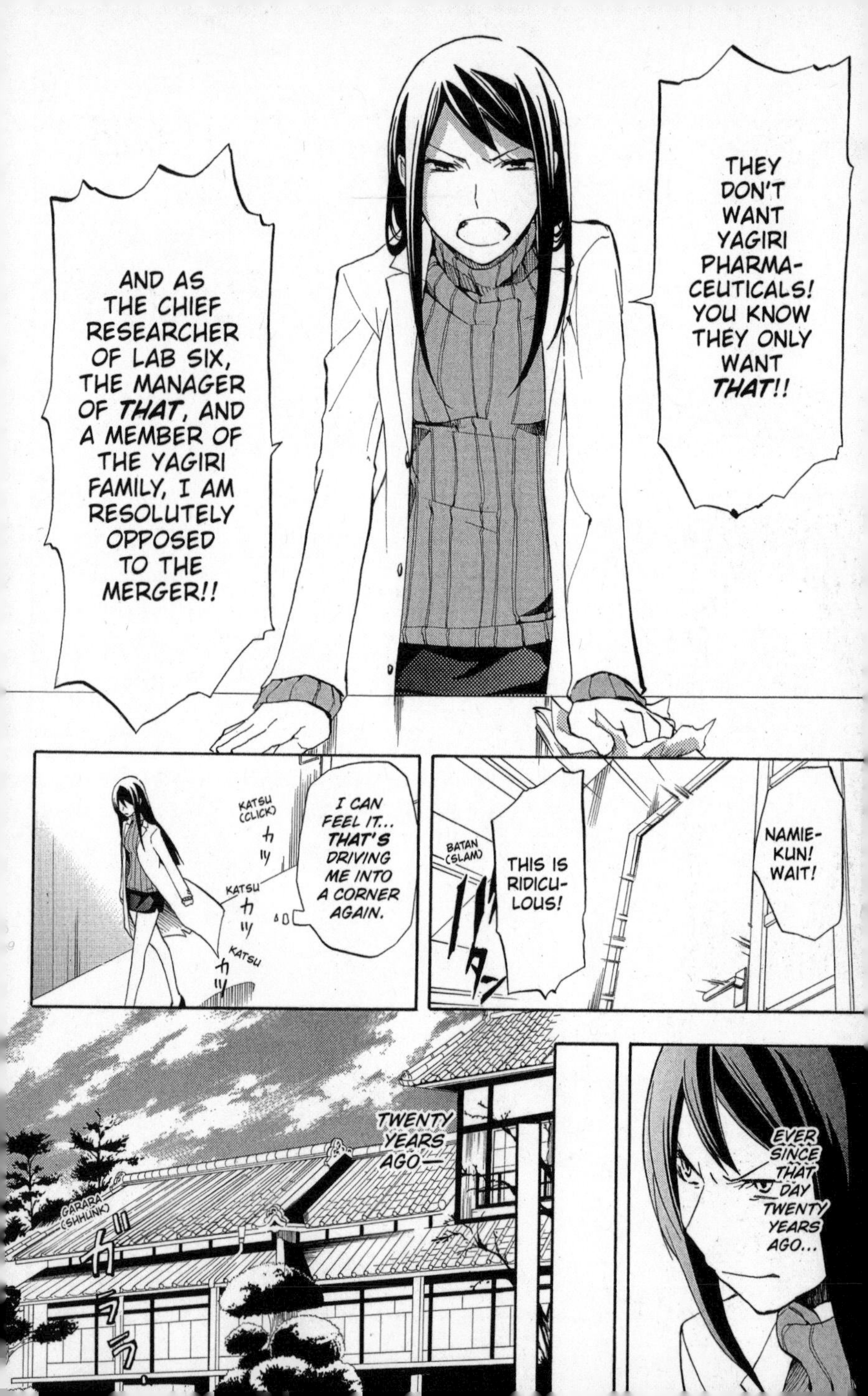
THEY DON'T WANT YAGIRI PHARMA-CEUTICALS! YOU KNOW THEY ONLY WANT *THAT*!!
AND AS THE CHIEF RESEARCHER OF LAB SIX, THE MANAGER OF *THAT*, AND A MEMBER OF THE YAGIRI FAMILY, I AM RESOLUTELY OPPOSED TO THE MERGER!!
NAMIE-KUN! WAIT!
BATAN (SLAM)
THIS IS RIDICU-LOUS!
KATSU (CLICK)
KATSU
KATSU
I CAN FEEL IT... *THAT'S* DRIVING ME INTO A CORNER AGAIN.
EVER SINCE THAT DAY TWENTY YEARS AGO...
TWENTY YEARS AGO—
GARARA (SHHLINK)

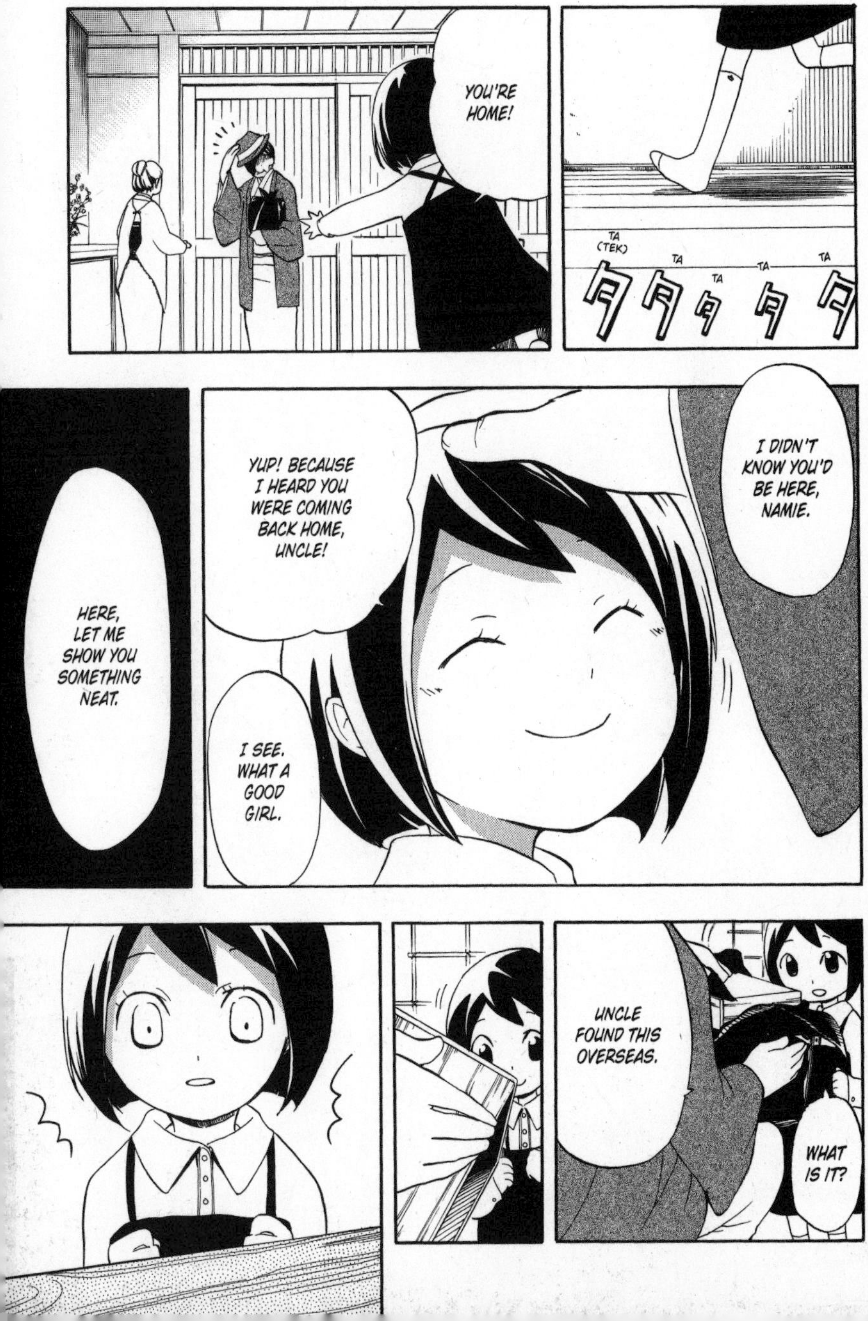
TA (TEK)
TA
TA
TA
TA
YOU'RE HOME!
I DIDN'T KNOW YOU'D BE HERE, NAMIE.
YUP! BECAUSE I HEARD YOU WERE COMING BACK HOME, UNCLE!
I SEE. WHAT A GOOD GIRL.
HERE, LET ME SHOW YOU SOMETHING NEAT.
UNCLE FOUND THIS OVERSEAS.
WHAT IS IT?

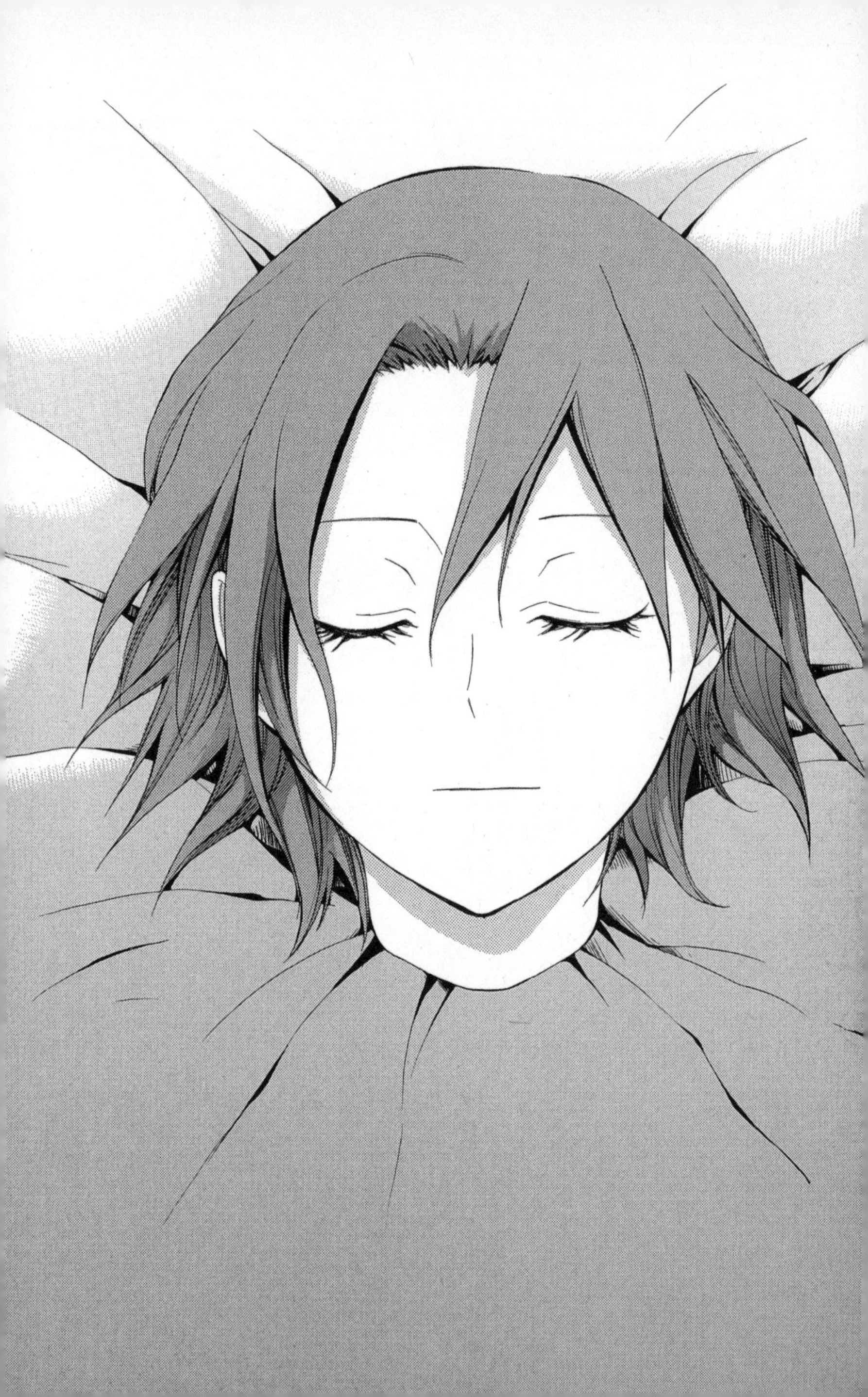

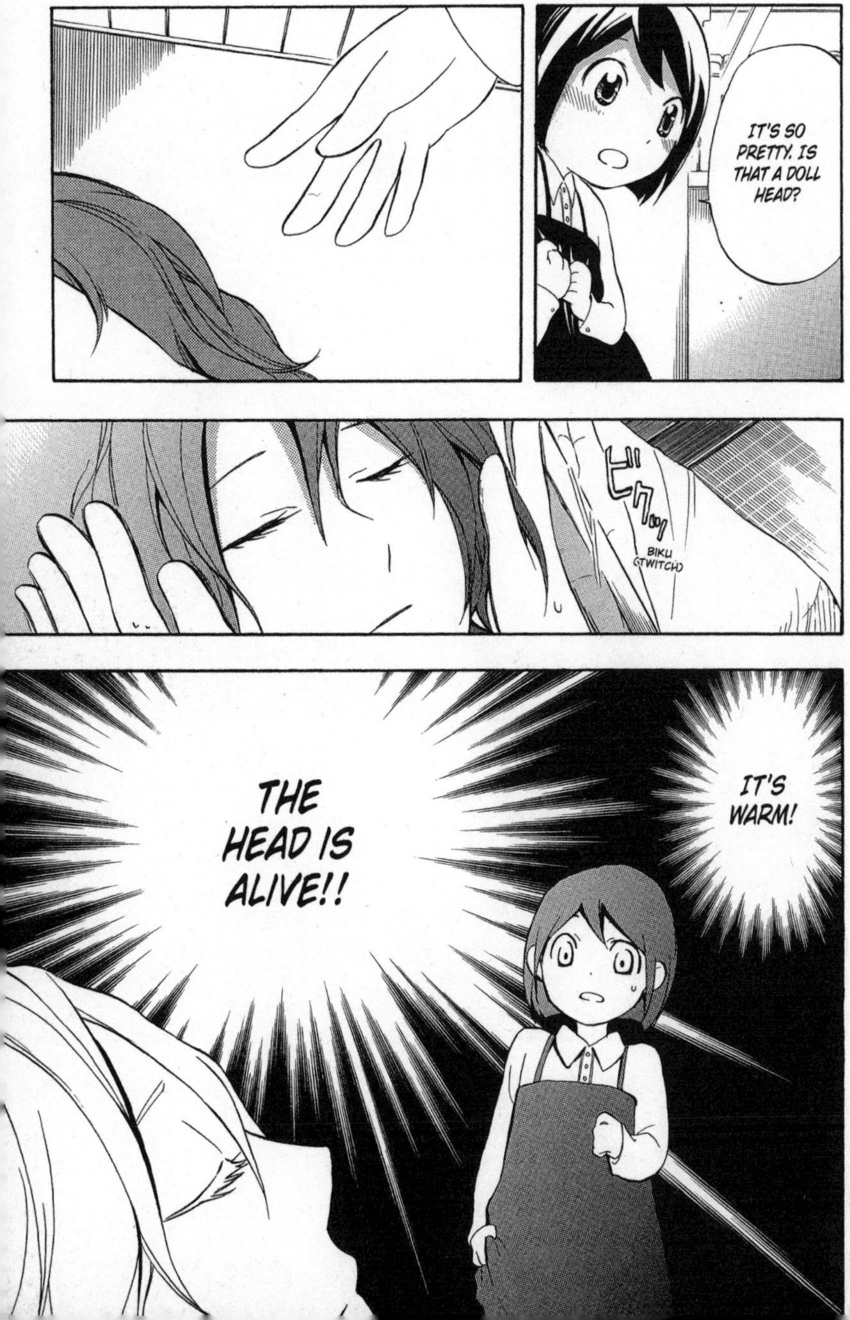
IT'S SO PRETTY. IS THAT A DOLL HEAD?
ビクッ
BIKU (TWITCH)
IT'S WARM!
THE HEAD IS ALIVE!!

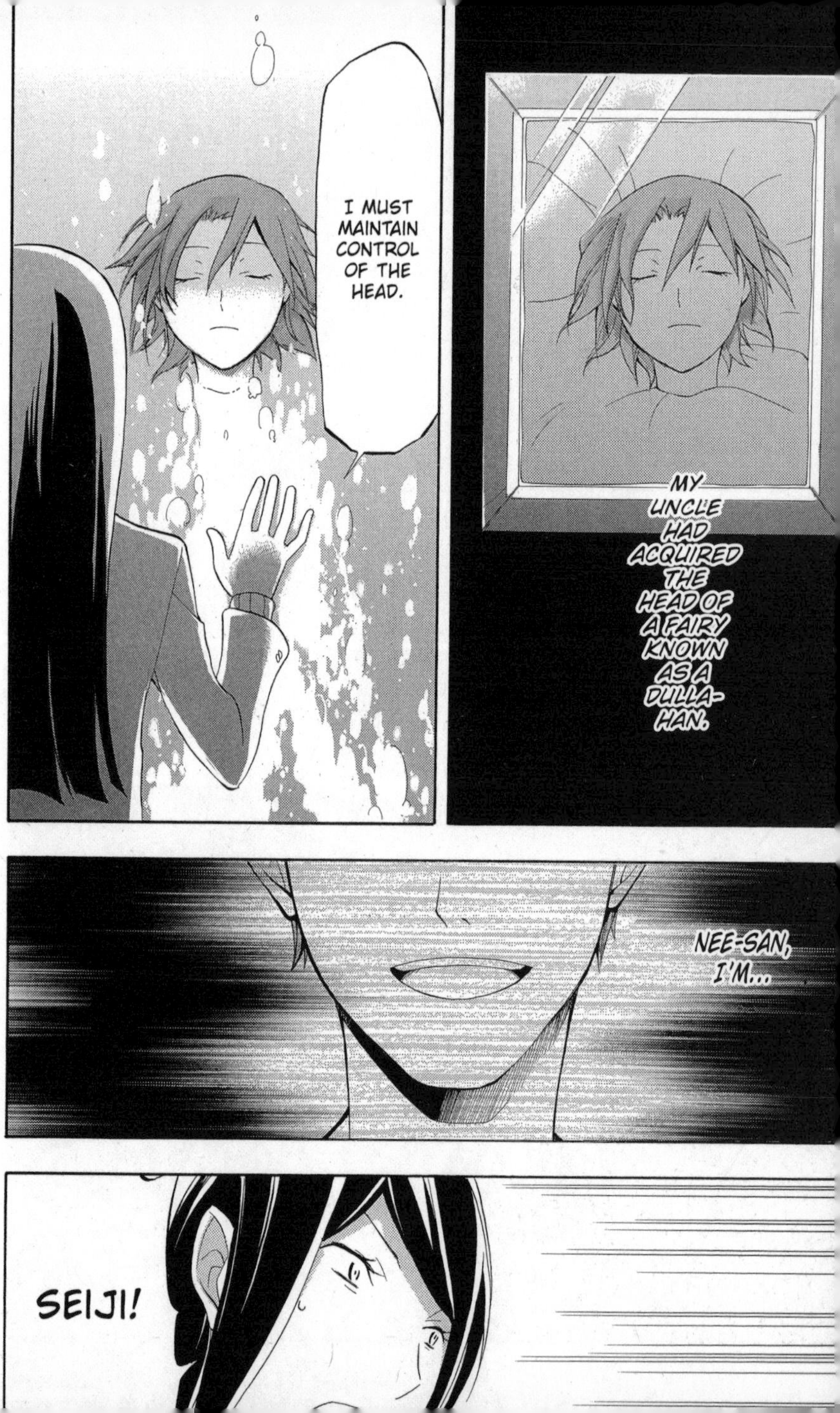
MY UNCLE HAD ACQUIRED THE HEAD OF A FAIRY KNOWN AS A DULLA-HAN.
I MUST MAINTAIN CONTROL OF THE HEAD.
NEE-SAN, I'M...
SEIJI!

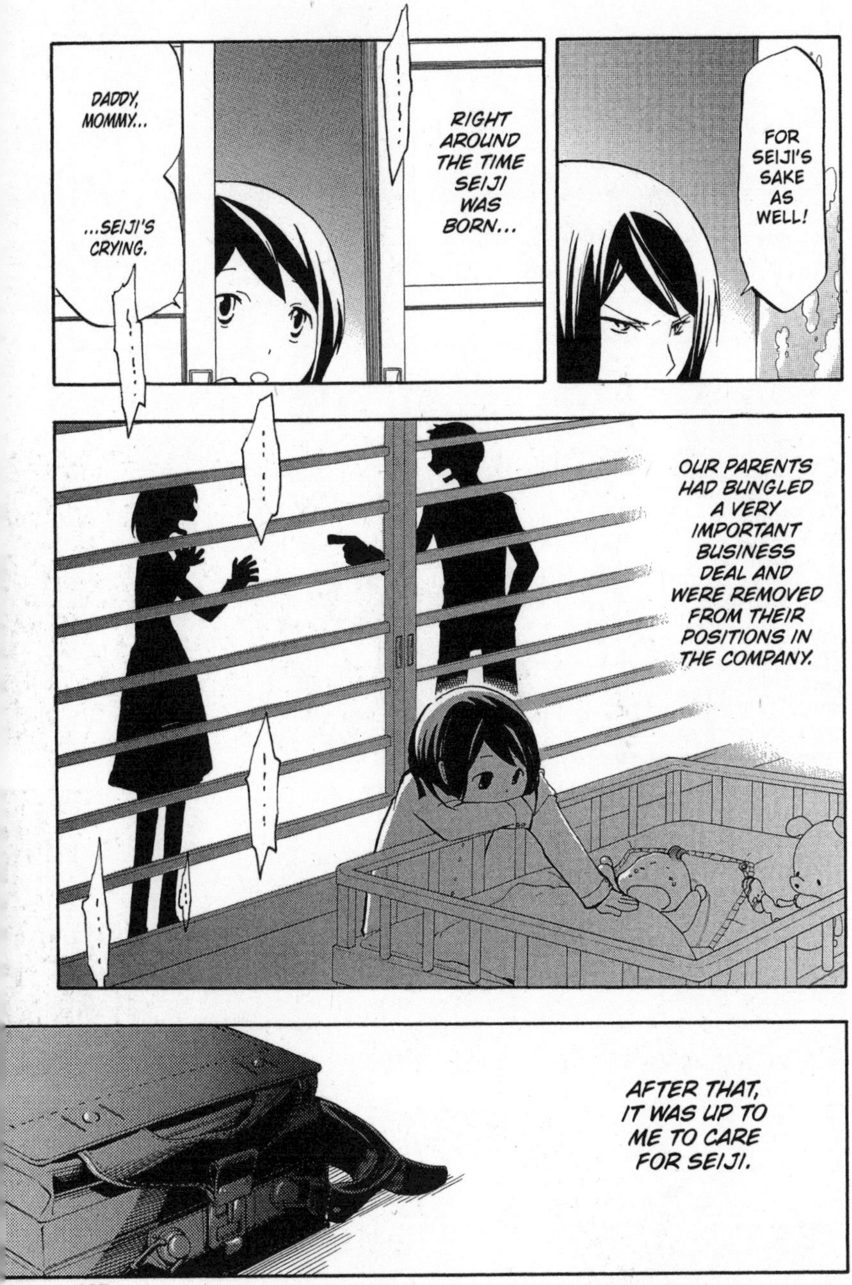
FOR SEIJI'S SAKE AS WELL!
RIGHT AROUND THE TIME SEIJI WAS BORN...
DADDY, MOMMY...
...SEIJI'S CRYING.
OUR PARENTS HAD BUNGLED A VERY IMPORTANT BUSINESS DEAL AND WERE REMOVED FROM THEIR POSITIONS IN THE COMPANY.
AFTER THAT, IT WAS UP TO ME TO CARE FOR SEIJI.

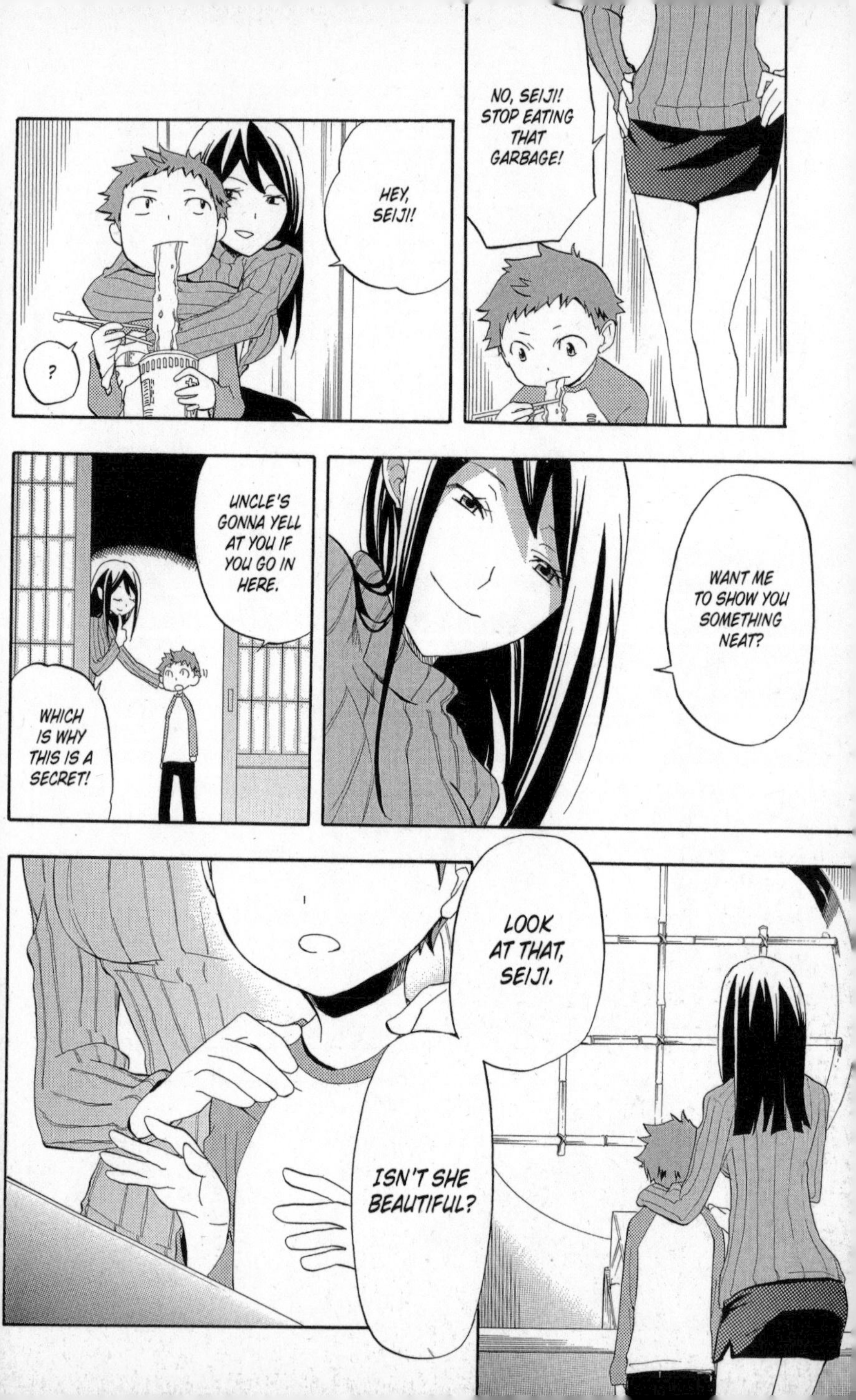
NO, SEIJI! STOP EATING THAT GARBAGE!
HEY, SEIJI!
?
WANT ME TO SHOW YOU SOMETHING NEAT?
UNCLE'S GONNA YELL AT YOU IF YOU GO IN HERE.
WHICH IS WHY THIS IS A SECRET!
LOOK AT THAT, SEIJI.
ISN'T SHE BEAUTIFUL?

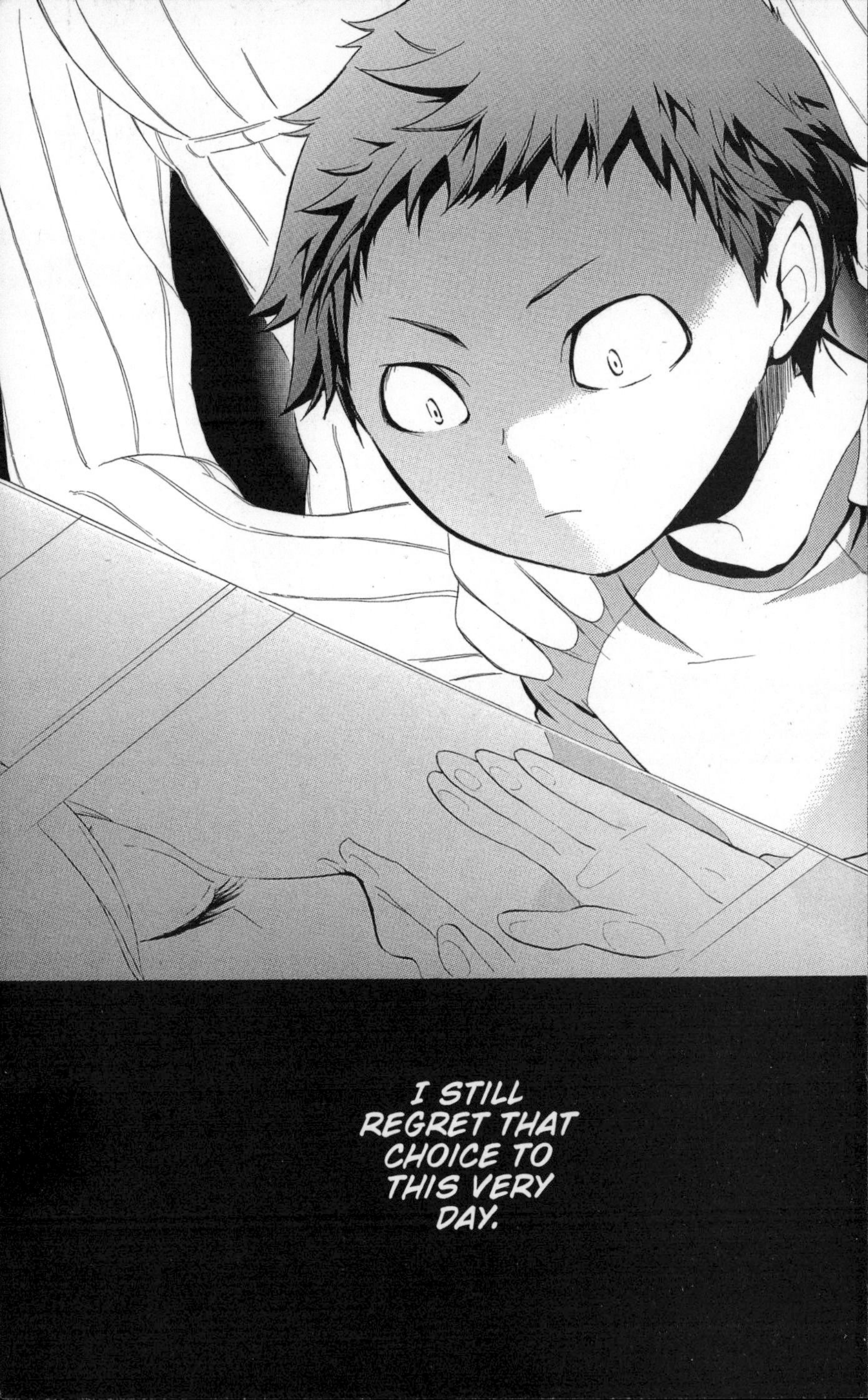
I STILL REGRET THAT CHOICE TO THIS VERY DAY.

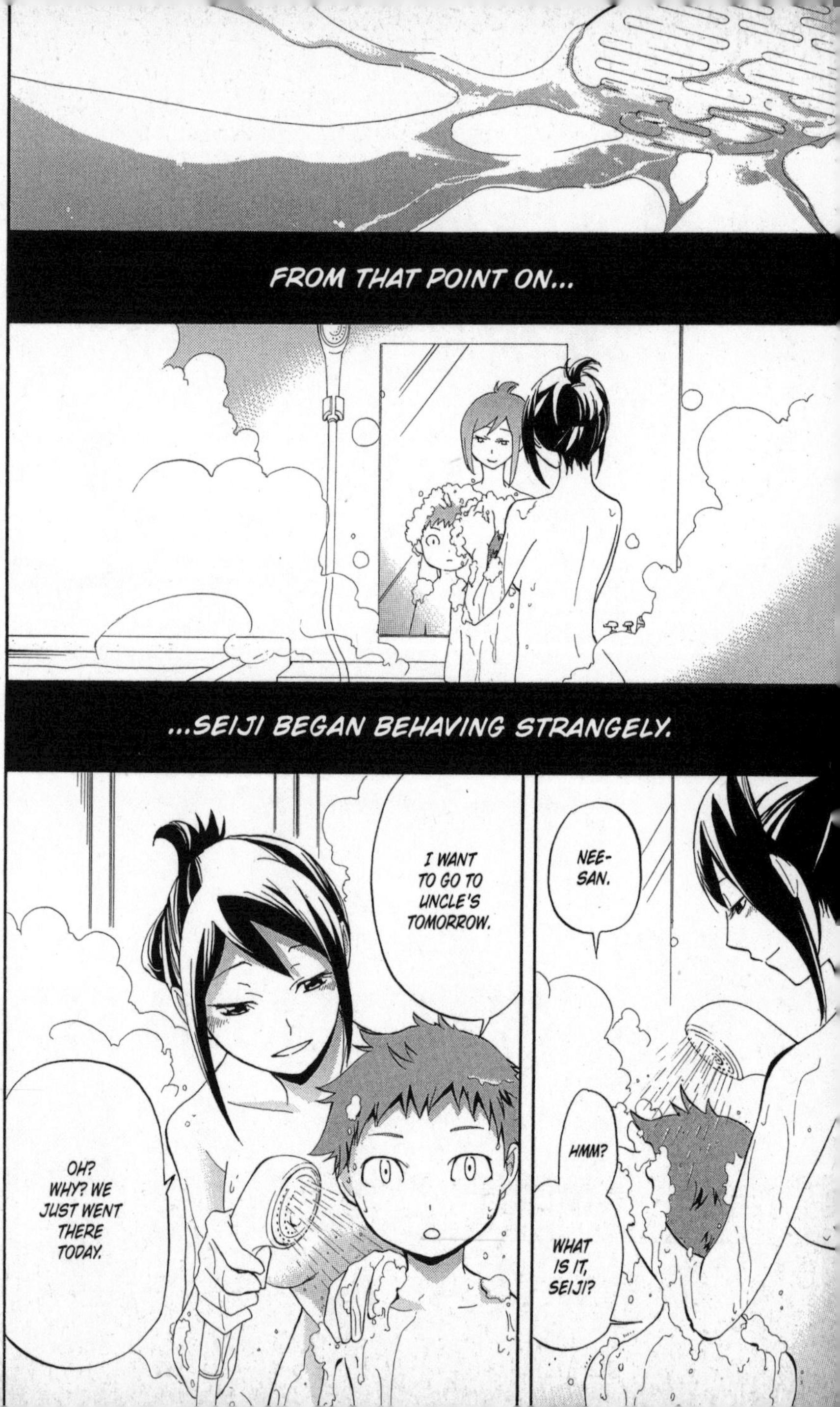
FROM THAT POINT ON...
...SEIJI BEGAN BEHAVING STRANGELY.
NEE-SAN.
HMM?
WHAT IS IT, SEIJI?
I WANT TO GO TO UNCLE'S TOMORROW.
OH? WHY? WE JUST WENT THERE TODAY.

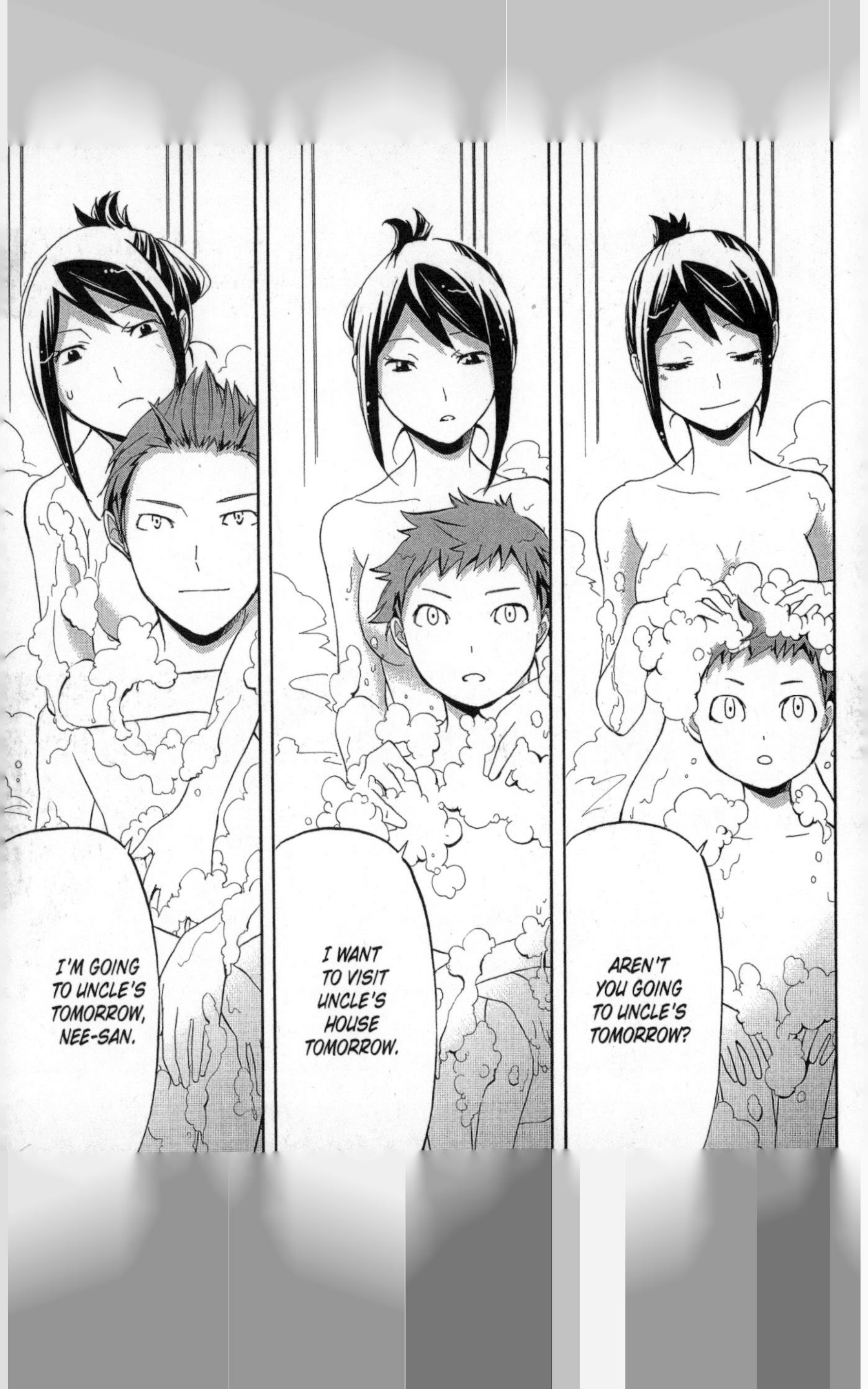
AREN'T YOU GOING TO UNCLE'S TOMORROW?
I WANT TO VISIT UNCLE'S HOUSE TOMORROW.
I'M GOING TO UNCLE'S TOMORROW, NEE-SAN.

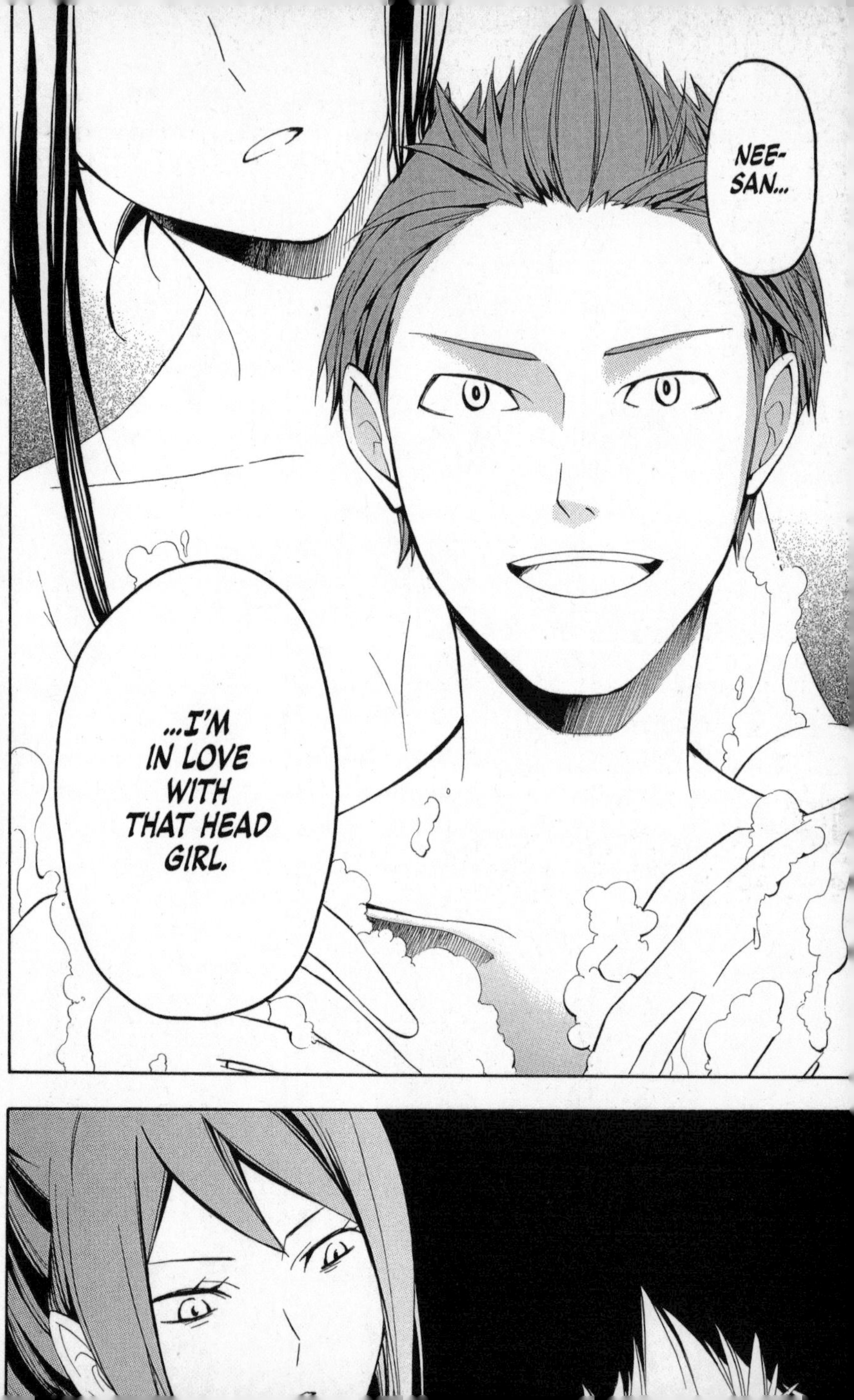
NEE-SAN...
...I'M IN LOVE WITH THAT HEAD GIRL.

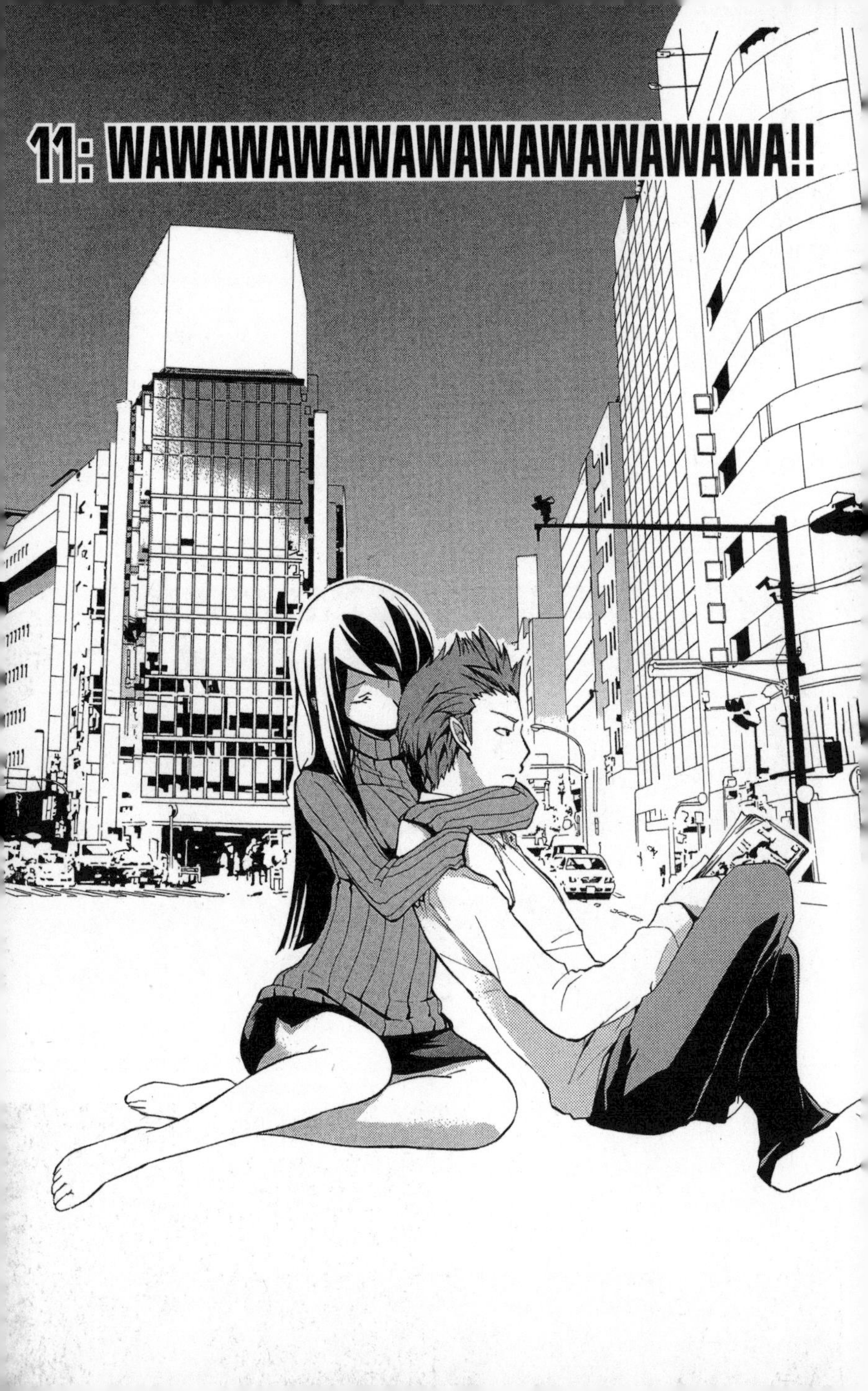
11: WAWAWAWAWAWAWAWAWAWAWAWA!!

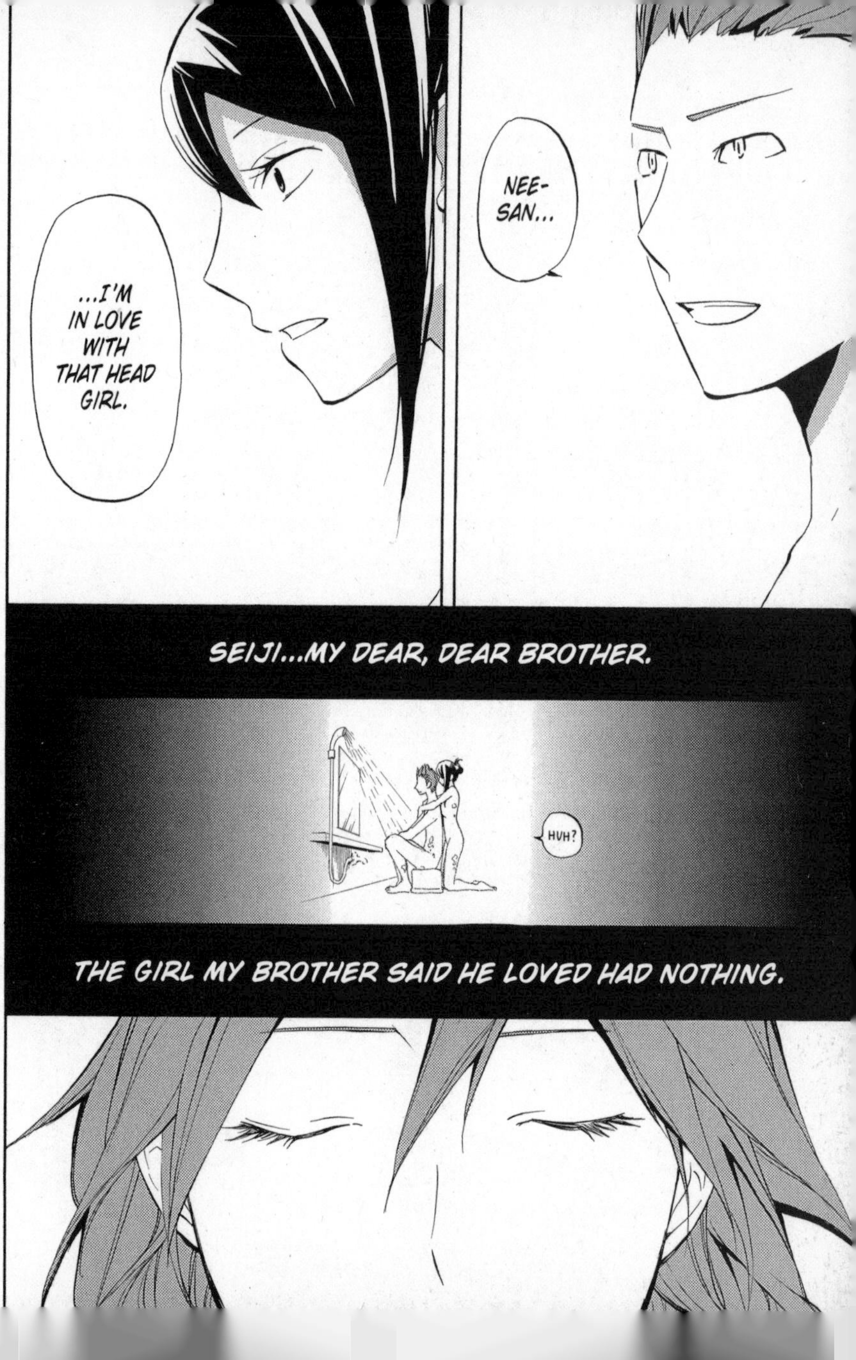
NEE-SAN...
...I'M IN LOVE WITH THAT HEAD GIRL.
SEIJI...MY DEAR, DEAR BROTHER.
HUH?
THE GIRL MY BROTHER SAID HE LOVED HAD NOTHING.

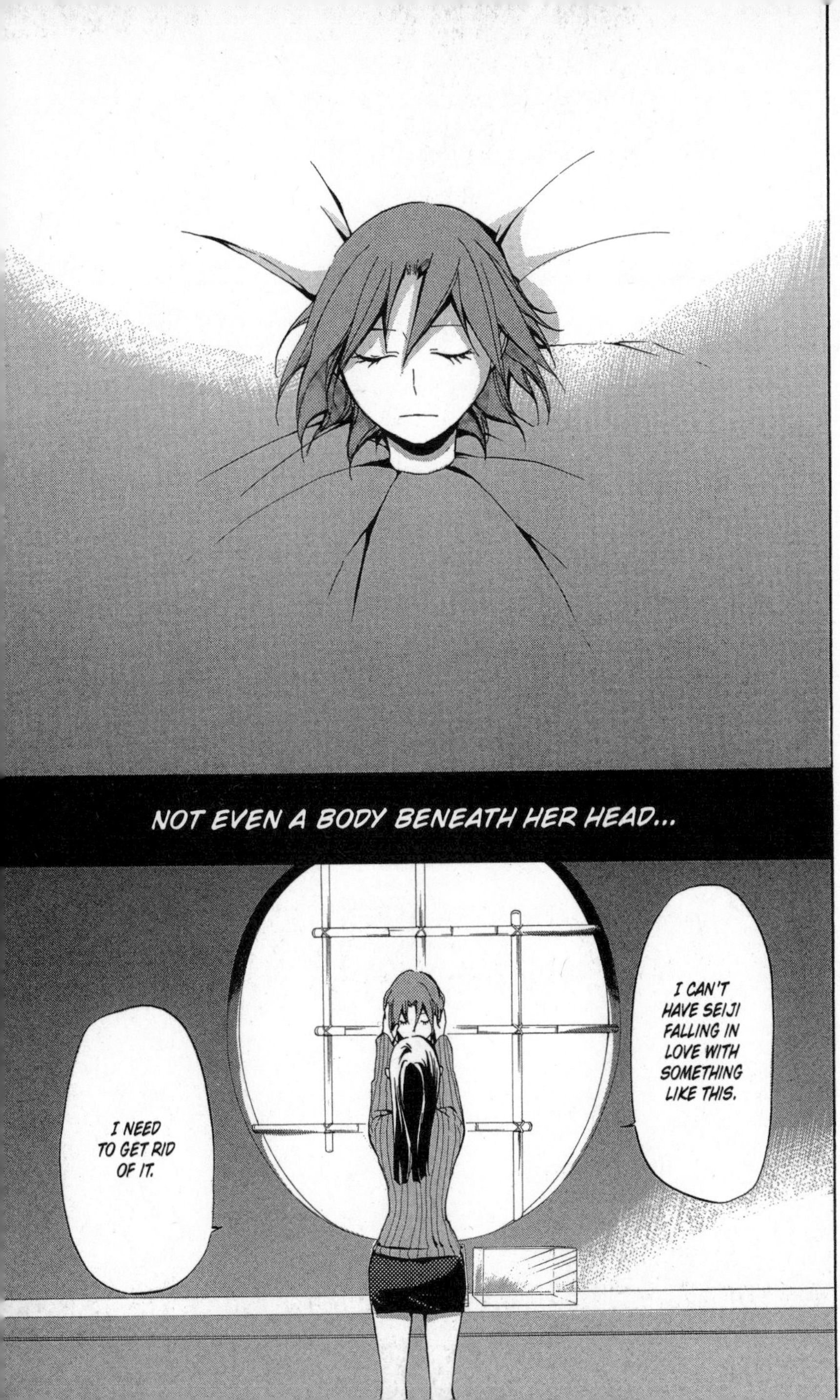
NOT EVEN A BODY BENEATH HER HEAD...
I CAN'T HAVE SEIJI FALLING IN LOVE WITH SOMETHING LIKE THIS.
I NEED TO GET RID OF IT.

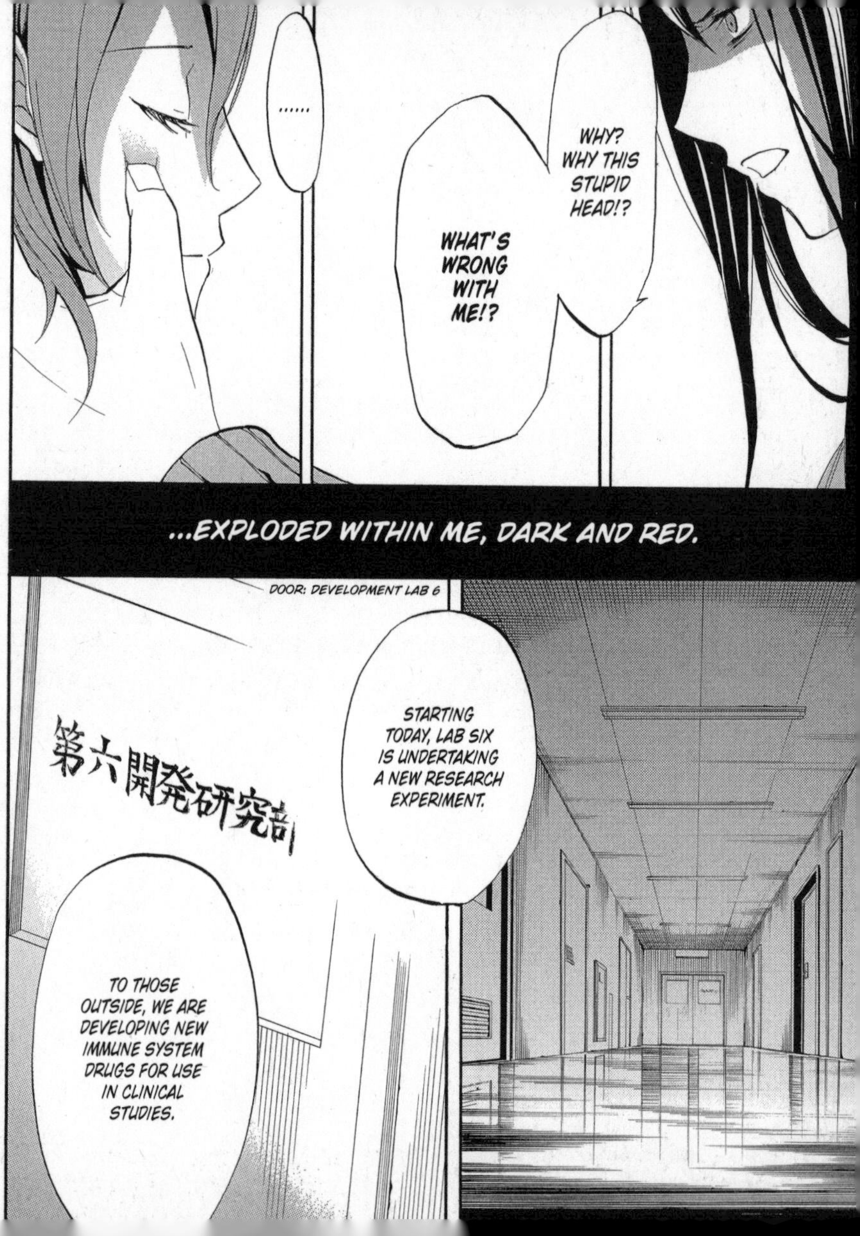
WHY? WHY THIS STUPID HEAD!?
WHAT'S WRONG WITH ME!?
......
...EXPLODED WITHIN ME, DARK AND RED.
STARTING TODAY, LAB SIX IS UNDERTAKING A NEW RESEARCH EXPERIMENT.
DOOR: DEVELOPMENT LAB 6
第六開発研究部
TO THOSE OUTSIDE, WE ARE DEVELOPING NEW IMMUNE SYSTEM DRUGS FOR USE IN CLINICAL STUDIES.

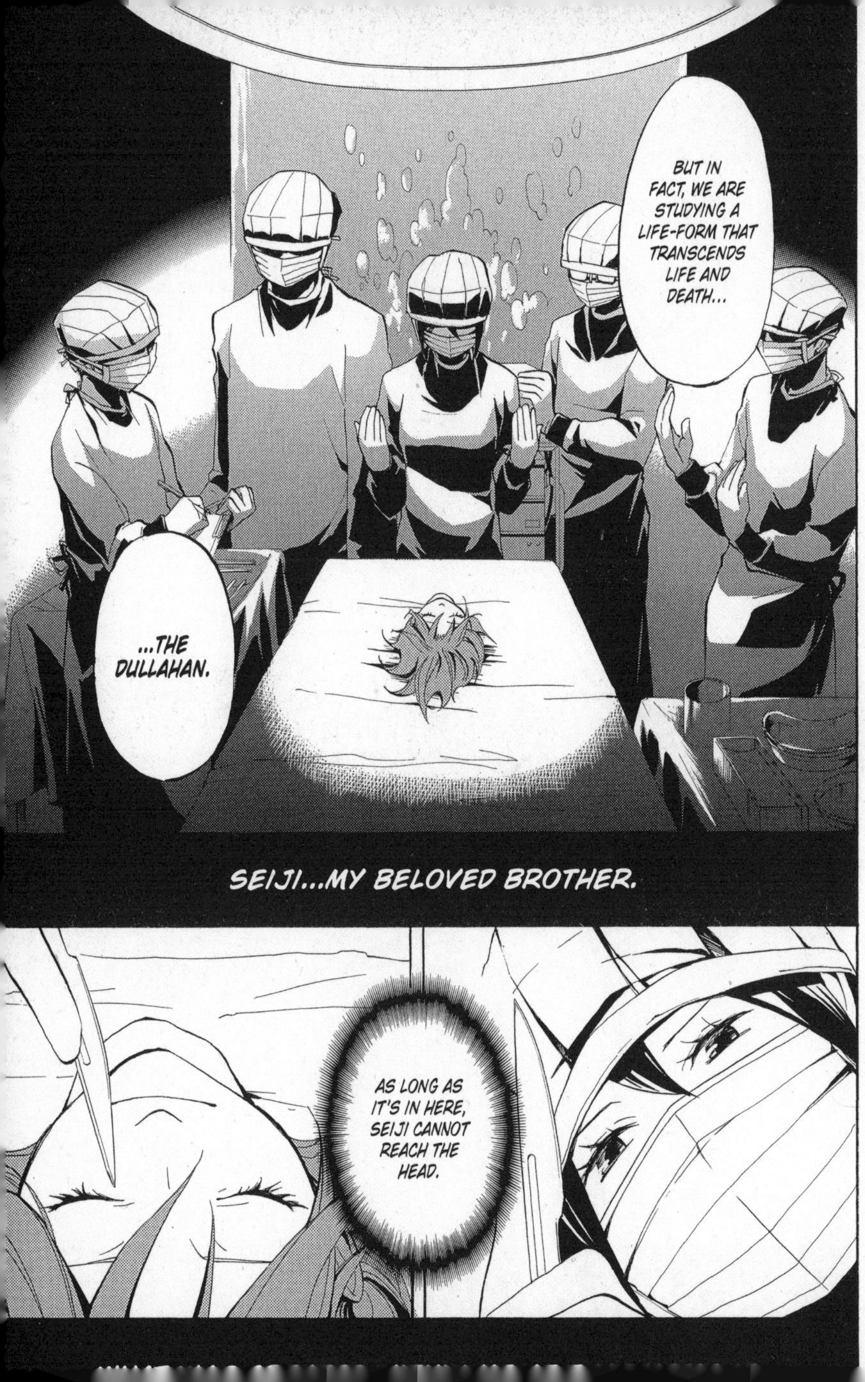
BUT IN FACT, WE ARE STUDYING A LIFE-FORM THAT TRANSCENDS LIFE AND DEATH...
...THE DULLAHAN.
SEIJI...MY BELOVED BROTHER.
AS LONG AS IT'S IN HERE, SEIJI CANNOT REACH THE HEAD.

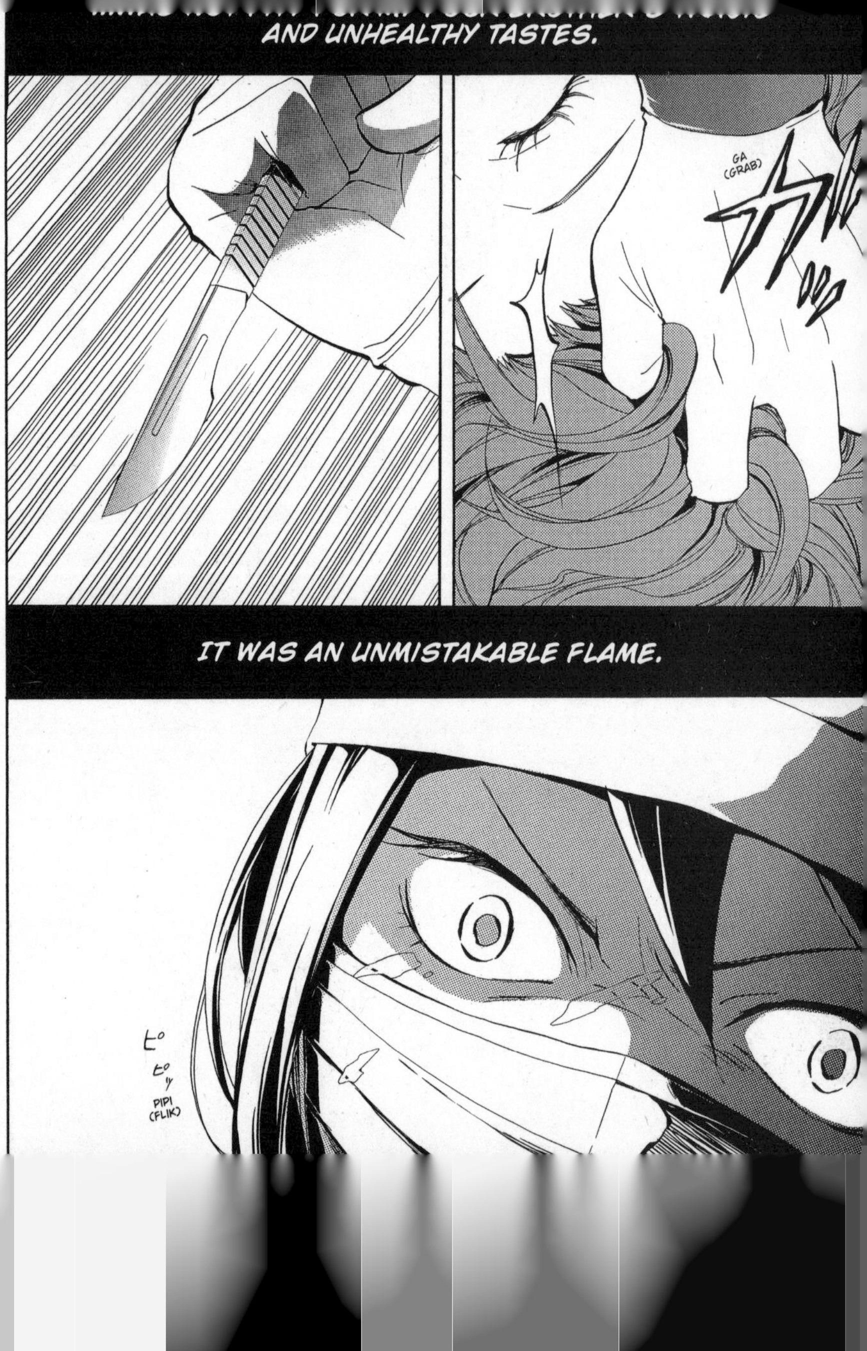
AND UNHEALTHY TASTES.
ガッ
GA (GRAB)
IT WAS AN UNMISTAKABLE FLAME.
ピピッ
PIPI (FLIK)

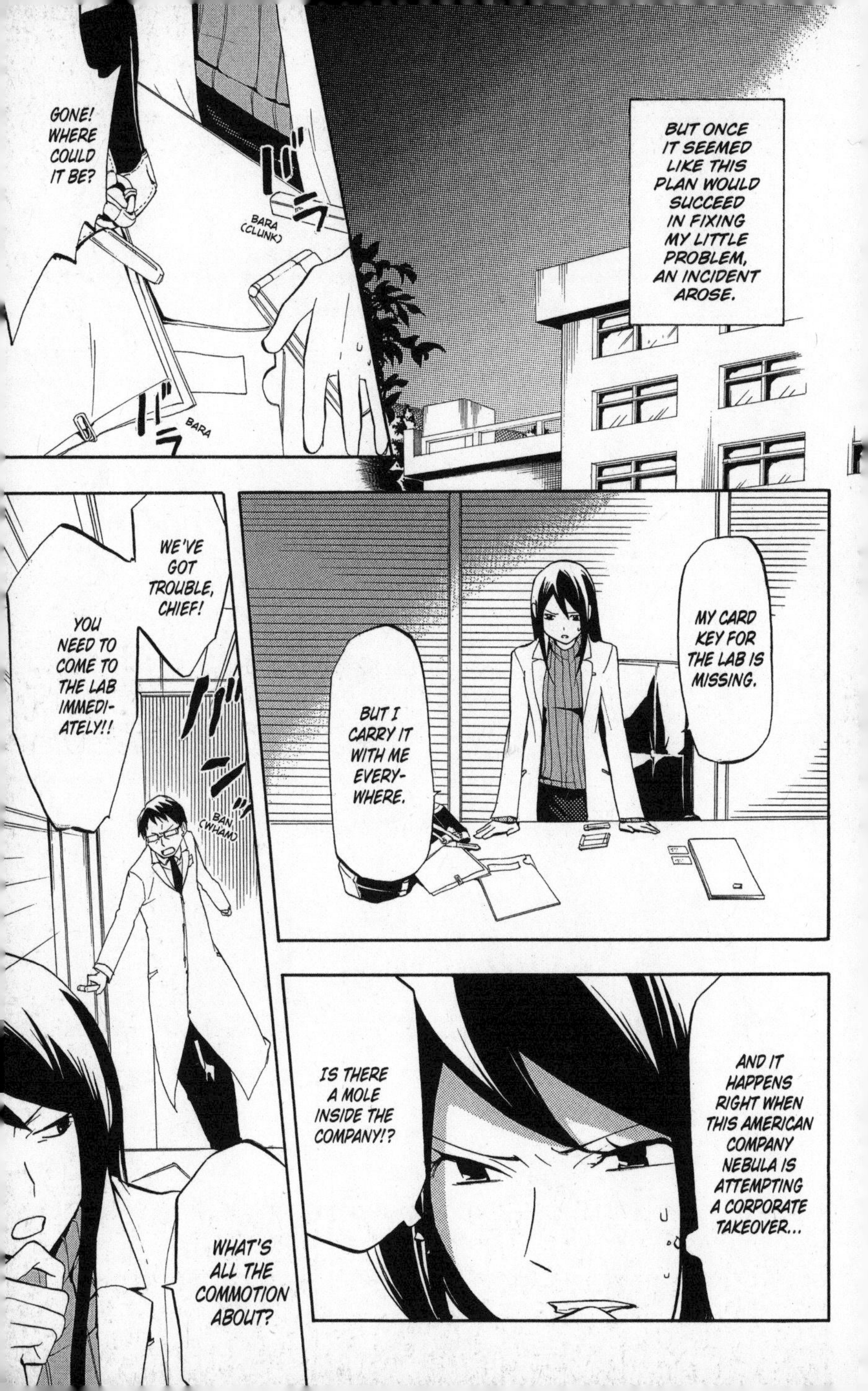
BUT ONCE IT SEEMED LIKE THIS PLAN WOULD SUCCEED IN FIXING MY LITTLE PROBLEM, AN INCIDENT AROSE.
GONE! WHERE COULD IT BE?
BARA (CLUNK)
BARA
MY CARD KEY FOR THE LAB IS MISSING.
BUT I CARRY IT WITH ME EVERYWHERE.
AND IT HAPPENS RIGHT WHEN THIS AMERICAN COMPANY NEBULA IS ATTEMPTING A CORPORATE TAKEOVER...
IS THERE A MOLE INSIDE THE COMPANY!?
WE'VE GOT TROUBLE, CHIEF!
YOU NEED TO COME TO THE LAB IMMEDIATELY!!
BAN (WHAM)
WHAT'S ALL THE COMMOTION ABOUT?

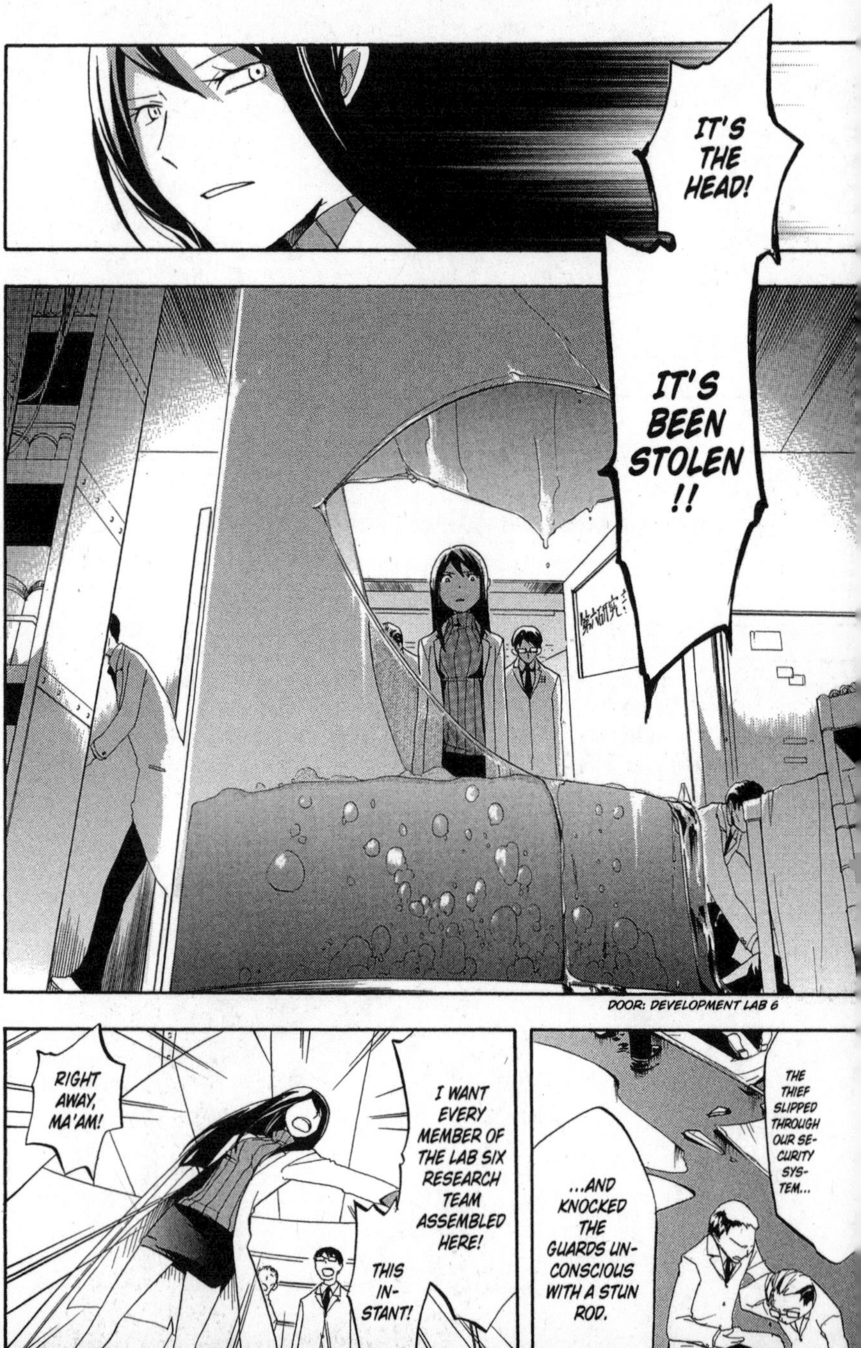
IT'S THE HEAD!
IT'S BEEN STOLEN!!
DOOR: DEVELOPMENT LAB 6
THE THIEF SLIPPED THROUGH OUR SE-CURITY SYS-TEM...
...AND KNOCKED THE GUARDS UN-CONSCIOUS WITH A STUN ROD.
I WANT EVERY MEMBER OF THE LAB SIX RESEARCH TEAM ASSEMBLED HERE!
THIS IN-STANT!
RIGHT AWAY, MA'AM!

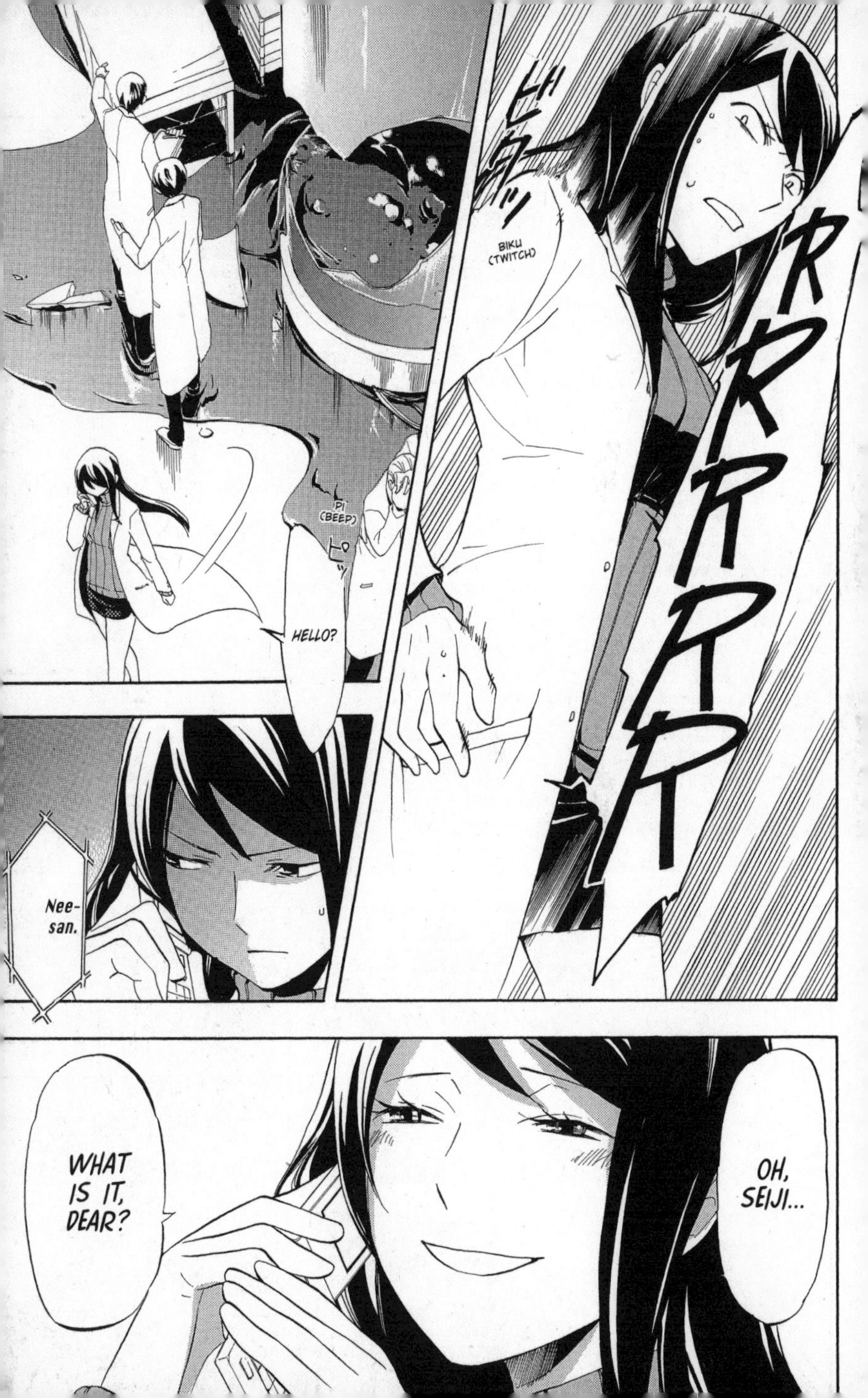
RRRRRR
ビクッ
BIKU (TWITCH)
ピッ
PI (BEEP)
HELLO?
Nee-san.
OH, SEIJI...
WHAT IS IT, DEAR?

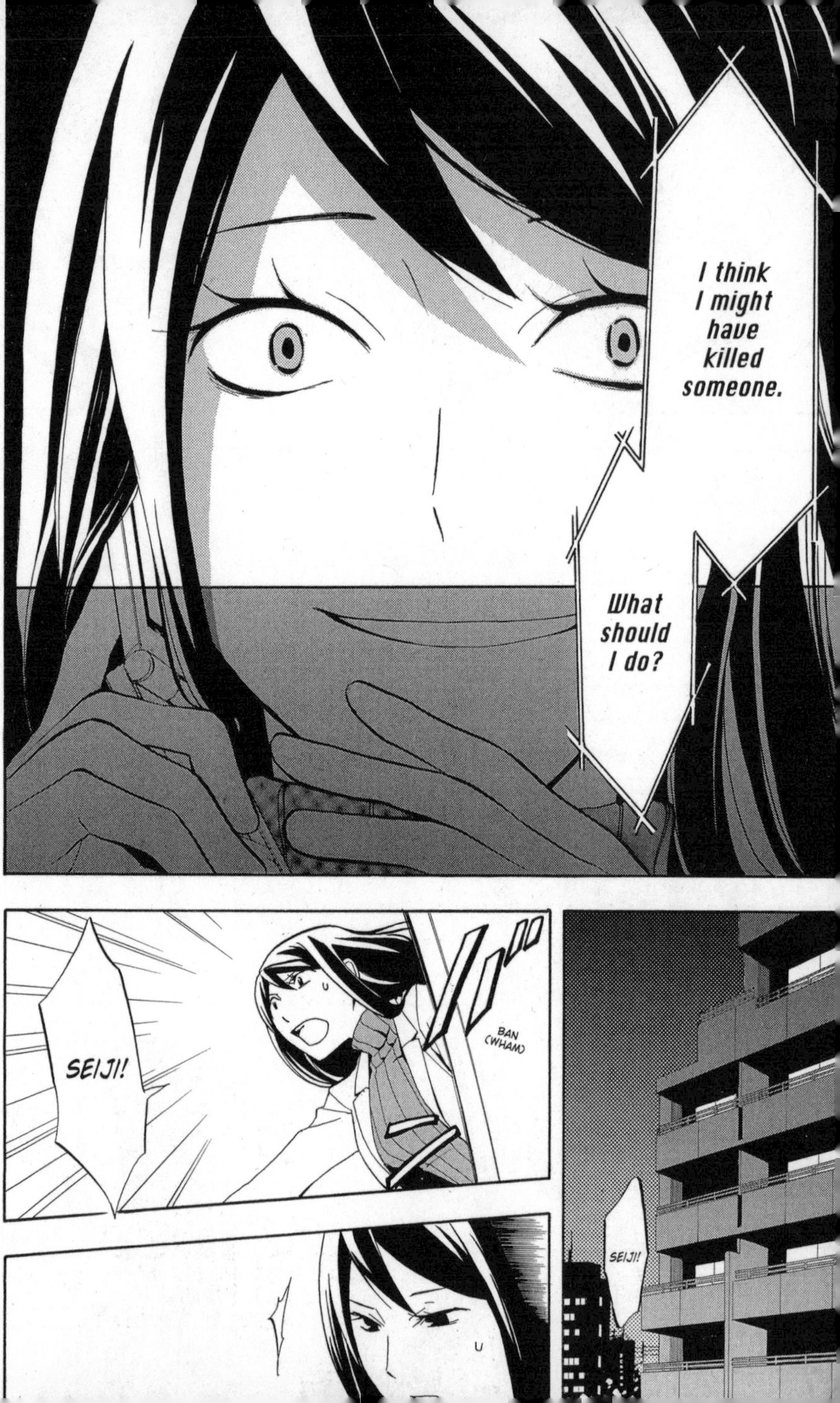
I think I might have killed someone.
What should I do?
SEIJI!
SEIJI!
BAN (WHAM)
U

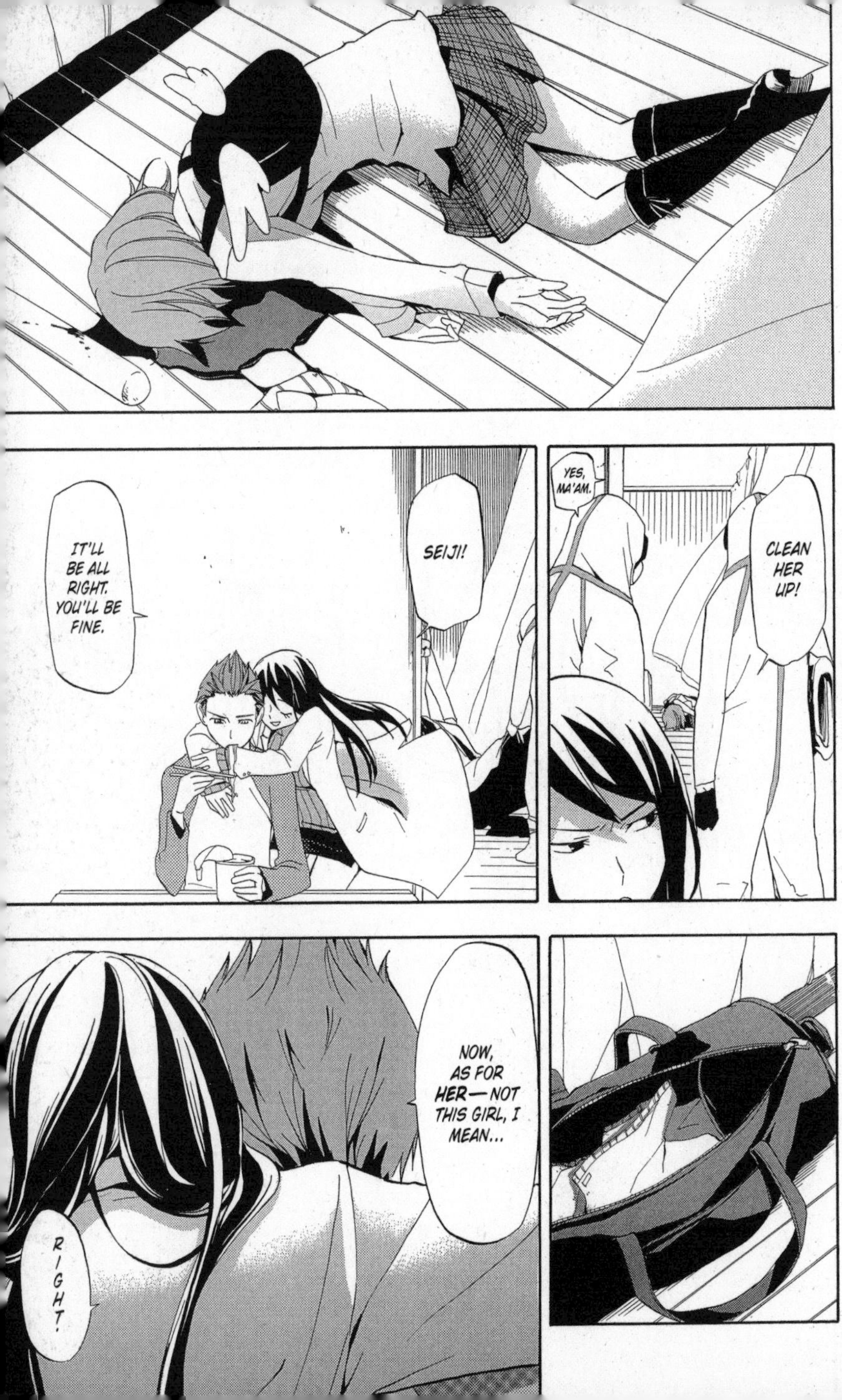
CLEAN HER UP!
YES, MA'AM.
SEIJI!
IT'LL BE ALL RIGHT. YOU'LL BE FINE.
NOW, AS FOR HER—NOT THIS GIRL, I MEAN...
RIGHT.

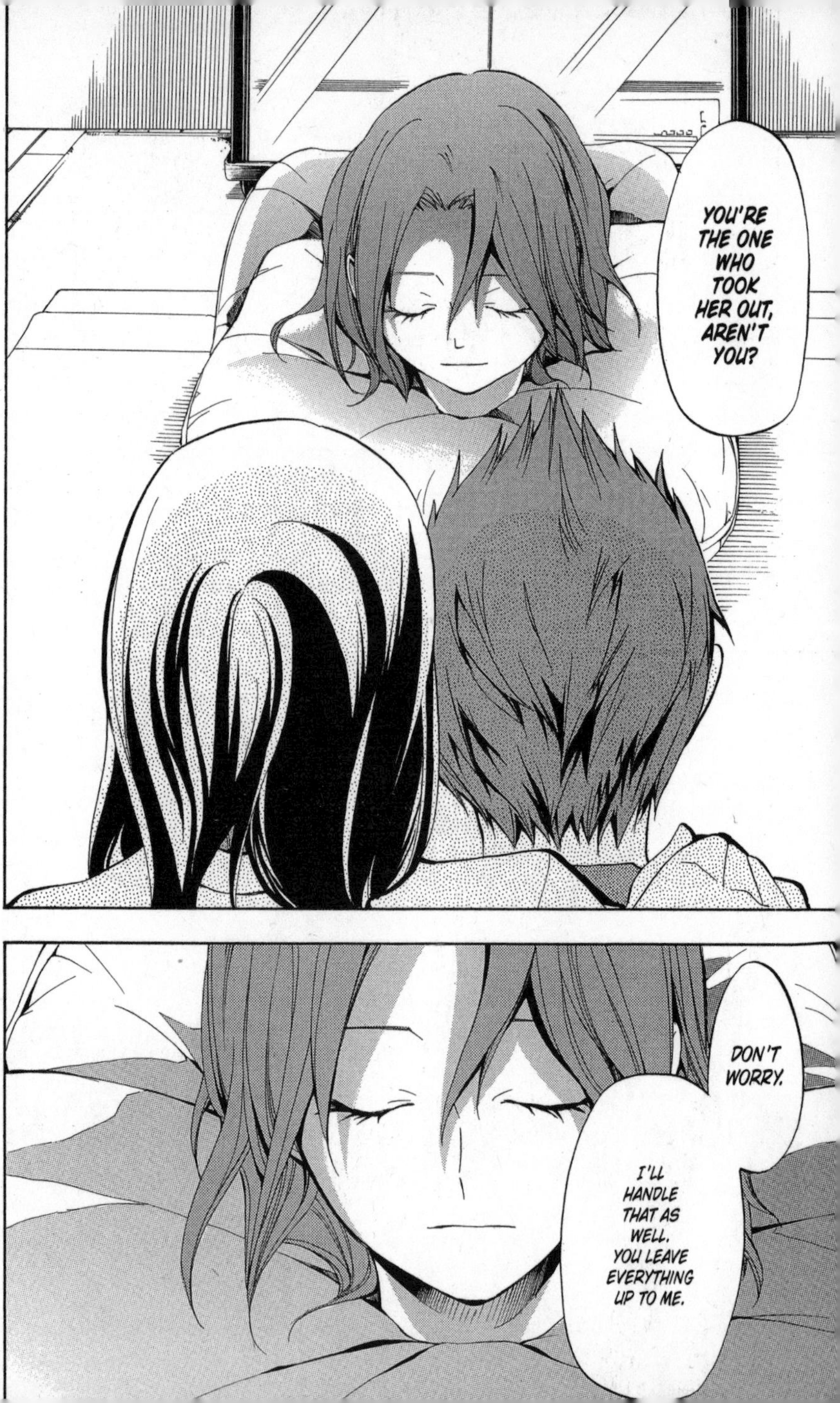
YOU'RE THE ONE WHO TOOK HER OUT, AREN'T YOU?
DON'T WORRY.
I'LL HANDLE THAT AS WELL. YOU LEAVE EVERYTHING UP TO ME.

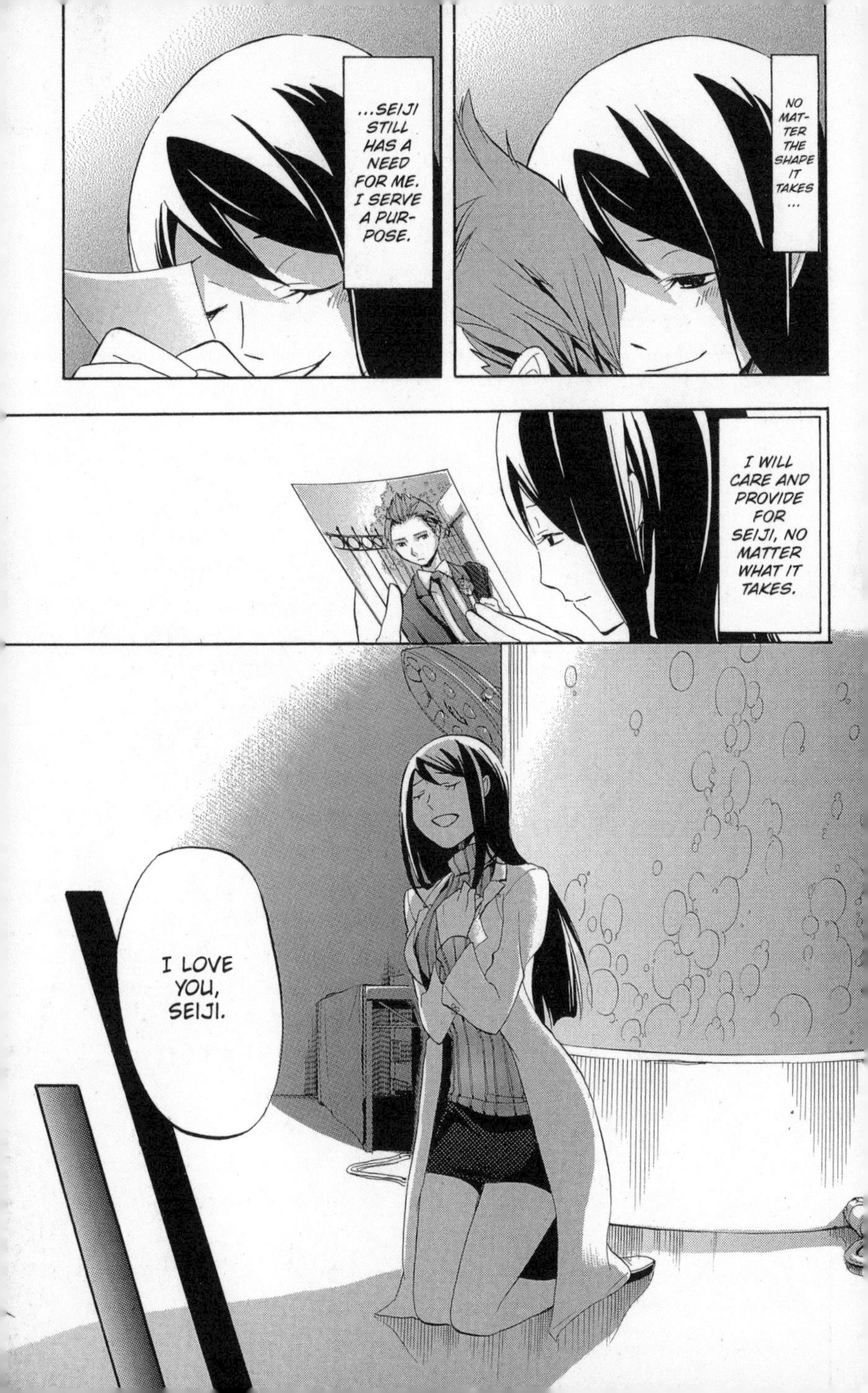
NO MATTER THE SHAPE IT TAKES...
...SEIJI STILL HAS A NEED FOR ME. I SERVE A PURPOSE.
I WILL CARE AND PROVIDE FOR SEIJI, NO MATTER WHAT IT TAKES.
I LOVE YOU, SEIJI.

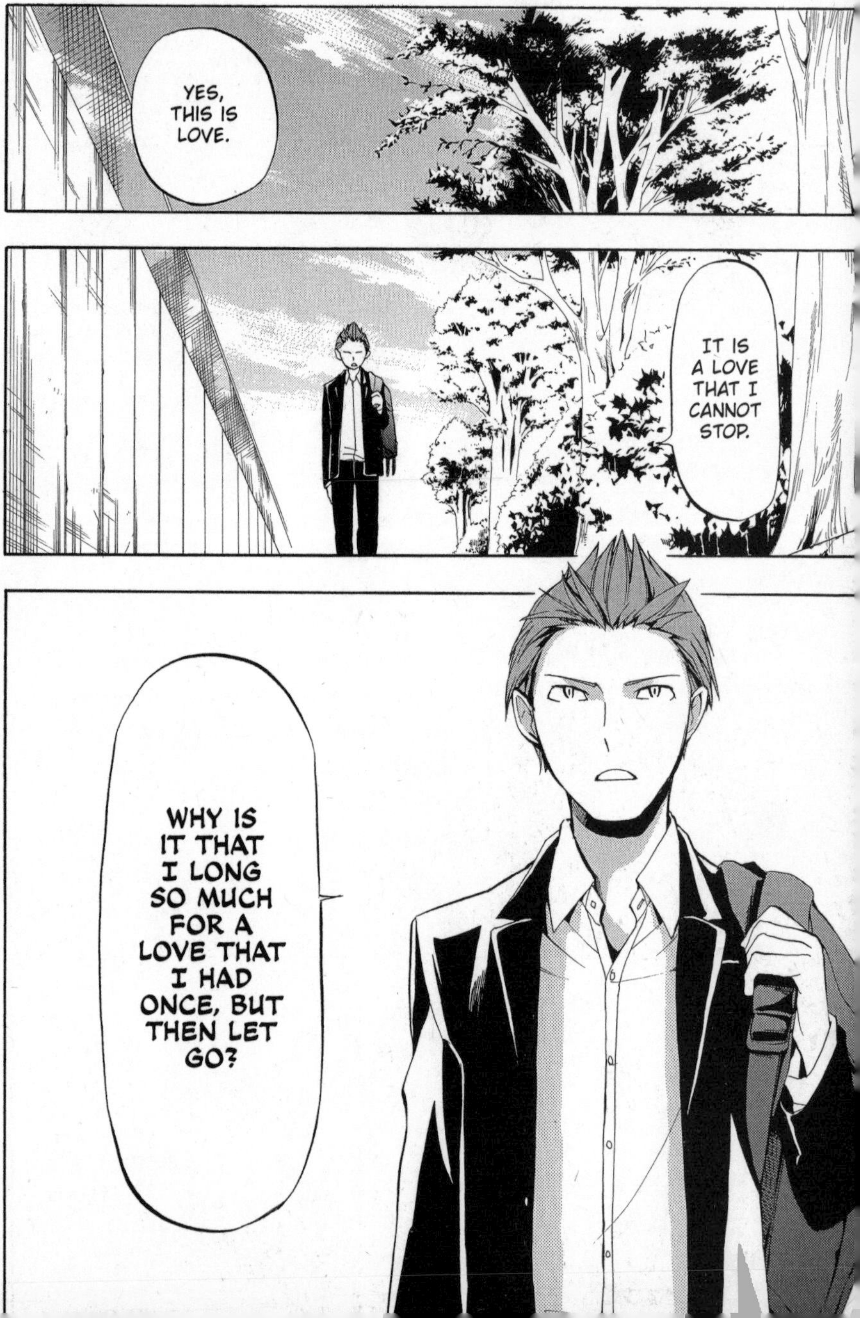
YES, THIS IS LOVE.
IT IS A LOVE THAT I CANNOT STOP.
WHY IS IT THAT I LONG SO MUCH FOR A LOVE THAT I HAD ONCE, BUT THEN LET GO?

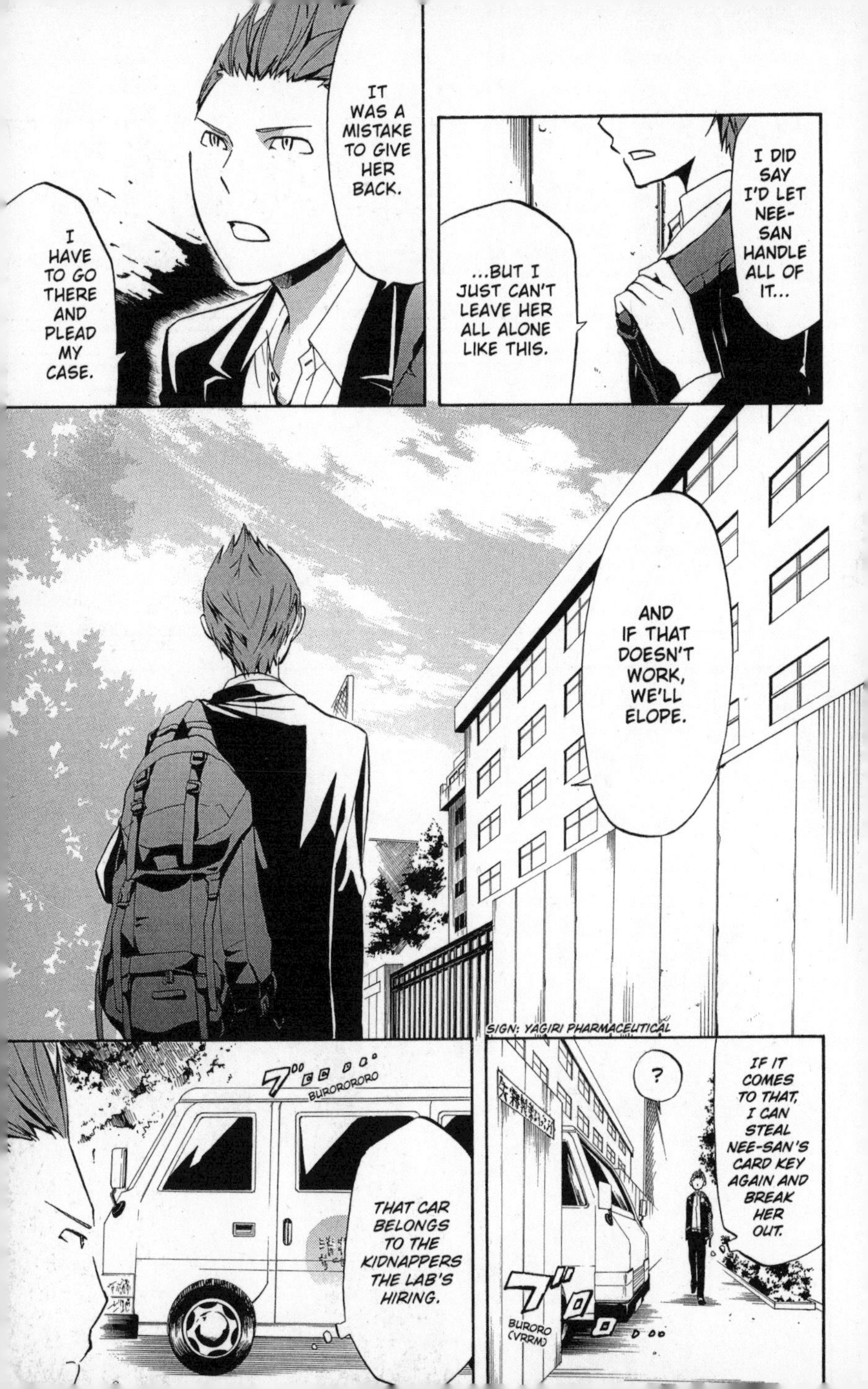
I DID SAY I'D LET NEE-SAN HANDLE ALL OF IT...
...BUT I JUST CAN'T LEAVE HER ALL ALONE LIKE THIS.
IT WAS A MISTAKE TO GIVE HER BACK.
I HAVE TO GO THERE AND PLEAD MY CASE.
AND IF THAT DOESN'T WORK, WE'LL ELOPE.
SIGN: YAGIRI PHARMACEUTICAL
IF IT COMES TO THAT, I CAN STEAL NEE-SAN'S CARD KEY AGAIN AND BREAK HER OUT.
?
BURORO (VRRM)
BURORORO
THAT CAR BELONGS TO THE KIDNAPPERS THE LAB'S HIRING.

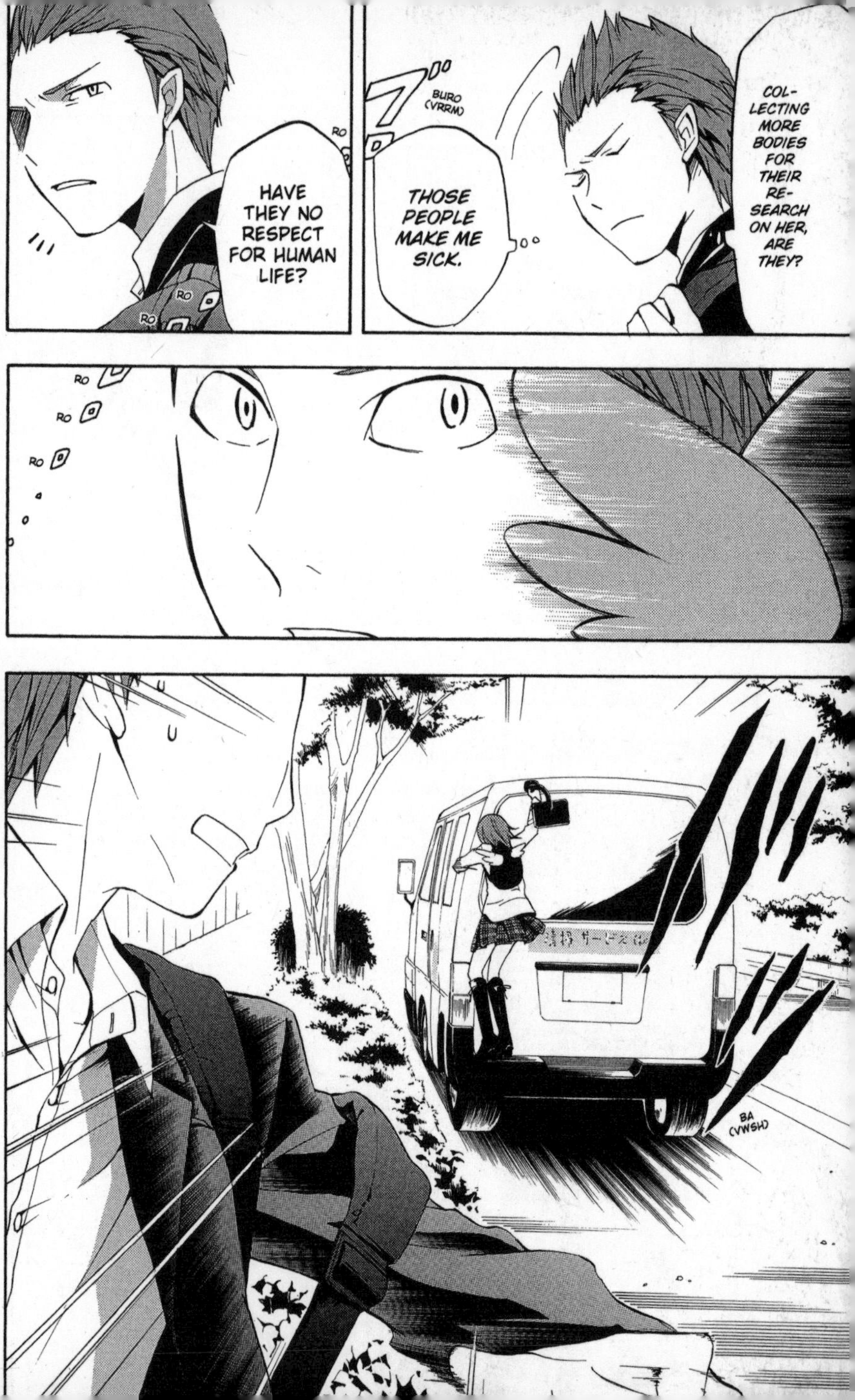
COL-LECTING MORE BODIES FOR THEIR RE-SEARCH ON HER, ARE THEY?
BURO (VRRM)
THOSE PEOPLE MAKE ME SICK.
RO
HAVE THEY NO RESPECT FOR HUMAN LIFE?
RO
RO
RO
RO
RO
BA (VWSH)

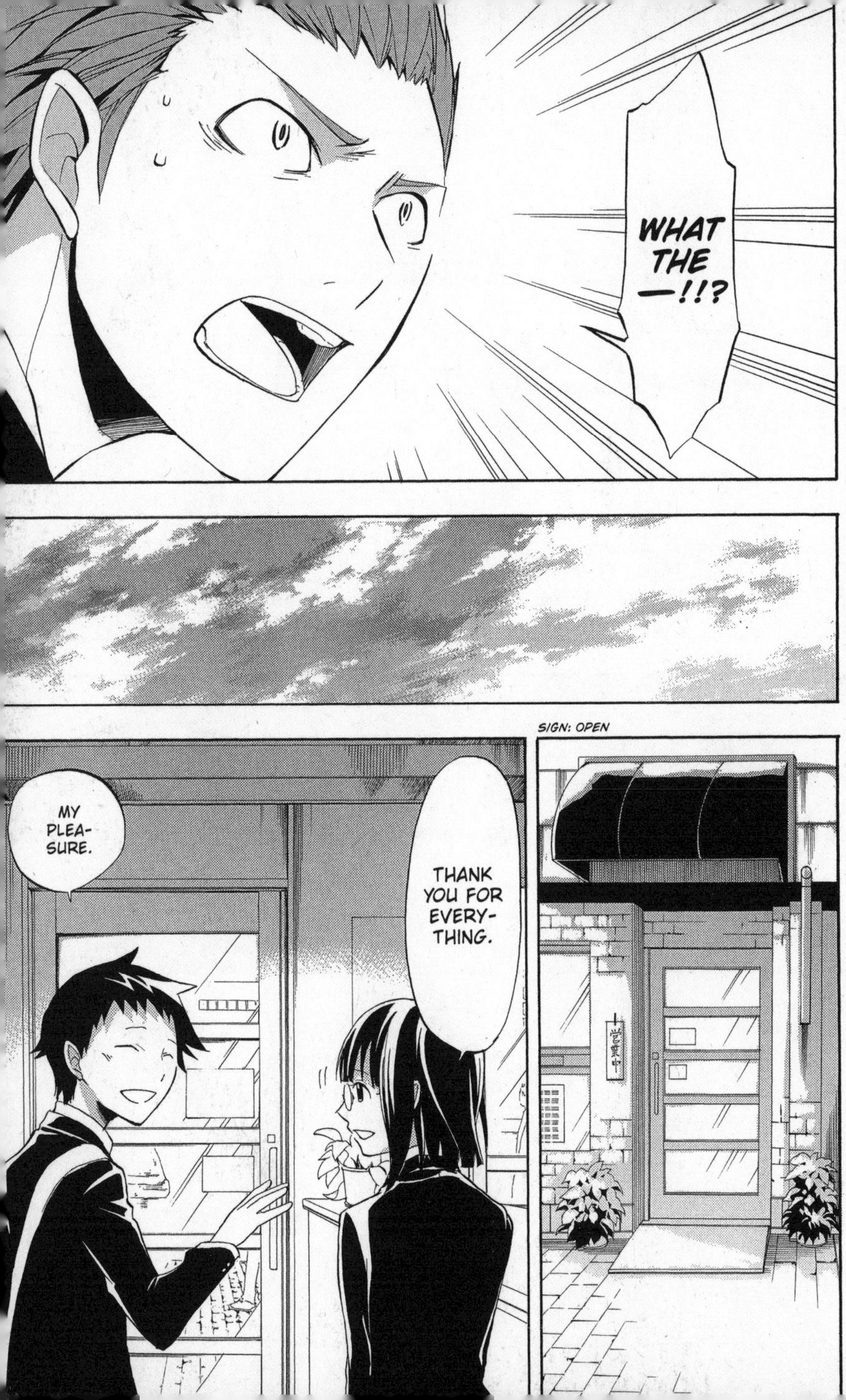

WHAT THE—!!?
SIGN: OPEN
THANK YOU FOR EVERY-THING.
MY PLEA-SURE.

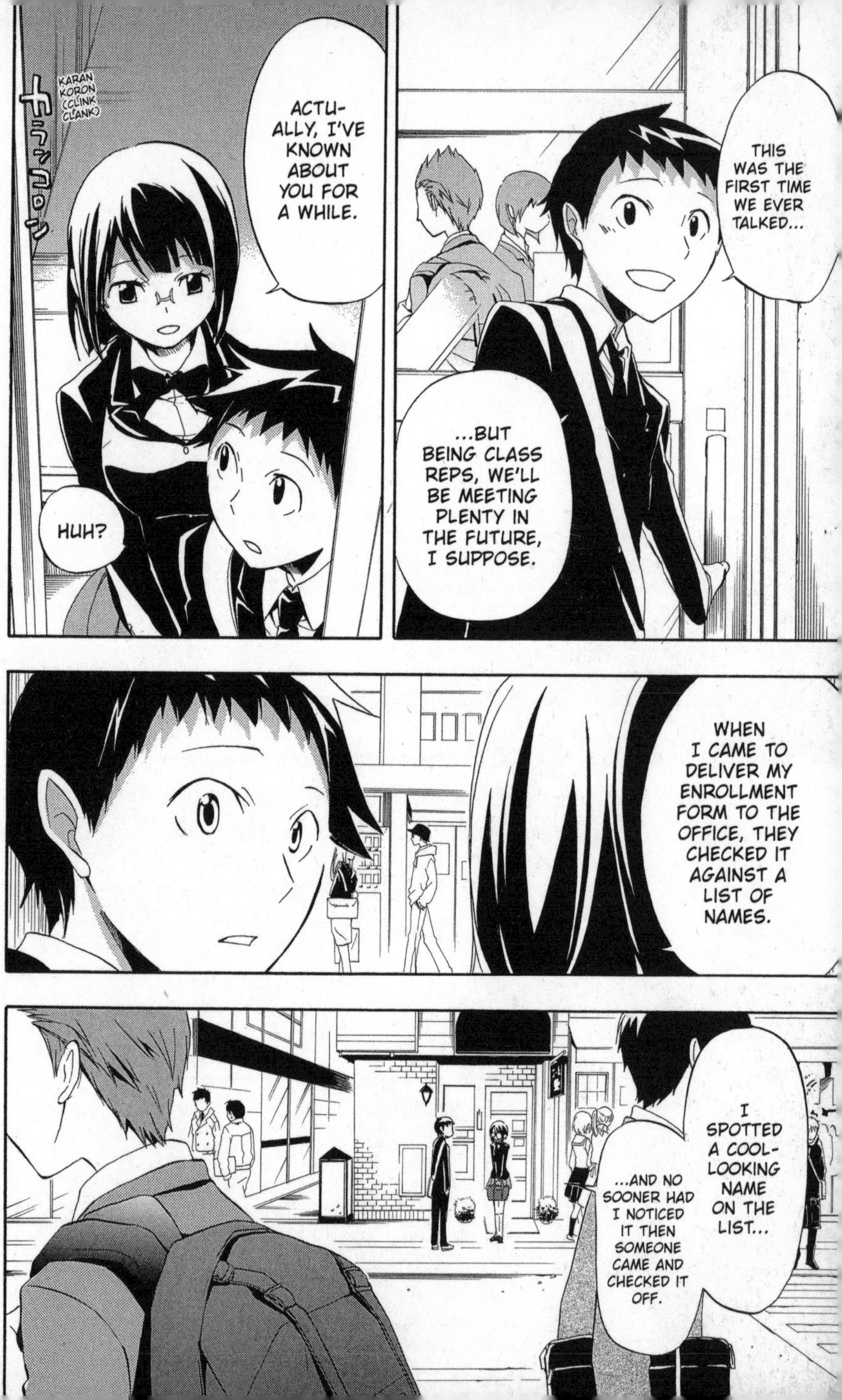
THIS WAS THE FIRST TIME WE EVER TALKED...
...BUT BEING CLASS REPS, WE'LL BE MEETING PLENTY IN THE FUTURE, I SUPPOSE.
ACTUALLY, I'VE KNOWN ABOUT YOU FOR A WHILE.
KARAN KORON (CLINK CLANK)
HUH?
WHEN I CAME TO DELIVER MY ENROLLMENT FORM TO THE OFFICE, THEY CHECKED IT AGAINST A LIST OF NAMES.
I SPOTTED A COOL-LOOKING NAME ON THE LIST...
...AND NO SOONER HAD I NOTICED IT THEN SOMEONE CAME AND CHECKED IT OFF.

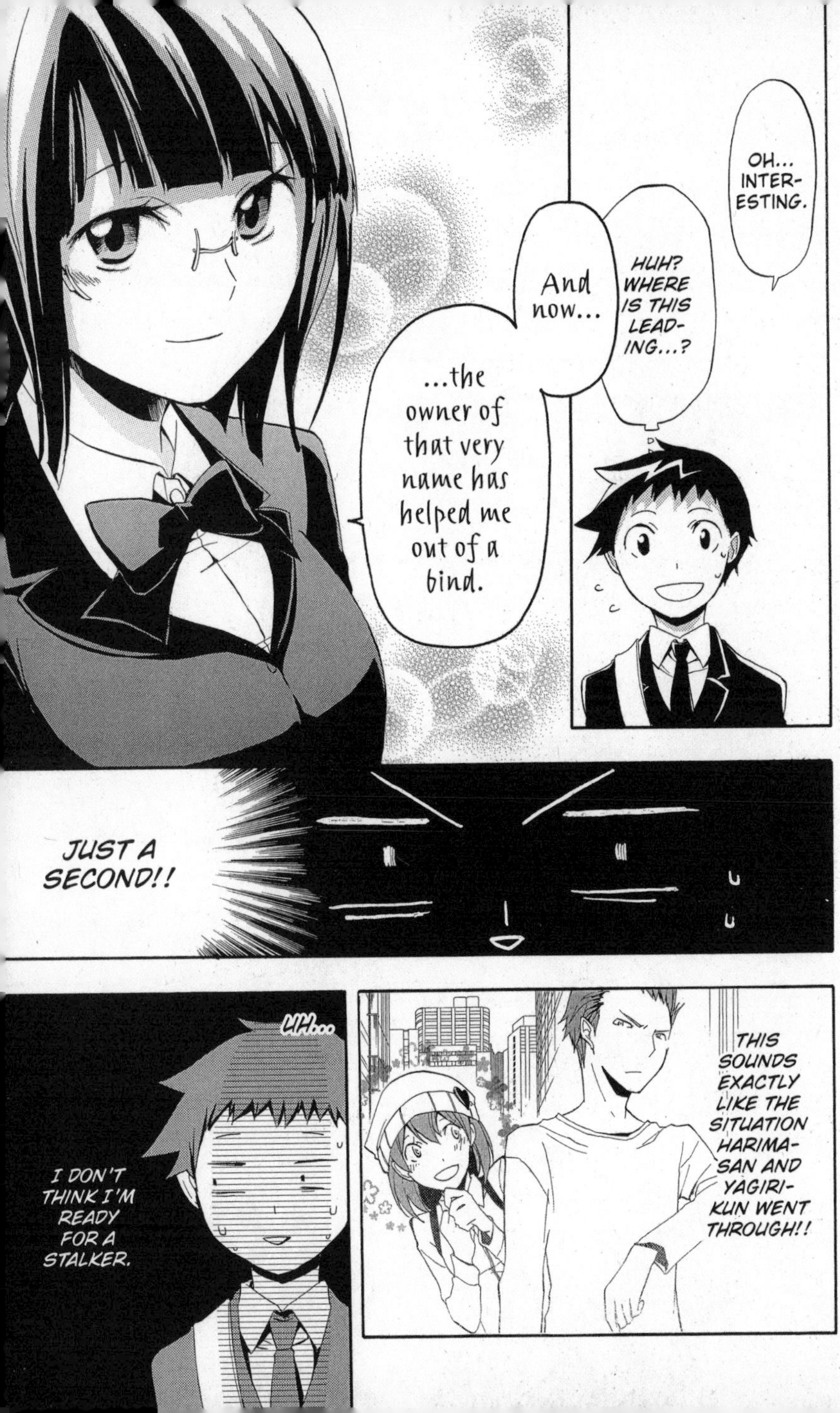
OH... INTERESTING.
HUH? WHERE IS THIS LEADING...?
And now...
...the owner of that very name has helped me out of a bind.
JUST A SECOND!!
THIS SOUNDS EXACTLY LIKE THE SITUATION HARIMA-SAN AND YAGIRI-KUN WENT THROUGH!!
UH...
I DON'T THINK I'M READY FOR A STALKER.

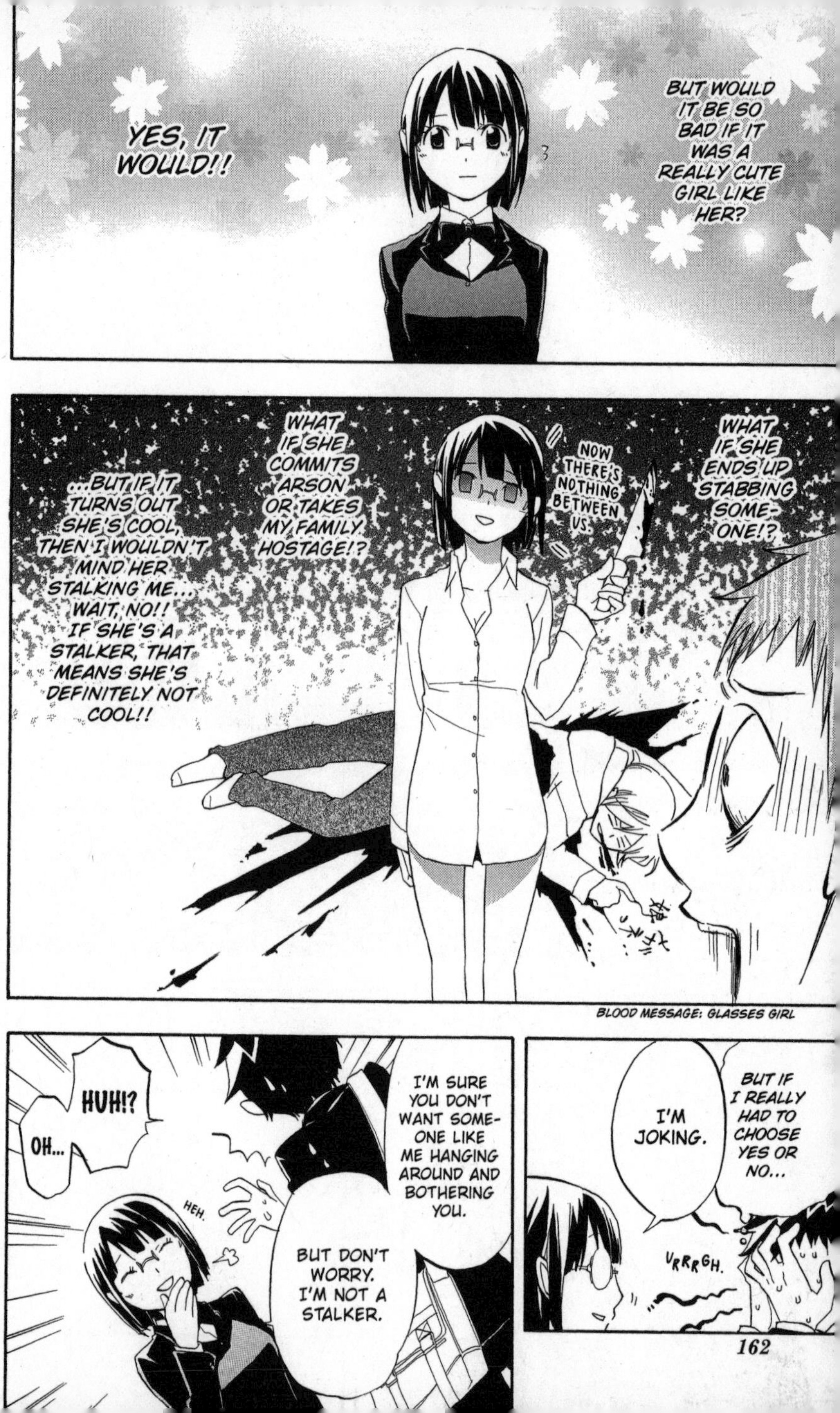
BUT WOULD IT BE SO BAD IF IT WAS A REALLY CUTE GIRL LIKE HER?
YES, IT WOULD!!
WHAT IF SHE ENDS UP STABBING SOME-ONE!?
NOW THERE'S NOTHING BETWEEN US.
WHAT IF SHE COMMITS ARSON OR TAKES MY FAMILY HOSTAGE!?
...BUT IF IT TURNS OUT SHE'S COOL, THEN I WOULDN'T MIND HER STALKING ME... WAIT, NO!! IF SHE'S A STALKER, THAT MEANS SHE'S DEFINITELY NOT COOL!!
BLOOD MESSAGE: GLASSES GIRL
BUT IF I REALLY HAD TO CHOOSE YES OR NO...
I'M JOKING.
URRRGH.
I'M SURE YOU DON'T WANT SOME-ONE LIKE ME HANGING AROUND AND BOTHERING YOU.
BUT DON'T WORRY. I'M NOT A STALKER.
HUH!?
OH...
HEH.

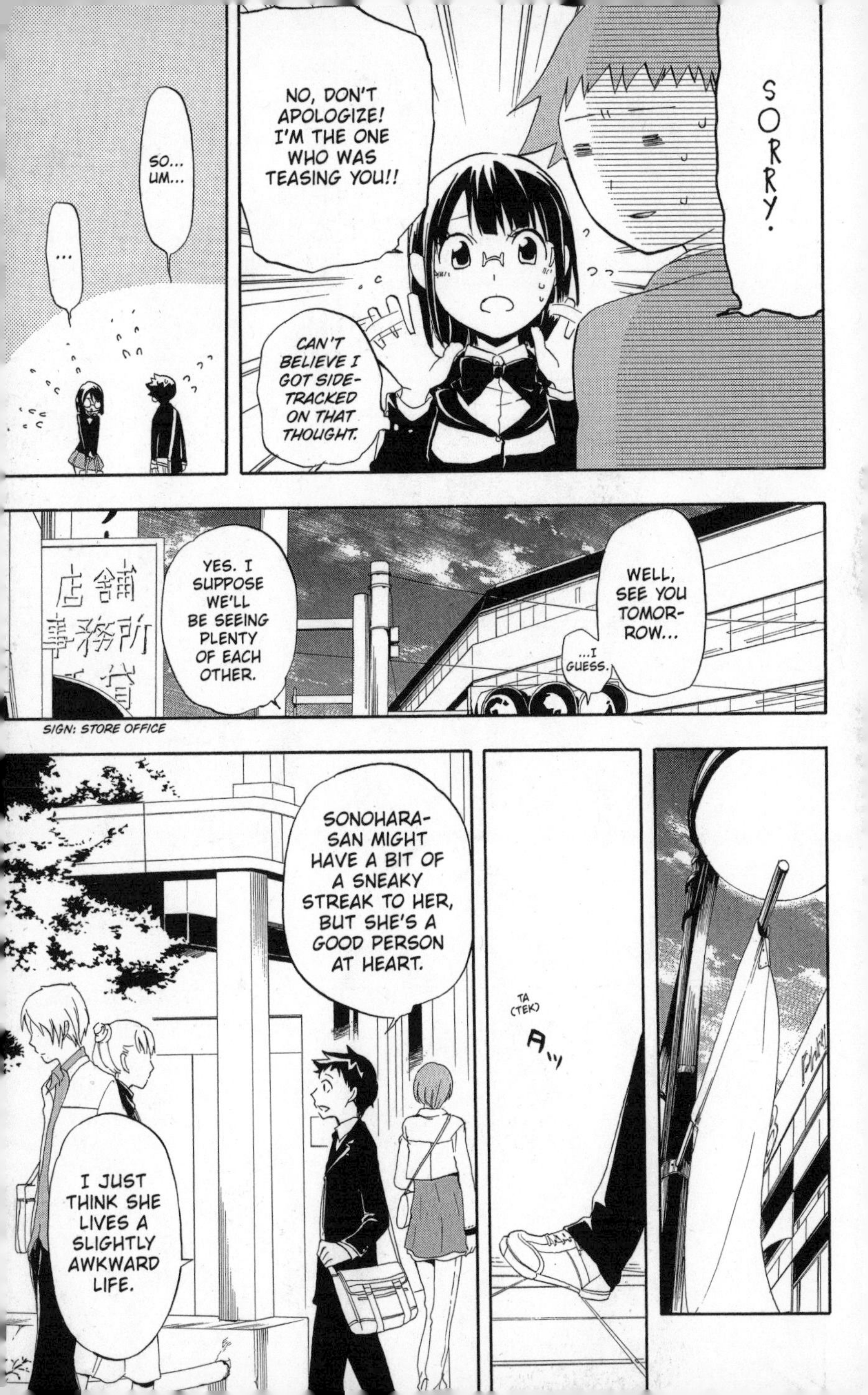
SORRY.
NO, DON'T APOLOGIZE! I'M THE ONE WHO WAS TEASING YOU!!
CAN'T BELIEVE I GOT SIDE-TRACKED ON THAT THOUGHT.
SO... UM...
...
WELL, SEE YOU TOMORROW...
...I GUESS.
YES. I SUPPOSE WE'LL BE SEEING PLENTY OF EACH OTHER.
SIGN: STORE OFFICE
TA (TEK)
SONOHARA-SAN MIGHT HAVE A BIT OF A SNEAKY STREAK TO HER, BUT SHE'S A GOOD PERSON AT HEART.
I JUST THINK SHE LIVES A SLIGHTLY AWKWARD LIFE.

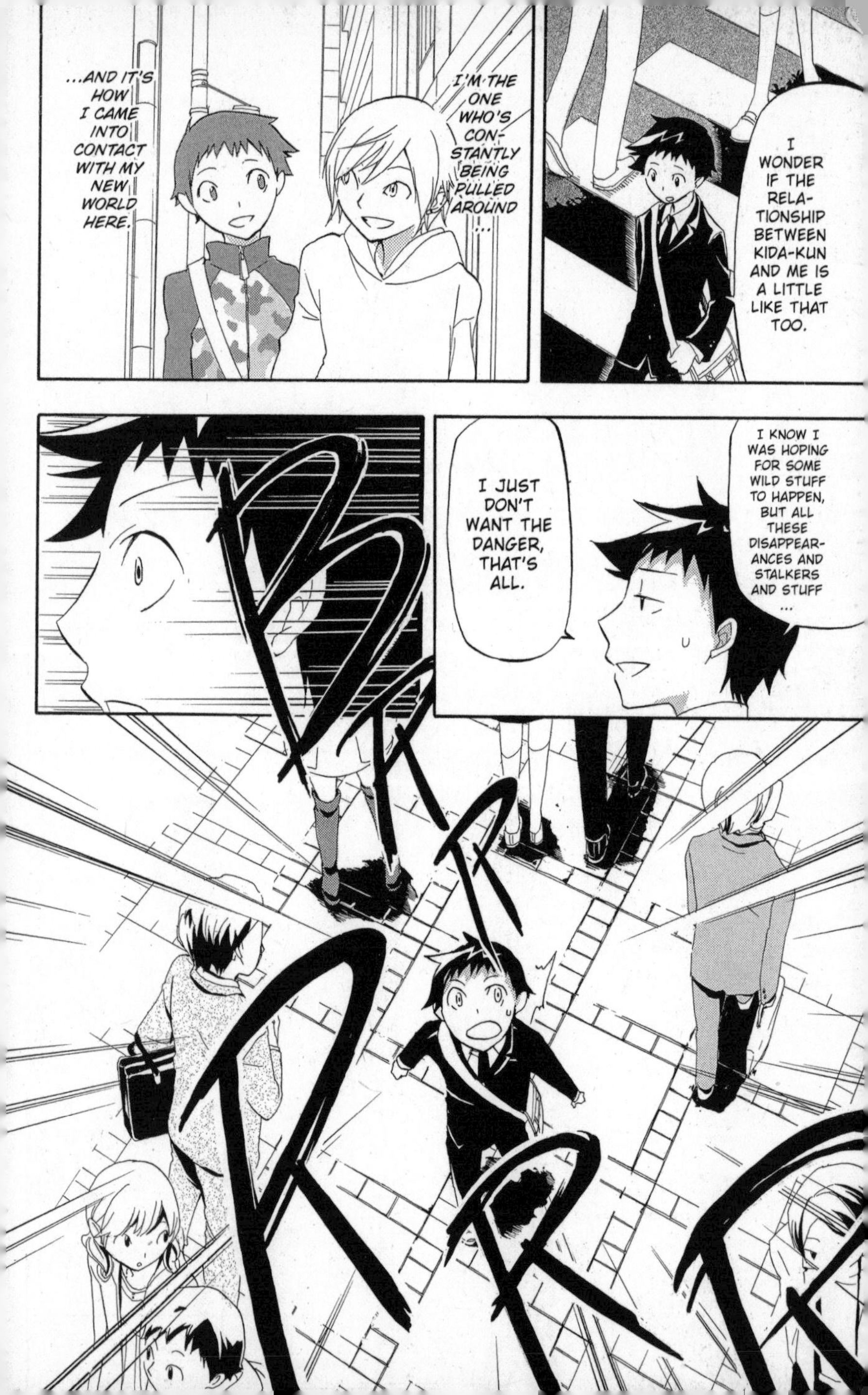
I WONDER IF THE RELATIONSHIP BETWEEN KIDA-KUN AND ME IS A LITTLE LIKE THAT TOO.
I'M THE ONE WHO'S CONSTANTLY BEING PULLED AROUND...
...AND IT'S HOW I CAME INTO CONTACT WITH MY NEW WORLD HERE.
I KNOW I WAS HOPING FOR SOME WILD STUFF TO HAPPEN, BUT ALL THESE DISAPPEARANCES AND STALKERS AND STUFF...
I JUST DON'T WANT THE DANGER, THAT'S ALL.
BRRRR

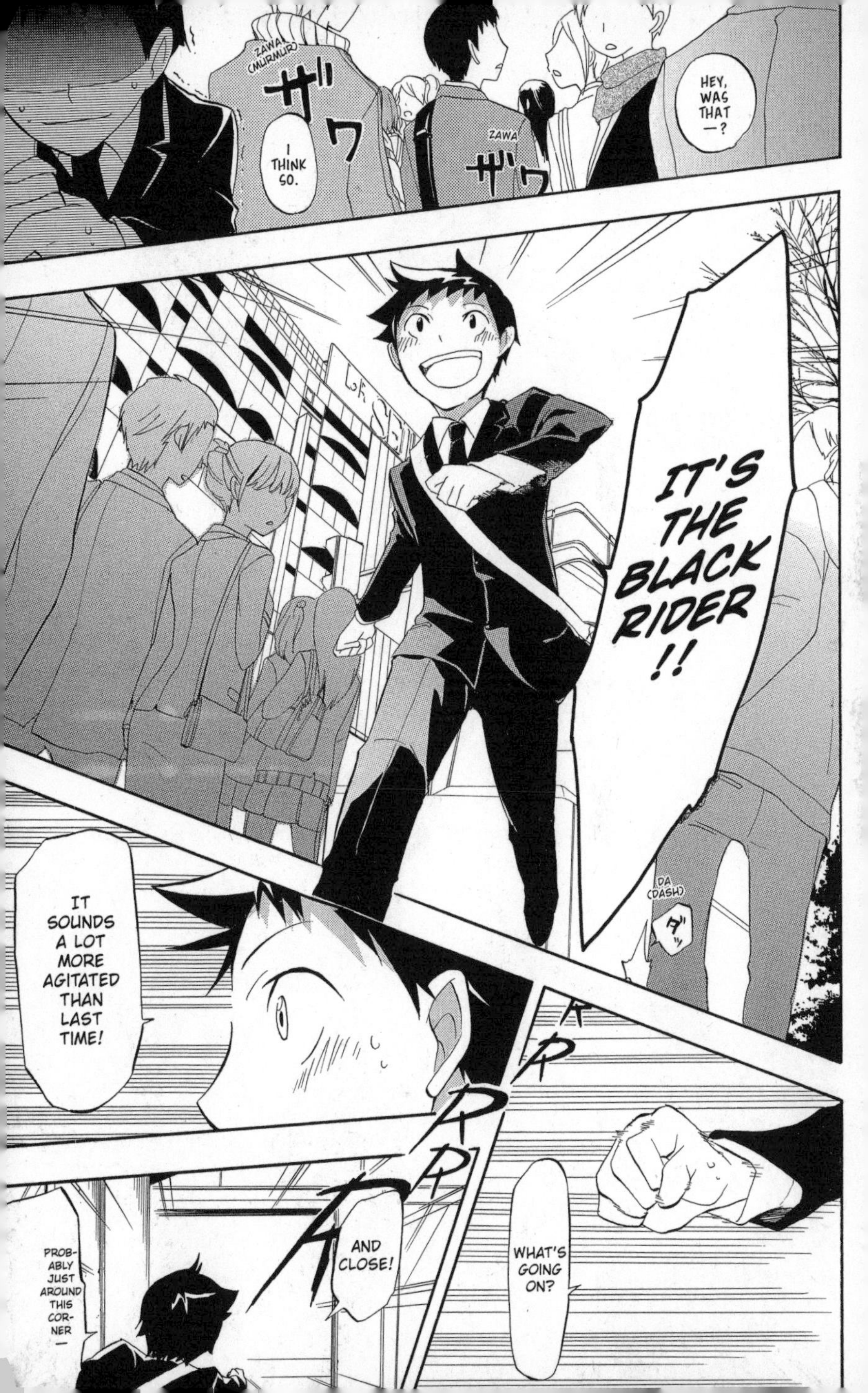
HEY, WAS THAT—?
ZAWA
ザワ
I THINK SO.
ZAWA (MURMUR)
ザワ
IT'S THE BLACK RIDER!!
DA (DASH)
ダッ
IT SOUNDS A LOT MORE AGITATED THAN LAST TIME!
WHAT'S GOING ON?
AND CLOSE!
PROB-ABLY JUST AROUND THIS COR-NER—

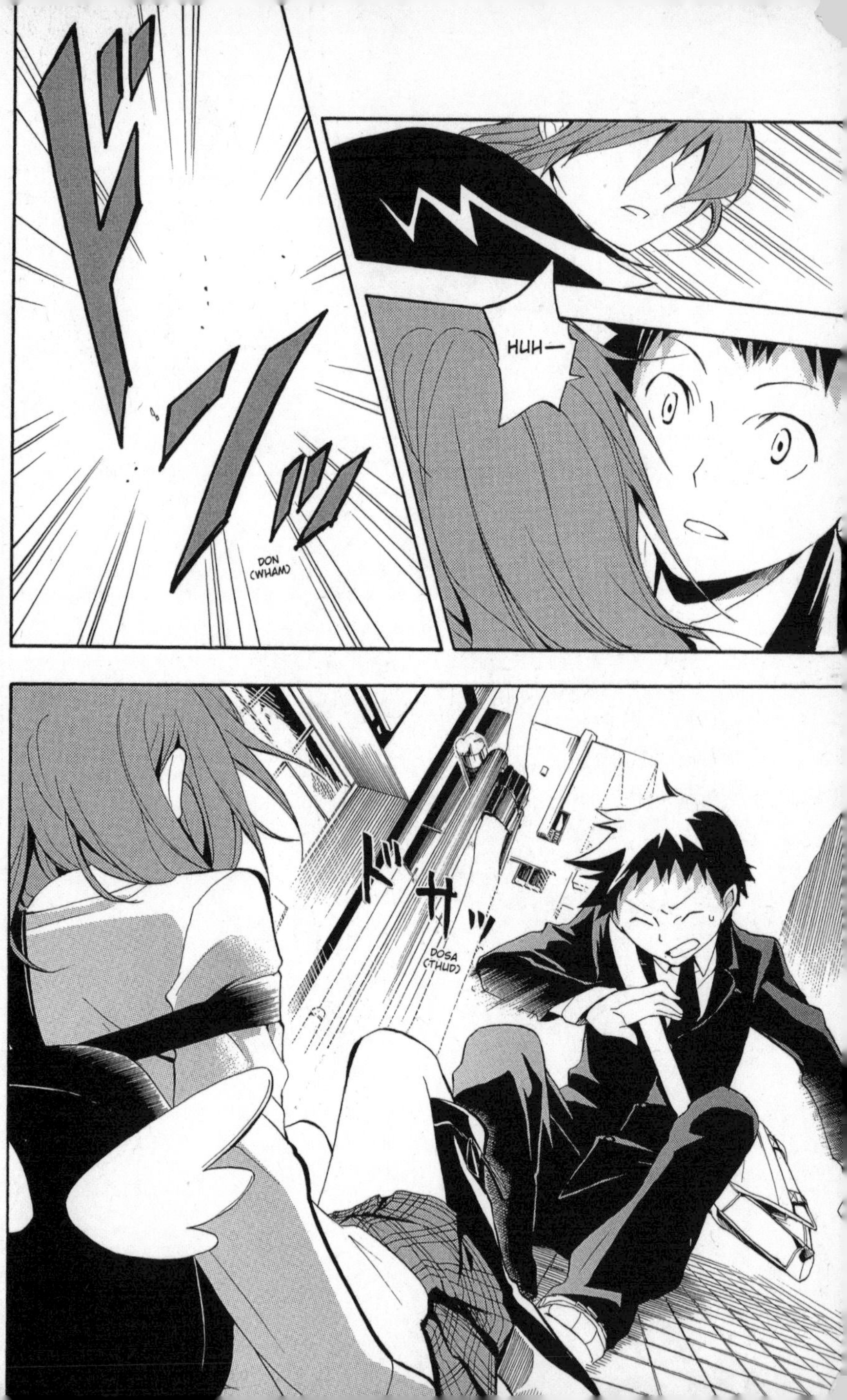
HUH—
ドン
DON (WHAM)
ドサッ
DOSA (THUD)

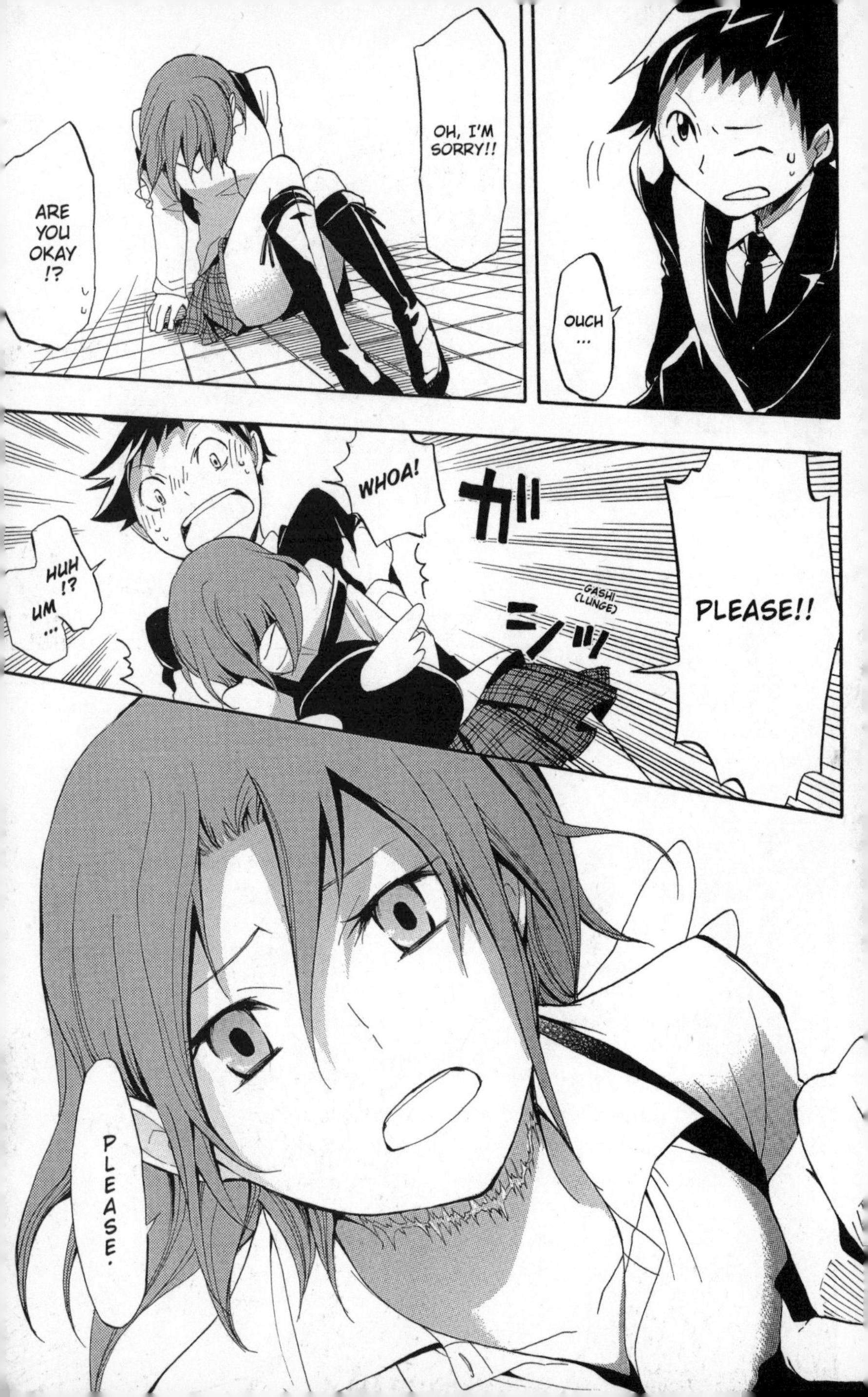
OUCH...
OH, I'M SORRY!!
ARE YOU OKAY!?
PLEASE!!
ガシッ
GASHI (LUNGE)
WHOA!
HUH!? UM...
PLEASE.

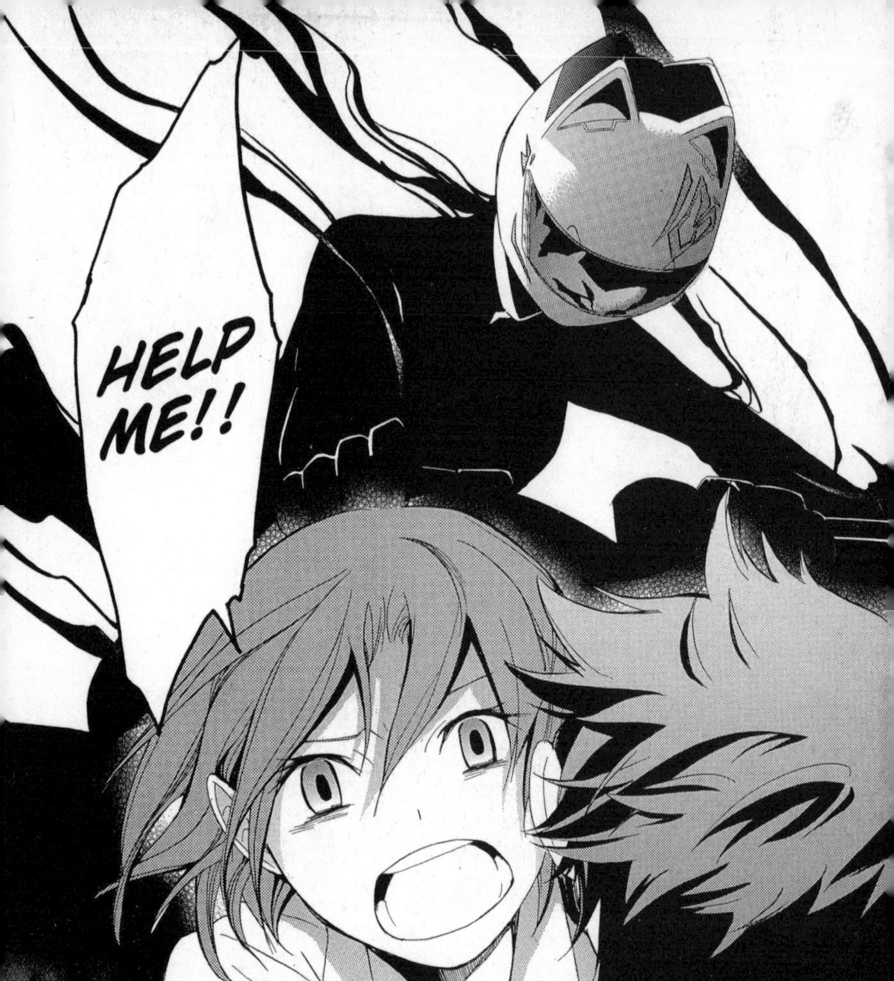
HELP ME!!
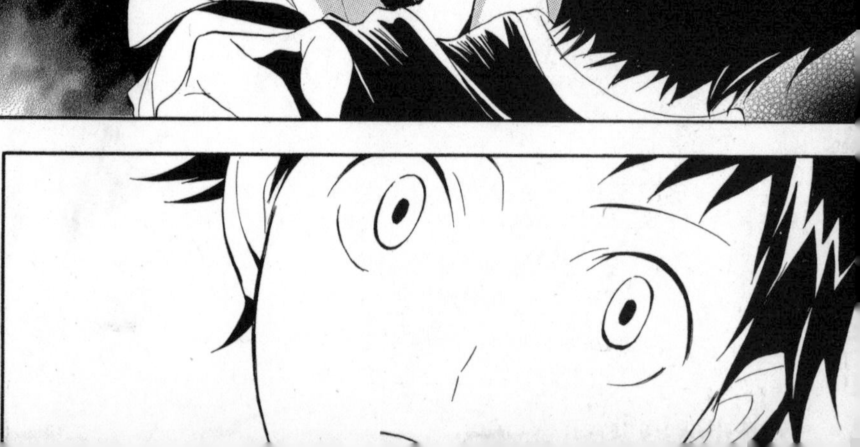

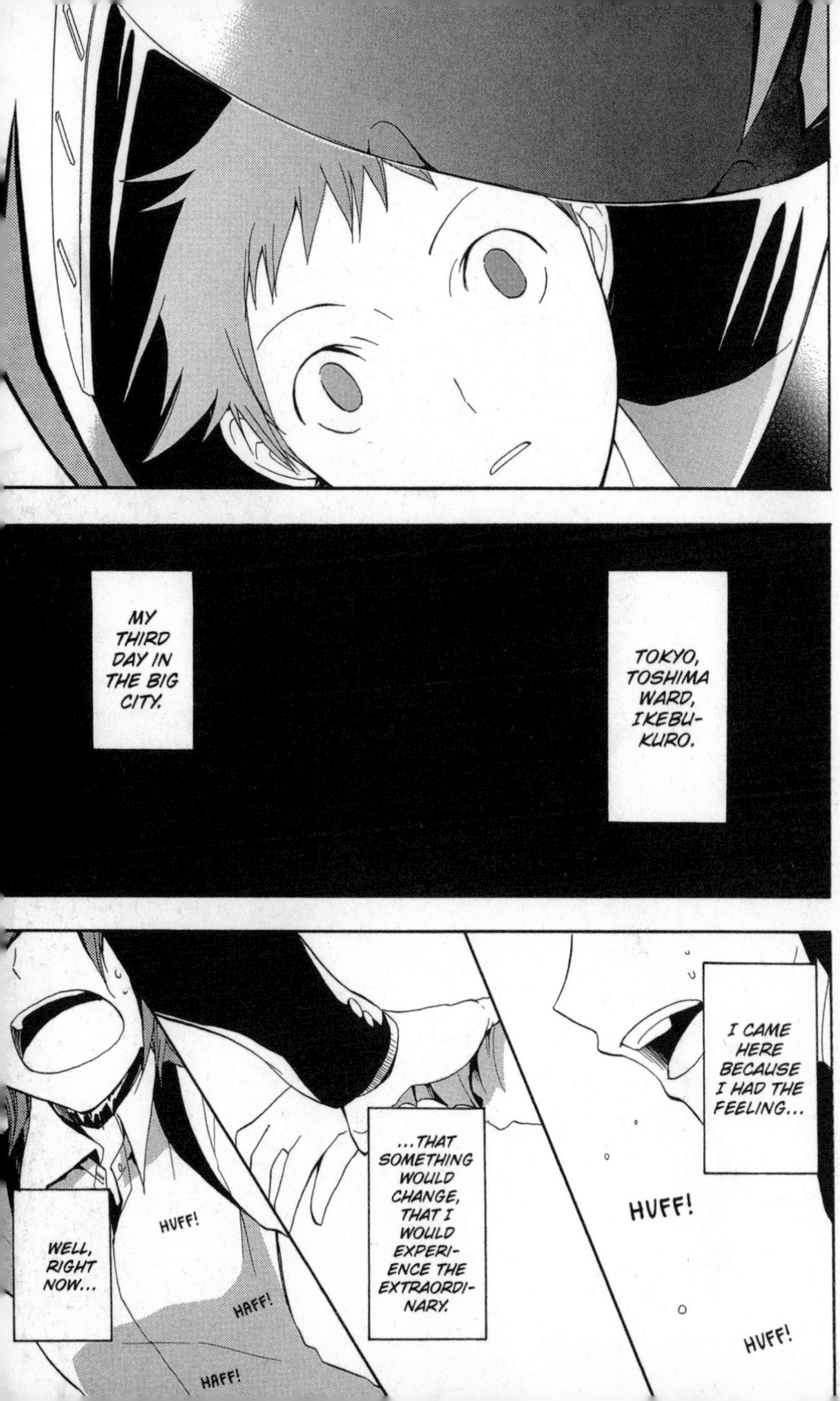
TOKYO, TOSHIMA WARD, IKEBUKURO.
MY THIRD DAY IN THE BIG CITY.
I CAME HERE BECAUSE I HAD THE FEELING...
HUFF!
HUFF!
...THAT SOMETHING WOULD CHANGE, THAT I WOULD EXPERIENCE THE EXTRAORDINARY.
HUFF!
HAFF!
HAFF!
WELL, RIGHT NOW...

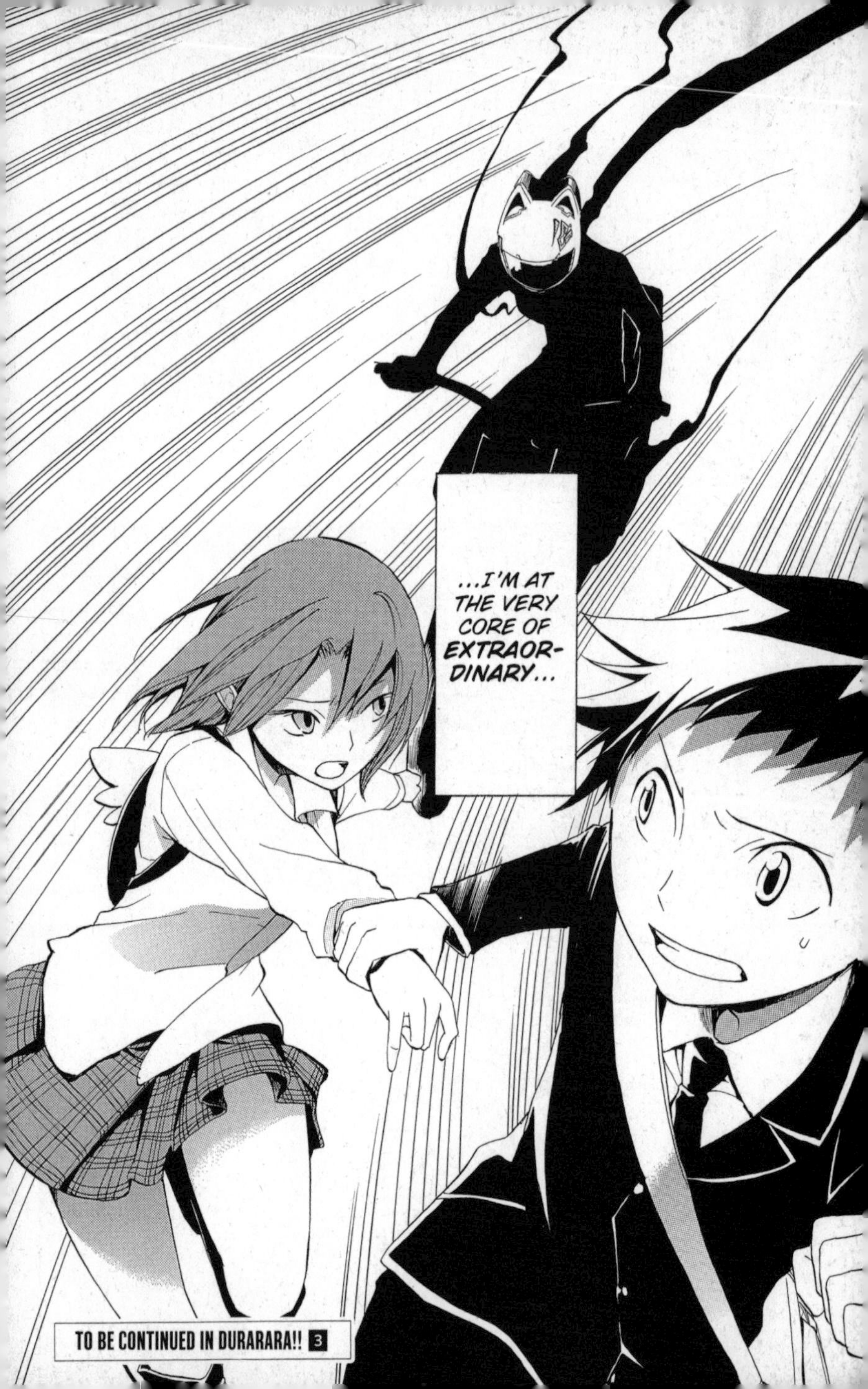
...I'M AT THE VERY CORE OF EXTRAOR-DINARY...
TO BE CONTINUED IN DURARARA!! 3

TRANSLATION NOTES

COMMON HONORIFICS

No honorific: Indicates familiarity or closeness; if used without permission or reason, addressing someone this way would constitute an insult.

-san: The Japanese equivalent of Mr./Mrs./Miss. If a situation calls for politeness, this is the fail-safe honorific.

-kun: Used most often when referring to boys, this indicates affection or familiarity. Occasionally used by older men among their peers, but it may also be used by anyone referring to a person of lower standing.

-chan: An affectionate honorific indicating familiarity used mostly in reference to girls; also used in reference to cute persons or animals of either gender.

PAGES 40-41

Gangan IXA: Based on the Japanese word for "battle" (*ikusa*), this is a manga magazine/line that focuses on fantasy stories with an East Asian/period background, rather than the European Middle style that is commonly associated with "fantasy."

All the books represented on this page are published by Square Enix (the Japanese publisher of the *Durarara!!* manga) or Dengeki Bunko (the publisher of the *Durarara!!* novels). The catchphrase "feel the lightning" (*kimi ni Dengeki!*) is the sales pitch of Dengeki Bunko.

PAGE 43

Bludgeoning Angel Dokuro-chan: A comedy novel/manga/anime series about a cute but violently unhinged angel who bludgeons to death the boy she's meant to protect at the slightest provocation, then brings him back to life.

Doubt: A horror manga published in *Monthly Shonen Gangan* in Japan about a survival game in which the participants, who are "rabbits," must identify the "wolf" among them or be killed one by one.

PAGE 44

Darker Than Black: A supernatural noir anime/manga series about Contractors, people with special powers that can be accessed by paying a "cost" that involves some special, obsessive-compulsive action that must be performed each time. The main character, Hei, has the ability to manipulate electricity, while the villain character in this particular manga adaptation, Harvest, can melt his victims and must swallow a round object the size of a golf ball to perform his special skill. Check out the *Darker Than Black* omnibus edition from Yen Press to see the action!

PAGE 45

Innocentius: A fire-based summoned being from the *A Certain Magical Index* anime/novel series.

PAGE 47

Black Butler: The demonic butler Sebastian in this anime/manga series is bound to his master by a pentacle, which is branded into his young master's eye. In the original Japanese dialogue, Walker Yumasaki's solder ("*handa*") pun is a reference to the character Ryu Handa from the series *Our Home's Fox Deity* (*Wagaya no Oinari-sama*). In translation, this reference was altered to the *Black Butler* character Baldroy, who is a former soldier and serves as cook at the Phantomhive Estate. *Black Butler* is now available from Yen Press!

PAGE 123

Yen conversion: While exchange rates fluctuate daily, a convenient conversion estimation is about ¥100 to 1 USD.

Cast:

Mikado Ryuugamine

Masaomi Kida

Anri Sonohara

Namie Yagiri

Seiji Yagiri

Mika Harima

Izaya Orihara

Shizuo Heiwajima

Simon Brezhnev

Walker Yumasaki

Erika Karisawa

Saburo Togusa

Kyouhei Kadota

Shinra Kishitani

Celty Sturluson

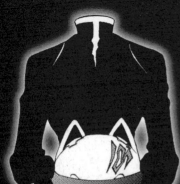

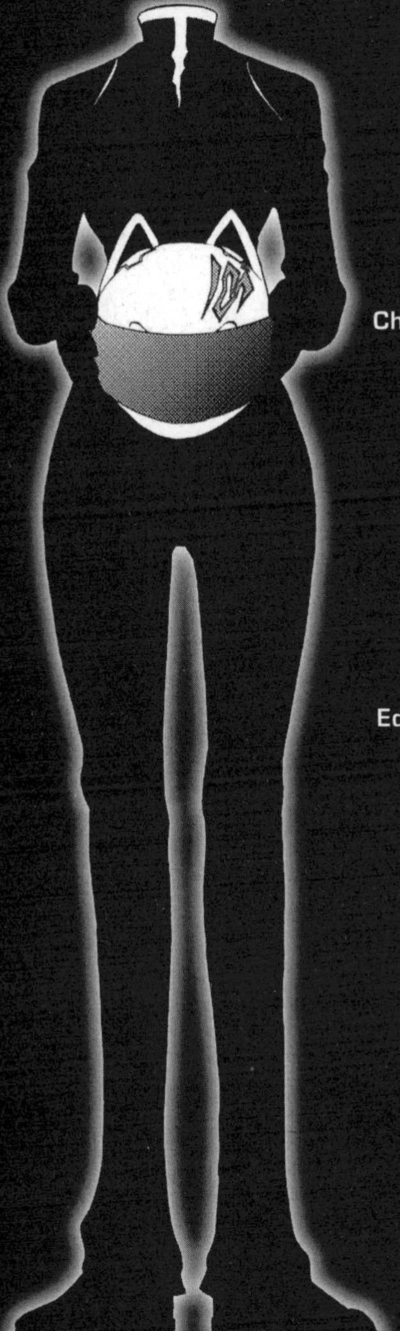

Staff:

Story: Ryohgo Narita

Character Design: Suzuhito Yasuda

Art: Akiyo Satorigi

Art Assistants:
Toka
Masako Shibata
Urata
Kotana
Kazuki
Satorigi's Family

Cover: Masayuki Sato
(Maniackers Design)

Editor: Takeshi Kuma (Square Enix)

Supervision: Atsushi Wada
(ASCII Media Works)

Publisher: Square Enix

special Thanks:

Masaki Okayu
Yoshiki Tonogai
Yuji Iwahara
Reki Kawahara
Kazuma Kamaike
Jin Shibamura
Tsukasa Fushimi
Yana Toboso
DTBG Production Committee
Dengeki Bunko
Ikebukuro Dollars

Hello, nice to see you again! I am Ryohgo Narita, the so-called "creator" of this mixed-media project called *Durarara!!*

So it's been almost a full year of serialization for the manga now, and the fact that this second volume exists is thanks to Satorigi-san, the *GFantasy* editorial office, and of course, all of you readers for supporting the series! Thank you...thank you so much!

In fact, I'm so full of gratitude that I could fill the rest of this page with thank-yous, but I'll refrain since I don't want it to seem forced or that I'm taking the easy way out of writing this afterword...

As a matter of fact, I've received quite a lot of inspiration from Satorigi-san's manga. Together with the anime, I feel like each version strengthens the other in the ideal form for a mixed-media project like this.

There are fantastic, kinetic details present in the manga that weren't in the novels (Simon grabbing the traffic pole that Shizuo threw, the Yagiri siblings bathing together) that make me like any other reader, eagerly anticipating the next month's chapter.

But most of all, I'm grateful to Satorigi-san for enabling this series to continue! When I saw the drafts of the first few chapters, it was such a detailed and faithful representation of the story that I thought, "Oh no! If this manga doesn't take off when it has such incredible direction and art, it's entirely the fault of my story!" I'm so glad it's been a success. In fact, it should be even better because I feel like the manga is filling in the spots that my novels have failed to cover. Oops, I'm starting to repeat myself.

By the time this volume is out, the anime will be nearing the airing of the final episode. As I speak, the *Durarara!!* project is partially leaving my hands to find its own place in the world.

The memorabilia and goods marketplaces are also exploding with perfume, *Durarara!!* dumplings, Heiwajima family curry, and a whole host of unfathomable items being produced and sold. Even in *GFantasy*, they're busy making a variety of trinkets to be packaged with magazine issues, something that makes me so thankful, I could spend the rest of this afterword just repeating...oops, there I go again.

In the last volume, I compared the anime, manga, and novels to a drill, but now I think of them more like the three primary colors that make up light. Depending on the combination of the three sources used for inspiration, the various goods, CDs, comic anthologies, and so on form their own colors that create a vibrant rainbow. Speaking of colors, the combination of the three primary colors makes white...and what should I write on this white canvas that is the entirety of the *Durarara!!* media project? What will Satorigi-san draw on it? What will the anime staff project on it? And what will the readers think of it? I hope you will conjure this image in your head as you enjoy *Durarara!!*

So in closing, once again, I hope you continue to enjoy Satorigi-san's manga version of *Durarara!!*

Ryohgo Narita

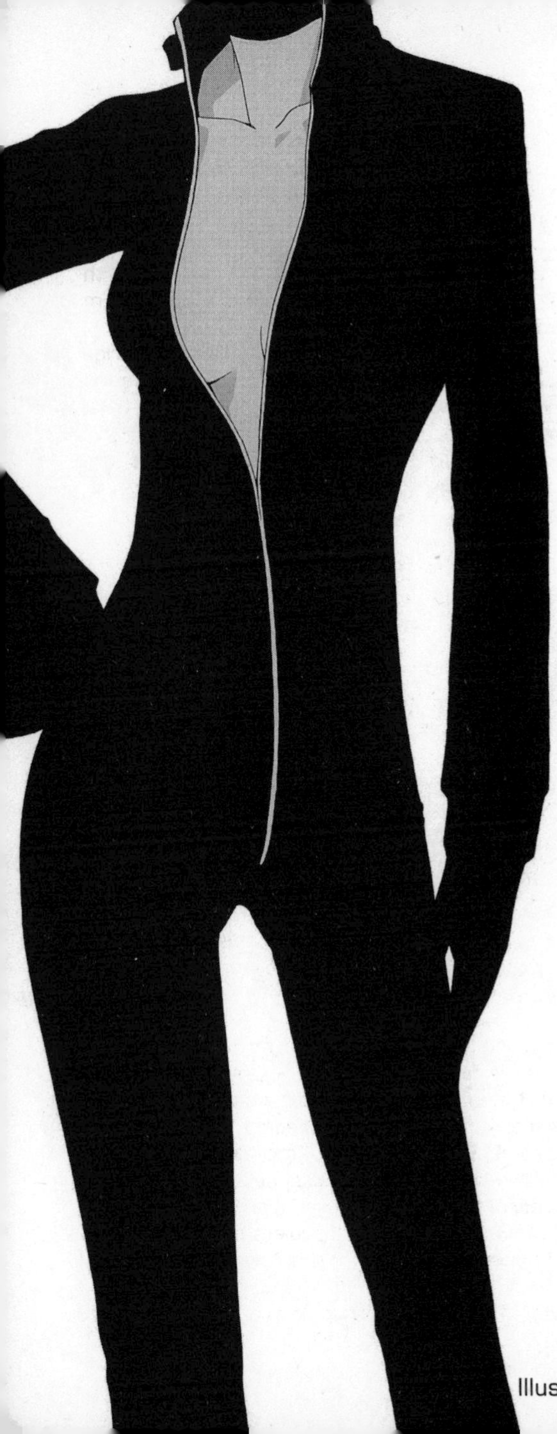

Illustration: Suzuhito Yasuda

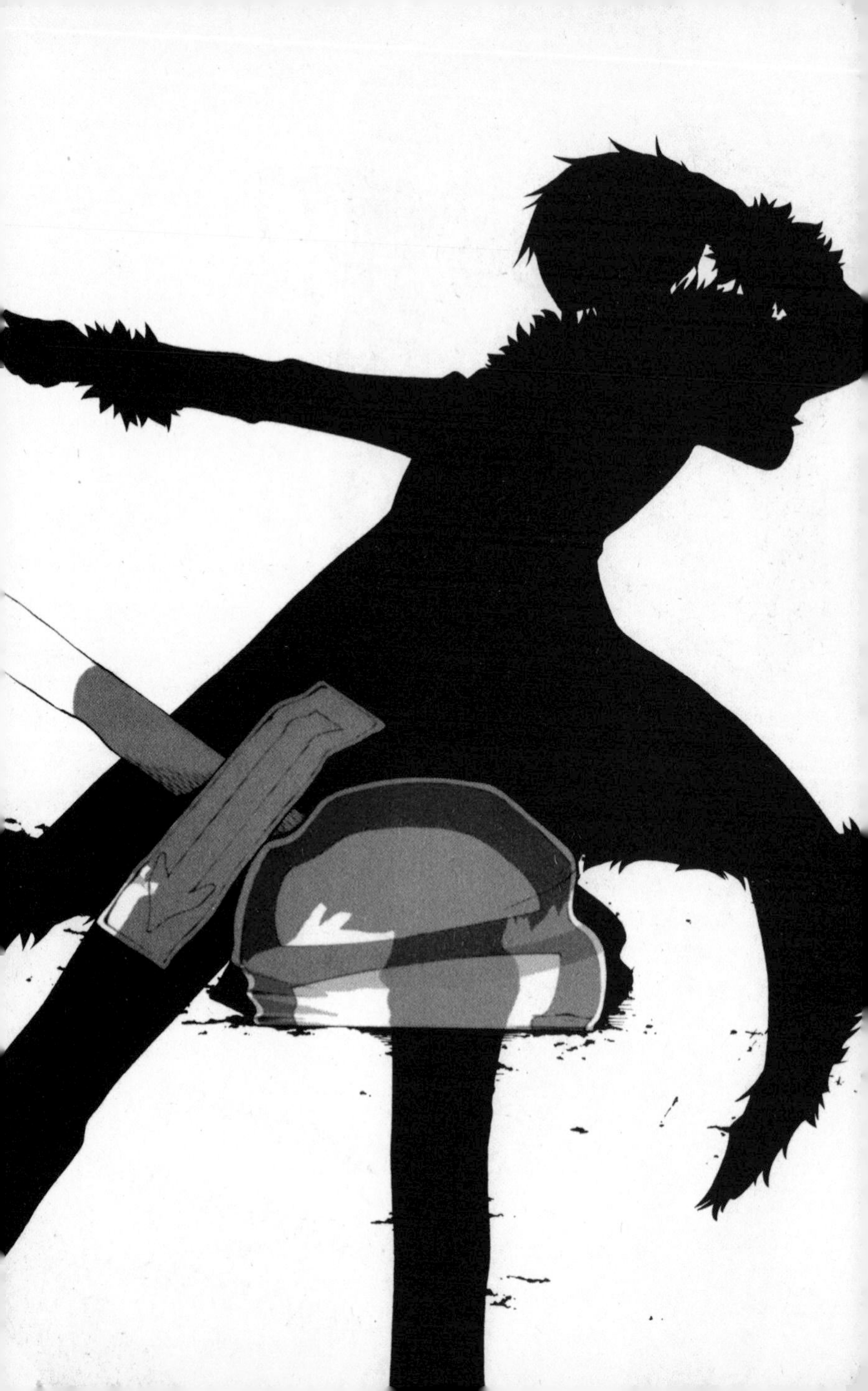

DURARARA!! 2

**RYOHGO NARITA
SUZUHITO YASUDA
AKIYO SATORIGI**

Translation: Stephen Paul

Lettering: Lys Blakeslee

DURARARA!! Vol. 2
© 2010 Ryohgo Narita
© 2010 Akiyo Satorigi / SQUARE ENIX
Licensed by KADOKAWA CORPORATION ASCII MEDIA WORKS
First published in Japan in 2010 by SQUARE ENIX CO., LTD. English translation rights arranged with SQUARE ENIX CO., LTD. and Hachette Book Group through Tuttle-Mori Agency, Inc.

Translation © 2012 by SQUARE ENIX CO., LTD.

Yen Press
Hachette Book Group
1290 Avenue of the Americas, New York, NY 10104

www.HachetteBookGroup.com
www.YenPress.com

Yen Press is an imprint of Hachette Book Group, Inc. The Yen Press name and logo are trademarks of Hachette Book Group, Inc.

First Yen Press Edition: April 2012

ISBN: 978-0-316-20931-1

20 19 18 17 16 15 14 13 12 11

BVG

Printed in the United States of America

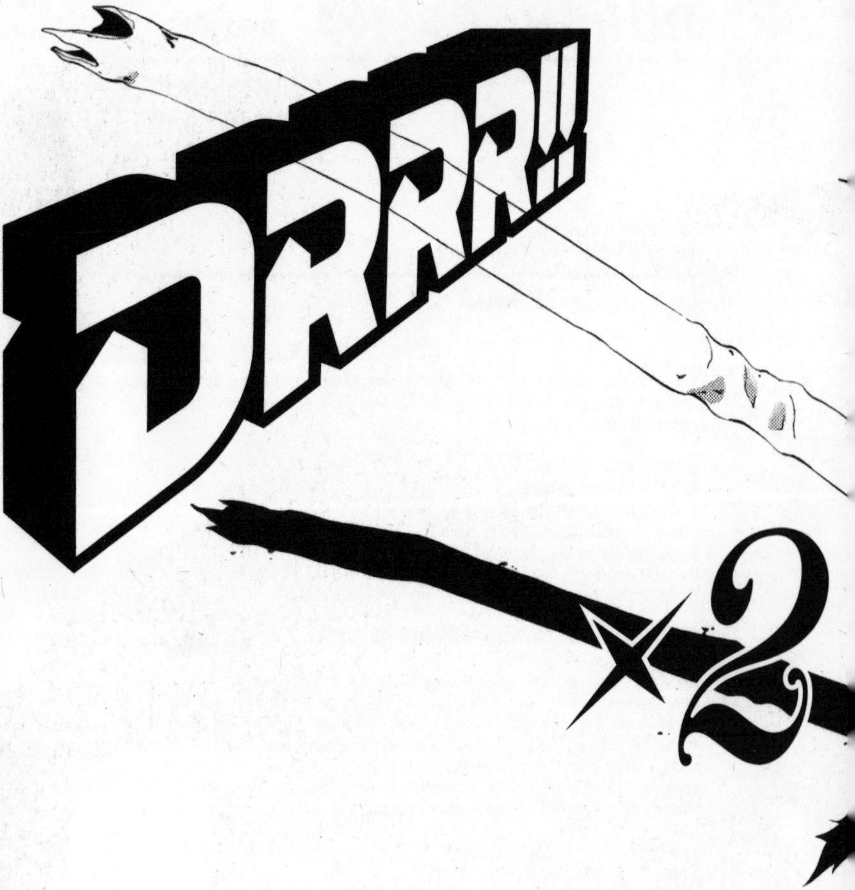
DRRR!!
×2

RYOHGO NARITA
×
SUZUHITO YASUDA
×
AKIYO SATORIGI

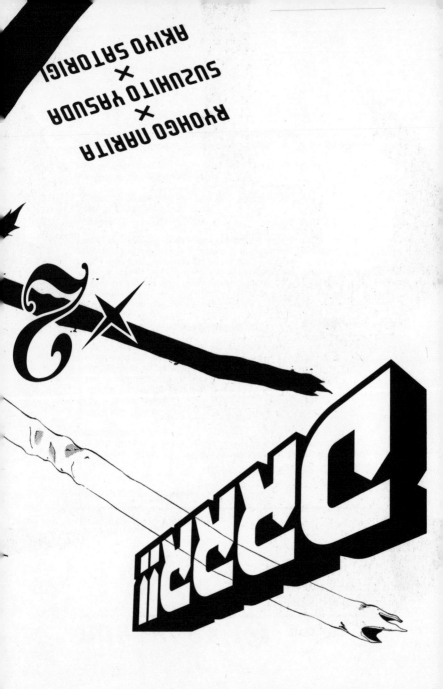